....

Fair Trade and Social Justice

....

Fair Trade and Social Justice

Global Ethnographies

EDITED BY

Sarah Lyon and Mark Moberg

NEW YORK UNIVERSITY PRESS

New York & London

NEW YORK UNIVERSITY PRESS
New York and London
www.nyupress.org

Library of Congress Cataloging-in-Publication Data
Fair trade and social justice : global ethnographies /
edited by Sarah M. Lyon and Mark Moberg.
p. cm.
Includes bibliographical references and index.
ISBN-13: 978–0–8147–9620–7 (cl : alk. paper)
ISBN-10: 0–8147–9620–6 (cl : alk. paper)
ISBN-13: 978–0–8147–9621–4 (pb : alk. paper)
ISBN-10: 0–8147–9621–4 (pb : alk. paper)
[etc.]
1. International trade. 2. Competition, Unfair. 3. Social justice.
I. Lyon, Sarah M. II. Moberg, Mark, 1959–
HF1379.F342   2010
382'.3—dc22   2009053609

New York University Press books are printed on acid-free paper,
and their binding materials are chosen for strength and durability.
We strive to use environmentally responsible suppliers and materials
to the greatest extent possible in publishing our books.

Manufactured in the United States of America

10 9 8 7 6 5 4 3 2 1

Contents

Acknowledgments

Virtually unheard of a few decades ago, fair trade has suddenly emerged as one of the fastest growing segments of the consumer market, with hundreds of agricultural and manufactured goods now certified as having been produced under socially and environmentally sustainable conditions. Recent years have witnessed annual growth rates of 30 percent or more in the global consumption of such goods, with sales now topping two billion dollars annually. Much that has been written of this rapidly growing phenomenon has taken as its point of departure the language of fair trade advocates in the now-developed world. Fair trade is seen as a means by which solidarity and mutual respect are created between producers and consumers in place of capitalist imperatives of competition and profit maximization. However, for all the value-laden discourse surrounding fair trade advocacy, only in the past few years have anthropologists and other scholars begun to examine critically how this movement actually operates on the ground, among those involved in fair trade networks. This book grew out of a panel organized by Sarah Lyon for the 2007 meetings of the American Anthropological Association. The panel brought together researchers whose ethnographic work spanned a wide range of locales and commodities involved in fair trade networks. The enthusiastic response of audience members encouraged us to assemble this work in a published volume, the first to examine a variety of fairly traded commodities from an anthropological perspective.

From the rich array of chapters contributed by our authors there emerged the central dimensions of fair trade around which the volume is organized: "Global Markets and Local Realities," "Negotiating Difference and Identity in Fair Trade Markets," and "Relationships and Consumption in Fair Trade Markets and Alternative Economies." To all our contributors we owe a debt of gratitude for their responsiveness to our suggestions and to those of the volume's external reviewers. Their receptiveness to these comments helped us transform a disparate collection of essays into a coherent and focused manuscript, one in which all of us learned from and drew upon one another's work. We also wish to acknowledge the enthusiastic support of our editor, Jennifer Hammer, and the staff of

NYU Press, who from the outset have guided this project with the utmost professionalism and alacrity. We truly appreciated Jennifer's placement of the manuscript with a series of knowledgeable yet critical external readers who compelled all of us, authors and editors alike, to refine and focus our arguments through the process of revision. The final manuscript was immeasurably strengthened by their suggestions, although we of course bear responsibility for any deficiencies that remain.

Ultimately, as anthropologists and authors, all of us owe our greatest debt to the many individuals—whether fair trade producers, activists, or consumers—who assisted us in the research on which this volume is built. The experiences of fair trade producers in particular are often represented to the consumers of their goods through the intermediaries of advertising and advocacy that extol the virtues of fair trade. As will be seen in the following chapters, when producers speak in their own voices, they often have a more nuanced story to tell. To them, and to all who aspire to the "new world" of social and economic justice promised by fair trade, we dedicate this volume.

What's Fair?

The Paradox of Seeking Justice through Markets

MARK MOBERG AND SARAH LYON

Fair Trade and Neoliberal Globalization: A Brief History

In recent decades, the growth of global markets for agricultural commodities, manufactured goods, and artisanal products has made available to residents of the developed countries an unprecedented array of consumer goods originating in diverse cultures and geographies. This seemingly endless expansion of consumer choice is rooted in the process of neoliberal globalization, a model of economic development now dominant among the world's governments, multilateral lending agencies, and trade bodies. Intended to promote global trade through neoliberalism as exercised through institutions such as the International Monetary Fund (IMF), the World Bank, and the World Trade Organization (WTO), globalization has dismantled most state policies regulating the movement of capital and commodities across national borders (Basch et al. 1994; Greider 1997; Brennan 2003). Implemented through regional trade agreements such as the North American Free Trade Agreement (NAFTA) and the Single European Market, neoliberal policies have also facilitated massive levels of transnational investment, most of which originates from financial centers in the developed North. Meanwhile, technological and transport innovations of recent decades, particularly jet air cargo and containerized shipping, have brought the fruits of such investment within the reach of consumers in the developed countries (Harvey 1989: 240ff.). The result has been a profusion of once-novel agricultural and manufactured goods on retail shelves, as well as traditionally available items originating in new sites of production: winter fruits and vegetables from Central America, cut flowers from Ecuador and Colombia, and fresh seafood from Asia have become routine items of consumption for North American shoppers (Fischer and Benson 2006; Ziegler 2007). This global sourcing of new products, combined with the ongoing volatility associated with markets for traditional bulk commodities such as coffee, tea, cacao, and bananas, has in turn heightened awareness of global wealth disparities. This awareness is a major impetus for the contemporary fair trade movement.

Neoliberalism[1] has largely supplanted earlier models of economic development rooted in state regulation of markets and international trade, a project whose origins date to the Bretton Woods conference of 1944 to plan a postwar global economy (Helleiner 1994). Bretton Woods endorsed Keynesian policies conferring a primary role for economic management on central governments, upholding controls on international transfers of capital to further national goals of investment and social welfare (ibid.). As independence movements swept colonized regions of the globe following World War II, newly installed national governments adopted Keynesian measures to regulate their countries' involvement in the global economy. Promoting industrialization at home through state-led investment, developing countries also pursued regulation to ensure more stable markets for their exports. The term *fair trade* first arose during this time to encompass an agenda among United Nations member states favoring more equitable exchange between the developed and developing worlds (Fridell 2007: 24). Arguing that the global South's reliance on primary product exports placed it at a disadvantage relative to the industrialized North, developing nations in the United Nations Economic Commission on Latin America (ECLA) and UN Commission on Trade and Development (UNCTAD) lobbied for commodity controls ensuring "fairer" prices for primary product exporters of the South (ibid.: 30). Hence, the fair trade movement in its earliest incarnation was opposed in principle to the deregulation embraced by later neoliberal policies.

During the 1980s, the Bretton Woods framework crumbled as national governments rescinded controls over international capital transfers, following the lead of the United States, which renounced such measures in 1973. Over the ensuing decade, severe trade imbalances due to deteriorating export prices and the rising costs of oil imports led many governments of the global South to default on foreign loans. In seeking assistance from the U.S.-dominated International Monetary Fund, developing countries averted bankruptcy only after agreeing to IMF Structural Adjustment Programs (SAPs) that diverted government spending into debt repayment. The effect was a forced imposition of neoliberal policies, as SAPs restricted the regulatory tools that national governments had earlier used to manage trade. Under the mandates of Structural Adjustment, developing countries were required to remove protective tariffs and restrictions over

foreign investment, suspend subsidies for domestic producers, and ori-
ent their agricultural and manufacturing sectors to export production—
all with the goal of maximizing export earnings in order to repay debts.
In effect, national governments lost sovereign control of their economies.
With the demise of the Soviet bloc in 1990, free trade—premised on the
absence of tariffs, quotas, or state intervention in labor and commodity
markets—emerged as the unchallenged economic paradigm virtually everywhere in the global economy. Upon the creation of the World Trade
Organization in 1995, neoliberal doctrines acquired the force of law, as
member governments could now sue others to force them to open their
markets and remove "illegal" restrictions on the transnational movement
of commodities. By that decade, the fair trade movement as originally
conceived, that is, a statist program challenging free trade, appeared to be
as moribund as the Keynesian policies on which it was based.

Yet with the expansion of neoliberalism the need for fairer international
trade has become ever more pressing to many people in the postcolonial
world. Free-market policies have brought millions of small-scale farmers
into competition with industrial agriculture, which enjoys greater productivity because of its technological advantages as well as subsidies in the
form of tax credits and price supports in the developed countries.[2] Usually unable to compete in deregulated markets with much larger corporate
farms, household-based farmers confront the alternatives of plummeting
earnings or a withdrawal from commercial farming altogether. National
governments throughout the developing world face new pressures to export goods and generate foreign exchange, further glutting global markets
for traditional export crops and depressing farmers' receipts below their
costs of production. The abandonment of longstanding multilateral efforts
to regulate commodity prices, such as the International Coffee Agreement
(ICA) and Lomé Convention,[3] has also forced producer prices for many
commodities to unprecedented lows (see Jaffee 2007: 42ff). These trends
have been exacerbated by the consolidation of retail power in the developed world—epitomized by the emergence of Wal-Mart as a multinational
supermarket chain—which has fueled intense price competition among the
surviving retailers for the consumer market (Barrientos and Dolan 2006).
By the 1990s, coffee growers experienced the lowest prices in a generation,
and the decade witnessed deepening material hardship and even starvation
in some coffee-growing regions (Charveriat 2001; R. Collier 2001). The
attendant effects of neoliberal globalization have included massive emi-
gration from rural areas (in turn lowering wages and living standards in

manufacturing sectors) and recourse to dangerous and often exploitative survival strategies, such as prostitution and the production of illegal drugs (Nash 1994; Baumann 1998; Farmer 1999; Collins 2000; Moberg 2008). Yet, in many areas of the world, small-scale farmers are unwilling to "go quietly into that dark night," at least not without resisting draconian neoliberal measures. It is no coincidence, for example, that the Zapatista rebellion in southern Mexico began on the very day that the North American Free Trade Agreement took effect. Zapatista leaders recognized that the dismantling of tariffs on cheap U.S. maize, one of NAFTA's provisions, would decimate Mexico's small farmers (G. Collier 1994).

Awareness of these global dislocations has given fair trade a rebirth in a nonstatist incarnation as an international movement that seeks economic justice and environmental sustainability through markets themselves. Thus redefined from government intervention to a market-based initiative, fair trade seeks to extend a preferred retail niche to products grown and manufactured under ethical conditions, thereby rewarding their producers with a higher return to their labor. As characterized by a coalition of European alternative trade organizations (ATOs) involved in the movement,

> Fair trade is a trading partnership, based on dialogue, transparency, and respect, that seeks greater equity in international trade. It contributes to sustainable development by offering better trading conditions to, and securing the rights of, marginalized producers and workers—especially in the South. Fair trade organizations (backed by consumers) are engaged actively in supporting producers, awareness raising and in campaigning for changes in the rules and practice of conventional trade. (Quoted in Moore 2004: 73)

By certifying the products of family farmers, cooperatives, and ethically run commercial farms as fair trade goods, ATOs claim to encourage more socially just and environmentally sustainable forms of production. Consumers of fair-trade-certified goods pay substantially higher retail prices for such items than for their conventional counterparts, with the difference ranging up to 100 percent or more for some fresh juice and produce (Stecklow and White 2004). Such prices are intended to generate greater earnings for family farmers and living wages on commercial farms. In addition, a portion of every fair trade purchase is returned to the producer's organization itself as a "social premium" to be invested in a community project of local design. Fair trade producers are required to satisfy sustainable environmental criteria, including restricted pesticide use and practices intended to reduce erosion and maintain watersheds. Thus, the contemporary fair trade movement claims to privilege the interests of small-scale producers and the environment over large-scale agribusiness. It does so not through state intervention in commodity and labor markets but by encouraging more ethical consumer choice among the many alternatives made freely available to shoppers by neoliberal globalization.

Although the use of the term *fair trade* for the pursuit of social justice through markets is relatively recent, such initiatives date back to the mid-twentieth century in efforts to improve the prices received by artisans in the developing world for goods exported to the developed North (Jaffee 2007: 12ff.). In the 1950s, handicrafts were sold through OXFAM in the United Kingdom, SOS-Kinderhof in Holland, and the U.S.-based Mennonite SELFHELP initiative (later to become Ten Thousand Villages) in ways that averted traditional middlemen, ensuring higher prices for artisans themselves. In the United States, the marketing of coffee along fair trade lines accelerated in tandem with the Central American solidarity movement of the 1980s. The most prominent of these initiatives, Equal Exchange, developed direct marketing relationships with Nicaraguan coffee cooperatives to offset the Reagan administration's trade embargo against the Sandinista government. North American fair trade groups at their inception focused on mail-order and later online systems of distribution and have only expanded into coffeehouses and other retail outlets within the past decade. Supermarket sales remain a small, albeit growing, segment of fair trade purchases in the United States. In contrast, three European ATOs, TransFair, Max Havelaar, and Fairtrade Mark, were promoting fair trade goods in mainstream supermarkets by the late 1980s. Over the following decade, fair trade labeling initiatives proliferated in seventeen nations of Europe, North America, and Japan, each geared to its respective national market. In 1997, these organizations sought to coordinate their efforts with the creation of an umbrella group, the Fairtrade Labelling Organizations International (FLO), based in Bonn, Germany. FLO is responsible for formulating consistent certification standards for fair trade products among its member organizations and creating a unified retail market through labeling and promotion (Raynolds 2000).

In order to receive the benefits of fair trade prices, producers must satisfy an array of criteria by which FLO attests that goods are grown or manufactured under conditions of social equity and environmental sustainability. Certification standards vary according to the commodity and the scale of the enterprise that produces it (see FLO 2008). Small-scale fair trade farmers must belong to democratically run producers' associations in which participation is open to all eligible growers, regardless of ethnicity, gender, religion, or political affiliation. Alternately, if fair trade products originate on larger commercial farms, farm owners are expected to abide by International Labor Organization (ILO) standards affirming the right to association (including union membership), freedom from discrimination, prohibition of child or involuntary labor, and workplace safety. In addition, a host of environmental criteria apply to the production of fair trade goods, all designed to minimize the impact of farming on watersheds, topsoil, and wildlife. Most fair trade farmers are prohibited from using herbicides and must maintain uncultivated zones adjacent to streams to reduce chemical runoff and soil erosion. Chemical inputs are limited to a narrow range of approved substances, and the amounts and frequency of their use must be recorded on each farm. These requirements originate with ATOs based in developed countries; they are monitored through on-site visits by representatives of FLO-Cert (a third-party auditing body reportable to FLO) and are subject to little or no alteration from farmers seeking certification.[4] In some cases, the standards have been criticized for their apparent arbitrariness and lack of transparency (Raynolds 2002; Calo and Wise 2005; Giovannucci and Ponte 2005; Lyon 2006).

By 2005, FLO had established certification standards for producers of coffee, tea, cacao, bananas and many other fresh fruit and vegetables, sugar, honey, orange juice, wine, cut flowers, and spun cotton, as well as for producers of some manufactured goods. All of these items are prominently displayed on supermarket shelves in the United Kingdom and continental Europe and are heavily promoted in broadcast and print advertising. A commitment to fair trade principles is also conspicuously advertised on European retailers' Internet websites as a measure of their corporate social responsibility (see Tesco 2008, Sainsbury's 2009). By 2005, the volume of fair trade sales in the developed world reached US$1.45 billion, a nearly fivefold increase in three years (FLO 2006: 12; FLO 2004). Sales increased another 42 percent in the following year, with the leading two fair trade markets being the United Kingdom and Switzerland (FLO 2007: 11). In 2006, annual per capita sales in Britain reached US$9.19, well below Switzerland's $25.67 but more than four times their per capita level in the United States (ibid.). Despite the still rudimentary size of the U.S. market—a reflection of fair trade's relatively late arrival in North America—it is now the fastest growing market worldwide in annual percentage terms.

Fair Trade and Neoliberal Paradoxes

The contemporary fair trade movement rests on a deep (and perhaps deepening) paradox. Many consumers of fair trade goods are motivated by a strenuous opposition to the effects of neoliberal globalization as measured in the growing poverty and environmental damage in many regions of the developing world. In seeking social justice and environmental sustainability, however, fair trade pursues a market-based solution to the very problems developing from free markets. As one recent observer notes, fair trade's "voluntarist, non-statist program has been viewed by public institutions and corporations as being fundamentally compatible with neoliberal reforms" (Fridell 2007: 21); indeed, market-based fair trade has been promoted by the World Bank as an alternative to commodity control schemes and government-enforced labor standards (ibid.: 94). In place of legal and policy remedies by states on behalf of the farmers and workers who reside within their borders, fair trade seeks social justice by embracing the deregulated markets that are themselves often responsible for deepening poverty in rural communities. Thus, its means of accomplishing social justice are constrained by the structure of existing markets and the entities that dominate them, leading in many cases to fair trade's cooptation by the very corporations that the movement formerly opposed.

In summarizing the rapidly growing scholarly and advocacy literature on market-based fair trade, Fridell (2007) identifies three emergent (and often overlapping) perspectives on the phenomenon.[5] Many advocates and sympathetic scholars have identified fair trade as a means of "alternative globalization," or a mechanism to establish a parallel trading system that enhances the well-being of developing world producers by returning to them a larger share of the final sale price of their goods (Raynolds 2002; Fisher 2004; Taylor 2005; Jaffee 2007). The goal of alternative globalization is to create markets that serve the interests of both producers and consumers by setting minimal social and environmental criteria for internationally traded commodities. Others view fair trade as a form of "decommodification" in that it purports to establish a bond between producers and the buyers of their goods, rupturing the impersonal nature of global markets and substituting values of community and solidarity for capitalist competition (Lappé and Lappé 2002; Jaffee et al. 2004). Accordingly, much of the labeling on fair trade items is devoted to information about the communities in which particular products originate (often down to the specific farm and even individual responsible for their production). Packaging for many goods certified by FLO for European supermarkets highlights the ways in which fair trade producer groups invest social premiums in local development projects, creating the impression that the consumers of such goods are themselves contributing to such efforts. Finally, fair trade is viewed more modestly as a form of "shaped advantage" by which a limited number of producers enter the global market under more favorable terms, utilizing enhanced institutional capacity and marketing skills to tap into a growing niche market. Despite the movement's lofty goals of social transformation, often expressed in promotional literature extolling the new world of solidarity and equity created by fair trade producer-consumer relationships, in practice the benefits of fair trade have been limited to the more humble goals of shaped advantage. Many of the essays in this volume explore this dimension of fair trade in practice.

For consumers who embrace one or more of fair trade's transformative goals, its appeal, and no doubt one reason for its phenomenal growth, lies in its ability to engage a newfound sense of agency and identity through consumption. As Appadurai writes in an influential essay on global culture and economy, a defining attribute of contemporary marketing is the "fetishism of the consumer . . . [who] is consistently helped to believe that he or she is an actor, where in fact he or she is at best a chooser" (1990: 307). Niche marketing draws on this illusion of choice by creating a multiplicity of brands and retail commodities, each superficially differentiated by packaging and minor product differences. Each, in turn, is targeted at selected demographic groups whose personal identities—including their political beliefs—increasingly center on the goods they consume (Klein 2000). Lyon identifies the appeal of certified shade-grown coffee to environmentally minded shoppers in precisely such terms, for "the dominant *modus operandi* of identity construction has become our 'lifestyle,' which we shape through our choices as sovereign consumers" (2006: 380). The "branding" of personal identities and beliefs through an ever-proliferating array of products and transitory fashions belies a continuing tendency toward the consolidation of wholesale and retail markets in the hands of fewer and fewer corporations. From the belief that individuals transform their social identities through branded consumption, it is but a short logical step to the conclusion that as consumers they can also transform the condition of society. Such claims are widely deployed in fair trade advertising, as is the case for a fair trade chocolate bar promoted with the message that "shopping can change the world!" (Dubble 2006).

While many fair trade activists view their consumption choices as a form of alternative globalization, fair trade's growing retail prominence and redemptive potential are seen as valuable opportunities by many of the same corporations initially opposed by the movement. The $2.2 billion in fair trade sales during 2006 alone (Downie 2007) represents a loss in potential earnings for Nestlé, Proctor and Gamble, Chiquita, Cadbury's, and other global middlemen. Fair trade's sustained 30–40 percent annual growth in sales since the late 1990s has attracted the attention of these and other companies eager to break into new markets and to rehabilitate their corporate images. In 2000, when fair trade remained a minuscule presence in the U.S. market and was largely limited to mail-order and Internet sales, Murray and Raynolds already warned that "transnational corporations [are] seeking to capture these initiatives and redefine them in ways that advance not progressive agendas, but their own private profits" (2000: 73). To an extent, fair trade's future may resemble earlier commercial exploitation of the civil rights and environmental movements: initially opposed by major corporations during the 1960s and '70s, both movements have subsequently seen much of their rhetoric and imagery appropriated for marketing purposes. Yet because fair trade, unlike the civil rights and environmental movements, does not wield a political presence or constituent community apart from the retail market, the risks associated with corporate cooptation are correspondingly greater. Grassroots civil rights and environmental activists have not been deterred in their work by the appropriation of movement symbols by corporations, although some organizations might be so constrained (see Dowie 1995 regarding corporate sponsorship of environmental groups). Should global agribusiness companies come to dominate the fair trade market, however, those who advocate fair trade as a mechanism to reform the world market are likely to see its goals changed beyond recognition. Instead of promoting social justice, fair trade runs the risk of becoming a niche market catering to relatively affluent consumers seeking commodified morality in their purchases (see Fridell 2003). Reluctant to surrender the tangible material gains that fair trade has achieved among certified producers, activists thus engage in a "dance with the devil" (Jaffee 2007: 199) by inviting corporate entities controlling the largest segments of world commodity markets to launch fair-trade-labeled products themselves.

Since the 1990s, corporate attitudes toward fair trade have changed rapidly from antagonism to appropriation, recapitulating the way in which business has dealt with past adversarial social movements. In 1999,

Starbucks, the largest specialty coffee retailer in the United States, was the target of a boycott campaign by the human rights initiative Global Exchange because of its coffee-buying policies. The campaign drew attention to the huge disparities between Starbucks's retail prices (between US$10 and $12 per pound of whole coffee) and rising profit margins, on the one hand, and the declining price it paid Central American growers for their coffee beans (then about $0.30 to $0.50 per pound) (Global Exchange 2000). Following a year of damaging informational campaigns that widened the boycott to Starbucks stores in the United Kingdom and Canada, the company announced that it would stock certified fair trade coffee in all its outlets. The resolution of the boycott left many fair trade advocates dissatisfied. Claiming that it lacks access to adequate supplies of fair trade coffee to sell it in brewed form (which makes up most of its retail sales), Starbucks relegates fair trade almost exclusively to sales of whole beans (Jaffee 2007: 200). The company's professed inability to locate sufficient volumes of fair trade coffee strikes many activists as implausible (ibid.: 200–201). As is the case for most fair trade commodities, there are substantially larger supplies of coffee grown by fair trade producers than there is market demand: indeed, about 80 percent of all coffee that could potentially be labeled as fair trade is instead sold through conventional channels at lower prices (Ten Thousand Villages 2007). While Starbucks boasts that it now imports 32 percent of the fair trade coffee entering the United States (Starbucks 2007), critics contend that this commitment is unimpressive when compared with the greater than 20 percent of the U.S. specialty market that the company commands (Global Exchange 2007). Notwithstanding persisting concerns within the movement about company policies, Starbucks has publicly recrafted its image from being an adversary of fair trade to becoming a supporter of it. Starbucks's annual report extols the decision to stock fair trade coffee "as one of the ways we demonstrate our commitment to smallholder farms, and work to sustain coffee farms. Starbucks and the Fair Trade movement share common goals—to ensure that farmers receive an equitable price for their coffee" (Starbucks 2007). Despite such claims, seven years after the end of the Global Exchange boycott, fair trade made up only 3.7 percent of Starbucks's coffee sales, less than fair trade's overall percentage share of the U.S. specialty market (Grant 2007). Nor is there any evidence that Starbucks's rhetorical embrace of fair trade has altered its other internal policies. While the company flaunts its reputation for social responsibility through fair trade, it also aggressively fights unionization efforts among its own employees, a right that, ironically, is guaranteed to Starbucks's fair trade coffee suppliers in the developing world (Jaffee 2007: 206).

This strategy of reaping public-relations benefits by incorporating a single fair trade item into a much wider line of products has been seized on by other global corporations. In 2004, Proctor and Gamble, the largest coffee distributor in the United States, announced that its specialty Millstone brand would include a certified fair trade selection. Constituting minuscule sales compared to the company's Folgers label, Millstone's fair trade offering allowed Proctor and Gamble to adopt a mantle of social responsibility without altering the way it purchases the large majority of its coffee. By 2007, McDonald's and Dunkin' Donuts announced plans to serve fair trade coffee in their stores on the U.S. East Coast, and even Sam's Club, the warehouse chain of Wal-Mart, had introduced its own brand of fair trade coffee (Downie 2007) and flowers (Ziegler, chap. 4, this volume). Other companies have adopted fair trade labels only after, like Starbucks, they had earlier vowed not to bow to pressure from fair trade advocates. Cadbury's, one of the world's largest chocolate manufacturers, responding to criticisms that it relied on repressive human rights climates in West Africa to source cacao below growers' costs of production, angrily asserted, "all our . . . chocolate products are produced fairly" (Tiffin 2002: 390). As criticism persisted, however, the company introduced a fair trade chocolate bar produced with Belizean cacao. While conferring fair trade respectability on a minute segment of the company's sales, the decision did not entail any change in Cadbury's supply or labor policies elsewhere. Few corporations have so audaciously redefined themselves with respect to fair trade as the Swiss multinational Nestlé, which controls significant shares of the world's coffee and cacao markets. Targeted by a consumer boycott over three decades for its marketing of infant formula in the developing world, the company has also acquired a reputation for labor repression in its Latin American and African divisions. Nestlé has adamantly refused to reform its marketing, labor, and pricing practices and has dismissed complaints about sourcing policies for its chocolate with the claim that "all Nestlé cocoa is fairly traded" (Tiffin 2002: 390). For more than ten years, the company opposed all fair trade initiatives in coffee as unwarranted violations of "free-trade policies" (O'Nions 2006). In 2005, Nestlé abruptly ceased its rhetorical battle with fair trade and introduced its Partners' Blend freeze-dried coffee into UK supermarkets. Partners' Blend is identified on its label as "coffee that helps farmers, their communities, and the environment." Out of more than eighty-five hundred products marketed by Nestlé, it is the only one certified to carry FLO's fair trade logo.

FLO's certification of a Nestlé product prompted angry exchanges within the European fair trade movement. A spokesperson for the UK-based Fairtrade Foundation (itself affiliated with FLO) praised the decision as "a turning point. . . . Here is a major multinational listening to people and giving them what they want—a fair trade product" (quoted in O'Nions 2006). Others perceive more than a trace of irony in FLO's certification of Partners' Blend. Because Nestlé's control of much of the global coffee industry has enabled it to force down producer prices, the company is widely believed to be responsible for the misery that made fair trade necessary in the first place. The UK-based World Development Movement responded to Partners' Blend with a challenge: "If Nestlé really believes in fair trade coffee, it will alter its business practices and lobbying strategies and radically overhaul its business to ensure that all coffee farmers get a fair return for their efforts. Until then, Nestlé will remain part of the problem, not the solution" (quoted in O'Nions 2006). Short of such measures, many critics feel that to certify a single product without reference to a company's wider behavior allows corporations with abysmal environmental and labor records to redeem themselves in the eyes of consumers cheaply while leaving most of their business practices unchanged. Consumer surveys indicate that FLO's fair trade logo and principles are recognized by about half of all UK consumers, but most respondents mistakenly believe that FLO certification extends not to producers of individual goods but to the companies that package and retail them (O'Nions 2006.). Such buyers may indeed assume that global corporations such as Nestlé have been certified as "ethical" by FLO, despite the fact that just one-tenth of one percent of the coffee sold by the company is acquired through fair trade channels.

FLO's decision to certify Partners' Blend points to a developing rift within the fair trade movement. Some segments of the movement, including representatives of TransFair, a FLO affiliate and the largest U.S.-based ATO, welcome the new marketing opportunities arising from the desire of multinational corporations to acquire a socially responsible image through some fair trade sourcing. Many activists outside the organization consider this view of fair trade as simply a niche market to be a betrayal of the movement's original intention to reform the whole global trading system. Following intense debate over these positions 'at the 2005 Fair Trade Futures Conference in Chicago, several groups broke away from TransFair to establish certifying ATOs of their own. Dean Cycon, founder of Dean's Beans Coffee, argued against a fair trade system dominated by multinational corporations in the following terms: "Is the goal of fair trade to have every roaster use five percent fair trade coffee, thereby dooming the other 95 percent of farmers to deepening debt? Or, is the goal to transform the world coffee market into a more just system of trade?" (quoted in Caldwell and Bacon 2006). Indeed, the former approach, which appears to be the emerging model, suggests another paradox in the fair trade movement, one that would be predicted from the classical economic models that inform neoliberalism. By stimulating the production of traditional exports, such as coffee, cacao, and bananas, fair trade may well contribute to the glut of such commodities on world markets. Ironically, this would depress prices for the large majority of growers lacking access to fair trade networks (Economist 2006). The demand for fair trade coffee, currently the most widely sold certified commodity, remains insufficient to absorb supplies on a glutted world market: FLO estimates that the capacity of producers worldwide who could meet certification standards is roughly seven times the current volume exported via fair trade channels (Murray et al. 2006).

The Organization of This Volume:
Fair Trade in Discourse and Practice

In recent years, poststructuralists in anthropology and other disciplines have characterized the "development encounter" as a form of hegemonic discourse originating in powerful institutions (e.g., the U.S. Agency for International Development or the World Bank) whose policies seek to reshape the cultures and economies of the postcolonial world (Ferguson 1994; Escobar 1995). Designed to re-create formerly colonized societies in the image of the now-industrialized countries, development from this perspective is seen as an imposition of Western assumptions that privilege scientific rationality over local knowledge and cultural traditions, not to mention over the desires of development "recipients" themselves. Illuminating as it may be to examine the ideological underpinnings of development through consideration of institutional policies and rhetoric, anthropologists whose research has centered on the "development encounter" itself point out limitations when this view is applied to the outcome of such projects (Mosse 1997; Woost 1997; Rossi 2006). A discursive approach can elucidate the means by which powerful institutions legitimate their actions to state sponsors and the broader public, but it offers little insight into the factional struggles waged within states, development institutions, and NGOs that determine how (or whether) those practices are put in place (Mosse 2004: 644). Indeed, by rendering development as a largely monolithic enterprise, discursive approaches betray at best a partial understanding of both decolonizing states and the workings of development agencies (see Grillo 1997: 20ff.), in turn precluding an appreciation of the contested nature of institutional policies and their implementation (Mosse and Lewis 2006: 4–5). "While [development knowledge] may function hegemonically," Gardner observes from her study of one such project, "it is also created and recreated by multiple agents, who often have very different understandings of their work" (1997: 134). Finally, and perhaps most seriously, discursive approaches do little to illuminate how the intended beneficiaries of development practices in the Global South interpret, accommodate, or resist these policies; nor do they explain why development programs yield results so often at variance with the discourse on which they are based (Little and Painter 1995: 605). It is here that the ethnographic imperative—rooted in the fine-grained documentation of communities and regions affected by institutional power, state policies, and markets—provides a more powerful insight into development in practice.

Not unlike discursive analyses of development, much that has been written of the fair trade movement has taken as its point of departure the language of fair trade advocates in the now-developed world. This discourse draws heavily from the "alternative globalization" and "decommodification" models elucidated by Fridell (2007), that is, those segments of the movement that challenge the free-market assumptions of neoliberalism and the impersonal nature of market-based relationships. Thus, fair trade advocates claim that the movement challenges processes "that devalue and exploit disadvantaged peoples and the environment" and aims to "re-embed commodity circuits within ecological and social relations" (Raynolds 2000: 298). It is seen as a means by which solidarity and mutual respect are created between regions, substituting these values for capitalist motives of competition and profit maximization (see Hudson and Hudson 2003; Fisher 2004). The ideological basis of fair trade has been identified as one of "moral economy" (Luetchford 2008: 152), much as Thompson (1971) and Scott (1976) described peasant resistance to the corrosive effects of markets on traditional livelihoods and social obligations. The movement is premised, Fridell writes, on nothing less than "a mixture of traditional and contemporary Christian values, the liberal human and

labor rights embodied in the conventions of the International Labor Organization and the UN, and a radical interpretation of the Enlightenment
values of social justice" (2007: 285). For all the value-laden, indeed moral,
discourse surrounding fair trade advocacy, however, comparatively little
attention has been paid to the processes by which these values are to be
established among fair trade producers and consumers. What is needed
to complement this discourse—most of which arises from the retail end
of the commodity chain and among those promoting fair trade in the developed countries—is an ethnographically grounded examination of how
fair trade operates in practice. Does it in fact attain the goals of social justice and environmental sustainability that fair trade advocates identify as
the movement's central premises? Does it create the kind of transparent,
reciprocal relationships between producers and consumers described in
much fair trade advocacy? What are the practical limits of certification-
dependent strategies within a neoliberal context in which many states
have abandoned their regulatory role? Do the producers' organizations
required of fair trade participants operate in the democratic, gender-in-
clusive fashion spelled out as a condition of certification? And finally, as
discursive approaches to development might ask, to what extent does fair
trade certification operate as a means of governance and control rather
than a mechanism of economic and social emancipation?

Spanning both the developed and developing worlds and an array of
"fairly traded" commodities, the ten case studies in this book juxtapose
fair trade in practice with the advocacy on which the movement is based.
We have organized the chapters around three broad themes emerging
from the discourse of fair trade and the producer-consumer relationships
established under certification. Each of these parts, in turn, is preceded
by a short introduction examining how our contributors approach these
themes. The first part, "Global Markets and Local Realities," involves
four ethnographic explorations of how fair trade actually operates on the
ground in different commodity systems—coffee, bananas, tea, and cut
flowers. These commodities entail vastly differing production arrangements, ranging from small-scale household-based farming (Moberg's
study of St. Lucian banana growers), to a mix of small-scale farms and
larger entities operated with wage labor (Smith's exploration of the specialty coffee market), to plantation-based producers (Besky's study of
Indian tea production), and finally highly capitalized commercial farms
(Ziegler's examination of the cut flower market). Each of these case studies
reveals in distinctive ways how disparities persist between the profound

social transformations that fair trade promotes in its public advocacy and the modest (or, in some instances, nonexistent) material improvements that it has attained for certified producers.

A second group of case studies is organized around the theme of "Negotiating Difference and Identity in Fair Trade Markets." In addition to redefining producer-consumer relationships, fair trade's certification standards have prioritized gender equality, community empowerment, and democratic participation within producer groups. Lyon's study of a Guatemalan coffee cooperative and Dolan's examination of Kenyan tea producers both raise questions about fair trade's ability to secure gender equity in a context of longstanding patriarchal domestic and economic arrangements. Ethnic identity forms the focus of Wilson's study of Ecuadorian craft producers, who either gain or are denied access to a lucrative fair trade market according to their ability to deploy "acceptably indigenous" behaviors. These case studies point to the continuing asymmetries in power between commodity producers and those who procure their goods for fair trade distribution. In Foucauldian terms, they suggest that the emancipatory discourses of fair trade entail systems of governance that operate by alternately benefiting or withholding benefits from those who are subject to them.

The final three chapters explore alternative trade from the vantage point of consumption and its meanings, embracing the theme of "Relationships and Consumption in Fair Trade Markets and Alternative Economies." Although the number of certified fair trade commodities has expanded dramatically in recent years, most goods remain entirely outside fair trade networks, notwithstanding great inequities involved in their production and sale. Papavasiliou's study of an alternative currency system in Ithaca, New York, suggests a direct counterpart to transnational alternative trade that seeks greater justice and strengthened bonds between producers and consumers. Like fair trade, however, the vast majority of commodities and exchanges in Ithaca remain outside the sphere of circulation of the city's alternative currency. Doane's examination of "relationship coffees" reveals how the meanings that roasters and consumers in North America impute to fair trade relationships are rarely shared among Mexican fair trade coffee producers themselves, again illustrating a gulf between the ways fair trade advocates and producers conceptualize the new trading system. Finally, M'Closkey demonstrates that the marketing of textiles on fair trade Internet sites has served to impoverish Navajo weavers whose designs are appropriated by lower-cost craft producers elsewhere, promoting the very "race to the bottom" that the movement was intended to challenge.

Emerging from all three sets of case studies in this volume are a number of conclusions regarding the local impact of fair trade networks and certification. Clearly, fair trade has provided measurable and in some cases significant economic benefits to small-scale household-based farmers with access to alternative markets. Because most producers of any given commodity lack such access, however, the differential distribution of higher fair trade prices is likely to result in heightened economic disparities within producer communities. Hence, prior constraints—whether personal or political, tenurial or agronomic—that limit the access of some producers to fair trade markets may well become the basis of growing local stratification. Besky's and Ziegler's studies of plantation-based production systems reveal that fair trade's benefits to wageworkers are far less evident and are probably inferior to what could be gained through greater state regulation. Although fair trade advocates claim to transform relationships among producers themselves, a closer examination reveals that in many ways they remain unchanged. Where women retain a significant role in export production and are often farm owners in their own right, as in St. Lucia, they have been able to take advantage of the benefits of fair trade markets at levels comparable to their male counterparts. Where more entrenched patriarchal traditions prevail, as in Guatemala and Kenya, fair trade's rhetorical commitment to gender equality appears to have largely failed to ameliorate the subordination of women within the public and domestic spheres, not to mention their role in production and marketing. Finally, these case studies reveal that the fair trade movement is failing to realize its most fundamental goal—the radical transformation of producer-consumer relationships through the elimination of exploitative middlemen. While fair trade advocates claim that it fosters greater equity and mutual respect, in reality this alternative market has created a new category of middlemen, foreign ATOs and certifiers. While producers may no longer suffer under the weight of coffee *coyotes* and other market middlemen, the case studies demonstrate that ATOs and certifiers exert equal power through their ability to extend fair trade market access and its attendant benefits to some producers while withholding them from others.

In Jane Henrici's concluding assessment, she steps back from the particulars of these case studies to outline a broader path toward a more equitable exchange system at both the global and local levels, one that would move beyond neoliberal conceptions of private governance. At present, she notes, trading rights supersede human rights in virtually all corners of the contemporary global economy. The right to make a profit takes precedence within most nation-states over other rights, such as the values of social justice and environmental sustainability endorsed by the fair trade movement. Henrici argues that those who sympathize with the goals of alternative trade need to articulate a set of universal trading rights, analogous and perhaps related to those of human rights as expressed in the charters of various multinational organizations. The challenge emerging from these case studies is to discover the common values on which to base our exchanges and thereby to make all of them more economically equitable as well as socially just. In the process, Henrici contends, we may reprivilege ourselves and our communities over the commodities we consume.

NOTES

1. By *neoliberalism* we mean doctrines or policies that accord the market rather than the state the main role in satisfying economic and other needs (see for example Edelman and Haugerud 2005).

2. Many fair trade advocates claim that the "free market" rhetoric employed by governments of the developed countries is essentially hypocritical. They note that such governments use multilateral agencies such as the IMF and WTO to impose a removal of subsidies in developing countries while retaining protectionist measures for their own economies (Lappé and Lappé 2002; Stiglitz 2002). Hence, governments of the developed North subsidize their agricultural sectors by an estimated one billion dollars daily, then dump much of their surpluses at low prices on deregulated markets in the global South, to the detriment of local producers (Fridell 2007: 92).

3. The ICA imposed export quotas and regulated coffee supplies on global markets to provide a price floor that covered most producers' costs of production. It collapsed in 1989 after the U.S. delegation to the agreement insisted on free-market reforms. The Lomé Convention regulated the importation of agricultural goods into the European market, imposing tariffs and quotas to protect export prices for items produced by countries that are former African, Caribbean, and Pacific (ACP) colonies of Europe. Many of these provisions were renegotiated following the creation of the Single European Market in 1993, while others, notably provisions protecting ACP banana producers, were challenged by the United States in the World Trade Organization (Clegg 2002; Josling 2003).

4. As we show in the cases of shade-grown coffee (Lyon 2006: 384) and fair trade bananas (Moberg 2005: 11), the environmental requirements of certification as mandated by ATOs in the developed North frequently strike producers in the developing world as inappropriate or irrational.

5. Similarly, Jaffee (2007: 26ff) distinguishes between segments of the fair trade movement who view it as a "market-breaking," a "market reform," or a "market access" mechanism, with each segment staking different ideological positions with regard to participation in existing global markets and the corporations that dominate them.

WORKS CITED

Appadurai, A.
  1990 Disjuncture and Difference in the Global Cultural Economy. Theory, Culture and
    Society 7(2): 295–310.
Barrientos, S., and C. Dolan
  2006 Transformation of Global Food: Opportunities and Challenges of Fair and
    Ethical Trade. *In* Ethical Sourcing in the Global Food System. S. Barrientos and
    C. Dolan, eds. Pp. 1–34. London: Earthscan.
Basch, L., N. Glick Schiller, and C. Szanton-Blanc
  1994 Nations Unbound: Transnational Projects, Postcolonial Predicaments, and Deter-
    ritorialized Nation-States. Amsterdam: Gordon and Breach.
Baumann, Z.
  1998 Globalization: The Human Consequences. New York: Columbia University Press.
Brennan, T.
  2003 Globalization and Its Terrors: Daily Life in the West. London: Routledge.
Caldwell, Z. T., and C. Bacon
  2006 Fair Trade's Future: Scaling Up without Selling Out? http://us.oneworld.net/
    article/view/123087/, accessed September 1, 2006.
Calo, M., and T. A. Wise
  2005 Revaluing Peasant Coffee Production: Organic and Fair Trade Markets in
    Mexico. Medford, MA: Global Development and Environment Institute, Tufts
    University.
Charveriat, C.
  2001 Bitter Coffee: How the Poor Are Paying for the Slump in Coffee Prices. London:
    Oxfam.
Clegg, P.
  2002 The Caribbean Banana Trade: From Colonialism to Globalization. Basingstoke,
    UK: Palgrave Macmillan.
Collier, G.
  1994 Basta! Land and the Zapatista Rebellion in Chiapas. Oakland, CA: Food First.
Collier, R.
  2001 Mourning Coffee: World's Leading Java Companies Are Raking in High
    Profits, but Growers Worldwide Face Ruin as Prices Sink to Historic Lows. San
    Francisco Chronicle, May 20: A1.
Collins, J. L.
  2000 Tracing Social Relations in Commodity Chains: The Case of Grapes in
    Brazil. *In* Commodities and Globalization: Anthropological Perspectives. A.
    Haugerud, M. P. Stone, and P. Little, eds. Pp. 97–109. New York: Rowman and
    Littlefield.

Dowie, M.
   1995 Losing Ground: American Environmentalism at the Close of the 20th Century.
      Cambridge, MA: MIT Press.
Downie, A.
   2007 Fair Trade in Bloom. New York Times, October 2: C1–5.
Dubble
   2006 Fairtrade. http://www.dubble.co.uk/fairtrade/, accessed October 24, 2006.
Economist
   2006 Good Food? 381(8507): 12.
Edelman, M., and A. Haugerud
   2005 Introduction: The Anthropology of Development and Globalization. In The An-
      thropology of Development and Globalization. M. Edelman and A. Haugerud,
      eds. Pp. 1–74. London: Blackwell.
Escobar, A.
   1995 Encountering Development: The Making and Unmaking of the Third World.
      Princeton, NJ: Princeton University Press.
Farmer, P.
   1999 Infections and Inequality: The Modern Plagues. Berkeley: University of Califor-
      nia Press.
Ferguson, J.
   1994 The Anti-politics Machine: Development, Depoliticization and Bureaucratic
      Power in Lesotho. Minneapolis: University of Minnesota Press.
Fischer, E. F., and P. Benson
   2006 Broccoli and Desire: Global Connections and Maya Struggles in Postwar
      Guatemala. Stanford, CA: Stanford University Press.
Fisher, C.
   2004 Report from the Field: Fair Trade and the Idea of the Market. North American
      Dialogue 7(2): 15–18.
FLO (Fairtrade Labelling Organizations International)
   2004 Impact. http://www.fairtrade.net/sites/impact/impact.html, accessed March 8,
      2004.
   2006 News Bulletin, July. http://www.fairtrade.net/news_bulletin.html, accessed
      September 17, 2006.
   2007 2006/7 Annual Report. http://www.fairtrade.net/uploads/media/Final_FLO_
      AR_2007_01.pdf, accessed September 3, 2007.
   2008 FLO International Standards. http://www.fairtrade.net/standards.html, accessed
      April 2, 2008.
Fridell, G.
   2003 Fair Trade and the International Moral Economy: Within and Against the
      Market. Toronto: Centre for Research on Latin America and the Caribbean, York
      University.
   2007 Fair Trade Coffee: The Prospects and Pitfalls of Market-Driven Social Justice.
      Toronto: University of Toronto Press.

Gardner, K.
  1997 Mixed Messages: Contested "Development" and the "Plantation Rehabilitation Project." *In* Discourses of Development: Anthropological Perspectives. R. D. Grillo and R. T. Stirrat, eds. Pp. 133–156. Oxford, UK: Berg.
Giovannucci, D., and S. Ponte
  2005 Standards as a New Form of Social Contract? Sustainability Initiatives in the Coffee Industry. Food Policy 30(1): 284–301.
Global Exchange
  2000 An Open Letter to Starbucks. http://www.globalexchange.org/campaigns/fairtrade/coffee/OpenLetterToStarbucks.html, accessed September 3, 2007.
  2007 Starbucks Campaign. http://www.globalexchange.org/campaigns/fairtrade/coffee/starbucks.html, accessed September 3, 2007.
Grant, J.
  2007 Does Fair Trade Coffee Work? The Environment Report, April 2. http://environmentreport.org/transcript.php3?story_id=3374, accessed September 3, 2007.
Greider, W.
  1997 One World, Ready or Not: The Manic Logic of Global Capitalism. New York: Simon and Schuster.
Grillo, R. D.
  1997 Discourses of Development: The View from Anthropology. *In* Discourses of Development: Anthropological Perspectives. R. D. Grillo and R. T. Stirrat, eds. Pp. 1–34. Oxford, UK: Berg.
Harvey, D.
  1989 The Condition of Postmodernity. Oxford, UK: Blackwell.
Helleiner, E.
  1994 From Bretton Woods to Global Finance: A World Turned Upside Down. *In* Political Economy and the Changing Global Order. R. Stubbs and G. R. D. Underhill, eds. Pp. 163–175. New York: St. Martin's.
Hudson, I., and M. Hudson.
  2003 Removing the Veil? Commodity Fetishism, Fair Trade, and the Environment. Organization and Environment 16(10): 413–430.
Jaffee, D.
  2007 Brewing Justice: Fair Trade Coffee, Sustainability, and Survival. Berkeley: University of California Press.
Jaffee, D., J. R. Kloppenburg, Jr., and M. B. Monroy
  2004 Bringing the "Moral Charge" Home: Fair Trade within the North and within the South. Rural Sociology 69(2): 169–196.
Josling, T.
  2003 Bananas and the WTO: Testing the New Dispute Settlement Process. *In* Banana Wars: The Anatomy of a Trade Dispute. T. E. Josling and T. G. Taylor, eds. Pp. 169–194. Cambridge, MA: CABI.
Klein, N.
  2000 No Logo: Taking Aim at the Brand Bullies. New York: Picador.
Lappé, F., and A. Lappé
  2002 Hope's Edge: The Next Diet for a Small Planet. New York: Putnam.

Little, P. D., and M. Painter
   1995 Discourse, Politics, and the Development Process: Reflections on Escobar's
      "Anthropology and the Development Encounter." American Ethnologist 22(3):
      602–616.
Luetchford, P.
   2008 Fair Trade and a Global Commodity: Coffee in Costa Rica. London: Pluto.
Lyon, S.
   2006 Migratory Imaginations: The Commodification and Contradictions of Shade
      Grown Coffee. Social Anthropology 14(3): 377–390.
Moberg, M.
   2005 Fair Trade and Eastern Caribbean Banana Farmers: Rhetoric and Reality in the
      Anti-globalization Movement. Human Organization 64(1): 4–15.
   2008 Slipping Away: Banana Politics and Fair Trade in the Eastern Caribbean. New
      York: Berghahn Books.
Moore, G.
   2004 The Fair Trade Movement: Parameters, Issues, and Future Research. Journal of
      Business Ethics 53(1): 73–86.
Mosse, D.
   1997 The Ideological and Politics of Community Participation: Tank Irrigation De-
      velopment in Colonial and Contemporary Tamil Nadu. In Discourses of Devel-
      opment: Anthropological Perspectives. R. D. Grillo and R. T. Stirrat, eds. Pp.
      255–292. Oxford, UK: Berg.
   2004 Is Good Policy Unimplementable? Reflections on the Ethnography of Aid Policy
      and Practice. Development and Change 35(4): 639–671.
Mosse, D., and D. Lewis
   2006 Theoretical Approaches to Brokerage and Translation in Development. In De-
      velopment Brokers and Translators: The Ethnography of Aid and Agencies. D.
      Lewis and D. Mosse, eds. Pp. 1–34. Bloomfield, CT: Kumarian.
Murray, D. L., and L. T. Raynolds
   2000 Alternative Trade in Bananas: Obstacles and Opportunities for Progressive Social
      Change in the Global Economy. Agriculture and Human Values 17(1): 65–75.
Murray, D. L., L. T. Raynolds, and P. L. Taylor
   2006 The Future of Fair Trade Coffee: Dilemmas Facing Latin America's Small-Scale
      Producers. Development in Practice 16: 179–192.
Nash, J.
   1994 Global Integration and Subsistence Insecurity. American Anthropologist 96(1):
      7–30.
O'Nions, J.
   2006 Fairtrade and Global Justice. http://www.grain.org/seedling/?id=430, accessed
      September 1, 2006.
Raynolds, L. T.
   2000 Re-embedding Global Agriculture: The International Organic and Fair Trade
      Movements. Agriculture and Human Values 17(3): 297–309.
   2002 Consumer/Producer Links in Fair Trade Coffee Networks. Sociologia Ruralis
      42(4): 404–424.

Rossi, B.
  2006 Aid Policies and Recipient Strategies in Niger: Why Donors and Recipients Should Not Be Compartmentalized into Separate "Worlds of Knowledge." *In* Development Brokers and Translators: The Ethnography of Aid and Agencies. D. Lewis and D. Mosse, eds. Pp. 27–50. Bloomfield, CT: Kumarian.
Sainsbury's
  2009 Sourcing with Integrity. http://www.j-sainsbury.co.uk/cr/index.asp?pageid=36, accessed October 21, 2009.
Scott, J. C.
  1976 The Moral Economy of the Peasant: Subsistence and Rebellion in Southeast Asia. New Haven, CT: Yale University Press.
Starbucks
  2007 Starbucks Corporation Fiscal 2007 Corporate Social Responsibility Annual Report. http://www.starbucks.com/aboutus/csrreport/Starbucks_CSR_FY2007.pdf, accessed October 20, 2009.
Stecklow, S., and E. White
  2004 What Price Virtue? At Some Retailers, "Fair Trade" Carries a Very High Cost. Wall Street Journal, June 8.
Stiglitz, J.
  2002 Globalization and Its Discontents. New York: Norton.
Taylor, P. L.
  2005 In the Market but Not of It: Fair Trade Coffee and Forest Stewardship Council Certification as Market-Based Social Change. World Development 33: 129–147.
Ten Thousand Villages
  2007 Fair Trade Sales Increase around the World! http://www.tenthousandvillages.ca/cgiin/category.cgi?type=store&item=pageZAAAB45&template=fullpage-en&category=news, accessed September 2, 2007.
Tesco
  2008 Tesco Corporate Information. http://www.tesco.com/corporateinfo/, accessed January 23, 2008.
Thompson, E. P.
  1971 The Moral Economy of the English Crowd in the Eighteenth Century. Past and Present 5: 76–136.
Tiffin, P.
  2002 A Chocolate Coated Case for Alternative International Business. Development in Practice 12(3–4): 383–397.
Woost, M. D.
  1997 Alternative Vocabularies of Development? "Community" and "Participation" in Development Discourse in Sri Lanka. *In* Discourses of Development: Anthropological Perspectives. R. D. Grillo and R. T. Stirrat, eds. Pp. 229–254. Oxford, UK: Berg.
Ziegler, C.
  2007 Favored Flowers: Culture and Economy in a Global System. Durham, NC: Duke University Press.

Part I
....

Global Markets and Local Realities
Regulating and Expanding Fair Trade

The first set of contributions in our volume, juxtaposed with the claims of much fair trade discourse, offers ethnographic explorations of how fair trade operates on the ground in four vastly different commodity systems: coffee, bananas, tea, and cut flowers. As the first and still most extensively marketed fair trade commodity, coffee fixes in the minds of many consumers the image of fair trade as a production system based on small-scale independent farmers employing family labor. Julia Smith notes that this perception remains widespread despite a growing trend toward fair trade certification of coffee marketed by transnational corporations such as Kraft and General Mills, which source the vast majority of their products from large commercial farms operated with wage labor. Meanwhile, many of the original aims of the fair trade movement, including commitments to sustained relationships with small-scale producers, infrastructure and development investments in farming communities, and returns above the world market price, have now been adopted in the specialty coffee market dominated by smaller, often locally based brands. Although specialty roasters operate outside the formal fair trade certification system, they may purchase the coffee of small growers at a price several times higher than the prevailing fair trade price, which has declined in real terms over the past two decades. As a distinct market niche, then, fair trade has lost much of its original significance, according to Smith, while the higher prices paid by specialty roasters have led many small-scale growers to forgo fair trade certification and its burdensome requirements in favor of the less hierarchical specialty market.

The St. Lucian banana growers featured in Mark Moberg's chapter are in many ways emblematic of the small-scale household-based producers traditionally associated with fair trade. Fair trade's claim to redefine the relationship between producers and consumers in equitable and reciprocal terms is belied by the nonnegotiable nature of the certification criteria to which Caribbean farmers must adhere. Throughout the region bananas growers frequently express resentment at fair trade's environmental requirements, which originate with European certifiers and are widely regarded as inappropriate and costly in an island context in which both land and labor are scarce. Compared with their conventional farming counterparts, however, fair trade banana producers have experienced measurable economic advantages in a region buffeted by neoliberal policies and trade wars in recent years, and for most farmers these material gains outweigh the costs of certification. Many in fact attribute their ability to persist in a deregulated European market to the benefits of higher fair trade prices. Moberg also finds some social benefits deriving from the workings of fair trade farmer groups themselves. Their newfound ability to invest social premiums in projects of their own design has had the unintended effect of enhancing local decision-making and freeing some communities from the vagaries and factionalism of island patronage politics.

In contrast, Catherine Ziegler's study of the cut flower trade shows how fair trade's recent extension of certification to nontraditional commodities from commercial farms has diluted the movement's original intent, much as Smith mentions for coffee. Unlike the small-scale growers associated with fair trade in the Caribbean and Central America, cut flower producers in South America and East Africa are owners of large, capital-intensive farms. These entities may employ hundreds of workers and generally rely on sophisticated marketing connections with retailers in the developed North. Ziegler notes that the high capital costs of the greenhouses and specialized technology required of flower production for export have excluded smallholding farmers from that sector. In cut flower production, the beneficial effects of social premiums that Moberg discerned in the Caribbean are largely absent, as fair trade has been unable to ensure that economic benefits flow to farm workers themselves. Further, because flowers of various sources are often mixed and sold as bouquets in flower shops and supermarkets, effective fair trade labeling becomes almost impossible at the retail level. The virtual absence of branding in turn undermines one of alternative trade's core assumptions by restricting the consumer's ability to choose between fair trade and conventional cut flowers.

Finally, Sarah Besky notes similar limitations in the distribution of fair trade benefits in Indian Darjeeling tea production, which is based on privately owned plantations rather than cooperatively organized small farmers. Not only are fair trade's certification standards for worker welfare weaker than the rights formerly granted plantation workers under Indian law, but most of the benefits of higher fair trade tea prices and marketing connections have accrued to owners rather than their employees. Indeed,

Besky notes that the harvest piece rate paid to tea plantation workers has not changed at all as a result of fair trade certification. In examining how fair trade operates in systems of plantation production, both Ziegler and Besky note the inability of market-based mechanisms to compensate fully for the neoliberal state's diminished role in regulating working conditions and wages. Comparison of the four cases suggests that fair trade does not appear to ameliorate inequality where it already exists (on commercial farms, for example) and may even contribute to inequality in small-scale farming communities. In the Caribbean, as Moberg argues, most banana producers were formerly on a comparable economic footing but are now witnessing economic disparities between growers who produce for fair trade markets and those whose land tenure arrangements prevent them from earning fair trade certification. On the plantations and commercial farms featured in Besky's and Ziegler's work, the fair trade market has benefited farm owners at least as much as, if not more than, the wage- and pieceworkers who provide the labor of planting, harvesting, and processing. Ironically, these are the very producers that fair trade is presumed to support.

Fair Trade and the Specialty Coffee Market
Growing Alliances, Shifting Rivalries

JULIA SMITH

The fair trade movement has achieved great success in creating a new set of rules for a corner of the coffee market; this change in rules has had positive effects for fair-trade-certified producers and vendors but has also had influence far beyond the formal fair trade market. This chapter examines the links between the formally defined (certified) fair trade market and two closely related markets. The first related market is the specialty coffee market, in which substantially higher prices are paid for coffee of exceptional quality. This chapter argues that, at least in the United States, the fair trade market has effectively come to be part of the specialty coffee market, adopting its quality standards. At the same time, the fair trade market has influenced both the terms of trade and the rhetoric of the specialty coffee market. The second related market, consisting of vendors who essentially market what they might call "fairer than fair trade" coffee, developed in response to the mainstreaming of the fair trade market and its perceived inadequacies and compromises. Not surprisingly, the shift from a small fair trade coffee market sold mostly through food cooperatives and church groups to a large fair trade coffee market solidly situated in supermarkets and large coffeehouse chains such as Starbucks has led to a variety of conflicts over the future of the fair trade movement and marketing system. The commonalities and conflicts between these three systems—the broad specialty market, the fair-trade-certified market, and these "fairer" vendors—and their rhetoric raise a set of issues about the nature of "fair trade."

The conflicts within the fair trade movement, one part social movement and one part a system of market certification, have been highlighted by a variety of authors (Jaffee 2007 and Raynolds and Long 2007 do a particularly nice job of discussing the terms of the conflict). This chapter does not focus on the conflict between activism and market orientation in the fair trade conflict but instead examines the ways in which various coffee vendors manipulate the content of this conflict to their own advantage in the marketplace of coffee rather than the marketplace of ideas. To do so, I first examine how the fair trade and specialty markets have grown together and affected one another. I argue that the fair trade market and the specialty coffee market have over time come to resemble each other, with fair trade sellers emphasizing quality and specialty sellers emphasizing their close relationships with producers and generosity in their financial negotiations with them. The end result is that a variety of specialty sellers can present themselves as equivalent to, or as even better than, fair-trade-certified coffee. Some of these non-fair-trade sellers offer terms and conditions that really are equivalent to fair trade terms, while others offer terms that sound similar but are in practice substantially worse. This variability means that the fair trade label still has value, as a guarantee of a certain set of terms; the alternative is essentially to attempt to evaluate the sellers' representations of their business individually, which is difficult even for the knowledgeable consumer. This underlines the importance of a certification system but also raises questions of how and whether to reward those who really do invest more in helping coffee farmers and their communities.

Molly Doane's chapter in this volume deals with some similar issues by focusing on recent ethnographic data from midwestern roasters and consumers. Here I employ a longer and broader perspective, situating this set of current fair trade issues within a wider context of shifting coffee markets and discourses around them. This chapter largely focuses on the analysis of publicly available figures and discourse, because it is specifically focused on the issues of how various coffee markets interact and how public rhetoric within them is similar and different. Nevertheless, the concerns with which it deals and the understandings offered here arise from ethnographic work.

The analysis presented here emerges from eighteen months of ethnographic fieldwork conducted in a coffee-producing community in southern Costa Rica in 1995, 1997–98, and 2005. As part of this work, I interviewed coffee producers, buyers, and promoters in Mexico, Central America, and the United States. In addition, I collected information from published sources and interviews regarding the shifts in the coffee market over the past fifteen years, both in the fair trade market and in the broader specialty coffee market. Accounts of southern Costa Rican experience with fair trade and conventional coffee markets have been published elsewhere (Smith 2001, 2007, 2009). Specifically, I have outlined (Smith 2001) the history of the local area and engaged questions of what kinds of environmentally sustainable practices have been integrated into production and under what circumstances. Elsewhere (Smith 2007), I have argued that farmers in southern Costa Rica have had mixed experience with fair trade markets. They did not receive as many benefits from the fair trade market as some groups have reported because they were already organized into democratic cooperatives under a national system that regulated how much of the price of coffee sales processors and exporters could retain as profits. Moreover, organizational problems limited their ability to take advantage of the fair trade market. On the other hand, their work with an American university to sell directly to North American consumers has been reasonably successful.

In Smith 2009, I focus on the attempts of farmers from southern Costa Rica and their neighbors in western Panama to find their footing in the specialty coffee market. I find that the structures described above, in which democratically organized cooperatives helped to shape the terms of the market and a regulatory system ensures that producers can retain much of the price of their coffee, allowed Costa Rican farmers to thrive in the conventional coffee market. However, this success led to struggles in the elite coffee market; structures created to produce large amounts of consistently good coffee stand in the way of creating the sorts of distinctive coffee that achieve high prices. This problem is exacerbated by the fact that climatic differences between this area and other parts of Costa Rica have made it hard to capitalize on successes by other Costa Rican coffees. In western Panama, on the other hand, a relatively poor position in the conventional coffee market created a flexibility that has given way to great success in the specialty coffee market, led by the famous Geisha from Hacienda La Esmeralda. This last project has led to my current interest in how coffee sellers create a discourse about coffee and its qualities, employing concepts of fair trade and other, more broadly defined ethical standards.

The Changing Nature of the Fair Trade Coffee System

The certification system developed within the fair trade system allows consumers to be confident about the ways in which the coffee was produced and how the producers were treated by the coffee retailer throughout the trading relationship. To be certified as fair trade coffee, vendors must agree to guarantee a "fair" minimum price (with appropriate increases when the world market price surpasses the minimum level) of $1.25 a pound for conventional and $1.45 for organic coffee (with slightly lower prices for dry processed *arabica* and all *robusta* coffee) (FLO 2009). In addition, they pay a premium—an additional $0.10 a pound, which goes to projects "enhancing [the area's] social, economic and environmental development." These payments are made to a certified producers' association, whose members must be small producers organized into a democratic cooperative who work to set and meet local "objectives for social, economic and environmental sustainability," which in practice generally means moving toward organic production (FLO 2008a, 2008b). In addition, fair trade buyers are encouraged to create "a long term and stable relationship" with producer cooperatives and required to provide financing for production equivalent to 60 percent of the purchase price (FLO 2008b).

In multiple ways, the fair trade movement has created solid and very significant successes for producers and for the market systems (Lyon 2005; Murray et al. 2003; Jaffee 2007). Perhaps the most important success lies in raising the volume of small-producer coffee sold through high-value markets. The volume of coffee sold through fair trade markets has increased astronomically, reaching over 114 million pounds worldwide and nearly three-quarters of a billion dollars in revenue (FLO 2007; TransFair 2007). Moreover, this growth came at a critical time; in 1998, when coffee prices were high, less than one hundred thousand pounds of coffee were certified in the United States (TransFair 2007). During the next several years, during which the world market price of coffee hit record lows, bottoming out at forty-one cents per pound of green coffee in September 2001 and not returning consistently to over a dollar a pound until late 2006 (ICO 2008), fair trade coffee sales grew exponentially, reaching over sixty million pounds in 2006. While the conventional coffee market slumped below the costs of production for years in much of the world, the fair trade system offered a way for small farmers to make ends meet and promised that coffee production would remain profitable in the future (Gresser and Tickell 2002).

Claims regarding nonmonetary benefits have been more contested, with some producers and producer communities reporting that they have received great benefits, while others have had much more mixed experiences. Elsewhere (Smith 2007), I have argued that the early adopters of fair trade in southern Costa Rica have had limited benefit from their experience with the fair trade market. Most cooperative members largely viewed it as a higher-value market with limited growth potential but were not aware of the nonmonetary benefits that theoretically accrue to fair trade cooperatives. Sales through a second "fair" but not certified system involving a partnership with an American university have had a far greater impact on the area. The relationships formed between researchers, student volunteers in the organization, and cooperative leaders are considered by most observers to be warm and productive (Smith 2007). Even within producer communities, benefits are unevenly distributed; in particular, individuals who take on leadership positions and thus build relationships with outside vendors, activists, and experts in the field often have stronger commitments to and better opinions of the fair trade system than do the rank-and-file members of cooperatives.

Twenty years ago, when the fair trade market entered onto the world stage, almost all small-producer coffee—indeed the vast majority of all coffee—passed through the conventional coffee market. In this market, prices are set through a small number of well-organized commodity markets (the most important is in New York), in which sales of coffee and coffee futures were traded on the large scale (Bates 1997; Pelupessy 1993). In this market, coffee was largely treated as a uniform good, with only minor differences in price based on the type of coffee, its country of origin, the altitude at which it is grown, and the amount of damage to it. Coffee might pass through a dozen hands between the producer and consumer, with each taking a cut. Little of the final selling price, or even of the world market price, reached the hands of the producer. As the fair trade movement began to take off, this coffee market was in some disarray. The International Coffee Agreement, which maintained relatively steady and high prices through a quota system (though one that had begun to spring leaks), collapsed completely in 1989 under the joint pressure of Central American producers and American consumers (Talbot 2004). New coffee from both traditional and emerging producers entered the market, and prices began to fluctuate wildly, increasing uncertainty among small producers.

A tiny amount of coffee, mostly produced by large-scale producers, bypassed this market and entered into the specialty coffee market. The specialty coffee market in several ways resembles the fair trade sector: commodity chains are short, with roasters often buying directly from producers and processors, and prices are generally significantly higher than those of coffee sold through the traditional commodity market. Of course, this market demands considerably higher quality coffee than the conventional market: defects of processing must be essentially nonexistent and the coffee of high drinkability (Roseberry 1996; Giovannucci 2001). Vendors generally create relationships with producers, both to ensure a consistent product from year to year and to help producers to improve the coffee they grow. When the specialty coffee market began, it was organized around a small number of relatively large estates located in prime coffee-producing regions, including Hawaiian Kona, Jamaican Blue Mountain, and Costa Rican Terrazu coffee. However, the specialty coffee market has grown considerably across the past twenty years, with the growth expanding in the past decade. As the specialty coffee market grew to hundreds of millions of pounds annually, it expanded far beyond these origins, to involve smaller producers and a wider variety of locations.

In the early days, the fair trade coffee market, which was mostly organized around outlets with a special concern for social justice, such as food cooperatives, church organizations, and the like, did not compete directly in the specialty coffee market. Instead, those who sold fair trade coffee saw themselves as drawing coffee consumers mainly from the conventional coffee market; people who might otherwise buy inexpensive supermarket coffee could be convinced to buy fair trade coffee for altruistic reasons. This meant that coffee quality was not a major concern, as long as its social justice credentials were impeccable, and subsequently fair trade coffees developed in some quarters a reputation for indifferent quality. However, it became clear that a substantial number of consumers were willing to pay prices equivalent to fair trade for high-quality specialty coffee. This led some fair trade vendors to begin to focus on recruiting these consumers. As a result, the fair trade market was effectively transformed into a subset of the specialty market: vendors began to focus on a wider variety of outlets and to focus on the quality of coffee. Competition among new cooperatives attempting to enter into or expand their sales to the fair trade coffee market as the world market price became more unstable in the early 1990s and then plummeted in the period after 1999 allowed fair trade buyers to demand higher-quality coffee. With the fair trade price in the period between 1999 and 2003 often rising to several times the price paid for coffee in the conventional market, it was easy for small-producer cooperatives to feel enthusiastic about meeting the demands for higher-quality coffee and for more organic and sustainable production.

As fair trade coffee improved in quality and expanded into the specialty coffee market, it played an important role in the diversifying coffee market. In the increasingly saturated coffeehouse market, where large chains such as Starbucks had aggressively moved to displace small roasters and vendors, fair trade coffee came to be a point of distinction for small vendors, just as it had for small producers. In recent years, Starbucks has been harshly criticized by activists for its lack of commitment to fair trade coffee, while smaller roasters boast of their commitment to fair trade. Fair trade, then, served as an introduction to the business, quality, and flavor demands of the specialty market for many groups of small producers, while helping small coffee roasters to find a market niche.

Changes in the specialty market have made it easier for small producers to enter it. Once, coffee was identified largely at the country level, with low defects and a neutral, balanced flavor the main requirements for market success. Today, a much wider array of coffee flavors and characteristics are prized, with "distinctiveness" highly valued. This distinctive coffee is sold in much smaller batches, which allows small and medium-sized producers to compete on more equal terms with the large producers that traditionally dominated this market (this is discussed more extensively in Smith 1996 and Smith 2009). In the 1980s and 1990s, fair trade certification served as the main entry point into this market for small producers and cooperatives. The new millennium, however, provided emerging routes through which smaller producers and cooperatives could enter the specialty market. The Cup of Excellence competitions were created in 1999 to bring previously unknown Brazilian coffee producers to the attention of the international market; since then they have spread to seven other Latin American countries (Spindler 2007). Winners of these competitions have included small-scale farmers and coffee cooperatives; the judged coffee is then auctioned, with winners often receiving bids of over ten dollars a pound for their coffee (Smith n.d.). The Quality Coffee and Best of Panama auctions sell small batches of coffee for record prices year after year; while small producers and cooperatives have not on the whole done as well as medium-sized producers in these auctions, they are well represented (Smith n.d.).[1]

The Changing Demands of the Fair Trade Market

These changes in the overall market and in the specialty market have had important effects on fair trade producers. The terms of exchange for fair-trade-certified coffee have deteriorated somewhat over the past decade. The base price for fair trade coffee remained stagnant at $1.21 a pound from 1989 to May 2008, at which point it increased to $1.25 a pound, representing only a 3 percent increase across twenty years. Simply to maintain its value in constant dollars, the price paid to producers for a pound of green coffee should now be over a $2.00 a pound.[2] The recent increase of $0.05 for the price differential for organic coffee and social premium improves the situation slightly but only brings the price increase to 10 percent across twenty years, well below the rate of inflation for that period.

While the fair trade price paid to producers has stagnated, the demands of the fair trade market have grown more challenging for producers to meet. As explained earlier, fair trade coffee increasingly functions as part of the coffee specialty market, competing with conventional specialty coffees through coffee shops, mail order, and supermarkets. Thus, fair trade purchasers required coffee that was similar in quality to specialty coffee as well as meeting the fair trade standards. This required cooperatives to improve the quality of their coffee, both through production and processing. Producing coffee of this quality for the fair trade market requires more care and hence expense. As the push to improve the quality of fair trade coffee occurred during a period of historically low prices in the conventional market, small producers had little choice but to comply. Indeed, large numbers of producer cooperatives were fighting to enter the fair trade market at that time; this combination made it impossible for producer cooperatives to resist the increased expense of producing coffee for this market or to demand supplementary compensation for the additional expenses of production and processing.

Furthermore, the costs of certification have increased for producers. The Fair Trade Labelling Organization (FLO) has asked producer cooperatives to assume more of the costs of their fair trade certification, which FLO used to provide without charge (TransFair 2008). The decision was presented as necessary to increase producer access to the fair trade market; FLO also allows (and encourages) producer organizations to seek certification before they have a buyer, which previously was not allowed. The expenses of acquiring and maintaining certification are not dependent on success in the fair trade market, so that it is possible that producer cooperatives can spend more in certification costs than they make selling fair trade coffee. While it is likely that only cooperatives that find the fair trade market profitable will maintain certification, the costs of initial certification must generally be paid before any possible income arrives from the fair trade market. In addition, organic certification has become a near necessity, with three-quarters of the fair trade coffee sold in the United States now organic (TransFair 2007: 7). The end result is that while the price paid to fair trade producers has remained nearly constant, falling behind when inflation is taken into account, the costs involved in producing fair-trade-certified coffee have continually risen.

This decline in the terms of fair-trade-certified coffee is certainly one of the criticisms leveled by those who argue that fair trade organizations have been overly friendly to corporate interests. From a market perspective, fair trade producers held a relatively weak position during the late 1990s and early years of the twenty-first century due to the historically low prices of the broader coffee market. As long as the conventional coffee market remained well under one dollar per pound, and this market remained the main alternative to fair trade for producer cooperatives, these cooperatives felt they had no real alternatives. The market situation, rather than the needs of producers, was determining the price.

However, in recent years, the situation has changed: the price of coffee in the conventional coffee market has returned to more normal levels of over one dollar per pound; the price that specialty coffee sellers report paying for specialty coffee sometimes exceeds the fair trade price; and new mechanisms, such as the Quality Coffee auctions, have created remarkable prices for coffee of exceptional quality, whether it is produced by small or larger producers. As a result, for some producers fair trade is no longer the best option in the marketplace, as the best coffee from small producers and fair trade cooperatives can be sold for higher prices through the system of Quality Coffee auctions, through direct sales to American consumers, or through creating close relationships with the right coffee vendors in the United States. Not surprisingly, many organizations of small producers are pursuing these alternatives, alternatives possible not because of a generic identification as a small producer deserving of social justice but because of an identification as a specific named producer or group of producers in a specific location growing a particular style of coffee.

Some of these alternative markets even offer many of the social advantages that the fair trade movement aimed to create. For example, the nature of buyer-producer relationships is one point of conflict within the contemporary fair trade movement. While fair trade certification has moved away from stressing the importance of substantive relationships between producers and consumers as well as ongoing relationships between roasters and producer cooperatives, alternative markets, such as the Cup of Excellence, can help foster meaningful connections between producers and Northern buyers.

Despite the current downplaying of buyer-producer relationships in the current fair trade certification standards, images of personal relationships continue to be potent in the discourse of fair trade and the specialty coffee market. Websites and advertising are strewn with images of coffee farmers, sometimes depicted with the company's buyers but often without. While the concept of relationships is an important part of the fair trade image, in practice non-fair-trade producers use their relationships with producers to depict themselves as being equivalent to fair trade, though ironically some fair trade vendors have little connection to the producers whose coffee they buy.

The Peet's Coffee website states that "some of Peet's relationships with growers 'are the same as or better than Fair Trade' because they have been working with some of them for more than 30 years" (Eng 2007). Intelligentsia, a company that has replaced fair trade coffee with its own ethical system, says, "For a coffee to be considered Intelligentsia Direct Trade™, there must be a true and tangible relationship between the growers of the coffee and Intelligentsia. A couple of emails and a phone call just won't cut it. . . . We usually visit every farmer or cooperative at least three times per year: before harvest to plan, during the harvest to monitor quality, and after harvest to recap and celebrate the successes." (Intelligentsia Coffee 2008). While some smaller specialty coffee vendors work closely with producers, only some of them focus on fair-trade-certified coffee. Some, such as Intelligentsia Coffee and Larry's Beans, have rejected the fair trade certification system for coffee in its current form, while continuing officially to follow trading standards based on fair trade principles and terms. Others, such as Sweet Maria's and Stumptown Coffee, sell both fair trade and non-fair-trade coffees, purchasing them through an array of personal connections, auctions, and competitions (for a discussion of how such producers buy coffee, see Meehan 2007). On the other hand, one small fair-trade-focused vendor says, "I don't want to get that involved on that level. Because it would be going to all these different farms and making sure that they were farming properly." Instead, her relationships with producers are impersonal: "I just leave it up to TransFair USA, which is the American labeling organization that certifies that it was bought in this way [according to fair trade standards]" (Farrelly 2004). The buyers with whom Molly Doane worked (see chap. 10, this volume) fall somewhere between these two: a bit cynical about the reality of close connections between coffee sellers and coffee producers but at the same time involved in helping churches to build relationships with Chiapas, Mexico.

National coffee competitions, such as the Cup of Excellence and Quality Coffee auctions, are organized by groups who have an interest in providing technical assistance to promising producers. The Coffee Quality Institute (2008) states that its main goal is providing technical assistance, with the associated coffee auctions a secondary goal. Even the competitions and auctions that do not directly provide assistance help to put producers in touch with buyers willing to pay for exceptional coffee (and often to make already good coffee even better), with other sophisticated producers who can share know-how, and with organizations that work to assist coffee producers. Clearly, these alternative markets are not a solution for all small producers, as many cannot produce coffee that can compete at this level. These programs do not aim to help producers who are not already at an elite level. However, increasingly all fair trade coffee producers must at least aspire to an elite level, if they hope to sell their coffee to vendors such as Starbucks. The days of relatively poor quality coffee sold only for social justice reasons are over; today fair trade coffee must meet the standards of specialty coffee.

It is quite easy to be overly critical of the fair trade movement on this issue: many of the small producers and cooperatives that are doing well in these new demanding specialty markets started out and built basic skills through the fair trade market. They learned to deal directly with wholesalers, learned how to meet the demands of the specialty coffee market, and through the fair trade market were able to make contacts with organizations and individuals who can open doors to these other opportunities. Many cooperatives that make connections with the right buyers through the fair trade market have had close and warm relationships with buyers. Others, however, have had to leave the fair trade system to find this support (Smith 2007 outlines one such example). However, it is not clear whether later entrants to the fair trade coffee market have found the same kinds of support and patience as did their predecessors as they struggle to learn these basic skills (though Martinez [2002] observes that producer problems in meeting fair trade demands are not a new problem).

Is Fair Trade Really Different?

Clearly other mechanisms have emerged to give small producers access to higher-priced markets and to the ears of foreign buyers. Fair trade, however, has led to this point. If the goal of the fair trade movement was to alter the way in which coffee was bought and sold, then it has succeeded beyond anyone's wildest dreams, at least within the specialty coffee market. Almost all specialty coffee vendors brag about how well they pay producers, the personal relationships they have created with producers, and the support that they have provided for producer communities. Small-scale coffee vendors often show themselves with the producers who grow the coffee they sell, on their websites, on their promotional materials, and on their products. Even Starbucks spends time and money to do this. Starbucks proudly observes that in 2005 it paid $1.28 per pound and that in 2006 it paid on average $1.42 per pound for its coffee, which is higher than the fair trade price (Starbucks 2007b). It loans millions of dollars to coffee farmers for production annually. It has established a foundation which gave $1.7 million in 2006 to improve coffee quality and life in general in coffee-producing communities. In addition, it has established its own set of standards, the CAFE (Coffee and Farmer Equity) Practices, which are intended to reflect the values of supporting communities and coffee farmers (Starbucks 2007a).

However, this very success has diluted the power of the fair trade label, as a variety of specialty coffee sellers make claims that suggest (or outright state) that their coffee meets or exceeds fair trade standards. The descriptions of prices paid, relationships created, and additional aid certainly sounds good to the typical consumer. Two cases make clear the difficulties in evaluating descriptions of the terms of coffee sellers. Starbucks boasts of paying a generous price of $1.42 per pound for its coffee, a price well above the fair trade price. However, this price includes money paid to importers, as well as that which goes directly to producers; an example of this can be found in Chiapas, where Starbucks paid $1.43 per pound for coffee from the Comon Yaj Noc Pic cooperative, but the cooperative only received $1.23 after Starbucks's buying agent took its cut (Malkin 2007). While Starbucks is not clear on the subject, the price it pays producers almost assuredly includes the cost of delivering the coffee to the United States, an expense that fair trade vendors assume in addition to the price paid to producers. Finally, the fact that this is reported as the "average" price makes it clear that a considerable number of producers—probably more than half—are paid less than that price. Thus, the superb overall price that Starbucks reports covers considerable variety, and many producers are paid well below the guaranteed fair trade price.

The other terms of trade fall even shorter of the fair trade package. Starbucks makes nearly $10 million available for financing coffee production; this is a great deal of money, but it represents only 2 percent of Starbucks's expenditures on coffee, while fair trade buyers are required to make 60 percent of the contracted sale price available for financing. Similarly, while Starbucks gives away a considerable amount of money ($36.1 million in cash and in-kind contributions in fiscal 2006, according to

Starbucks 2007a), much of that generosity is focused on the United States. All money given to coffee-producing communities, including money donated to disaster relief in coffee-growing countries ($1 million in addition to the $1.7 million that goes to coffee-growing communities), amounts to only 0.5 percent of the amount that Starbucks pays for coffee, while the fair trade social premium is well over 6 percent of the purchase price (Starbucks 2007a; FLO 2009; all calculations are the author's). This demonstrates how large vendors are able to create the appearance of an investment in producers equivalent to the fair trade requirements—millions of dollars is a big number, after all—while actually expending far less than fair trade requirements.

Starbucks is not unique, of course; other vendors do the same. Starbucks, in fact, offers a great deal of transparency about its dealings, which allows this kind of evaluation. The bulk of smaller-scale sellers, which are not publicly traded companies, generally do not make available information that allows their claims to be evaluated. The requirements of public reporting mean that it is easier to point to the differences between presentation and practice for large companies. But many smaller companies' lack of transparency certainly suggests that, just as with Starbucks, their terms of trade would not compare favorably with fair trade terms. However, distinguishing sellers who exceed fair trade terms from those who fall far short is nearly impossible for the typical coffee consumer, which underlines the importance of the fair trade certification system.

The problem of differentiation and evaluation of claims plays out with organizations that are "fairer than" fair trade as well. Some high-end smaller fair-trade-focused coffee vendors have withdrawn from the fair trade certification system to create systems that they perceive to be fairer. Larry Larson, owner of Larry's Beans, asserts, "We left TransFair in 2004 because we did not want to be confused with companies like Starbucks that only offer a small selection of fair trade coffee. TransFair USA certifies only specific batches of coffee, not companies" (Larry's Beans 2008). Instead, Larry's Beans is affiliated with the Fair Trade Federation, an association of fair trade businesses, and depends on independent auditors to demonstrate that its prices and terms of trade are equivalent to fair trade standards. Another system is Intelligentsia Coffee's "Direct Trade" system, which guarantees a price 25 percent above the fair trade price and focuses on sustainability and transparency, though not on privileging small producers, providing production loans, or working with democratically organized cooperatives. The company dismisses fair trade as follows:

Experience has shown us that we can achieve better results through our own efforts and attain a higher level of transparency than we could by simply purchasing Fair Trade coffees. . . . Many of our coffees come from cooperatives that are Fair Trade certified, and we could easily make them Fair Trade coffees. If we did so, Intelligentsia would pay a commission to Fair Trade for the use of the Fair Trade logo. Our belief is that the money makes a bigger and more positive difference when it goes directly into the hand of the producer. Instead of buying the right to use a label we just give the money to the grower. (Intelligentsia Coffee 2008).

This variety of experience and philosophies, underpinning claims of being "like" fair trade, all make it difficult and confusing for consumers to evaluate the claims made about the coffee sold and its qualities. In a 2007 review of fair trade coffees, Davids ends by observing that two of the sampled coffees are not certified by FLO but rather carry the label of the Fair Trade Federation (these were probably coffees from Larry's Beans). He concludes with the words, "Whether the use of the Fair Trade Federation seal (it looks a lot like the TransFair seal) and claims made by the roasters who offer these uncertified coffees are a slippery duplicity taking unfair advantage of someone else's investment in developing public awareness or a justifiable alternative approach to the same goals is a call concerned consumers will need to make" (Davids 2007). In this case, Davids clearly sees these beans as less "fairly traded" than certified beans, though the seller would almost assuredly disagree strongly, arguing that they are more fairly traded than many certified coffees.

Intelligentsia Coffee (2008) openly asks the question, "How does the consumer know that we do what we say?" Its answer is not encouraging: "The proof is in the cup. Quality is not an accidental thing, and does not happen without very careful attention to detail at every step of the way." The same thing can be said to be true of most specialty roasters, whatever the conditions under which the coffee is bought. While there is no reason to doubt Intelligentsia's claims as to how it deals with coffee producers (in 2007, it was reported by Sudo 2007 that the company had hired an independent auditor, though no reports seem to have been made publicly available), it is difficult for an uninformed consumer to distinguish between the variety of claims made by sellers about fair-trade-certified coffee, Intelligentsia's Direct Trade, Starbucks's CAFE system, and Larry's Beans' independent certification system.

Conclusions

Clearly fair trade has had important effects on the way that the specialty coffee market has evolved, helping to shape a relatively just and fair system of exchange as the norm rather than the exception. However, the ability of the fair trade movement to be the main trendsetter in the market for socially concerned consumers is under pressure. The challenge for the fair trade certification and marketing system remains the problem of balancing the pressure of an increasingly large and profit-focused market on the one hand against the push to continue to make the terms of trade more just for small producers. Otherwise, the market for fairly traded products will continue to fragment and force producers and consumers alike to depend on the "good name" of the seller of coffee to be assured that the claims made regarding how producers are treated and compensated are justified. Since in the current market, exaggerated claims are regularly made, it is unlikely that any but the most discerning and educated consumers will be able to sort out the "good" sellers from those who simply know what to say.

At the same time, the argument for certification remains strong. The large number of specialty coffee vendors, both large and small, that make claims about how much they do on behalf of and with small producers makes it clear that there is a demand for coffee that is fairly traded, in the broad sense. The current variety of claims about prices paid for coffee, about the benefits provided to producers and their communities, and about the ways in which vendors contribute to the sustainability of coffee-producing communities create confusion. For those vendors that are often less generous than fair trade terms, many of them the largest companies with the biggest name recognition and the greatest ability to advertise their "generosity," this may be a plus. However, for smaller coffee vendors, it is a more dangerous game. The leaders of the movement to reject fair trade labeling in the name of fairly trading may do well individually, as they receive positive press as a result of their position. However, a market for fairly traded products that requires producers and consumers to depend on the "good name" of the vendor of coffee to be assured that the product is truly fairly traded is a market open to abuse.

For the fair trade system to continue to grow and thrive, it must continue to respond to the realities of the current market, including finding ways to reward those who engage in fair trading practices that exceed fair trade standards while penalizing those who use fair trade rhetoric without following the standards. While the fair trade system continues to grow rapidly, its proponents must ensure that they can continue to defend the standards as superior to the alternatives, whether direct trading systems that pay more to producers while cutting the Fairtrade Labelling Organization out of the loop or company-specific standards such as CAFE that mimic fair trade terms at a lower level of investment and benefit. Otherwise, proponents may find themselves under attack both from above and from below, unable to shape terms of trade for fairly traded coffee. And while it is clear that there are important differences in how those standards are interpreted and enforced by different vendors, without a common set of terms for what constitutes fairly traded coffee, all parts of the system—producers and vendors alike—would be worse off. Relatively minor differences would rapidly increase, leaving consumers confused and discouraged that their choice of coffee would make any real difference to the lives of coffee producers.

NOTES

1. Smith n.d. is based on analysis of part of the extensive data available at http://www.cupofexcellence.org and some of the Q and Specialty Coffee Auctions available at http://auction.stoneworks.com/.

2. Based on calculators at the Bureau of Labor Statistics (data.bls.gov/cgi-bin/cpicalc.pl) from inflation in the Consumer Price Index. The European HICP would suggest a price of around $1.90.

WORKS CITED

Bates, Robert H.
1997 Open-Economy Politics: The Political Economy of the World Coffee Trade. Princeton, NJ: Princeton University Press.
Coffee Quality Institute (CQI)
2008 About CQI. Electronic document, http://www.coffeeinstitute.org/about_cqi.asp, accessed March 5, 2008.
Davids, K.
2007 Fair Trade Coffees: The Controversy and the Cup. Coffee Review. Electronic document, http://www.coffeereview.com/article.cfm?ID=136, accessed March 5, 2008.
Eng, M.
2007 All's Not Always "Fair" in Coffee Labeling. Chicago Tribune, April 19.
Fairtrade Labelling Organizations International (FLO)
2007 Shaping Global Partnerships: Annual Report 2006/7. Electronic document, http://www.fairtrade.net/uploads/media/Final_FLO_AR_2007_03.pdf, accessed November 10, 2007.

2008a Fair Trade Standards for Coffee for Small Farmers' Organizations. Electronic document, http://www.fairtrade.net/fileadmin/user_upload/content/Coffee_SF_January_2008_EN.pdf, accessed April 5, 2008.

2008b Generic Standards. Electronic document, http://www.fairtrade.net/fileadmin/user_upload/content/Generic_Fairtrade_Standard_SF_Dec_2007_EN.pdf, accessed April 5, 2008.

2009 Fairtrade Minimum Price and Fairtrade Premium Table. Version 26.05.2009. Available at www.fairtrade.net, accessed June 11, 2009.

Farrelly, M.

2004 Fair Trade Coffee. Voice of America. Electronic document, http://www.larrysbeans.com/fair-trade-coffee, accessed March 5, 2008.

Giovannucci, D.

2001 Sustainable Coffee Survey of the North American Specialty Coffee Industry. Electronic document, http://www.scaa.org/pdfs/Sustainable_Coffee_Report_NA.pdf, accessed March 29, 2006.

Gresser, C., and S. Tickell

2002 Mugged: Poverty in Your Coffee Cup. Electronic document, http://www.oxfamamerica.org/newsandpublications/publications/research_reports/mugged/mugged_coffee_report.pdf, accessed April 5, 2008.

Intelligentsia Coffee

2008 Origin—Intelligentsia Direct Trade™. Electronic document, http://www.intelligentsiacoffee.com/origin/directtrade, accessed March 5, 2008.

International Coffee Organization (ICO)

2008 Historical Data: Monthly Averages of ICO Indicator Prices in US Cents per Lb. Electronic document, http://www.ico.org/asp/display10.asp, accessed March 1, 2008.

Jaffee, D.

2007 Brewing Justice: Fair Trade Coffee, Sustainability, and Survival. Berkeley: University of California Press.

Larry's Beans

2008 FAQ (Frequently Asked Questions). Electronic document, http://www.larrysbeans.com/faq/, accessed March 5, 2008.

Lyon, S.

2005 Maya Coffee Farmers and the Fair Trade Commodity Chain. Ph.D. dissertation, Department of Anthropology, Emory University.

Malkin, E.

2007 Certifying Coffee Aids Farmers and Forests in Chiapas. New York Times, April 22. Electronic document, http://www.nytimes.com/2007/04/22/world/americas/22coffeeweb.html, accessed March 5, 2008.

Martinez, M.

2002 Poverty Alleviation through Participation in Fair Trade Coffee Networks: The Case of the Tzotzilotic Tzobolotic Coffee Coop Chiapas, Mexico. Electronic document, http://www.colostate.edu/Depts/Sociology/FairTradeResearchGroup/doc/tzotzilotic.pdf, accessed March 29, 2006.

Meehan, P.
   2007 To Burundi and Beyond for Coffee's Holy Grail. New York Times, September 12. Electronic document, http://www.nytimes.com/2007/09/12/dining/12coff.html, accessed March 5, 2008.
Murray, D., L. T. Raynolds, and P. L. Taylor
   2003 One Cup at a Time: Poverty Alleviation and Fair Trade Coffee in Latin America. Electronic document, http://www.colostate.edu/Depts/Sociology/FairTradeResearchGroup/doc/fairtrade.pdf, accessed March 29, 2006.
Pelupessy, W.
   1993 El mercado mundial del café: El caso de El Salvador. San Jose, CR: Departmento Ecuméncio de Investigaciones.
Raynolds, L., and M. Long
   2007 Fair/Alternative Trade: Historical and Empirical Dimensions. *In* Fair Trade: The Challenges of Transforming Globalization. Laura Raynolds, Douglas Murray, and John Wilkinson, eds. Pp. 201–224. New York: Routledge.
Roseberry, W.
   1996 The Rise of Yuppie Coffees and the Reimagination of Class in the United States. American Anthropologist 98(4): 762–775.
Smith, J.
   n.d. Calculating Costs and Payoffs in Coffee Markets. Unpublished manuscript, Department of Geography and Anthropology, Eastern Washington University.
   2001 Towards Sustainability: Small Scale Coffee Production beyond the Green Revolution. Ph.D. dissertation, Department of Anthropology, University of Pittsburgh.
   2006 Small Producers in the Specialty Coffee Market. Paper presented at the Annual Meeting of the American Anthropological Association, San Jose, CA, November 16.
   2007 The Search for Sustainable Markets: The Promise and Failures of Fair Trade. Culture and Agriculture 29(2): 89–99.
   2009 Shifting Coffee Markets and Producer Responses in Costa Rica and Panama. Research in Economic Anthropology 29: 201–224.
Spindler, S.
   2007 Our History (Cup of Excellence). Electronic document, http://www.cupofexcellence.org/WhatisCOE/OurHistory/tabid/148/Default.aspx, accessed November 11, 2007.
Starbucks
   2007a Corporate Social Responsibility: Fiscal 2006 Annual Report. Electronic document, http://media.starbucks.com.edgesuite.net/dotcom/csr_reports/OMR-005_FY06_CSR_AR.pdf, accessed November 11, 2007.
   2007b Starbucks Leads Global Coffee Industry in Paying Premium Prices for Sustainably-Sourced Coffee. Electronic document, http://www.starbucks.com/aboutus/pressdesc.asp?id=738, accessed November 11, 2007.
Sudo, C.
   2007 Chicagoist Grills: Intelligentsia Coffee & Roasting Works CEO Doug Zell. Chicagoist. Electronic document, http://chicagoist.com/2007/02/13/chicagoist_grills_intelligentsia_coffee_roasting_works_ceo_doug_zell_.php, accessed January 29, 2009.

Talbot, J. M.
   2004 Grounds for Agreement: The Political Economy of the Coffee Commodity Chain. Lanham, MD: Rowman & Littlefield.
TransFair USA
   2007 Fair Trade Almanac 1998–2006. Electronic document, http://www.transfairusa.org/pdfs/2007FairTradeAlmanac.pdf, accessed November 11, 2007.
   2008 Producer Certification. Electronic document, http://transfairusa.org/content/certification/producer_certification.php, accessed April 5, 2008.

A New World?

Neoliberalism and Fair Trade Farming in the Eastern Caribbean

MARK MOBERG

Unlike the United States, where fair trade sales are still largely limited to coffeehouses, co-ops, and online retailers, a wide array of fair trade items has been available in mainstream European supermarkets for more than a decade. Most of these goods bear the logo of Fairtrade Labelling Organizations International (FLO), which currently certifies more than 1.5 million producers of about one thousand different items originating in fifty-eight countries (FLO 2008: 11). In 2007, global fair trade retail sales exceeded $3.4 billion, a seventy-fold increase in ten years (ibid.: 3). Although fair trade has had a significant and growing impact on the retail market, especially in Europe, consumers generally must take as an article of faith that their purchases of fair trade goods actually benefit those who produce them. In part, that is because much of what has been written about fair trade has examined it from either the endpoint of consumption or in terms of the movement's discursive claims. This literature has raised important questions about the nature of fair trade as a social movement and its relationship to other forms of exchange (e.g., Moore 2004; Fridell 2007; Fisher 2007); it tends less often, however, to examine whether the movement's social justice and economic priorities are realized on the ground. This chapter attempts such an assessment through a controlled comparison of banana producers in St. Lucia's Mabouya Valley, the Eastern Caribbean country's largest banana-producing region. In addition to ethnographic research in the area over three periods from 2000 to 2004, this project involved an extensive survey of demography, economic activities, and attitudes among fifty-eight certified fair trade and seventy-five conventional banana growers residing in the valley.[1] The research reveals that fair trade in practice falls considerably short of the new world of mutuality and transparency in producer-consumer relationships promised by many of the movement's advocates in the developed North. Nonetheless, it also demonstrates that the fair trade market has offered unequivocal material and social advantages to Caribbean farmers.

Fair trade principles are often upheld by antiglobalization activists as alternatives to neoliberal policies guiding institutions such as the World Trade Organization and International Monetary Fund.[2] In few areas of the global economy have the two ideologies collided as directly as they have in the Caribbean banana industry. Together with St. Vincent, Dominica, and Grenada, St. Lucia is one of four newly independent Commonwealth countries in the Windward Islands of the Eastern Caribbean. Throughout the region, export agriculture has been dominated by a "reconstituted peasantry" formed after the end of slavery (Mintz 1984), a process occurring in distinct ways on each of the islands. During the eighteenth century, St. Lucia changed hands between the French and British fourteen times before being finally ceded to Britain in 1815. The period of contested colonial occupation is reflected in the continued use of a French-based Creole (known as Kwéyòl or Patwa) beside the official language of English as well as land tenure laws based on French precedents. Unlike in other sugar-producing islands with a continuous history of British occupation, in St. Lucia the estate system was controlled early on by French expatriate planters. Faced with competition from lower-cost sugar elsewhere during the nineteenth century, cash-poor landlords divided their estates among former slaves, who cultivated the land under a sharecropping arrangement known as *metayage*. By the twentieth century the declining viability of sugar allowed sharecroppers to negotiate more favorable contracts with landlords or to purchase land from them outright. Smallholder farming was also promoted by colonial policies that distributed Crown Lands to create a politically "stable" peasantry, a recommendation arising from the 1897 West India Royal Commission investigating poverty and social unrest on the islands (Lobdell 1988).

During the 1950s, as the region's remaining sugar exports collapsed, Britain encouraged smallholding banana production in the Windwards as a source of income for islands that otherwise constituted a drain on central government revenues. The region's bananas were granted protected status in the United Kingdom to avert monopoly control of the retail market by Fyffes Ltd., then the country's largest fruit importer and a wholly owned subsidiary of the U.S. multinational Chiquita (Clegg 2002). St. Lucia's banana industry was consolidated after the attainment of internal self-government in the 1960s, as the nationalist leader John Compton won power by mobilizing the votes of rural residents. Largely to reward

Compton's rural voter base, government agricultural policy and development aid heavily favored banana farmers until the 1990s. Similar forms of political patronage and voter mobilization spurred the growth of banana production among small farmers on the other Windward Islands during this time.

In contrast to Central America, where single banana plantations often comprise thousands of acres and employ hundreds or thousands of workers, Windwards banana farms are labor-intensive, family-run operations. The average St. Lucian farm is about four acres in size and employs fewer than two full-time workers (St. Lucia 2002). Their lack of irrigation and other capital investments, combined with steep hillside slopes, place Caribbean farms at a competitive disadvantage with Central and South American plantations. While the latter may annually produce twenty-five tons or more of fruit per acre, St. Lucian farms average only about one-third that amount (Sandiford 2000: 12). In addition, labor costs in the Eastern Caribbean (between fifteen and twenty U.S. dollars per day) far exceed prevailing wages in Central America, where even unionized banana workers earn less than seven dollars per day. Despite the high costs of production in the Windwards, Britain's protected market and a lack of ready agricultural alternatives left the region heavily dependent on banana exports for employment and revenue. In 1991, at its historical peak of production, St. Lucia produced about 25 percent of the United Kingdom's market share for bananas, with another 40 percent sourced from the other Windwards (Nurse and Sandiford 1995: 28). At that time approximately 8,200 St. Lucians operated banana farms (OAS 1995), and the industry generated more than 60 percent of the country's export earnings and directly employed 35,000–40,000 persons out of a population of 140,000 (Jn Pierre, personal communication, 2000).

Until 1993, the region's farmers were shielded from direct price competition with much cheaper Latin American fruit by virtue of the Lomé Convention, a series of treaties dating from 1976 that established market preferences for numerous agricultural imports into Europe. Among Lomé's many provisions, it stipulated that bananas from former African, Caribbean, and Pacific colonies of Europe (the so-called ACP countries) could be imported free of duty, while levying a 20 percent tariff on Dollar Area fruit, as Latin American bananas are known (Tangermann 2003: 26). Yet what was supposed to be a common trade policy masked divergent interests among European states. Britain, France, Spain, and Italy, all of which maintained strong ties to banana producers in former colonies or overseas departments, imposed additional preferences in the form of restrictive import quotas of Dollar Area fruit. Countries lacking former colonies, such as Germany, Austria, and Sweden, obtained an exemption from the common tariff and declined to impose quotas of any kind. In between these extremes were countries such as Denmark, Ireland, Belgium, and the Netherlands, which imposed no quotas on Dollar fruit but maintained the 20 percent tariff (ibid.: 28). In practice, Latin American bananas saturated markets everywhere except in those countries, such as Britain, that erected quotas. The creation of the Single European Market (SEM) in 1993—itself a significant neoliberal objective—was intended to remove most trade barriers between European Union (EU) member states. In that year, national differences in banana trade policy were negotiated out of existence in favor of a continent-wide import regime. Lomé was reformulated to provide transferable import licenses to importers, with quotas established for all fruit by country of origin. To the extent that ACP countries did not fulfill their quotas, licenses for the balance could be sold to other importers, including the U.S. multinationals Chiquita, Dole, and Del Monte. This resulted in a flood of Dollar fruit imported into the United Kingdom from other European countries, with an attendant drop in retail prices. These trends, in turn, drove producer prices in the Windwards to unprecedented lows after 1993.

Despite the increased access afforded to Dollar fruit by the SEM, in 1996 the United States and several Latin American governments, acting at the request of Chiquita, challenged the EU's tariff-quota system as an unfair trade practice in the World Trade Organization.[3] Two years later, the WTO ruled in favor of the plaintiffs, signaling an end to more than half a century of quota-protected markets for Windward Islands banana producers. After several unsuccessful appeals by the EU, all parties agreed to defer introduction of a WTO-compliant tariff-only arrangement to 2006, providing a transition period for Caribbean farmers to improve their productivity. Long before this date, the glutting of European markets with Dollar fruit had driven most Caribbean growers' earnings below their production costs. By the end of the decade, most of the region's growers had abandoned banana production because of a continued downward slide in prices and widening pessimism about the industry's future in the wake of the WTO ruling. From approximately twenty-eight thousand active growers in the four islands in 1992, only about forty-five hundred Windwards farmers remained in production in 2003, with export production having ceased entirely on Grenada (NERA 2003). Total exports from the region declined nearly every year since the SEM, from about 280,000 tons in 1993 to 85,000 tons in 2004 (Edmunds and Shillingford 2005).

From the outset, fair trade initiatives in the Windwards were contemplated as a direct response to the effects of free-trade policies. The Windward Islands Farmers Association (WINFA), a regional nongovernmental organization (NGO) based in St. Vincent, first sought alternative markets for Caribbean bananas soon after the creation of the SEM. The later WTO ruling added greater urgency to these efforts. In 1999, WINFA began working with FLO to organize fair trade producers' groups on each island. Within a year, the first labeled fair trade fruit was being delivered by the islands' exporter WIBDECO (Windward Islands Banana Development and Exporting Company) to British supermarkets. Much as Chiquita and the U.S. government became the objects of outrage in the Caribbean during the WTO suit, the U.S. position in the "banana war" was also widely criticized in the British press. Amid media accounts portraying U.S. actions as a Chiquita-inspired assault on family farmers, retailers exhorted their customers to express solidarity with the former British West Indies by purchasing fair trade bananas. A ready-made market was born out of such sentiments, and by 2003, fair trade already made up about 15 percent of all retail banana sales in the United Kingdom (Hoggarth, personal communication, 2003). By 2006, that figure had nearly doubled, and several supermarkets announced that they would henceforth stock only certified fair trade bananas (FLO 2007). With the expansion of fair trade certification, the number of active banana farmers in the Windwards has finally stabilized and even increased slightly since 2004.

New Masters or a New World?

Apart from two frenetic harvest days each week, banana farms in the Mabouya Valley are serenely quiet places that belie the economic turmoil wrought by the WTO ruling. Employing neither the mechanized cableways nor the spray irrigation systems found in Central America, on most farms the only sounds heard, other than the banter of those who work on them, are the rustle of the breeze and sporadic drumming of raindrops on banana leaves. Since the 1980s, when farmers replaced most hand weeding with herbicides, even the steady rhythm of farmers chopping undergrowth with "cutlasses" (machetes) has gradually disappeared. That silence was broken in mid-2000 by sputtering two-cycle motors and whirring monofilament grass cutters, sounds more often associated with manicured suburban lawns than with banana farms in the tropics. The gas-powered weed eaters testify to a host of new production requirements facing fair trade banana farmers. Under FLO's environmental criteria, most of the chemicals formerly used in the area are now banned in the production of fair trade bananas. These include paraquat, a highly toxic herbicide linked to the disappearance of fish and other wildlife from agricultural watersheds, and all commercially available nematicides, which are implicated in birth defects and cancer in many banana-producing regions (Bérubé and Aquin 2005). At FLO's urging, the weed eater has emerged as the most widely used tool for a job formerly performed with herbicides dispensed from backpack sprayers. The Mabouya Valley Fair Trade Group owns eight of the machines, which rotate among members according to a list maintained by the group's secretary. If the weed eater is emblematic of the changes that farmers have had to adopt in becoming fair trade certified, it also symbolizes their ambivalence to that process. Overwhelmingly, farmers state that they are grateful for the higher prices they receive from fair trade sales. In the same breath, most express frustration with the weed eater as an impractical tool imposed by European certifiers possessing little knowledge of the realities of local farming or the labor constraints under which they operate. Conventional farmers, who remain outside the fair trade group, continue to use herbicides, and all have spurned weed eaters as alternatives to chemicals.

With 119 members, comprising about 40 percent of all local banana growers, the Mabouya Valley Fair Trade Group is the largest of five such associations on St. Lucia. Four years after the introduction of FLO's no-herbicide policy, it continued to dominate discussion during meetings of the fair trade group, with most complaints focusing on the resulting labor demands and pest control problems. Older farmers protest that they lack the strength required to operate the thirty-five-pound weed eaters for a period long enough to clear the undergrowth from their farms. The average age of the valley's fair trade farmers is 50.9 years, significantly greater than the average of conventional farmers (40.1 years). More than 46 percent of fair trade growers are 51 years of age or older; three are in their 70s, and the oldest is 83. To comply with the herbicide ban almost all older farmers hire younger men to operate weed eaters in clearing secondary growth, a task they had previously performed themselves with chemicals. The only alternative approved by FLO would be to return to hand weeding by cutlass, a practice abandoned by most farmers in the 1980s. This method also involves increased labor requirements and compels farmers regardless of age to hire more workers. A majority (55 percent) of fair trade farmers report that their wage costs increased as a result of the herbicide ban, with each spending an average of EC$116 (about US$44) more per fortnight.[4]

Because of limited demand for fair trade bananas in the United Kingdom, less than half the fruit produced by the valley's fair trade farmers is actually labeled as such. Like other fair trade groups on St. Lucia, the Mabouya Valley group maintains a roster in which members are assigned to sell fair trade bananas in one out of every three harvests, which on most farms occur every two weeks. Even during those harvests in which farmers pack fair trade fruit, they will also pack fruit for two or even three other price and label categories for a UK banana market highly specialized by supermarket brand and product niche. In any given shipment, then, some fruit may earn fair trade prices, while other bananas from the same farm, and even the same plant, will be packaged differently and sold at lower prices. To further complicate matters, each grower sells his or her fruit to one or more of four privately owned, island-based banana companies, which act as intermediaries between the grower and WIBDECO.[5] As originally formulated, FLO's environmental criteria were to apply to all certified growers regardless of the amount of fair trade fruit they sell or the frequency with which they sell it. Hence, the criteria require farmers to accept continuously higher production costs, despite the fact that those higher costs are only occasionally offset by fair trade's higher prices. Given that labor costs and availability are the concerns most often mentioned by farmers, after the costs of inputs and price of bananas, it is no surprise that many claim that FLO's environmental policies have aggravated their economic circumstances.

Soon after adopting the weed eater, growers learned that the new farming methods caused an unanticipated agronomic problem in the form of an introduced weed, *Commelina*, or watergrass. Easily eradicated by herbicides, *Commelina* propagates new roots when its stems are sliced by weed eaters and cutlasses. The weed in turn acts as a host species for nematodes, minute worms that destroy banana plants by burrowing into their roots and corm. Because FLO prohibits the use of existing nematicides, many farmers argue that its policies have amplified weed and pest problems without providing effective alternatives to chemical use. Farmers who are able to demonstrate the presence of nematodes on their farms may apply limited amounts of one of the less-toxic nematicides to affected areas, but only after an inspection and dispensation granted by FLO's certification officer. For most farmers, the added bureaucracy required in gaining authorization for a decision that they would ordinarily make on their own involves a delay of at least a week in treating their farms, during which time they are unable to halt the widening infestations. As a result, affected farmers experience production losses that could easily be otherwise averted.

The restriction on chemicals is one component of a fair trade protocol that has radically changed the way farmers grow bananas. The rationales for these changes are poorly understood by most farmers, and even the Windwards-based certification officer responsible for enforcing them acknowledges that some rules are inappropriate for local conditions. Among these is a requirement that farmers maintain a twenty-meter-wide buffer zone adjacent to streams and roads to minimize soil erosion and protect watersheds. FLO crafted these rules to apply worldwide to all "small farmers' organizations" (FLO 2009) receiving fair trade certification. While the twenty-meter rule may be feasible in regions with larger units of production, on a four-acre Caribbean farm it requires growers to remove a significant amount of their land from production. The certification officer himself describes the mandate as "an unreasonable economic demand." After vociferous complaints, WINFA obtained a modification of the policy to offset farmers' losses. The revision permits the buffer zone to consist of tree crops having commercial value, such as citrus and coconuts. The trees require at least five years to reach bearing maturity, during which time the farmer recoups no earnings from the buffer zone on his or her farm. Hence, even the modified requirement poses a continued economic sacrifice for many farmers.

Concerns about the new environmental criteria are discussed at length during meetings of St. Lucia's five fair trade farmers' groups. As required by FLO, each group convenes meetings at least once per month, with attendance required of all members other than those excused for legitimate reasons. At any given meeting of the Mabouya Valley group, which generally lasts between two and four hours, about 70 percent of the members are present. Most attendees, however, appear to be engaged in the animated discussions that ensue. Meetings are presided over by President Cornelius Lynch and Secretary Daniel Sandiford, both of whom are younger and possess much more formal education than most members. As a university-trained agronomist and former extension agent, Lynch was assigned for a time to educate farmers around the island on fair trade principles, and he played a key role in organizing the Mabouya Valley group. At monthly meetings, members share information, debate uses for social premiums in local projects, and formulate requests for information or resources from umbrella organizations such as the National Fair Trade Committee and WINFA.

As president, Lynch's work has shifted from educating farmers about fair trade to defending the certification process over their often fervent opposition. During the August 2003 meeting, he announced a change in the rotation schedule for the group's weed eaters, the result of two machines having broken down in as many weeks. The announcement was the third of its kind that year and provoked a chorus of complaints. Fitz Roy Alexander, also one of the group's younger members, took the opportunity to challenge the herbicide ban altogether. Alexander claimed that his labor expenses regularly exceeded those of his conventional-farming neighbor, the difference being the increased labor requirements of weeding without chemicals. "I weed eater [*sic*] my whole farm, but I only get to ship fair trade a third of the time. So what's fair about fair trade when the farmer who weed eaters has to pay more to grow his bananas but doesn't get the benefits?" Alexander's comment was met by angry affirmations from others unhappy with the policy. In response, Lynch sought to justify the ban by drawing a contrast between local farmers and their corporate adversaries in Latin America:

> We, as fair trade farmers, we use the weed eater because we are more concerned about the environment, and we want to leave a decent world for our children. Do you think Chiquita cares about this? Do you? You should be proud that we are not like those big companies poisoning the environment with their chemicals and their pollution. Remember we are getting a social premium because we are fair trade farmers. The minute we stop taking care of the environment we are no longer fair trade farmers and we will no longer receive the social premium.

Murmurs of disagreement greeted this explanation, and Alexander persisted in his challenge. "But look here, our grandmothers and grandfathers grew bananas and they cared about the environment. Who are these people from outside to tell us they know better than we how to take care of the environment and grow bananas?" This assertion was met by approving calls of "that's right, that's right!" from several members, leading Lynch to look about the room as if for allies. "That's where I would disagree with you," he called out over a growing chorus of discontent. "Our grandparents and parents did *not* take good care of the environment. They cut down forests; they planted on slopes and next to streams. As fair trade farmers we can't do those things. Now you can grow fruit the way your grandparents did, and you can use herbicide *and still* export to England, but you can't be a fair trade farmer if you choose to do that."

The meeting dissolved into half a dozen animated arguments between members and the president. As was usually the case when members departed from the meeting's agenda, the discussion gravitated from the formal meeting's English into Kwéyòl, from which the English word "weed eater" occasionally surfaced as an epithet. Gradually regaining the floor, Lynch offered a compromise. "Here's an idea that has been discussed with the National Committee,[6] and I know that WINFA has approved it. Maybe the solution is to divide your farm and use herbicide on one side, while you use the weed eater on the other one. Then, when you harvest fair trade fruit, it would come just from that part of the farm. But if you do this, it is crucial that you *never* take fruit from the conventional side of your farm and box it as fair trade bananas." If pesticide residues were detected on even a single box of fair trade bananas in Britain, he warned, all growers' reputations would be damaged. Lynch also cautioned members that their unique identification numbers meant that every box of fruit could be traced back to the farm that produced it.[7] "Now the supermarkets are just asking us to keep our word when we call ourselves fair trade," he continued. "Let me warn you: if anybody here puts fruit that has Gramoxone[8] on it in a fair trade box and I find out about it, I will *personally* ensure that that member is delisted as a fair trade grower."

Interviewed after the meeting, Lynch admitted that he had long known of the compromise of dividing farms between fair trade and conventional sections. He had hesitated to announce it until the strenuous opinions of some farmers made him fear that they would simply defy the ban in its entirety. Yet he worried about the effect of the compromise on farmers eager both to reduce their soaring production costs and to garner the benefits of fair trade prices. "What if you have two acres grown conventionally and one acre that uses no herbicide?" he asked during the interview. "Maybe your quota is forty boxes, but you only have twenty boxes available from the fair trade part of your farm. You see how tempting it would be to divert fruit from the other part of your farm and label it as fair trade? The alternative is to lose twenty boxes at the fair trade price. We only have to get a single box of bananas misrepresented in that way to destroy the fair trade market" (Lynch, personal communication, 2003).

While forced to defend the new environmental requirements during meetings of the fair trade group, Lynch also sympathized with farmers' discontent. Since the late 1980s, farmers have witnessed a massive loss of autonomy in the realm of production, as exporters and supermarkets dictated the way in which Caribbean bananas were to be grown and passed the costs of elaborate new postharvest procedures to island farmers (see Grossman 1998; Slocum 2006; Moberg 2008). In private, Lynch acknowledged that the fair trade requirements meant that farmers were once again finding their actions dictated by powerful "outsiders" who make what most consider to be unreasonable demands on their labor and resources:

> Look, you can talk all you want about fair trade as a partnership between the customer in England and the grower in the Caribbean. I've seen the websites; I know what they say. But from the farmer's perspective, it looks like more of the same old thing. First WIBDECO tells them how to grow the fruit. Then the supermarkets tell them how to pack it, and they have to pay for the privilege of using the supermarket's boxes and materials. Then EUREP-GAP comes along and tells them to put toilets and first-aid kits in their farms.[9] Now it's FLO telling them to use weed eaters and keep buffer zones. Can you blame farmers for viewing the fair trade people as a new set of masters? For them, anything that reduces their independence, anything that comes from "outside," causes resentment. Because in their experience the effect is always the same: more work, higher costs, less control over their time, lower earnings. (Lynch, personal communication, 2004).

Reflecting farmers' ambivalence toward fair trade certification, many of them responded rapidly to the suggestion that they divide their farms into conventional and fair trade sections. This policy was authorized reluctantly by FLO, and only after WINFA representatives warned the ATO's certifiers of the threat of widespread defiance of the herbicide ban among disaffected growers. By May 2004, more than a third of the valley's fair trade farms were already divided into "conventional" and "fair trade" parcels. Less than eight months had passed since Cornelius Lynch had offered the compromise at the meeting of the fair trade group.

Building Community

If FLO's environmental criteria require significant changes in agricultural practices, its social criteria have promoted a form of cooperative development that is also without recent precedent. Small-scale fair trade growers are required to participate in producers' associations that are democratically organized, self-governing, and nondiscriminatory with regard to gender, age, ethnicity, religion, or political identity. With few exceptions, formal cooperatives in rural communities of the Windwards either did not exist or were moribund prior to the formation of fair trade farmers' associations. Moreover, the fate of those cooperatives that had been organized in the past may not seem to augur well for the new producers' groups. In the 1930s, church-based organizations promoted cooperatives and credit unions throughout the Caribbean in an attempt to offset the effects of the global depression on the region's poor. Following World War II, cooperatives were embraced by British authorities to enhance rural economic viability and prepare island residents for limited self-government in the waning years of colonialism. This commitment survived the era of decolonization, and most Caribbean governments maintained field staff and entire departments devoted to cooperative promotion and development well into the 1990s. With few exceptions, however, the region's agricultural cooperatives have exhibited a poor record of viability. Few survived for more than a few years, usually because of the meager prospects of production for domestic markets, to which most cooperatives were oriented. Where local demand for food crops is limited, as on most Caribbean islands, there are few advantages to be gained by cooperative marketing efforts. Indeed, a farmer's best chance for disposing of produce when markets are glutted is to fall back on his or her individual contacts and wiles. In contrast, bulking produce with other farmers for sale—a customary strategy of marketing cooperatives—simply leads to lower prices for all. Against this record, the region also presents some notable instances of commercially successful cooperative ventures, mostly oriented toward export production. Among them are the fishing cooperatives of Belize (King 2004), the Jamaica Banana Producers' Association prior to its disruption by Chiquita during the 1930s (Holt 1992), and all of the Windward Islands' Banana Growers' Associations before they came under government control in the 1960s (Romalis 1975).[10] Nonetheless, by 2000, when the first fair trade groups were introduced into rural areas of St. Lucia, they arrived without any precedent of producers' cooperatives, successful or otherwise, in recent memory.

Fair trade farmers' groups, unlike the co-ops that preceded them a generation ago, have the potential to make a tangible material contribution to rural life by allocating social premiums, a portion of the final retail price that is returned to the fair trade association for investment in local needs. Any member may propose health, education, or infrastructure projects to be funded with social premiums, and such proposals are voted on by the group's membership at large. Among the first uses of social premiums by fair trade groups was the purchase of weed eaters to comply with FLO's certification requirements, an expenditure that one grower likened to "robbing Peter to pay Paul." Since then, most social-premium-funded projects have not been agricultural in nature. A novel health insurance fund has been established through a joint effort involving all fair trade groups on the island. This initiative provides reimbursement of farmers' households for medical expenses up to EC$1,000 (US$375) that are not covered by public clinics and hospitals. Another project initiated by the Mabouya Valley group seeks to increase secondary-school attendance for fair trade members' high-school-aged children. Rural teens are much less likely than their counterparts in town to attend high school because of the costs of transportation to and from school. A scholarship fund offsets travel and some other educational expenses for farmers' children who make progress toward graduation. A large share of the group's social premiums is also targeted to projects serving the broader community, where approximately 60 percent of farming residents do not participate in the fair trade group at all. In this vein, premiums have been used to purchase equipment for schools, to improve roads, to create and maintain sports fields, to provide lighting in crime-prone areas, and to offer vocational training for rural youth.

Apart from investment in agriculture, services, and infrastructure, social premiums support activities that "help to build community," according to Herbert Rosarie, an extension officer who formerly organized fair trade groups on the island. In the Mabouya Valley, these include events such as sports competitions, talent shows, dances, holiday celebrations, and "Seniors' Days," which honor the valley's senior citizens for their contributions. Fair trade farming groups underwrite such events by providing food and drink, entertainment, educational materials, T-shirts, trophies, and other services that help to generate a sizeable turnout. Rosarie notes that the investment of social premiums also fills a void in health care and education created in recent years by the state, whose programs and very presence in rural areas have contracted under neoliberal policies. "It used to be that people looked to government to do these things," Rosarie explains.

But since the '90s, when the bottom fell out of bananas, government tells us it doesn't have the funds. It can't even provide essential services, like schools and roads. Government tells us that we have to get used to living in a new age, a time of self-reliance. So where does that leave us? Sometimes political parties do these things, but only in a partisan way, a way that poisons relationships. . . . As for most people, especially the ones in rural areas, they are hurting even more than government. How can you be self-reliant if you have your livelihood kicked out from under you? So fair trade groups are stepping into this vacuum. They're providing services and development that don't come from anywhere else. What we're seeing is the creation of civil society; this is people themselves building up community. We've never experienced anything like this before. This . . . is the most exciting part of fair trade. (Rosarie, personal communication, 2003)

The magnitude of fair trade contributions to community development is considerable and rapidly growing, even as the overall prospects for the region's banana industry remain uncertain. Each box of fair trade fruit exported from St. Lucia generates a US$1.75 social premium, of which $0.20 is allocated to WINFA and $0.55 to the St. Lucia National Fair Trade Association (SLNFTA), an NGO representing all islandwide fair trade farmers. The remaining net social premium of US$1.00 per box is deposited into the accounts of farmers' groups according to their share of the island's fair trade output. The SLNFTA incurs some administrative costs, notably salaries for three staff members and rent for a modest office. Much of its share of the social premium is ultimately returned to local fair trade farmers' groups, however. Most expenses required of EUREP-GAP compliance were offset by direct grants from the SLNFTA to each fair trade group, as are some of the costs of establishing the buffer zones required by FLO. Reflecting the rapid expansion of the fair trade market in Britain, between 2000 and 2005, annual imports of certified fair trade bananas to the United Kingdom increased from 43,000 to over 1.33 million boxes. By the latter year, fair trade bananas accounted for nearly half of all the fruit exported by Windwards growers, generating US$2.33 million in social premiums. Of this amount, US$1.33 million was returned to farmers' groups for use as members saw fit to benefit local agricultural or community development.

In the Mabouya Valley, farmers state that social premiums have encouraged them to become more involved in community concerns than in the past, as the fair trade group has remained outside partisan divisions often stoked by other development interventions. For many of the farmers, fair trade offers the first opportunity they have had to participate in a democratically run organization not affiliated with political parties or their surrogates. Since the 1990s, the Mabouya Valley has been the site of various European Union–funded initiatives, including temporary public-work and community-infrastructure programs, most of which have sought to ameliorate poverty from the decline of the banana industry. While the EU provided most of the funding for the programs, the projects themselves are administered by the St. Lucian government, which has been criticized by the political opposition for allocating development projects and anti-poverty assistance to communities and individuals known to support the ruling party. In contrast, social premiums provide farmers with a chance to design and fund their own projects rather than compete for whatever largesse that the state, political parties, and NGOs intend for them. From this process has emerged an identity that extends beyond the benefits of higher producer prices. Fair trade farmers are often recognizable by their lapel pins bearing the same logo that FLO displays on all the products it certifies. Survey data corroborate that these outward distinctions between fair trade and conventional growers are evident in their material circumstances as well as their outlook on the banana industry and its future.

Fair Trade and Conventional Farmers Compared

Among Caribbean and EU governments, there is general agreement about securing some future for the Windward Islands banana industry. Most resulting policy recommendations center on questions of agricultural economics, notably, costs of production and yields per acre as well as macroeconomic issues such as the permissible level of tariff protection following the WTO ruling. In the midst of this animated policy debate, a fundamental issue affecting the industry's future, its aging demographic structure, is rarely mentioned. Yet to attend any gathering of banana growers on St. Lucia is to be in the presence of many people who are beyond their prime working years, leading the most casual observer to note how few young men and women now select farming as a way of life. If a Caribbean banana industry of any size is to survive beyond the immediate future, it must demonstrate its viability to younger farmers. To the extent that fair trade benefits those that it purports to help, it may well determine whether future growers survive in a deregulated global market. Data from the 2004 survey address this question through a comparison of fair trade and conventional farmers living and working side by side in the Mabouya Valley.

Some differences between fair trade and conventional farmers are so striking that the two groups might be taken for entirely separate populations. The survey results indicate that, on average, fair trade farmers are significantly older (by 10.8 years) than their conventional counterparts and have been farming in the valley for a significantly longer period of time (for twenty-five versus seventeen years). In contrast to the Kenyan and Guatemalan cases analyzed by Dolan and Lyon in this volume, women participate at least as fully in St. Lucia's fair trade system as do men, a fact that reflects a longstanding regional tradition of female-headed households and female participation in agriculture. On an island in which approximately one-third of all registered banana growers are female, women are even more heavily represented among fair trade farmers. Nearly half (48 percent) of the Mabouya Valley's fair trade growers are female, compared to 28 percent of conventional farmers. There is virtually no difference in the amount of land cultivated in bananas by either fair trade or conventional farmers or in the number of parcels that each farms. Yet these outward similarities conceal huge underlying differences in land tenure. Fair trade farmers, on average, individually own more than twice the amount of land owned by conventional farmers, while the latter on average utilize more than five times the amount of "family land," in which they share ownership with kinsmen in other households. Family land, or *ti familie* in Kwéyòl, is formally recognized in the island's inheritance law, which is derived from eighteenth-century French precedents. The law specifies that when a landowner dies without a will, all his or her heirs inherit an equal share of the land. The parcel usually remains undivided and cannot be sold without permission of all coowners, who may number in the dozens. As I point out elsewhere (Moberg 2008: 28), this provision strongly inhibits the sale and consolidation of land, in effect impeding the process of social differentiation in agriculture. On the other hand, policymakers have often viewed family land as an impediment to investment, as those who rely on it enjoy much less discretion over land use than do farmers with free and clear ownership. Many of these investments represent the very commitments expected of farmers under the fair trade regime.

Several reasons explain why fair trade farmers represent the older, more female, and most heavily invested segment of the valley's farming population. Chief among these is the manner in which farmers were recruited into the fair trade group when it was formed in 2000. Since the late 1970s, the region had been the site of the Mabouya Valley Development Project (MVDP), an ambitious integrated rural development initiative by the St. Lucian government that was funded in part by the Organization of American States. The project's overriding goal was to promote agricultural "modernization" in the form of individualized (rather than family) land tenure and technological change. Participating farmers were afforded an opportunity to purchase five-acre parcels from a government-owned estate in the valley with low-interest loans, to receive subsidized irrigation services,[11] and to participate in "grassroots" community associations linked to the MVDP. Among the most active participants in these associations were local women who formed a "sewing circle" and organized a still-active interdenominational mutual-aid society, known as Dorcas.[12] Although not formally operating as a cooperative, the MVDP promoted a degree of common interest and familiarity through monthly meetings of valley farmers with government officials, Ministry of Agriculture extension agents, and staff of the Banana Growers' Association (BGA). The project was winding down at about the same time that WINFA and the St. Lucia Banana Corporation began promoting fair trade farming in 2000 through the MVDP project headquarters at Riche Fond. That office served as a meeting place for the first informal gatherings of what was to become the valley's fair trade group, which continues to meet in a building at the same site. Hence, the first farmers to participate in fair trade were those who had previously participated in the MVDP; as such, they were also among the most established local farmers in terms of their individualized land tenure, farming experience, length of valley residence, and, for women, prior participation in mutual-aid groups. When they were asked how they had first learned about fair trade, 66 percent said they had been told about it directly by the MVDP office or by another farmer associated with the project. While networking of this sort played a critical role in recruitment to fair trade farming, the group has managed to stay clear of the political and religious divisions that often have ensnared other cooperatives. Elsewhere in the Caribbean, cooperatives have been known to draw their members from a single political party or religious affiliation, resulting in an inequitable distribution of benefits that heightens village factionalism and class divisions (Feuer 1984; Moberg 1991). Although valley residents acknowledge some persisting acrimony dating back to a series of mass protests by farmers against the Compton government in 1993, the fair trade group itself draws members from both political parties as well as most of the valley's churches.

The absence of partisanship in the fair trade group does not imply that all farmers enjoy equal opportunities to join it. Some certification requirements preclude participation by the many farmers who lack individual titles to land, a factor that mitigates against fair trade certification of farmers who had not been involved in the MVDP. Over 60 percent of fair trade farmers own all or some of their land individually, while 72 percent of conventional farmers lack individual ownership over any land, relying on either rental arrangements or family land. Farmers without individual discretion over land use find it difficult to comply with some fair trade environmental criteria. To comply with the buffer-zone requirement, a farmer occupying family land would have to secure the permission of all other family members sharing rights to his or her parcel to leave a portion of it uncultivated or planted in tree crops. Similarly, he or she would have to secure the agreement of other users not to spray prohibited chemicals on the parcel. Such arrangements are almost certain to be opposed by other kin who rely on the same land for subsistence or income. Indeed, the most commonly encountered complaint by those who cultivate family land regards the pressure placed on a given parcel by many competing demands from kinsmen. Similarly, few farmers would willingly invest in planting tree crops on land that they rented on an annual basis but did not themselves own. Because the buffer-zone requirement presupposes that farmers have complete discretion over the use of their land and would solely benefit from improvements such as tree crops, it has in effect limited participation in the fair trade group mostly to those who exercise independent ownership of their land.

Because fair trade and conventional farmers are so distinct in terms of demography and land tenure, it might be anticipated that the impact of fair trade on banana farmers is confounded by these variables. Yet, in the amount of land cultivated in bananas, fair trade and conventional farmers are virtually identical (both averaging 4.3 acres under bananas). Whatever other differences characterize the groups, then, their returns and expenses from banana production could be attributed to whether or not they participate in fair trade. Table 3.1 summarizes some of these differences. Fair trade farmers report that their labor requirements have increased as a result of FLO's herbicide ban, which is borne out by their greater wage expenses. The average 17 percent greater amount of fruit sold by fair trade growers over a given fortnight (eighty-two versus seventy boxes) points to a critical difference between the groups with regard to incentives for production. The box price paid to growers for premium conventional bananas during 2004 lagged between 12 and 16 percent below that of fair trade fruit, while fruit for the wholesale market sold for 40 percent less. These lower prices discourage increased banana production among conventional farmers, whose labor often brings a higher return when deployed off the farm than on it, especially during the early part of the year, when fruit prices are lowest. This fact, which is reflected in their higher average off-farm incomes, means that conventional farmers seasonally reduce their labor contributions to farming, which in turn reduces their average output. The difference in productivity, combined with higher producer prices, corresponds to significantly higher earnings for fair trade growers. Gross sales receipts of fair trade farmers every fortnight average 53 percent higher than those of conventional growers (the equivalent of US$547 versus $363). After deductions for inputs and labor, net returns from banana sales per fortnight remain significantly higher for fair trade than conventional farmers (US$291 versus $201).

TABLE 3.1

Economic Characteristics: Fair Trade and Conventional Farmers
(all figures in Eastern Caribbean dollars; EC$1.00 = US$0.38)

		N	Mean	Std. Deviation
Annual nonfarm income	Fair Trade	58	2,141	7,553.7
	Conventional	75	3,095*	8,587.5
Paid nonharvest workers on farm	Fair Trade	58	2.8*	1.0
	Conventional	75	2.4	0.9
Wages paid fortnightly	Fair Trade	58	$410*	324.5
	Conventional	75	$285	195.5
Gross sales from most recent harvest	Fair Trade	57	$1,458*	1074.8
	Conventional	74	$968	703.3
Net earnings from most recent harvest	Fair Trade	57	$776*	544.3
	Conventional	74	$538	400.1
Most recent shipment (boxes)	Fair Trade	58	82.7*	51.4
	Conventional	75	70.1	63.6

* t-statistic significant at p < .05
Source: Author's survey data.

Conclusions: A Changed Outlook

The material benefits associated with fair trade translate into what industry representatives call "a changed outlook" in many banana-producing
communities. This can be characterized as a degree of optimism conspicuously absent from most industry participants since 1993. During this time,
conventional farmers have sought to diversify their sources of household
income, with a resulting decline in their attention to farming and farm investments. In comparison, fair trade farmers remain committed to banana
farming as a livelihood, notwithstanding the costly changes expected of
them by the new environmental protocols. Over 62 percent of fair trade
farmers reported that they were growing the same or a greater amount of
bananas than five years earlier, compared to 56 percent of conventional
farmers. Given the demographic composition of the fair trade farmers,
it is notable that most of them have maintained or increased their commitment to banana production in recent years. As noted earlier, fair trade
farmers in the Mabouya Valley are disproportionately older and female.
These are the very segments of the rural population that have otherwise
reduced their reliance on banana farming in recent years as compared
to younger male growers. The improved outlook that industry observers
have attributed to fair trade growers is borne out by fair trade growers'
own perceptions of their near-term economic prospects, which reveal
much more optimism than among their conventional counterparts. Asked
whether they expected to remain in banana production in five years' time,
fair trade growers were significantly more likely than conventional farmers to answer affirmatively.

The contributions that fair trade groups have made to island economies, in terms of both higher export earnings and social premiums, have
gained the attention of governments formerly distrustful of social movements organized outside the political party system. Until 2004, the stated
position of the St. Lucian government toward banana-industry revitalization emphasized state-directed technological change based on irrigation-
dependent High Yielding Varieties (HYVs) of imported tissue-culture bananas. This policy offered little accommodation for low-chemical farming
as emphasized under fair trade. Many observers predicted that the HYVs,
with their greater labor and input costs, would, like other Green Revolution innovations, achieve higher productivity at a steep social cost in
stratification. Having witnessed fair trade's contributions in rural incomes
and community development, the government now accepts its expansion

as a key to the industry's salvation. This policy shift signals an implicit endorsement of social and environmental sustainability in place of the government's earlier promotion of an industry involving a smaller number of larger, more "efficient" farms. Over the long term it remains to be seen whether the material benefits of fair trade will entice a new generation to enter farming after the present, aging generation has retired. For those who remain in the industry, however, there is general agreement that fair trade represents the most promising avenue for the survival of family farmers in a liberalized global market.

On January 1, 2006, the last vestiges of the tariff-quota system were eliminated, a moment once predicted to be the death knell of the Caribbean banana industry. Ironically, by that point there were signs that the remaining farmers had weathered the worst of liberalization. Soon two of the largest supermarket chains in the United Kingdom, Sainsbury's and Waitrose, announced that they would exclusively carry fair trade bananas in their stores, with fruit to be sourced from the Windward Islands, the Dominican Republic, and Colombia. The announcement anticipated the eventual conversion of all remaining growers in the Windwards to fair trade certification. Elsewhere (Moberg 2005) I have noted the limits to fair trade's promises to transform the global market or to alter the position of commodity producers in it. Particularly in the realm of certification, Eastern Caribbean realities fall painfully short of fair trade's claims to create a "new world" of transparency and mutual respect in the world economy. Farmers see little difference between the new standards to which they are held by FLO and the previous dictates of WIBDECO and European retailers to which they continue to be subject, all of which they characterize as arbitrary, costly, and authoritarian. Yet what distinguishes fair trade from these previous directives is that for the first time the benefits—both in producer prices and social premiums—have offset the costs of compliance. Whereas all previous mandates over production and postharvest handling were accompanied by a steady attrition of growers, the promised expansion of fair trade certification to the remaining growers has finally stanched the losses of the past two decades. It also prompted a modest but measurable return to cultivation among farmers who had dropped out of production over previous years. By early 2007, according to the WINFA, the number of commercially active banana farmers in the Windwards had reached 3,347 (FLO 2007), marking the first time since 1990 that the industry's productive base had grown instead of declined. No one anticipates that the industry will ever constitute more than a fraction of its size during the heyday of protected markets, a time that island residents nostalgically recall as "Green Gold." For the farmers who remain, however, fair trade has become, in the words of one Mabouya Valley resident, "our last, best chance to survive here."

NOTES

1. This research was funded by the University of South Alabama Research Council and National Science Foundation (grant BCS-0003965 and Supplement). To ensure a cross-section of active growers, farmers were interviewed as they delivered their fruit to the buying depot at La Caye, which services all valley farms. Three area residents, all having some experience with banana farming, were recruited as ethnographic interviewers. They also prepared a Kwéyòl version of the survey instrument, which was administered in that language in about 70 percent of all cases. The sample represented a third of all active growers in the valley, according to data maintained by St. Lucia's Banana Emergency Recovery Unit (BERU). In the sample's demographic characteristics and proportion of fair trade and conventional farmers, it closely approximates the parameters of the farming population as indicated in BERU's database of all valley growers (St. Lucia 2002).

2. Fridell (2007:21) points out that neoliberal policies are in fact compatible with fair trade, an observation born out by the fact that fair trade is encouraged by the World Bank as a nonstatist, market-based, and voluntary approach to social justice.

3. Nurse and Sandiford (1995) provide a comprehensive discussion of marketing arrangements predating the WTO suit. An extensive literature has examined the development of the U.S.-EU trade dispute over European banana imports (Josling and Taylor 2003; Raynolds 2003; Wiley 2008), including the role played by campaign contributions in the decision of the Clinton White House to file the WTO suit (see Moberg 2008: 82ff.).

4. As harvests typically occur every two weeks on island banana farms, most growers measure their production, income, and expenses by fortnight.

5. Fair trade farmers' groups in the Windwards act as associations for disseminating information and allocating social premiums; they do not have a marketing function per se.

6. Lynch was referring to the National Fair Trade Committee, which is composed of representatives from each of the fair trade farmers' groups on the island.

7. Fruit is inspected prior to sale in the islands, and a subsample of boxes is inspected again upon arrival in England. Some of this fruit is tested for chemical residues, so violation of the herbicide ban can be easily traced back to a specific farmer.

8. Gramoxone is the trade name for paraquat.

9. At the beginning of 2004, St. Lucian farmers, like all exporters of agricultural produce to Europe, were required to implement costly new practices to comply with the European Retailer's Good Agricultural Practices (EUREP-GAP). The requirements include the provision of toilets, secure chemical storage areas, and first-aid kits on farms, among many other measures, and on average cost each farmer US$1,130.

10. Elsewhere (Moberg 2008), I argue that the St. Lucian government effectively seized control of a democratically governed Banana Growers' Association in 1967 because it had become too inclusive of small farmers and too independent of the party in power.

11. These efforts at irrigation failed due to engineering errors made by the original contractor. All of the irrigation lines now operating in the valley resulted from a more recent initiative by the European Union in the late 1990s.

12. Mentioned in the Acts of the Apostles, Dorcas was a Christian woman of Joppa revered for her almsgiving and good works.

PERSONAL COMMUNICATIONS

Hoggarth, Marcus, Head Produce Buyer, Sainsbury's Supermarkets. London, UK, March 13, 2003.

Jn Pierre, Tony, Communications Director, St. Lucia Banana Corporation. Castries, St. Lucia, May 16, 2000.

Lynch, Cornelius, President, Mabouya Valley Fair Trade Farmers Group. Osdan, St. Lucia, August 12, 2003, and Riche Fond, St. Lucia, June 18, 2004.

Rosarie, Herbert, Field Officer, St. Lucia Banana Corporation. Castries, St. Lucia, August 8, 2003.

WORKS CITED

Bérubé, N., and B. Aquin
    2005 Chiquita's Children. In These Times, May 10. http://www.inthesetimes.com/ article/2096/, accessed August 17, 2007.
Clegg, P.
    2002 The Caribbean Banana Trade: From Colonialism to Globalization. Basingstoke, UK: Palgrave Macmillan.
Edmunds, J. F., and C. Shillingford
    2005 A Program for the Resuscitation of the Windward Islands Banana Industry and Recommendations to Contribute to Its Sustainability in World Trade. http:// www.da-academy.org/banana_project.html, accessed January 21, 2007.
Feuer, C. H.
    1984 Jamaica and the Sugar Worker Cooperatives: The Politics of Reform. Boulder, CO: Westview.
Fisher, C.
    2007 Selling Coffee, or Selling Out? Evaluating the Consequences of Different Ways to Analyze the Fair-Trade System. Culture and Agriculture 29(2): 78–88.
FLO (Fairtrade Labelling Organizations International)
    2007 2006/7 Annual Report. http://www.fairtrade.net/uploads/media/Final_FLO_ AR_2007_01.pdf, accessed September 3, 2007.
    2008 2007 Annual Report. http://www.fairtrade.net/uploads/media/FLO_AR2007_ low_res_01.pdf, accessed August 11, 2008.
    2009 Producer Standards. http://www.fairtrade.net/fileadmin/user_upload/content/ Jan09_EN_Generic_Fairtrade_Standards_SPO.pdf, accessed February 2, 2009.
Fridell, G.
    2007 Fair Trade Coffee: The Prospects and Pitfalls of Market-Driven Social Justice. Toronto: University of Toronto Press.

Grossman, L. S.
  1998 The Political Ecology of Bananas: Contract Farming, Peasants, and Agrarian Change in the Eastern Caribbean. Chapel Hill: University of North Carolina Press.
Holt, T. C.
  1992 The Problem of Freedom: Race, Labor and Politics in Jamaica and Britain. Baltimore: Johns Hopkins University Press.
Josling, T. E., and T. G. Taylor, eds.
  2003 Banana Wars: Anatomy of a Trade Dispute. Cambridge, MA: CABI.
King, T.
  2004 Success and Transformation: Collective Marketing and Common Pool Credit in a Belizean Fishing Cooperative: An Empirical Example of a Multi-tiered Collective Action Problem. Ph.D. dissertation, Department of Anthropology. Pennsylvania State University.
Lobdell, R. A.
  1988 British Officials and the West Indian Peasantry, 1842–1938. In Labor in the Caribbean: From Emancipation to Independence. M. Cross and G. Heuman, eds. Pp. 195–207. London: Macmillan Caribbean.
Mintz, S.
  1984 Caribbean Transformations. Baltimore: Johns Hopkins University Press.
Moberg, M.
  1991 Citrus and the State: Factions and Class Formation in Rural Belize. American Ethnologist 18(2): 215–233.
  2005 Fair Trade and Eastern Caribbean Banana Farmers: Rhetoric and Reality in the Anti-Globalization Movement. Human Organization 64(1): 4–15.
  2008 Slipping Away: Banana Politics and Fair Trade in the Eastern Caribbean. New York: Berghahn Books.
Moore, G.
  2004 The Fair Trade Movement: Parameters, Issues, and Future Research. Journal of Business Ethics 53(1): 73–86.
NERA
  2003 Banana Exports from the Caribbean since 1992. London: National Economic Research Associates.
Nurse, K., and W. Sandiford
  1995 Windwards Islands Bananas: Challenges and Options under the Single European Market. Kingston, Jamaica: Friedrich Ebert Stiftung.
OAS (Organization of American States)
  1995 Background Information for Project Entitled: Technological Modernization of the Banana Industry in the Caribbean. Castries: Inter-American Institute for Co-operation in Agriculture.
Raynolds, L.
  2003 The Global Banana Trade. In Banana Wars: Power, Production and History in the Americas. S. Striffler and M. Moberg, eds. Pp. 23–47. Durham, NC: Duke University Press.

Romalis, R.
  1975 Economic Change and Peasant Political Consciousness in the Commonwealth
      Caribbean. Journal of Commonwealth and Comparative Politics 13(3): 225–241.
Sandiford, W.
  2000 On the Brink of Decline: Bananas in the Windward Islands. St. Georges,
      Grenada: Fedon Books.
Slocum, K.
  2006 Free Trade and Freedom: Neoliberalism, Place and Nation in the Caribbean.
      Ann Arbor: University of Michigan Press.
St. Lucia
  2002 Survey of Banana Agro-Ecological Zones. Cul de Sac, St. Lucia: Banana
      Emergency Recovery Unit, Ministry of Agriculture.
Tangermann, S.
  2003 The European Common Banana Policy. *In* Banana Wars: The Anatomy of a
      Trade Dispute. T. E. Josling and T .G. Taylor, eds. Pp. 45–66. Cambridge, MA:
      CABI.
Wiley, J.
  2008 The Banana: Empire, Trade Wars, and Globalization. Lincoln: University of
      Nebraska Press.

Fair Flowers

Environmental and Social Labeling in the Global Cut Flower Trade

CATHERINE ZIEGLER

On chilly winter days, many American supermarkets welcome their entering customers with displays of fresh cut flowers. Urban convenience stores brighten sidewalks with buckets of orchids, roses, tulips, lilies, and even tuberoses on late winter mornings. Occasionally these fresh flowers are labeled with country of origin—Colombia, Costa Rica, Taiwan, Ecuador, Holland—but most are not. A rare few are branded in other ways: with a retailer's name or by the bouquet maker who packages the flowers. A tiny fraction of the many billions of commercial cut flowers sold annually in the United States and Europe are also labeled by one or another of several environmental and social certifying organizations such as Flower Label Program or Max Havelaar in Europe and just recently VeriFlora and Fair Trade in the United States. These labels have emerged since the early 1990s to legitimate and certify the products of the global cut flower industry. This chapter focuses on the recent arrival of fair trade flowers in the United States and examines the development of alternative flower-labeling organizations and their ethical aims and standards for flower farms. What have been the effects of these certifications? Certifying authorities have undoubtedly changed the behavior of participating growers by promoting environmentally sustainable agricultural practices including reduced use of toxic chemicals. Fair trade has larger ambitions than other flower-certifying entities. Among other things, it aims to use market forces to change South-North trading relationships, to empower Southern producers, to bring them fairer prices, and to change conditions for their farm workers and communities. All the various certifications also calm troubled consumers by assuring them that their purchases of labeled bunches of flowers reward ethical farms with healthy environments and smiling workers. Yet it is still uncertain whether they are more effective as a mechanism for

environmental and social change or as a marketing tool for flower plantation owners and flower retailers.

This chapter examines the development and effects of these certifications within the global cut flower industry in order to contribute to two
issues raised by research on fair trade and other ethical certifications
(Moore 2004; Barrientos and Dolan 2006; Fridell 2007; Jaffee 2007; Raynolds et al. 2007). First, how does fair trade certification differ from competing certifying organizations in the flower industry, and what benefits
do these certifications bring to growers, farm workers, and consumers?
Do competing labels lead to confusion and possibly disenchantment with
certification systems? Second, has the expansion of fair trade certification
in the flower industry, with its plantation agriculture and associated marketing through big retailers, contributed to "the co-option and dilution of
fair trade" and its core objectives? (Jaffee 2007: 255).

The chapter is based on research conducted in 2008, including semistructured interviews with flower growers, U.S. wholesalers, retailers, and
executives of certifying and grower organizations. Many of these interviews were conducted at a four-day flower trade show in Miami during
March 2008 where growers from the Netherlands, Kenya, Mexico, Colombia, Ecuador, and other Latin American countries displayed their fin-
est flowers. Several VeriFlora and a couple Fair Trade participants also attended the show. Email correspondence with other informants provided
data and opinions. Casual conversations with supermarket staff were also
useful as I monitored supermarket floral displays, primarily in the New
York metropolitan area, but also in the United Kingdom, Florida, and
California, This case study is also informed by data and interviews from
earlier research on the global cut flower industry (Ziegler 2007).

The Evolution of the Global Flower Trade

Fresh flowers, especially out-of-season flowers, flow round the world to
wealthy places and to prosperous people. Until the second half of the
twentieth century only a few people enjoyed this luxury, but over the past
forty years increasing prosperity, global production, and relatively declining prices have allowed many more people to enjoy year-round flowers.
Two characteristics distinguish fresh cut flowers from other global crops.
First, flowers in the international flower trade come in hundreds of different species and varieties including abundant popular flowers such as
roses, carnations, freesias, orchids, and lilies. Second, flowers are highly

perishable and short-lived, so they must reach consumers within very few days of harvesting and in absolutely unblemished condition. These characteristics create growing and trading challenges not faced by uniform, nonperishable fair trade crops such as coffee or tea.

Most fresh cut flowers are temperate-climate crops, so perhaps it is not surprising that the Netherlands leads the world in flower growing and exporting by a substantial margin, claiming about 44 percent of the world's total in 2005. France, Italy, Spain, Israel, Belgium, and Germany also produce large quantities of cut flowers for internal consumption and for export. Developed nations are responsible for about 55 percent of the world's cut flower exports (AIPH 2007). Colombia (13 percent), Ecuador (6 percent), and Kenya (5 percent) are also among the world's largest flower exporters, and their flower farms are the focus of a number of environmental and social certifying organizations such as Flower Label Program (FLP) and Fair Trade.

The export flower trade focuses on the closest markets and strongest trading relationships. In 2007, almost all Kenyan flowers ended up in the Netherlands (68 percent), United Kingdom (20 percent), and other European countries (Grey 2008). About 80 percent of flowers exported from Colombia, Ecuador, and other Latin American countries were sold in the United States, with 12–18 percent crossing the Atlantic to Europe and Russia (Expoflores 2008; Asocolflores 2009).

Flower Growers

The number of export flower growers, the size of flower farms, and marketing arrangements vary from country to country. The Netherlands, for example, has about twenty-four hundred cut flower growers, typically with just a few intensively cultivated hectares under glass greenhouses. Most thrive because they can market their flowers through Floraholland, the larger of the two remaining Dutch cooperative auctions (Ziegler 2007). In Kenya, Colombia, and Ecuador, in contrast, flowers for the international trade grow on large plantation-style farms. Often ten to fifty hectares in size, some farms may reach a hundred hectares and employ hundreds, and occasionally thousands, of workers. These Southern growers arrange their own sales, and the largest have their own sales and marketing staff. Kenya has over one hundred growers on about twenty-five hundred hectares.[1] But fewer than ten firms dominate flower exporting

(Ngige 2008). Colombia and Ecuador have about five hundred and three hundred flower growers, respectively (Velez Koppel 2006). Almost all are privately owned, family-run, but sophisticated businesses—even the largest grower in Colombia, Dole Fresh Flowers, a division of Dole Foods, is privately owned. The tight profit margins, unpredictability, and risk involved in flower growing and trading have discouraged participation by large public corporations. Dole Fresh Flowers has owned flower farms for ten years but is still not profitable (Ziegler 2007).

Comparing European and U.S. Delivery Chains

About 70 percent of the fresh flowers in U.S. stores are imported. Three-quarters come from Colombia and Ecuador, while most of the remaining 30 percent are grown in California. Most Latin American growers connect to the seventy or so American supermarket chains, to big stores such as Sam's Club, and to the fifteen thousand retail florists through intermediary importers, wholesalers, and bouquet makers (many in Miami) and have no direct relationship with a retailer. These longer, fragmented delivery chains affect the ultimate condition of the flowers. Consequently, branding flowers for retail is rare in the United States—dying flowers in Dole or A&P or even fair trade packaging are not good for business. So introducing certified or branded blooms also involves establishing speedier distribution chains in order to sustain quality, brand integrity, and consumer appeal.

Most fresh flowers sold in Western Europe today are grown within Europe. Imports come primarily from Kenya and Israel, with small amounts from Colombia, Ecuador, and other nations. Flowers travel between European countries in water-filled buckets in refrigerated trucks, arriving at their final retail destinations more swiftly and in better condition than in the United States, where most flowers have been dry-packed and transported in part by plane.

Principal forms of flower retailing also differ from country to country. Germany, the largest importer of fresh flowers in Europe, sells over 80 percent of its flowers through retail florists, with only about 15 percent of flower sales passing through its five major supermarket chains (the figure is similar for the Netherlands). In contrast, in the United Kingdom, five major supermarket chains dominate and are responsible for over 60 percent of cut flower sales (Van Kooten 2007).

Social and Environmental Monitoring

In 1990 the United Kingdom passed the Food Safety Act requiring trace-ability in horticulture chains, including flower supply. This prompted the large supermarket chains such as Tesco to establish strong relationships and integrated supply chains with a few large Kenyan growers so they could more easily verify the conditions on their source farms (Hughes 2000). Also in the early 1990s, European environmental and labor groups began scrutinizing workers' wages and exposure to agricultural chemicals on distant food and flower farms. Their television and print media revelations about poor conditions and environmental degradation produced a variety of public and private responses aimed at assuring the public that changes were being instituted and monitored. For example, grower organizations in Colombia, Ecuador, and Kenya responded by establishing certification programs that are briefly described later in this chapter (Asocolflores 2009; Ngige 2008). The Colombian and Ecuadorian governments also gradually increased their regulation of flower growers.[2] In both nations, however, regulations are poorly enforced, and some growers (perhaps many) ignore them.

Asocolflores, the Colombian flower growers' trade association, established its Florverde program in 1996.[3] The program is entirely voluntary, and about 170 farms are presently involved. By early 2008, independent inspectors had certified about eighty growers as fully compliant, with about ninety other companies participating at different levels (Asocolflores 2009). Florverde-certified growers constitute only about 36 percent of Asocolflores members (16 percent of all Colombian growers), but they include some of the largest flower-growing companies and biggest exporters, such as Dole Fresh Flowers.[4] The Florverde brand has been aggressively marketed in the United States, and in 2008 Florverde-certified bouquets were visible in several U.S. supermarket and grocery chains including A&P and Trader Joe.

Ecuador's flower growers' association Expoflores established a similar certification program named FlorEcuador.[5] Expoflores's 167 members (out of about 300 grower companies in Ecuador) tend to be the larger growers, collectively owning 70 percent of total flower-farm hectares. All members automatically participate in the FlorEcuador program, and in theory, all gradually work toward full certification. By January 2009, ninety members were FlorEcuador certified at some level (54 percent of Expoflores members and 30 percent of all Ecuadorian flower growers) (Expoflores

2008).⁶ Among the fully compliant farms allowed to use the FlorEcuador label are some of the best-known, including Nevado and Agrocoex (both fair trade certified) and Esmeralda Farms.

The Kenya Flower Council was established in 1996, and most Kenyan growers are members, including the largest, Homegrown/Finlays and Os-erian. Many are certified by the principal social and environmental organizations (described later in this chapter) in the Netherlands and the United Kingdom, Kenya's largest markets.

In effect, all three growers' associations—Asocolflores, Expoflores, and Kenya Flower Council—set standards and mandate services for their member farms that in other flower-growing regions such as the Netherlands and California are regulated, enforced, and provided by government agencies and market-based organizations. Their standards and improvement projects roughly correspond with those of the three principal Western European certifying organizations—Milieu Project Sierteelt (MPS), Flower Label Program (FLP), and Max Havelaar/Fair Trade Labelling Organizations—that by the mid-1990s had focused on improving the environmental and social conditions on Southern flower farms. Initially, these European organizations focused on either environmental conditions (Milieu Project Sierteelt) or social conditions (Flower Label Program), but today all include components of both (Petitjean 2006). Each of them is aimed at a specific national consumer audience and is an important marketing tool for the wholesalers and retailers in these nations and for growers seeking access to Northern markets.

European Certifying Organizations

Milieu Project Sierteelt (MPS), one of the first nonprofit environmental labeling programs, was established in the Netherlands in 1993. It currently has about five thousand member growers around the world, with about half of them in the Netherlands. Initially its auditors monitored members' fertilizer, pesticide, and energy use, but subsequently they evaluated the *types* of chemicals used on the basis of their environmental impact and encouraged reductions in overall chemical use. MPS gradually expanded internationally and added a social and quality component to its basic environmental compliance standards. Standards are adjusted to local conditions, with Dutch growers, for example, held to a different and higher standard than growers in Kenya. Today, according to MPS's managing director, the program is "in a position to bring appropriate answers to the whole range of society matters of concern." With all Dutch growers now in compliance, 70 percent of the flowers and plants passing through the enormous Dutch flower market are certified in some way by MPS (Petitjean 2006).

The Flower Label Program (FLP) was established in Germany in 1998 by German flower wholesalers and retailers partly in response to concern generated by a television documentary detailing workers' conditions on flower farms in developing countries. FLP inspects and certifies fifty-two farms in Ecuador, three in Kenya, and one in Portugal. Colombian and Zimbabwean members have all recently dropped out of the program. It is reasonable to assume that all the FLP-certified farms aim for the German market (Flower Label Program 2008).

FLP's requirements for certification are among the most stringent, specific, and detailed of all the certifying organizations. FLP specifies in detail its standards governing the social conditions of production such as living wages, safe working conditions, working hours, training, and freedom to form trade unions, as well as environmental practices including chemical use, worker exposure to chemicals, composting, and recycling. Again different standards apply to growers in different nations (in Ecuador, for example, very few farm workers are unionized), and compliance is verified by independent inspectors.

The Max Havelaar Foundation, based in Switzerland, was established in 1992 by several nongovernmental aid organizations and is a member of the Fairtrade Labelling Organizations International (FLO). Max Havelaar successfully opened a Swiss market for producers of a range of products including coffee, chocolate, bananas, and in the late 1990s, flowers. Like all fair trade organizations, Max Havelaar was conceived as an alternative trading system that established a more direct relationship between the producer, retailer, and consumer, promising ethical and environmentally sustainable practices in production. The Max Havelaar Foundation products are sold principally in Switzerland, where there is high consumer recognition of the label.[7] Under rules revised in October 2008, Max Havelaar, like all FLO affiliates, stipulates that buyers pay a 10 percent premium on flower-farm prices. That premium is earmarked for a fund overseen by a joint committee of management and employees and is allocated to projects that improve working or living conditions of employees and others in the source community.[8] In February 2004 the first fair trade flowers from Kenya were sold in the United Kingdom by Tesco Supermarkets. Their introduction was a supermarket response to public anger following a 2003 BBC television documentary exposing environmental and labor abuses on

Kenyan flower farms (Dolan 2007). According to Dolan, "UK supermarkets embarked on a campaign to refurbish their reputation by diversifying their product portfolio into a range of ethically produced wares, including Fair Trade flowers from Kenya" (Dolan 2007: 244). The United Kingdom quickly became the second-largest market for fair trade flowers after Germany (FLO 2008a).

By January 2009 eighteen Kenyan growers were certified by the Fairtrade Labelling Organizations (of forty-two flower growers worldwide, up from twenty-six in 2006), including the largest exporters, Oserian Homegrown/ Finlays Flowers and Longonot Horticulture (FLO-Cert 2009). Desirable though the fair trade label may be, there are limitations for many Kenyan growers. The "issue is that it is an expensive label," explained Jane Ngige, CEO of the Kenyan Flower Council (Ngige 2008). A comparison of labeling costs for Ecuadorian growers supports this contention, suggesting that annual costs for FLO certification were about $5,000 per year, compared with an average of about $2,500 for other certifications (van der Ploeg 2008).[9]

TransFair USA

In the United States, flower consumers remain largely unaware of the issues that have galvanized European legislators, flower consumers, and traders. There has been no outcry for certification programs to calm consumers, yet by February 2008 TransFair USA was overseeing fresh-cut-flower transactions that among other things guaranteed that "farmers and farm workers behind Fair Trade Certified goods were paid a fair, above-market price" (TransFair USA 2009). TransFair USA's website lists twelve flower growers: nine in Ecuador, one in Colombia, and two in Kenya, out of the total of twenty-eight listed by FLO for these countries. A TransFair representative explained the organization works with five more Kenyan growers that are not listed (Barrow 2009).[10] Puzzlingly, some growers listed as separate entities are actually part of the same company (for example, Agrocoex and Agroganadera Espinosa Chiriboga). These growers have all been certified by Max Havelaar, FLP, MPS, and several other organizations, as well as the appropriate national certifications such as Florverde or FlorEcuador. Several of the Ecuadorian growers sell their flowers in Switzerland, where the Max Havelaar label is an important marketing tool, or in other European countries and to a few high-end wholesalers in the United States for whom the fair trade label is irrelevant since they buy from these growers for their quality and varieties. Consequently, these growers are unlikely to send many roses to the (lower-priced) U.S. supermarkets or Internet sites. Some of these Ecuadorian fair trade growers have no website, suggesting they do not need additional marketing aids for their flowers. Some with websites fail to mention their fair trade certification.

Only a few of the listed Ecuadorian growers are large enough to supply the quantities of blooms essential to fulfilling orders on the scale demanded by samsclub.com and supermarket chains. Nevado and Agrocoex are among them. Nevado produces over twenty million blooms annually; and Agrocoex, over eleven million (van der Ploeg 2008). Both are exemplary growers, already certified by a range of organizations including FlorEcuador, VeriFlora (see below), FLP, Max Havelaar, and Fair Flowers Fair Plants (FFP) (see below).

Currently TransFair USA certifies only roses and carnations, and interested U.S. consumers may buy them from six Internet retailers (samsclub. com, 1800flowers.com, FTD, One World Flowers, Prairie Crocus Design, and Organicbouquet.com [these fair trade flowers are not necessarily organic]) (TransFair USA 2009). The TransFair USA website also lists seven regional and one national supermarket chain: Roche Bros., Massachusetts; Giant, Pennsylvania; Ukrops, Virginia; Kings Super Markets, New Jersey; Heinen's, Ohio; Metropolitan Markets, Seattle, Washington; New Seasons Market, Oregon; and Whole Foods, a national chain (TransFair 2009; Barrow 2009). The majority of the fair trade flowers marketed in the United States are probably sold through samsclub.com and 1800flowers. com. Samsclub.com has two sites for web sales. One, aimed at consumers, offers gift bouquets of a dozen fair trade roses for about sixty-four dollars including shipping—only slightly more than the fifty-eight dollars samsclub.com asks for a dozen conventional roses. Ecuadorian roses and Colombian carnations are also available in minimum quantities of 48–150 stems. The other site targets bulk buyers such as retail florists, and it offers fair trade roses and carnations in minimum quantities of 100–300 stems. Of the eighty-eight different recent offerings at this site, seven were fair trade flowers (Sam's Club Online 2009). This is not a vast choice of fair trade flowers, but Sam's Club's commitment is encouraging, even if it is motivated more by marketing than by ethical concerns, as seems likely for a large retail corporation. 1800flowers.com recently offered about sixty bouquets, of which between one and four (at different times) were fair trade roses apparently from Kenya, although their country of origin was not identified.[11]

A test of 1800flowers.com's fair trade roses was disappointing. The roses themselves were satisfactory and lasted for several days. However, nothing identified them as fair trade roses. There was no fair trade trademark on the blooms or even a helpful insert to advise that because of fair trade monitoring, the recipient could "feel good about the source of your flowers—that workers receive fair wages and protection from pesticides, that growers are taking steps towards sustainability and that the community is benefiting directly from your purchases," which is the message conveyed on the TransFair website. The roses could as easily have come from an uncertified farm in Colombia rather than a fair trade farm in Kenya. Such experiences raise doubts about the benefits of "mainstreaming" fair trade products without substantial organizational oversight or commitment on the retailer's part (Moore 2004). A purchase from organicstyle.com was disappointing in a different way. The simply gorgeous "Wanted" roses were labeled "organic," with no mention whatsoever of fair trade.[12] Internet flower purchases are almost entirely gifts, and as with all gifts, they express certain values and sentiments (Ziegler 2007). In choosing fair trade roses and paying a higher price for them, it is quite possible the giver intends to communicate some aspect of his or her values or acknowledge the sensitivity of the intended recipient to the social or moral ideals of the fair trade program. Such a message, however, would be lost in a gift of (hypothetically fair trade) roses from 1800flowers.com or organicstyle.com.[13]

Few supermarket chains in the United States mirror the ethical commitment of the Co-operative Group or Waitrose in the United Kingdom (Barrientos and Smith 2007). Whole Foods Markets comes closest, and the corporation embarked on a fair trade rose program in mid-2007 as part of its "Whole Trade" program that brought fair trade roses into its New York stores for around twenty dollars a dozen during 2008 (Whole Foods Markets 2009). These roses apparently came from one of the Agrocoex farms in Ecuador, and their transparent plastic sleeves and prominent point-of-sale signs were branded "Whole Trade." Initially bouquet sleeves also featured the fair trade icon, but by the end of 2008 the icon had been removed, leaving only the Whole Trade logo. The fair trade icon was now confined to a tiny tag wrapped around one of the blooms. Adjacent bouquets, also under the Whole Trade banner, were identified as Colombian flowers grown under "sustainable" conditions and bore similar small tags featuring the "Rainforest Alliance" icon. Even if consumers noticed these different tags, few would be able to specify the ethical differences between these two types of "Whole Trade" bouquets. Whole Foods Markets partners with TransFair USA in this program, and presumably perplexed consumers rely on the corporation's reputation and assurances about sourcing. Indeed by branding the flowers in this way, Whole Foods Markets theoretically undertakes responsibility for the sources of the flowers and the environmental and social conditions in which they are grown. Yet the "fair trade seal is the key element that allows consumers to distinguish fairly traded products from their superficially similar competitors" (Jaffee 2007: 162), so its shrinking visibility is a cause for concern. Whole Foods Markets also offers roses with another U.S. certification—VeriFlora. In March 2008 VeriFlora blooms cost about nine dollars a dozen—or less than half the price of the Whole Trade roses. Nearby convenience stores were selling a dozen visually similar but unlabeled roses for even less.

It is too soon to know whether the premiums generated by U.S. sales of fair trade flowers contribute to the kind of "community-led development" mentioned on the TransFair USA website. According to TransFair USA, in 2008 fair trade flower imports into the United States were valued at about one million dollars and generated one hundred thousand dollars in premiums sent to the various farms' Joint Bodies (Barrow 2009). In theory, TransFair USA also helps the two Ecuadorian growers, Nevado and Agrocoex, to gain access to a specialized market in the United States. But as Roberto Nevado pointed out in a recent *FloraCulture International* article, sales of certified blooms are still tiny. Even the most successful Ecuadorian farms sell less than 15 percent of their production as certified flowers (for all certifications), and for many farms such sales are less than 2 percent (van der Ploeg 2008).

It is not clear why TransFair USA chose this moment to add fair trade flowers to its roster of products sold in the United States. American media and NGO criticism of the international flower trade has been muted compared with their European counterparts, and consumers have not demanded fairly produced flowers. FLO's determination to move more fair trade products into supermarkets where the majority of people shop may partially explain this development (Moore 2004; Jaffee 2007). Raynolds estimates recognition of fair trade at 20 percent in the large U.S. market, and total consumption of fair trade products (overwhelmingly coffee) is certainly growing—to almost one-third of total world sales in 2007 (Raynolds 2007). But per capita fair trade consumption in the United Kingdom is still five times that of the United States, and in Switzerland it is ten times that of the United States.

Rainforest Alliance

An environmental conservation organization, Rainforest Alliance began certifying flowers quite recently after a four-year research process conducted in partnership with the Sustainable Agriculture Network. Rainforest Alliance presently certifies twenty-three flower farms in Ecuador, including Nevado, fourteen in Colombia, and only one, Finlays, in Kenya. This certification focuses on environmental and conservation issues aiming to "ensure that the [flower] farms are good neighbors to rural communities and wildlands" (Rainforest Alliance 2009). Social standards with respect to workers and local communities are far less rigorous and specific than FLP, Fair Trade, or VeriFlora standards (see Jaffee 2007 for a comparison to Fair Trade). Yet retailers such as Whole Foods Markets give the two certifying organizations equal consideration in their floral offerings, leaving confused consumers to puzzle out the differences.

VeriFlora

Introduced in 2004, VeriFlora is the principal U.S. floral certification system (excluding straightforward production labeling such as "organic") competing with Fair Trade for U.S. consumer attention. It developed from a desire among a small group of growers, wholesalers, and retailers to encourage growers supplying the U.S. market to adopt proven environmental, social, and accountability practices, similar to those established by the certifying organizations described earlier. However, it differs importantly from other certifications in its requirement that growers progress toward organic production for at least part of the farm's output and also create "a unified path for organic and sustainable agriculture." "Organic" is defined as the control of pests without "reliance on *dangerous* farm chemicals" (emphasis added). This represents a confusing dilution of the standards associated with organic production. Still, it is an attainable, if costly, objective for U.S. growers, but it may be far more difficult and risky for offshore growers, whose flowers must pass stringent phytosanitary searches for lingering insects as they enter the country. This requirement seems to have confused some journalists (and retailers) who praise VeriFlora flowers as "organic," which is not yet the case. Some journalists also assume that fair trade flowers are organic.[14] Others have noted the problems for Southern producers in converting crops to organic standards, including the time involved and the limited guarantee of a return on investment when selling such crops in "highly volatile world markets and in competition with conventional products" (Moore 2004: 79).

By January 2009, VeriFlora had certified thirty-one cut flower growers (up from twenty in May 2008): seventeen Ecuadorian, six Colombian, and eight in the United States (VeriFlora 2009). Nine wholesale flower companies were also members, and along with retail members they "give contracts, pay a premium [price] so [growers] have market assurance that if they grow it someone is willing to buy it and pay more for it" (Prolman 2008). The multiply certified fair trade grower Nevado is among Veri-Flora's Ecuadorian growers and probably had little difficulty in meeting VeriFlora standards, although the grower still needs to pay for the costly audits. Many of the others are also well-certified leading growers in California, Ecuador, and Colombia known for their exceptional farm practices and high-quality flowers. A few, however, are smaller farms with no other certifications. VeriFlora's certified growers have a substantial marketing advantage in their huge variety of flowers (not just roses and carnations as with fair trade offerings in the United States).

Some growers mentioned in conversations that their noteworthy farm environmental practices and social programs actually preceded their association with VeriFlora, but the organization's oversight has helped them to create a structure for accountability and improvement and a long-term process for adopting a "best practices program" (Johnson 2008). As one Ecuadorian VeriFlora grower explained, in a well-run business it is important to keep workers happy:

> To produce a good rose (and we are considered one of the premium farms) you need very happy and contented workers, because it is not easy [for them]. So we have over three hundred employees, and we take very good care of them. We are constantly doing courses on everything from how to produce the rose, how to cut them, all the way to family planning and finance and computers, because we want them to feel part of the team and we want them to be happy and stay at the farm. But the basis for all that is happy people who are committed to the company and who are going to stay and not go off to work somewhere else every three months. (Johnson 2008)

Without a certifying label these expensively produced "good roses" are hard to distinguish from others, and VeriFlora certification offers recognition of these attitudes. Members hope they will be compensated for their ethical behavior, environmental commitment, reliability, and consistent supply and for the quality of the flowers that happier workers, dedicated growers, and "handlers" and a speedy supply chain can bring to retailers and consumers. VeriFlora members acknowledge that there is currently little demand from American consumers for flowers that have been certified as ethically or "sustainably" produced. However, most are confident the demand will emerge in the future, and they want to help that process and be ready with the right flowers. Others, acknowledging unethical behavior among some of their fellow growers, fear that eventually flowers produced for American consumers will be subjected to the same scrutiny as their European counterparts. Like Fair Trade flowers, VeriFlora blooms are offered to U.S. consumers through a limited number of large retailers such as Whole Foods, a few small retailers, and Internet sites.[15]

Complex Standards

Comparing the standards of these many certifying organizations is a complicated task. Fair Trade's, Flower Label Program's, and VeriFlora's long lists of requirements illuminate some of their differences. VeriFlora's claims and standards are broad. For example, its flowers are produced under "sustainable" social and environmental conditions.[16] "Sustainability" is defined as the ability to "meet the needs of the present without compromising the ability of future generations to meet their own needs" (VeriFlora 2009).[17] In contrast, FLO's social standards released in October 2008 are very specific and include minimum requirements for hired labor on flower farms. These mandate three weeks' annual leave (as do FLP's standards), whereas VeriFlora requires only conformity with national laws, which are significantly less demanding in Colombia and Ecuador than in the United States. Similarly, FLO requires annual medical exams for all employees with quarterly examinations for employees handling agro-chemicals, whereas VeriFlora requires only the on-site availability of a health professional and financial contribution to a worker health program. FLO and FLP both require that uniforms be provided and changed and washed at the workplace. They also specify free transportation or a transportation allowance, whereas VeriFlora more vaguely requires that transportation needs be "addressed" (FLO 2008b; Flower Label Program 2008; Scientific Certification Systems 2008; van der Ploeg 2008; VeriFlora 2009). The broad nature of VeriFlora's standards is partly attributable to its certification of both Latin American and U.S. flower farms. VeriFlora may need to develop different standards for these different settings. The clearest difference among the three certifying organizations, however, is that only Fair Trade provides for the social premiums that have brought documented improvements for flower workers from sales of fair trade flowers in Europe (but not yet in the United States).

Obviously there is considerable overlap in the standards of all the major certifying authorities. However, because retailer involvement and consumer recognition tend to be country specific, a grower selling flowers in Germany and Switzerland may need both FLP and Max Havelaar certification. Consequently some growers in Colombia, Ecuador, and Kenya with varied markets may carry six or more labels, bolstering the membership counts of FLP, MPS, Max Havelaar, VeriFlora, FlorEcuador, and so on, but not necessarily expanding the numbers of workers who benefit from these programs. Furthermore, each organization mandates separate expensive audits and expensive and time-consuming records and statistics requirements.

Union Fleurs, an umbrella organization of flower growers based in Brussels, is attempting to harmonize the major certifying programs under the umbrella label Fair Flowers Fair Plants (FFP). Growers, traders, and retailers may all belong to FFP, and at present most members are from the Netherlands, Germany, Austria, and Sweden. This umbrella label would be most helpful if the grower organizations in Kenya, Colombia, and Ecuador could also meet its standards, and this seems to be their objective (Nevado 2007). Nevado and Agrocoex are among the half-dozen Ecuadorian farms already certified by FFP, but as Roberto Nevado explained to *FloraCulture International,* after three years of certification no Ecuadorian member had sold a single FFP flower (van der Ploeg 2008).

Who Gains from Certification?

To return to one of my original questions, what have been the effects of these certifications? Participating farm owners, flower-farm workers, retailers, and consumers all benefit in some ways. However, there is some evidence of grower skepticism and resentment of the increasingly burdensome nature of the requirements imposed on developing nation flower growers by distant institutions. Rod Evans of the Kenya Flower Council recently complained to *FloraCulture International,* "It is our considered opinion that many of the audit bodies are self-perpetuating and fail to add value. Our concern is that they simply provide employment and finance to their commercial enterprises based in the northern hemisphere" (Isaza 2007).

Farm Owners

Undoubtedly, emphasis on sustainable production methods and accountability standards has aided farm efficiency and productivity. Another fundamental requirement of all these programs, reduced chemical use, is gradually improving worker and community environments on member farms. VeriFlora may ultimately have the most environmental impact with its emphasis on a gradual shift to organic production.

Growers in developing nations hoping to penetrate higher-priced national markets—Germany, Switzerland, the Netherlands, and the United Kingdom—agree that certifications are an important marketing tool and may be useful—possibly essential—in accessing certain markets (see also Moore 2004). But for growers targeting the U.S. market the situation is a little different, and they must choose carefully. A few Ecuadorian growers originally joined FLP or MPS but found no consumer recognition in the United States because these organizations do not promote their products there. Some flower growers considering fair trade certification may derive little benefit from TransFair USA's current marketing structure because they do not produce flowers in large enough quantities to satisfy the bigger retailers. Yet growers who do qualify for Fair Trade or VeriFlora standards may face difficulty in recovering the costs involved, given the limited demand for certified flowers and the risk of oversupply.

Growers also mentioned a rarely discussed problem: the mingling of certified and uncertified flowers by traders in the destination country. As noted earlier, it is impossible to distinguish certified from uncertified blooms (as in my experience with purchases of unlabeled fair trade blooms). However, the higher prices of these labeled flowers and their value to consumers in terms of assurances of social and environmental responsibility depend on the vigilance of the certifying authority and of all those involved in the extended delivery chain including the retailers. Perhaps in response to this concern, certified flower bouquets are increasingly labeled and packaged at the farms, minimizing some of the confusion.

Flower Workers

Flower workers, who are the primary objective of these certified social programs, certainly gain from healthier, less toxic working environments and improved services. FLP members and fair trade websites offer warm testimonials to the benefits of their health and scholarship programs and the other benefits their premiums bring to workers. Flower growers, traders, and industry experts share anecdotal accounts of daycare centers, microlending programs, and other projects linked to one or another certification. Jane Ngige, for example, was enthusiastic about a daycare center on a fair-trade-certified farm which was open to the entire community, not just the workers' children. This, she proposed, would eventually improve local standards because when "you have these children who are very well taken care of during the day the parents want to sustain the same standards in their homes. . . . At the end of the day you uplift the quality of living standards in this community" (Ngige 2008).

Workers in Colombia and Ecuador readily change jobs, seeking employment at farms that offer them higher wages and better working conditions, such as at farms producing Fair Trade, FLP, or VeriFlora blooms. However, these are the fortunate few. The fact remains that in Ecuador and Colombia most farms do not participate actively in any certification program. So the majority of flower farming's poorest participants, those who work on smaller farms or on badly managed farms or for labor contracting services are untouched by certification systems. With respect to fair trade flowers in particular, it is not clear how the modest quantities sold in the United States (far less than 1 percent of all imported flowers) can substantially contribute to the broad reform of social conditions that fair trade enthusiasts desire (Jaffee 2007).

Retailers and Consumers

Without doubt, certifying organizations and retailers in Europe have enlarged the market for certified flowers among ethically concerned consumers. Consumer response has been especially positive in the United Kingdom, Germany, and Switzerland, where there has been sustained consumer education at the retail level (Petitjean 2006; Dolan 2007).

This is not quite the case in the United States, where the introduction of ethical labeling of fresh cut flowers seems to have created confusion, primarily because consumer education is lacking. While consumer recognition of the most well known certifier, Fair Trade, is growing, it is still far behind Europe's and is confined to the well-educated, upper middle classes (Hira and Ferrie 2006).[18] Thus far, neither the various certifiers, with their limited promotion budgets, nor the large retail corporations seem committed to a sustained consumer-education program for ethically produced flowers. A founding VeriFlora retailer acknowledged the high investment in building awareness of an ethical certification: "We want to support all good causes," he explained, "but our costs are already significantly higher. . . . It makes things hard as a business strategy. We have invested millions of dollars to build this market and create awareness" (Prolman 2008).

As Moore and others have pointed out, large retailers are averse to risk (Moore 2004; Hira and Ferrie 2006), and it is a challenge to persuade them to make a long-term commitment to a line of expensive ethical floral products for which there is little apparent demand. Even a retailer such as Whole Foods Markets, known for its commitment to social and environmental responsibility, is not promoting the fair trade program as such but is arguably diluting the value of the fair trade label (if not the movement's ideals) by promoting its own "Whole Trade" ethical-sourcing brand. On the other hand, small flower retailers rarely demand ethically produced flowers, in part because they are perplexed by the thicket of certifications and terms such as *sustainable, organic, environmentally friendly,* and just plain *eco.* Some assume, for example, that all certified flowers are fair trade and organic.

Even media coverage of ethical cut flower consumption is very uneven. It occurs primarily during the week before Valentine's Day or Mother's Day and then is abandoned for the rest of the year (see for example Navarro 2008). Journalists who claim to educate consumers on these topics muddle matters further by sometimes conflating the different certifications under a "fair trade" banner (see for example Losure 2007).

So it is not surprising that U.S. consumers are bewildered by the flower certifications they encounter in supermarkets and are still unaware of the opportunity to improve the lives of distant flower workers through selective flower buying. Confusion can lead to disenchantment or simply opting for the least expensive flowers, especially as flower purchases are primarily governed by the freshness of the flowers. Even the most ethically concerned consumer will hesitate to buy wilted fair trade roses if the adjacent bouquet of uncertified blooms looks fresh and colorful.

Conclusion

Fair Trade and other certification systems add gloss to the global flower-trading system, especially at the retail end in Europe. They also help to improve the lives of flowers workers and reward ethical growers by opening new market areas. British and Swiss supermarket connections undoubtedly helped the rapid expansion of fair trade flowers with their advertising and promotion of fair trade blooms (Hira and Ferrie 2006; Patton 2008). By 2006 the United Kingdom accounted for close to 30 percent and Switzerland about 50 percent of total global fair trade flower sales (FLO 2008a). Possibly, with a sustained education campaign, the same sort of demand will eventually develop in the United States. Pioneering certifications such as Flower Label Program and Max Havelaar have encouraged sustainable production, fair wages, health and daycare programs, integrated pest management, and other good agricultural practices. TransFair USA's major contribution has been to introduce the rigorous new FLO standards into the U.S. fresh-cut-flower system. This could raise the bar for other certifications in the United States, especially if consumers understand the differences represented by their labels and make purchasing decisions accordingly.

Yet, over the long term, supermarkets that promote their own brands of ethical flowers and larger retailers such as samsclub.com may be unstable channels for fair trade flowers, as they tend to place difficult production and pricing demands on their suppliers over time. For this reason, growers of high-quality blooms on smaller farms (including some of the Max Havelaar–certified farms) avoid them. As one Ecuadorian grower, who does not supply flowers to chains, commented during our discussion of fair trade certification,

> As flower producers we have all this pressure from these chains, but in reality they are looking at it both ways: at one point they are [asking for] Fair Trade [and other ethical labels], but on the other hand it is a price war. They squeeze the margins so much [that] a producer has to be very careful with the costs, and that affects their employees and the whole fair trade thing directly. But it starts at the top of the chain with Sam's Club. (Johnson 2008; see also Ziegler 2007)

In addition, higher-priced flowers are very vulnerable to retail and consumer demand fluctuations. Economic downturns quickly slow demand for discretionary luxuries such as fresh flowers. Supermarket-chain price wars and renewed focus on goods with better returns are also threats (Hawkes and Elliott 2008; Kesmodel 2008). In March 2008, for example, the British supermarket Tesco offered five fair trade bouquets on its website, but in May it discontinued website flower sales altogether. In June and July 2008, Tesco still offered a few fair trade bouquets in its largest stores, but they were obscured by many other bouquets of better quality. They also competed for the attention of consumers newly concerned with an antiglobalization movement. Prominent bouquets of fresh, locally grown flowers conspicuously labeled and certified as "British Blooms" seemed very popular.

Several other problems are apparent with the U.S. fair trade program for fresh cut flowers that point to inconsistencies with fair trade's core aims. First, as noted earlier, imported flowers seldom pass directly from grower to retailer because of their perishable nature, growers' distance from markets, and the general structure of the delivery systems. Instead, intermediate importers, wholesalers, or fulfillment centers often organize delivery to retailers or, in the case of Internet sales, to consumers.[19] This is inconsistent with fair trade's fundamental aims of eliminating middlemen, creating direct relationships, and improving prices for producers. At the same time, these intermediary layers may undermine the entire enterprise by contributing to an unacceptably high (for many American consumers) final price. Second, worker participation in Joint Bodies may encourage initiative and social and decision-making skills among the few workers involved, but there is a risk that the fair trade model may distract workers from organizing in other ways to change underlying conditions. Trade unions, for example, are highly unpopular among flower-producing companies in both Colombia and Ecuador.[20] Third, in the United States, fair trade currently offers only roses and carnations, two types of flowers that are widely available at extremely low prices. Consequently it may be difficult to persuade more than a handful of ethical consumers to respond to moral consciousness and pay higher prices for fair trade roses or carnations.

Finally, the relative quantities of fair trade flowers are still very small: 237 million stems of fair trade flowers were sold throughout the world in 2007, almost all in Germany and the United Kingdom. Although more than double the 2004 volume, this number still represents a tiny percentage of the production of Colombia, Ecuador, and Kenya and a minute fraction of the billions of commercial fresh flower stems traded globally (FLO 2008b). The volumes of fair trade flowers sold in the United States in 2008, as noted earlier, were inconsequential. To date FLO has certified about 4 percent of total Ecuadorian flower-farm acreage and far less in Colombia, so there is a long way to go to make a significant impact on working conditions for the majority of flower workers (van der Ploeg 2008). Even with such limited production, actual demand for flowers grown under fair trade conditions is so small in the United States that (because of flowers' short postharvest life) certified farms are forced to sell them unlabeled, through a different market channel, for less than optimum price and without a social premium—benefiting neither farm owners nor their workers (van der Ploeg 2008).

Clearly much remains to be done in order to increase demand for certified fresh cut flowers. Some observers have suggested that other remedies such as freer international trade or enforcement of existing regulations would do far more than the efforts of certifying organizations to improve the working and environmental conditions of the majority of flower workers (Sidwell 2008).[21] However, in view of the persistent absence of truly free trade or adequate enforcement of laws and government regulations in some of the flower-growing nations discussed here, reinvigorated support of ethical flower growing by Fair Trade, Flower Label Program, VeriFlora, Florverde, FlorEcuador, and other certifying authorities, even with their limitations, may be the better option.

NOTES

1. This figure includes about two thousand hectares under cover and about five hundred hectares for field-grown flowers.

2. In Ecuador, for example, government regulations mandate a forty-hour work week, minimum wages and overtime pay, medical services on large farms, and maternity leave (as in Colombia, about 60 percent of Ecuadorian flower workers are women). Employers must provide contracts and pay social security, and terminated employees must be given one month's salary for each year of work. Furthermore 15 percent of the company's profits must be shared with workers at the end of the year, although the mechanism for this is unclear. The Ecuadorian government also regulates pesticide use and other environmental matters in both flower growing and other farming enterprises such as banana and potato growing. However, government enforcement is weak, and farmers, especially potato growers and certainly some flower farmers, ignore these rules and use a variety of chemicals (Sawers 2005). In Colombia the mandated work week is longer—forty-eight hours—but laws provide similarly for contracts and social security payments, maternity leave, and so on. These standards evolved over time along with a few environmental regulations (Friedemann-Sanchez 2006).

3. Asocolflores's approximately 220 members (of about 500 flower growers) are responsible for about 75 percent of the country's flower exports.

4. Florverde's environmental requirements include such things as the reduction of chemical pesticide use through integrated pest management, including the biological control of pests, careful monitoring of insect populations, and the introduction of beneficial predator insects to consume unwanted pests. Composting and recycling are also part of the program. The social component includes occupational health and safety programs and practices. In addition to the Florverde program, Asocolflores has introduced childcare centers at farms, microloans to farm workers, and programs on building self-esteem among women workers and resolving family conflict (Asocolflores 2009).

5. FlorEcuador's environmental program similarly encourages integrated pest

management, reduced chemical use, and improvement in water and soil quality. It has also helped to introduce worker health insurance plans on some farms. http://florecuador.soho.ec/, accessed June 8, 2008.

6. Most of the growers who do not participate own very small farms and possibly see no benefit to membership. However, a few very large farms are also uninterested in Expoflores. Membership statistics change regularly. Unless otherwise noted, I am citing figures from 2008 and early 2009.

7. This certification sensibly avoids duplicating the standards and inspections of other flower-labeling organizations by requiring that members first participate in either the Dutch Milieu Project Sierteelt (MPS) or the German Flower Label Program (FLP).

8. According to the standards established by FLO in October 2008, importing wholesalers (or retailers, if the retailer buys directly from the farm) pay a premium of 10 percent of FOB value in addition to the price paid to the grower. Premiums are sent directly to the bank account of the farm's Joint Body (FLO 2008b). Buyers also pay a fee of roughly 2 percent to TransFair USA.

9. Several other major certifying programs are also based in Europe, where they enjoy broad recognition and acceptance. GLOBALGAP (formerly EUREPGAP), for example, was initiated by British and European supermarkets, again in response to consumer pressure. It provides growers with standards of Good Agricultural Practice (GAP) and allows supermarkets to assure customers that their flowers (and other agricultural products) meet approved labor and environmental standards (GLOBALGAP 2009). The Ethical Trade Initiative (ETI) is another. Retailers, trade unions, NGOs, and grower organizations have devised a code of conduct aimed at improving social conditions in companies supplying the British market (Petitjean 2006).

10. Some retailers such as A&P are also not listed. TransFair USA attributed this omission to understaffing and other factors.

11. In January 2009, 1800flowers.com's main page offered sixty bouquets, none of them fair-trade-certified flowers. A site search uncovered four bouquets of fair trade flowers in a small separate section. http://www.1800flowers.com, accessed March 4, March 22, and May 18, 2008, and January 10, 2009.

12. Organicstyle.com was very responsive to my enquiries about this. Through several telephone conversations and emails, they explained that the Nevado farms in Ecuador supply both organic and fair trade roses to organicstyle.com. They assured me that the premium on my dozen roses had been paid to the farm.

13. A similar purchase of Kenyan roses from the website of John Lewis in United Kingdom was delivered in a box prominently labeled "fair trade." In June 2008, the Fairtrade U.K. website listed eleven Internet retail sources for fair trade flowers. However, only John Lewis (a department store associated with Waitrose supermarkets, both strong supporters of fair trade) and two others actually offered fair trade flowers, the remaining eight sites (including Tesco and Sainsbury's, as noted earlier) having apparently abandoned Internet-based sales.

14. See for example Sarah Terry-Cobo, "Fair Trade Roses Sell, Smell Sweet," *Contra Costa Times,* November 24, 2007.

15. Organic Bouquet at organicstyle.com is the principal Internet supplier listed on the website. Fair Trade flowers and VeriFlora flowers are not yet certified organic, although it

is possible they may have been produced to organic standards. http://www.veriflora.org, accessed between March 18, 2008, and January 10, 2009.

16. VeriFlora was founded by a group of growers and U.S. wholesaler and retailers, but it is actually a trademark of Scientific Certification Systems (SCS), a partner company that certifies a range of "sustainably" produced goods. SCS established the criteria for VeriFlora's certification and also inspects and certifies compliance. http://www.veriflora.org, accessed February 19, 2008.

17. VeriFlora requirements include, for example, protection in and around the farm of species and habitats "of high ecological value" as well as "culturally significant areas," and farms must provide workers "with access to key services as needed." VeriFlora's standards were developed after consultation with a variety of organizations including the International Labor Rights Fund, but they could be open to wide interpretation; therefore, much depends on the SCS audits. http://www.veriflora.com/about.asp, accessed March 15, 2008, and January 10, 2009.

18. Other authors give different estimates. Raynolds (2007) puts recognition of fair trade at 20 percent in the United States.

19. World Flowers, for example, handles much of the packaging and delivery for some of the major UK supermarkets. http://www.world-flowers.co.uk, accessed January 9, 2009.

20. There may also be a slight risk that over time the fair trade premium—rather than the farms themselves—will become the source of funding for daycare centers and other worker benefits. Other research on FLP certification has suggested that workers are often poorly informed or skeptical about the benefits of certifying programs. See *Codes of Conduct in the Cut-Flower Industry*, an ILRF Working Paper, September 2003.

21. See also *Codes of Conduct in the Cut-Flower Industry*, an ILRF Working Paper, September 2003; and discussion in Moore 2004.

WORKS CITED

AIHP
  2007 International Statistics, Flowers and Plants. International Association of Horticultural Producers/Union Fleurs. Hanover, Germany.
Asocolflores
  2009 http://www.asocolflores.org, accessed January 7, 2009.
Barrientos, S., and C. Dolan
  2006 Ethical Sourcing in the Global Food System. Sterling, VA: Earthscan.
Barrientos, S., and S. Smith
  2007 Mainstreaming Fair Trade in Global Production Networks: Own Brand Fruit and Chocolate in UK Supermarkets. *In* Fair Trade: The Challenges of Transforming Globalization. L. T. Raynolds, D. L. Murray, and J. Wilkinson, eds. Pp. 103–122. New York: Routledge.
Barrow, K.
  2009 TransFair USA. Email exchange, January 10–23.
Dolan, C.
  2007 Market Affections: Moral Encounters with Kenyan Fairtrade Flowers. Ethnos 72(2): 239–261.

Expoflores
   2008 http://www.expoflores.com, accessed June 8, 2008.
FLO
   2008a Annual Report 2007. http://www.fairtrade.net/uploads/media/FLO_AR2008.pdf,
      accessed June 8, 2008.
   2008b Fairtrade Standards for Flowers and Plants for Hired Labour. http://www.
      fairtrade.net/fileadmin/user_upload/content/Flowers_and_Plants_HL_Oct_08_
      EN.pdf, accessed June 8, 2008.
FLO-Cert
   2009 http://www.flo-cert.net, accessed June 8, 2008.
Flower Label Program
   2008 http://www.fairflowers.de, accessed March 10, 2008, and January 9, 2009.
Fridell, G.
   2007 Fair Trade Coffee: The Prospects and Pitfalls of Market-Driven Social Justice.
      Toronto: University of Toronto Press.
Friedemann-Sanchez, G.
   2006 Assembling Flowers and Cultivating Homes. Lanham, MD: Lexington Books.
GLOBALGAP
   2009 http://www.globalgap.org, accessed January 10, 2009.
Grey, D.
   2008 Kenya Marches On. Floraculture International, May.
Hawkes, S., and V. Elliot
   2008 Stores Fire First Shots in Food Price War. The Times, June 27.
Hira, A., and J. Ferrie
   2006 Fair Trade: Three Key Challenges for Reaching the Mainstream. Journal of
      Business Ethics 63: 107–118.
Hughes, A.
   2000 Retailers, Knowledges and Changing Commodity Networks: The Case of the Cut
      Flower Trade. Geoforum 31: 175–190.
Isaza, J. C.
   2007 All in for Auditing Harmony. FloraCulture International, February.
Jaffee, D.
   2007 Brewing Justice: Fair Trade Coffee, Sustainability, and Survival. Berkeley: Univer-
      sity of California Press.
Johnson, R.
   2008 Ecuadorian VeriFlora grower. Interview, March.
Kesmodel, D.
   2008 Whole Foods Net Falls 31% in Slow Economy. Wall Street Journal, August 6.
Losure, M.
   2007 Roses Are Green: Fair-Trade Flower Market Grows. WCVB TV, Boston. http://
      www.thebostonchannel.com/news/14695107/detail.html, accessed June 8, 2008.
Moore, G.
   2004 The Fair Trade Movement: Parameters, Issues and Future Research. Journal of
      Business Ethics 53: 73–86.
Navarro, M.
   2008 To Pull a Thorn from the Side of the Planet. New York Times, February 3.
Nevado, R.
   2007 Asamblea de la Union Fleurs en Dusseldorf La Flor de Expoflores.
      October–November.

Ngige, J.
    2008 Chief Executive Officer, Kenyan Flower Council. Interview, March 7.
Patton, D.
    2008 Fairtrade Gives Flowers an Edge in UK. http://allafrica.com, accessed January 9,
        2009.
Petitjean, M. F.
    2006 Taking Responsibility. FloraCulture International, September.
Prolman, G.
    2008 CEO of Organic Bouquet Inc. Interview, August 11.
Rainforest Alliance
    2009 http://www.rainforest-alliance.org/agriculture.cfm?id=ferns_flowers, accessed
        January 15, 2009.
Raynolds, L. T.
    2007 Fair Trade Bananas: Broadening the Movement and Markets in the United
        States. In Fair Trade: The Challenges of Transforming Globalization. L. T.
        Raynolds, D. L. Murray, and J. Wilkinson, eds. Pp. 63–82. New York: Routledge.
Raynolds, L. T., D. L. Murray, and J. Wilkinson, eds.
    2007 Fair Trade: The Challenges of Transforming Globalization. New York: Routledge.
Sam's Club Online
    2009 http://www.samsclub.com, accessed January 10, 2009.
Sawers, L.
    2005 Sustainable Floriculture in Ecuador. American University, Department of
        Economics, Working Paper Series. Washington, DC.
Scientific Certification Systems
    2008 VeriFlora Standard 3.0. http://www.veriflora.com, accessed April 20, 2008, and
        January 14, 2009.
Sidwell, M.
    2008 Unfair Trade. London: Adam Smith Institute.
TransFair USA
    2009 http://www.transfairusa.org, accessed January 10, 2009.
van der Ploeg, R.
    2008 Strong Faith in Their Future. FloraCulture International, December.
Van Kooten, O.
    2007 Value Added Business Chains. FloraCulture International, September.
Velez Koppel, E.
    2006 Floriculture in Colombia: A Case of Competitive Entrepreneurship with Social
        and Environmental Responsibility, in a Country with Difficult and Changing
        Conditions. Ellison Chair for International Floriculture Lecture, Texas A&M
        University.
VeriFlora
    2009 http://www.veriflora.org, accessed January 8, 2009.
Whole Foods Markets
    2009 The Whole Trade Program. http://www.wholefoodsmarket.com/products/whole-
        trade.php, accessed January 10, 2009.
Ziegler, C.
    2007 Favored Flowers: Culture and Economy in a Global System. Durham, NC: Duke
        University Press.

Colonial Pasts and Fair Trade Futures

Changing Modes of Production and Regulation on Darjeeling Tea Plantations

SARAH BESKY

On a cold winter night over milky, sugary cups of tea, I talked with fair trade plantation workers about politics in the Darjeeling district of West Bengal, tucked in the Himalayan foothills.[1] Like on many evenings, we argued about the effectiveness of Darjeeling's political parties and politicians. Slamming his hand down on the sticky plastic table, Pranit said, "They eat all the money and buy new clothing and cars with it." "Wrong! We will get our separate state and help us get better wages on the plantation," said Kancha, cigarette hanging out of his mouth as he heaped white rice onto a plate. Someone else chimed in: "All that happens are cultural programs—dance, dance, dance; clothes, clothes, clothes—that is all they want to talk about."

"Darjeeling life is like that," said an old woman crouched in the corner without looking up from her dented stainless-steel cup filled with tea.

Later, the cups were filled with military-issue whiskey, and our conversation turned to the politics of the plantation itself. Jethi told the story of a friend: "he couldn't get a loan to fix his house. . . . The company used to give loans."

"Isn't that what the 'fair trade committee' [Joint Body] does?" I asked.

"Not anymore. . . . The company eats all the money, and we drink this black, black tea," she replied, referring to the cheap CTC tea we were drinking, produced in plains south of Darjeeling.

Everyone turned to Gautam. We all knew him as one of the few people privileged with knowledge of the higher-level functions of the plantation. Silence. "What is the Joint Body anyway?" I asked. Silence. I kept looking at him.

"*Manpardaina*" (I don't like it), he said, shaking his head and hands.

"Why?" I asked.

"*Man-par-dai-na*," he repeated deliberately. I gave him a puzzled look. After some contemplation, he explained, "You know the problem with Darjeeling politics?" with obvious reference to the last conversation. "That is why I don't like it [the Joint Body]," and the conversation screeched to an uncomfortable halt.

The plantation is the primary land tenure system for Indian tea, particularly in Darjeeling. Sloping green hillsides of neatly lined tea bushes surround the towns of the Darjeeling district. Where one of the eighty-seven plantations begins and another ends is often marked only by a narrow tree line or a natural drainage ditch running down the mountainside, if at all. Whether the plantations are conventional or fair trade certified, their tasks and organization are roughly the same. Most large plantations contain not only fields of tea bushes but also processing factories. While some men work as field laborers, women dominate the fields and the plucking of tea by hand. In the factory, men operate the machines and pack tea in the factory, while women hand sort the tea after processing. The average Darjeeling plantation has approximately seven hundred permanent factory and field laborers and hires additional seasonal help during the boom in production that comes with the monsoon rains. Permanent workers receive a daily wage that remains constant throughout the year. Each one of these laborers often supports four or more family members, who do not work on the garden but reside in one of the several plantation villages, which vary in proximity to the factory, towns, and roads.

Fair trade has made little impact on Darjeeling tea plantations.[2] The most positive effect of certification is that people feel free to talk, albeit behind closed doors and in cryptic statements, about how deplorable and often illegal the conditions of their life and employment really are.[3] In this chapter, I use a regulation approach to discuss the obstacles of certifying a plantation as fair trade. If democracy is at the core of the fair trade movement and the articulation of its standards, then how can a plantation, an inherently unequal land-tenure system, ever really be fair? Darjeeling plantations have taken steps toward becoming more "fair," but these steps were not the result of international certification schemes, such as fair trade, which have left workers little tangible benefits. Fair trade, as I argue in this chapter, is instead enmeshed in neoliberal economic practices (Fridell 2007).

Longstanding, colonial-inspired institutions still play a major role in regulating how Indian tea plantations operate. Tea is generally auctioned in large centers across the country, where bidders and brokers argue over and set the prices for all grades and regions of Indian tea. After Indian independence, national laws, specifically the Plantations Labor Act of 1951, were put in place to protect workers from mistreatment at the hands of plantation owners. In Darjeeling, these regulatory institutions—tea auctions and labor laws—are currently being upset by fair trade certification. Labor law and the auction system work within the parameters of the plantation system, an unequal land-tenure system in which the owners' economic best interest is to cut production costs and to maximize profits. These regulatory institutions serve as a check on this behavior; they serve to balance the inequities of the plantation system.

Today, planters seek to "update" the "irrelevant" sections of the Plantations Labor Act (PLA), namely, the social welfare clauses that dictate that owners provide workers houses, medical facilities, firewood, and food rations, which burden the owners with what they call "social costs." Owners believe that existing government structures could absolve them of this financial burden. Members of the Darjeeling Tea Association, the plantation owners' organization, are lobbying the central government to rewrite the PLA so that they do not have to bear these social costs and provide such support. The owners contend that workers should provide these things for themselves. Even as they lament paying the "social costs," these plantation owners are seeking fair trade certification. Not only does fair trade certification attest to the equitable treatment of workers, but it also provides owners a way to get their tea directly to foreign and boutique markets, circumventing the auction system. In this chapter, I discuss the problems that fair trade certification, with its emphasis on direct trade, has created for workers on Darjeeling tea plantations. I make a rather counterintuitive suggestion: perhaps colonial institutions and modes of regulation, such as tea auctioning and colonial-inspired labor codes, can be more effective regulators of social justice and fair prices than neoliberal regulatory institutions such as fair trade, with its emphasis on individual rights and empowerment. These regulations, unlike those of fair trade, account for the power of individual owners to manipulate the system to maximize profits. In Darjeeling, fair trade standards from the Fair Trade Labelling Organizations International (FLO) have undermined what local laws and government labor officers have done to promote social justice in Darjeeling.

Further complicating the Darjeeling tea market is that prices of Darjeeling tea fluctuate dramatically throughout the year because of what growers refer to as "flushes." There are four flushes, or seasons—first (mid-

March–mid-April), second (mid-April–May), monsoon (June–August), and autumn (September–November). Darjeeling's first and second flushes are the most prized and produce some of the highest priced teas in the world. Managers have explained to me that a Darjeeling garden makes all its annual money before the start of the monsoon at the end of May, when the heavy rains start and the quality of the leaf changes, becoming bigger and more fibrous. Furthermore, certain gardens are deemed more desirable according to the direction they face, the valley they are in, or their general *wastu* ("property," implying their position in the cosmic geography of the universe). A garden can make anywhere from Rs. 18,000 ($474) to Rs. 200 ($5) or less per kilogram for leaf-grade teas at the Kolkata auction. Finding meaningful statistics is difficult for two reasons: First, there are several grades of leaf tea, all yielding different prices—from STGFOP (Special Tippy Golden Flowery Orange Pekoe), FTGFOP (Fine Tippy Golden Flowery Orange Pekoe), TGFOP, GFOP, FOP, to OP (Orange Pekoe), broken leaf, and fannings. Second, it is difficult for the Tea Board to report on private sales, the dominant method of marketing among fair-trade-certified tea producers in Darjeeling. During my research in 2008 and 2009, I occasionally heard the prices at which traders bought directly from fair trade gardens, but even these prices fluctuated greatly, depending on the nature of the "long-term buying relationships" between traders and plantation owners. People in Darjeeling who make their living either directly or indirectly from the fair trade tea industry, although they know little about direct sales, continue to argue about the business. Some contend that the plantation owners, who are not from Darjeeling, are making windfall profits from private sales of premium-priced fair trade tea but are telling the public otherwise. Supporters of the owners, however, believe that labor costs have reduced profits. Judging by recent changes in fair trade tea standards regarding the distribution of fair trade premiums, FLO seems to believe the owners and their supporters.

This chapter is organized into three sections. I follow a regulation approach, the basics of which I outline in the first section, in which I also discuss how colonial tea production, despite gross inequalities, left independent Indian tea gardens with two key regulatory institutions: the auction and labor laws. In the second section, I describe how fair trade both challenges and furthers neoliberalization, a new "regime of accumulation" in the global market that brings with it new regulatory institutions. In the third section, I compare these neoliberal and colonial institutions and their ability to regulate social justice on Darjeeling tea plantations. I argue that in the case of plantation tea production fair trade is actually a destabilizing force, which erodes the headway that older, colonially rooted modes of regulation have made in maintaining the quality of life on plantations.[4]

The Old Regime: Colonial Tea Production and Regulation Theory

After the Opium Wars of the mid-1800s, the British, seeking to satisfy burgeoning demand for tea within the Empire, set up agricultural experimental stations and botanical gardens to test the potential of tea and other cash crops across India. The scientists at Lloyd Botanical Gardens in Darjeeling deemed that the environment of the Himalayan foothills was conducive to growing tea of the China *jat* (variety), the more prized variety of tea compared to the Assam *jat*, which grew wild in the jungles of Assam and was later cultivated on Assam plantations. Tea quickly became the most lucrative crop in the Darjeeling hills. Along with other tea-growing regions across India, Darjeeling supplied demand back home in Britain as well as the growing demand across the new colonies. Tea was a global commodity from the beginning. It was a lucrative export crop and the model British colonial agricultural product. While many other agricultural products of the British Empire, such as cinchona and timber, were used within the colony, tea and its companion, sugar, were produced for consumption for the European and American markets outside the colony (Mintz 1986).

In order to maintain their plantations, the British had to recruit laborers from outside Darjeeling. The reaction of Nepal's monarchy to British incursions on its territory facilitated this recruitment. After the Anglo-Nepalese Wars (1814–1816), the British annexed most of the lowland Terai, the most fertile part of contemporary Nepal (Burghart 1984: 113), and in 1817 they annexed present-day Darjeeling town from Sikkim. To offset the loss of land, Nepal's king pressed for the reclamation and agricultural intensification of less fertile lands in the eastern middle hills by high-caste Hindus, thus marginalizing those living in these peripheral hill regions (English 1982: 258). Lacking the resources to pay domestic taxes, many eastern hill people migrated to Darjeeling. The British need for labor steadily increased as their plantations developed in Darjeeling. To supply this need, the British began to increase the incentives for laborers to leave their families and homes in Nepal. Promises of housing, health care, land for cultivation and herding, and good schools for their children lured Nepalis to Darjeeling plantations (English 1982: 264; Griffiths 1967: 88). For most of the nineteenth century, the British stably accumulated wealth and maintained a willing labor force in the Darjeeling hills as a result of the way they structured their plantation system.

In an analysis of the differences between industrial wheat farms and family wheat farms in the United States, Harriet Friedmann elaborated a theory of accumulation that hinged on the idea of reproduction: "Reproduction occurs when the act of production not only results in a product, such as wheat, but also recreates the original structure of social relations so that the act of production can be repeated in the same form" (1978: 555). For Friedmann, industrial reproduction depended on the stability of a wage relation between the buyer of labor power on one side and the seller of labor power on the other. The British Empire successfully cultivated this relationship in India, making it the most financially successful colony in the Empire for over one hundred years. The social relations that defined capitalism reproduced themselves in a stabilized way through extensive bureaucracies and paternalistic welfare practices. Colonial social welfare codes in India facilitated the extraction of tea for a global market. This reproduced social relations between consumers of Darjeeling tea in London and sellers of tea and their labor power in Darjeeling.

Friedmann's focus on the stable accumulation of capital is central to a regulation approach, which is a valuable tool for exploring how institutions influence the flow of capital and shape economic and social relationships. Regulation theorists, drawing on Althusserian Marxism, emphasize the role of institutions, such as families, laws, and bureaucracies, in perpetuating people's willingness to participate in fundamentally unequal systems of production and consumption. Following Althusser, regulation theorists see institutions and regulatory social mechanisms, rather than individual agents, as drivers of social reproduction, thus paralleling Althusser's theoretical concerns with "ideological state apparatuses" (Althusser 1971). Institutions, rather than individual agents, are drivers of social reproduction. While recognizing that capitalist systems, resting on uncertain and unequal arrangements between labor and capital, tend toward crisis, regulation theorists are interested in the long periods of time when capital is accumulated stably. These unwavering periods are called "regimes of accumulation." The regime of accumulation is stabilized (1) at the individual level, by *habitus*, people's willingness to embody shared social values evidenced in daily practices of movement, labor, and social interaction (Bourdieu 1977), and (2) at the institutional level, by a *mode of regulation*. The mode of regulation includes wages, tax policies, international agreements, laws, unions, and other things that help reproduce capital accumulation. Instead of focusing on the *habitus*, regulation theorists scale up their analysis to an institutional level to focus on modes of regulation that enable the stable accumulation of capital. Modes of regulation define a particular relationship between production and consumption and characterize a particular regime of accumulation.

A crisis in a regime of accumulation implies a failure of regulation, the consequence of a deterioration of a mode of regulation and an institution's ability to accumulate capital stably (Goodwin and Painter 1996: 639). The fall of the colonial regime of accumulation in British tea production resonates with the collapse of the Fordist regime of factory production in the United States, the original object of analysis for regulation theorists. What separated Fordism as a distinct regime of accumulation was that capitalists recognized the link between mass production and mass consumption, which led to "a new system of the reproduction of labour power, a new politics of labour control and management, a new aesthetics and psychology, in short, a new kind of rationalized, modernist, and populist democratic society" (Harvey 1989: 126). Fordism hinged on the ability of the workers to purchase the products they produced. The disintegration of Fordism was caused by two factors. First, transactions became more international. Fordism was a "rigid" nation-centered regime; production and consumption were spatially linked. Second, factory owners were not making enough money from production because they were paying their workers high wages and providing welfare through, for example, pensions and health care (Harvey 1989: 142).

Much like the collapse of Fordism, the collapse of colonialism and colonial tea production was instigated by the financial infeasibility of the project. When the British left India, they took their demand for tea with them, turning to their remaining colonies in Kenya (see Dolan, chap. 7, this volume) and Sri Lanka to supply their domestic demand. The tight relationship between production and consumption was broken apart. During the colonial era, the British controlled all aspects of production and marketing. After India gained independence, the British slowly turned their Darjeeling tea plantations over to elite Indians, who quickly found that they did not have enough capital to maintain the plantations. The last British planters and their companies left in the late 1960s, at which point the industry is said to have "collapsed." After the fall of the colonial regime in India, new Indian plantation owners from outside Darjeeling had a surplus of tea and less people to buy it.

Colonialism did not leave India with a strong government, but it did leave it with the infrastructure necessary for a vibrant tea industry. Even after the British left, regulatory institutions that were central to the colonial project, namely, labor codes and tea auctions, remained. In 1951, shortly after independence, India's central government drafted the Plantations Labor Act, which adapted colonial labor policies into the constitution of independent India. The Plantations Labor Act continues to guarantee plantation workers' social welfare, insisting that owners provide workers housing, health care, food rations, and schooling for their children. It is the positive legacy of an otherwise exploitative colonial regime. During the production crisis that lasted from the 1960s until the late 1990s, tea continued to be sold at auction in Kolkata, much like it had for the past one hundred years. Many tea plantation owners gained the attention of fair trade certifiers because their relative adherence to the Labor Act made them viable candidates for fair trade certification, which attests to the social welfare of hired agricultural laborers.

The New Regime: Neoliberalism Meets Fair Trade

When fair trade certifiers first came to Darjeeling in the 1990s, fair trade seemed like an optimal way to solve the ills of postcolonial tea production, but it has been far from effective in this regard. Like factory owners under Fordism, Darjeeling planters told me that they are not able to give their workers the benefits that they once were and that labor law should be revised to absolve them of such obligations. They saw fair trade, which emphasizes the equitable treatment of laborers, as a way to avoid these costs and solve marketing woes. Although the loss of the colonial market produced an accumulation crisis in the tea industry, today's market for Darjeeling tea, touted for its health benefits, is rapidly growing. Fair trade certification attracts owners because (1) FLO encourages owners to sell directly to buyers, enabling them to circumvent the auction system; (2) the money for government-mandated welfare schemes can come from fair trade premiums; (3) demand for fair trade products is high: much like colonial products, there is a built-in market for socially conscious goods; in other words, the relationship between production and consumption has tightened back up; (4) fair trade standards are more flexible than labor law, and since there is minimal oversight, owners can often cut corners on labor practices and still keep fair trade certification.

Fair trade, with its reliance on transnational nongovernmental certi-fiers and its emphasis on universal notions of social justice and individual rights through "direct trade," reflects many of the philosophical tenets of neoliberalism. According to many social scientists, notably geographers, neoliberal theory frames today's regime of accumulation (Jessop 2002; McCarthy 2006; Zimmerer 2006; Harvey 2007). Rooted in neoclassical economics, neoliberalism upholds the free market—a market that is free of obstacles to trade such as national government policies and a market that privileges the power of private interests over publicly held institu-tions. Neoliberal theory maintains that institutions that preserve strong private-property rights and free markets can best protect individual lib-erty and freedom. Proponents of neoliberalism claim that the state should not be involved in the economy; instead, the state should use its power to preserve private-property rights and the free market. Neoliberal logic privileges nonstate actors, such as fair trade certification agencies, as the best regulators of capital. It encourages the state to promote the free flow of capital, orienting state power toward capital circulation rather than nationalist protectionism. Not only can nonstate actors accomplish this more effectively, according to neoliberal logic, they can distribute capital in more equitable ways.

To date, most studies on the production of fair trade products have focused on coffee in Latin America and have highlighted how fair trade is an alternative to neoliberal economic policies (Bacon 2005; Lyon 2007; Murray et al. 2006; Renard and Pérez-Grovas 2007; Renard 2003; Rice 2000; Smith 2007; Whatmore and Thorne 1997). Coffee and tea are very different, but boxes of fair trade organic coffee, tea, and other products all explain that consumer revenue goes straight into the pockets of produc-ers, described on the packaging as "empowered small farmers." Despite an emphasis on small-scale agriculture, FLO allows some products such as bananas and tea to be grown in "hired-labor situations," fair trade par-lance for "on a plantation." In hired-labor situations, the workers are sup-posed to democratically elect a body, called the Joint Body, which will de-cide how to spend the fair trade premium. Darjeeling tea plantations still have Joint Bodies, but the January 2008 FLO mandate has severely eroded the little power they had to control premium spending, as I describe later.

Fair trade certification has created alternative markets for small produc-ers' goods outside the mass market propagated by neoliberal orthodoxy. Often the literature on fair trade and other socially and environmentally friendly products focuses on marketing (Barrientos and Smith 2007; Lyon 2006a, 2006b; McDonagh 2002); consumption, specifically how people identify purchasing fair trade or organic commodities with environmentalist practices (Elkington and Hailes 1989; James 1993; Loureiro and Lotade 2004); resistance to conventional production (Shreck 2005); or class distinction (Roseberry 1996). Labels distinguish these alternative markets. Scholarship shows that "fair trade" and "organic" labels act as symbols that affirm consumers' belief that consumption can be a political act (Fisher 2007; Getz and Shreck 2006; Shreck et al. 2006; Howard and Allen 2006; Loureiro and Lotade 2004; Shreck 2005). Geographer Julie Guthman explains that grades and standards in the organic food industry have caused farmers to abandon sustainable methods (1998) or have undermined farmers' attempts to farm in a less intensive manner (2004). Guthman (2007) further argues that voluntary food labels, verifying environmental, social, or geographical values, are intended to counter neoliberal forms of governance. In this volume, however, Smith and Moberg (chaps. 2 and 3) discuss the problems of consumer perceptions that arise from corporate interests such as Starbucks, Chiquita, and Dunkin' Donuts labeling *some* of their products "fair trade." They may have the largest sales volume of fair trade products, but these products make up a tiny portion of their overall sales. A label has power, in this case, to shift the perceptions of consumers about companies that are only marginally committed to the social and economic conditions of the agricultural communities from which they source. As Smith points out (chap. 2, this volume), consumers are confident about what they purchase because of the standardization of fair trade certification, which is embodied in the fair trade label. Still, many buyers I spoke to said that they did not pay a fair trade premium for the tea they bought from fair trade gardens. On their packaging or marketing materials, they explain that the tea "comes from a fair trade certified estate." It is not "Fair Trade Darjeeling Tea." To a consumer this makes little difference, but to a producer it does. Producers do not receive a premium for tea that is not marked with FLO's or another certifying agency's "fair trade" label.

Despite fair trade's symbolic creation of alternative consumer markets, as Fridell (2007) argues, fair trade is not only an alternative movement. It is also enmeshed in larger processes of neoliberal, consumer-driven social justice. Yet, as a regulation approach shows, fair trade is also part of what Peck and Tickell call "roll-out liberalization," characterized by the "roll-out of new forms of institutional 'hardware'" (2002: 389). The institutional "hardware" of fair trade certification includes "social" policymaking strategies, led by nongovernmental organizations, aimed at opening trade to the Global South. Fair trade, however, also presents an alternative to neoliberal policies because it seeks to empower those not conventionally empowered in a free-market system. Fair trade aims to direct capital into the hands of empowered small farmers. This ideology of individual freedom and empowerment within a global market is a key tenet of neoliberal orthodoxy. This paradox is not lost on contemporary scholars, and overcoming it is essential for maintaining the fair flow of goods and capital on the global market.

Neoliberalism, as a regime of accumulation, requires both consumers and laborers to accept new regulatory institutions rooted in ideas of individual empowerment through democracy, the free market, and environmental protection. Neoliberalism favors nongovernmental regulatory institutions, including fair trade certifiers. Kamat explains:

> A fundamental cultural transformation involved in the transition from state-led development to a deregulated market economy is that citizens have to forego their sense of entitlement and have to acquire an entrepreneurial citizen identity that derives from liberal values of independence and autonomy. . . . The new economic institutions are engaged in this process of advancing a new citizen culture, aiding in the development of an active and dynamic civil society in which all citizens, including the poor, are encouraged to be enterprising and seize the opportunities of the global economy. (2004: 164)

Through certification programs, fair trade links consumers to producers in new ways, reinforcing the idea that a single consumer can empower a single producer through his or her consumption practices. Even though fair trade aims at challenging the inequities of neoliberal accumulation, fair trade philosophy resonates with that of the neoliberal regime of accumulation because, on one hand, the individual farmer is the object of empowerment and the individual consumer is the agent of that empowerment. On the other hand, however, both fair trade and neoliberal philosophy require the farmer to become the "subject" of empowerment. This philosophy is reflected in the numerous "success stories" displayed on the FLO website, one of which I discuss later in this chapter. In the next section, I show how fair trade, as it straddles neoliberalism and its more socially conscious alternatives, has neither gotten rid of farmers' "old" reliance on the state for social welfare nor eliminated the social welfare shortcomings of postcolonial production.

Out with the Old, in with the New? Fair Trade and the Clash of Regimes

Whereas the colonial regime of accumulation was stable, the neoliberal regime has trouble maintaining stability because it lacks transparent means to ensure social, economic, and environmental development. In the language of regulation theory, fair trade has weakened existing "regulatory institutions" that guaranteed the continued consent of plantation workers to labor in a hierarchical, factory-like system. Fair trade certification has indirectly contributed to the erosion of social, economic, and environmental security. By damaging workers' faith in both the old colonial power structure and the new NGO-based neoliberal one, these weaknesses have the potential to cause a crisis in each or in all three of the areas FLO claims to be "developing." Fair trade is both a challenge to neoliberalization, in that it seeks to create new modes of regulation, and a reinforcement of neoliberalism, because it displaces older regulatory frameworks regarding the role of the state and public institutions to regulate the flow of capital. It is fair trade's tenuous straddling of neoliberalization and consumer-driven social justice that contributes to this destabilization. In this section, I follow the three organizing themes outlined in FLO's *Generic Fairtrade Standards for Hired Labor* (FLO 2007b): social development, economic development, and environmental development. I outline the clash of incoming and outgoing modes of regulation, and highlight that fair trade standards have not bolstered social welfare on Darjeeling plantations, despite FLO's claims. I argue that older institutions of the colonial regime of accumulation are currently doing a better job of bolstering social welfare.

Social Development and Fair Trade Knowledge

According to FLO (2007b), a Joint Body is "an elected group of worker representatives and management representatives who are responsible for jointly managing, investing, and spending the fair trade premium." The Joint Body must (1) "inform and consult all workers of the company about fair trade standards and the fair trade premium and its use" and (2) "manage and invest the fair trade premium transparently and responsibly." The

Joint Body must be democratically elected through "regular" elections. FLO does not concretely define the intended regularity of meetings. At one fair trade plantation, workers with whom I discussed the Joint Body claimed that there were never elections. Instead, members were "appointed" by the owner. According to FLO, the composition of the Joint Body should reflect the composition of the work force, meaning that on a tea garden, where over 50 percent of the workers are female tea pluckers, the Joint Body should contain a proportional number of pluckers. However, Joint Body members and plantation residents said that the membership comprised few pluckers. Some cynically said that the Joint Body had ceased to exist. All the money, they said, had been "eaten."

FLO states that knowledge about fair trade is a central component of effective certification. Within one year of certification, all levels of plantation staff must know about the aims and objectives of fair trade as well as the functions of the Joint Body and fair trade premium. The management is supposed to provide this information. On several fair trade plantations, many general laborers knew neither about the aims and missions of fair trade nor what a Joint Body was. A select number of community members who worked in the office or had direct contact with an ecotourism project on the plantation had some idea that there was a Joint Body; however, they understood Joint Body members to be only those that are "in the *malik*'s [owner's] hand." If they knew that there was a Joint Body, there was no knowledge about who served on it, let alone what it did. Those workers I interviewed who had heard of the Joint Body said that they believed it got its money from foreign donations. On one plantation, workers conflated the Joint Body and all workings of fair trade with a development project on the plantation called the Community Health and Advancement in India (CHAI) program, funded by Tazo Tea (a subsidiary of Starbucks).[5] Some said that the Joint Body gave money to CHAI. Community members showed little knowledge about what fair trade was and how it operated, let alone voiced opinions about how fair trade should work or their confusion about aspects of its operation. This contrasts with some of the evidence in this volume, including Lyon's descriptions of Guatemalan women's opinions about the diversification of fair trade buying relations (chap. 6) and Moberg's explanation of farmers' thoughts on the economics of pesticide use in the Caribbean (chap. 3). Dolan explains that Kenyan tea-cooperative workers were frustrated with "retrocertification" because it prevents them from planning premium disbursement (chap. 7, this volume). As in Kenya, on Darjeeling plantations of any kind, workers were unclear about where tea went. Workers said that it went to Kolkata, the site of the port, airport, and auctions, and then to outside countries.

Indian labor laws adapted from the colonial regime require that each plantation have a labor welfare officer, whose job is to translate labor law, which is written in English, into the local language, Nepali. Across Darjeeling, however, owners installed labor officers as assistant managers and saddled them with other duties on top of their obligations to laborers. On Darjeeling fair trade gardens, the labor welfare officers were also appointed as the "fair trade officers" of the Joint Body. FLO requires that each Joint Body have such an officer to organize educational events and spread knowledge about fair trade. These individuals now have three obligations, but those I interviewed told me that their primary obligation is to be a good manager. Fair trade, to adopt regulation theory's use of Althusser's term, is an "ideological apparatus" that is supposed to convince workers to invest their time, labor, and capital into the plantation, but in the case of the Darjeeling tea plantations, it does not seem to be doing as effective a job as other examples in this volume. In practice, the involvement of ownership and state labor officers in the Joint Body have undermined rather than promoted workers' ability to access knowledge about their labor rights.

Economic Development

Fair trade has failed to build knowledge about workers' rights. This lack of knowledge, as I argue in this section, has been compounded by (1) a lack of an effective implementation of FLO's minimum price system, (2) a lack of an effective bargaining mechanism for workers because of the owners' co-opting of the Joint Body, and (3) a lack of market transparency in FLO's emphasis on direct trade. In each instance, colonial and neoliberal regulatory institutions are clashing in a mutually destructive manner. FLO's fair trade standards are not effectively arbitrating as a meaningful alternative to either regime.

In January 2008, FLO set the fair trade minimum prices for tea and premiums for dust, leaf, and CTC-grade teas. (CTC, "Cut-Thresh-Curl," is a low-grade tea primarily used domestically with milk.) Darjeeling tea gardens, however, have been exempted from minimum pricing schemes for tea. At coffee cooperatives, workers receive a floor price for unroasted green coffee, as discussed by Lyon and Smith in this volume (chaps. 6 and 2). The minimum price, championed as the keystone to fair trade in coffee, means little to Darjeeling tea laborers, the only group exempt from minimum pricing. Fair trade minimum pricing would mean little for workers in hired-labor situations in the first place. Whether a kilogram of tea sells for Rs. 18,000 or Rs. 200, the Darjeeling tea worker makes exactly the same amount of money, his or her daily wage, regulated by state wage negotiations and labor law. The West Bengal wage talks in 2008 raised the wage from 53.90 rupees a day to 58 rupees a day, just over a dollar a day (according to 2009 rates of exchange). Even in FLO's hired-labor standards, it talks about minimum pricing schemes as if they actually make a difference. All profits on Darjeeling plantations go into the pocket of the plantation owner, not the workers. Fair trade is not changing the wage-labor rate or employment relationship. Workers on fair trade gardens receive the same daily wage as those at conventional gardens. Unlike fair trade, the Indian labor law, adapted from the colonial regime of accumulation, regards the plantation much like a factory, guaranteeing workers a daily wage, not per unit payments. There are several clauses addressing how workers should be paid for overtime and holiday time. Labor law attempts to concretize socially just wages, whereas FLO's "minimum prices" only benefit cooperative farmers, who do not work for wages.

While drinking tea at tea stalls, having a pastry at a fancy Darjeeling bakery, or plucking tea, individuals across social classes and both those directly associated with the tea industry and those just living in Darjeeling told me the plantation owners have misled the community by claiming that the industry is in crisis, which prevents them from raising workers' wages. Unlike the coffee and banana contexts discussed in this volume, fair trade tea workers need to live off the daily wage provided to them by owners. They do not benefit in any direct way from the higher prices received from direct buying relationships. Despite the fact that Darjeeling tea is some of the priciest tea in the world, in West Bengal, where the Darjeeling district is located, tea laborers are paid India's lowest wages. Other tea-producing states in India, such as Kerala and Assam, produce lesser-quality tea, which sells for less on the domestic and international markets. Sanjay Bansal, owner of the fair trade company Ambootia and president of the Darjeeling Tea Association, described the 2008 wage hike to 58 rupees a day as "unprecedented," far too high for the economic conditions of the area, setting an unhealthy trend for future negotiations. Throughout my fieldwork, Bansal and owners of both conventional and fair trade gardens continued lobbying to get the social welfare structures removed and fighting to keep the wages of the workers down.

According to FLO, until there is a fair trade minimum price set for Darjeeling tea, there will be an exception "made in the case of Darjeeling where basic needs for the workers (e.g., housing, water, and sanitation) may be partly financed through the Fairtrade Premium. This is due to the critical economic situation in Darjeeling" (FLO 2007a: 3). Without further explanation of the "critical economic situation," FLO has now made it possible for owners to use fair trade premiums to provide facilities dictated by the Plantations Labor Act of 1951, facilities that they should be providing from their own profits. The fair trade premium is covering the social costs, yet owners are still lobbying for the removal of labor codes.

Even before January 2008, when FLO decided that it was acceptable for Darjeeling plantation owners to use fair trade premium money for the general upkeep of their gardens, FLO had posted another fair trade tea "success story" from a plantation in the Western Ghat Mountains of South India. The press release describes fifty-eight-year-old Manickam, a long-time plantation worker who signed up for a retirement project funded by fair trade premiums, which "gained him the right to receive a monthly pension for the next 15 years—a novelty in a country like India" (FLO n.d.). FLO's press release claimed that workers must leave the plantation after they retire. This is not the norm in Indian tea production. The story explains that retiring is almost impossible in India because there is little access to pensions. Under the fair trade pension scheme in the Western Ghats, workers received Rs. 800 a month if they work for twenty years and Rs. 1,200 a month for thirty years of service. FLO's claims that India does not have pension-fund projects, particularly on tea plantations, overlooks the roles of the institutions that already exist. According to existing Indian law, in addition to their wages, workers on all plantations are entitled to a "provident fund" (essentially a pension), a "gratuity" upon retirement, and an annual bonus for the holiday season. In India, the Employees' Provident Fund Organization of India (EPFO), established after independence, mandates that all owners set aside a percentage of workers' wages in a provident fund to be given to the worker upon retirement.

FLO mandates that unions or some form of democratic organization, outside the Joint Body, collectively bargain for wages and equitable treatment. On Indian plantations, no single union represents all laborers. Instead, unions are affiliated with political parties, so there can be a few contending unions on any one plantation. As mentioned earlier, wages are negotiated every three years in state capitals, and once instituted, unions comply until the next wage talk approaches. In the summer of 2008, before the wage talks of August 2008, the ruling political party told its union leaders to have workers enact a hunger strike for higher wages. I sat with these laborers, and for hours they asked me about how much their garden's tea costs in the United States. On this day, hunger strikes took place on every garden in Darjeeling, but they had particular resonance on this fair trade plantation. One of the effects of a recent ecotourism project on the plantation is that workers have begun to learn more about the market for tea from consumers. They know that their tea sells for $10 a cup in New York City at TSalon, a vendor that has a direct buying relationship with the plantation, but they only make $1.50 a day. "Do *you* pay that much for a cup of tea?" a worker asked me while sitting on hunger strike. "Just the tea? Not the milk and sugar?" a woman asked. Another man interjected, "No, only rich people can afford this tea, like the people who stay in the owner's house." It is important to note that this and other strikes were not wholly against the owner. Instead, workers saw themselves as striking against the state of West Bengal, because they saw the state as the agent who should provide for them. Attempting to diffuse the strike, the owner tried to use Joint Body meetings to discuss the union's wage complaints. After waiting, scheduled meetings, and then canceled meetings, the issues put before the Joint Body by striking workers were dropped. The wage talks proceeded later in the summer of 2008, but many pluckers doubted the efficacy of the strike. Sitting outside with a retired tea worker one afternoon, I asked her whether the hunger strikes ever had any effects. "Ahhh," she said, batting her hand in the air. "[The union politicians] would rather have the owner fill their bellies."

A look at the makeup of a Joint Body helps explain the woman's cynicism. On all fair trade plantations managers served in the other office positions, and on one garden, the Joint Body "president" was the owner himself. FLO's website explains that on Makaibari Tea Estate's Joint Body, ten out of the sixteen members are women; however, this figure does not include two permanent fixtures: the owner and his wife (FLO 2005). On the Makaibari Joint Body, there were more women then men, but these women overwhelmingly came from one village, the one closest to the factory and to the owner's house. This village is also the most visible from the road, and it is where all the guests stay when they come, often as guests of members of the Joint Body. As Lyon discusses in this volume (chap. 6), the fair trade movement holds gender equality and women's issues at the forefront. FLO claims that women at Makaibari who wanted to develop ecotourism to diversify their income decided to build eco-lodges and develop homestays in villages so that visitors could "glean a whiff of the Makaibari mystique." I found, however, that several of the homestays were benefiting members of the Joint Body individually and that as of 2008, the only "eco-lodges" had been built by Tazo Tea's CHAI development project, with financial contribution from the villagers in addition to an unspecified investment from the Joint Body. Community development was accomplished through the bolstering of a select few people in a village, nominated by the Joint Body. If anything, the Joint Body has only empowered a few of its members, who other villagers describe as "in the *malik*'s hand." The formation of the ecotourism projects, intended as economic development, did little more than remind workers of the great distance between prices and wages.

There is little demand domestically for Darjeeling tea, since the price of the tea is much higher than the price of tea produced at larger Indian tea plantations. These plantations specialize in CTC-grade teas for drinking with milk and sugar, the preferred preparation in India. Tea from small Darjeeling plantations as well as from these large plantations in Assam, Jalpaiguri, and the Dooars, goes up for sale at the Kolkata auction. For producers, there is a degree of uncertainty regarding how much a particular lot of tea will fetch on a given week at the auction because Indian marketing companies buying the tea understandably want to buy the best quality for the lowest price. Unlike coffee, tea is a geographically undifferentiated market. "Earl Grey" and "English Breakfast" are popular teas. These tea types can be sourced from any tea-growing region or grade. These more everyday teas, along with the teas marketed by the two most powerful buyers, Tata (Tetley) and Hindustan Unilever (Lipton), make up the bulk of the market. The Darjeeling planters I interviewed found that fair trade certification was an effective and lucrative means of reaching U.S. and other European markets without participating in the auction system.

Fair trade *can* shorten the commodity chain and allow plantations to trade directly with international retailers, though it is hard to say if this is beneficial for the workers whom fair trade aims to empower. Of course, tea-plantation laborers are not engaging in trade themselves. All financial arrangements go directly through owners and management. Fair trade does not address this paradox in the certification of plantations. The owner of the plantation acts as a middleman, a barrier not only to free trade but also to fair trade. Most fair-trade-certified gardens run marketing houses abroad, which market the tea to other smaller retailers such as online sellers or boutique teashops. It is difficult to ascertain how much tea a garden sells as "fair trade." In one public meeting, a community member asked a fair trade plantation owner what his average sales were. The owner claimed that his sales, both direct and at auction, averaged around Rs. 100 per kilogram. If this were the real average price, it would be absolutely impossible for the owner to run his garden. Rs. 100 per kilogram is far lower than the cost of production (between Rs. 150–200 per kilogram) and far lower than the average auction sales of the lowest grades of the worst gardens in Darjeeling. The residents of Darjeeling know this and believe that owners turn much larger profits, particularly through direct trade, but fair trade representatives have accepted the owners' low figures, even though the math does not make sense. Darjeelingers inside and outside of the tea industry continued to be suspicious of plantation owners' claims about low market prices creating a "crisis" in the industry. With the onset of fair trade and direct trade, the lack of transparency about pricing has only increased these suspicions. Direct buying relationships in Darjeeling are anything but open and transparent. Workers do not have anything to say about either the auction or direct buying, but at least the auction prices are public knowledge and made accessible by all the brokers in Kolkata. Neither of these clashing modes of regulation has made a difference to plantation laborers' quality of life. It is evident, however, that direct buying is causing more problems that it is solving.

Environmental Development and Human Sustainability

The environmental situation is less acute than the social or economic one, but a lack of transparent concern from either the Indian state or FLO is creating a slower, silent crisis. Neither the colonial nor the neoliberal mode of regulation has effectively dealt with environmental issues. Indian land-reform laws protect the forests within the plantations. This prevents owners from logging their own forests to provide firewood, one of the rations mandated by labor law. This limitation on logging, while protecting the forests, theoretically forces owners to buy firewood from other sources. However, in the research site the legislation seems to be having little impact as owners continue to cut down trees to provide firewood for their employees. There are few other state-driven environmental regulations for plantations. Although the colonial system comes short of promoting environmental sustainability, fair trade's emphasis on a division between the "natural" and the "human" environment, coupled with its philosophical emphasis on individual empowerment, has also limited its success in environmental development.

FLO emphasizes *sustainability* of the "natural" and "human" environments in its standards for environmental development. For the "natural" environment, fair trade environmental standards focus on environmental protection, sustainable farm inputs, reforestation, and reducing soil erosion. Tea has long been a mono-crop in Darjeeling. The hillsides of Darjeeling are clear-cut slopes covered in rows of neatly planted tea bushes, often one hundred years old. Fair trade standards include a long prohibited-substances list, which prohibits the use of chemical pesticides and pushes producers toward organic and sustainable production. Unlike in the case of banana farms in the Caribbean (see Moberg, chap. 3, this volume), this environmental hurdle to fair trade certification was not difficult to surmount, because all Darjeeling fair trade gardens were certified organic before becoming certified fair trade. Most continue to operate without chemicals; however, some have had to revert to conventional production, citing the production costs as too high.

According to FLO, whenever possible, producers should use renewable energy. In Darjeeling, the processing machines and plucking methods are the same ones used in the 1850s and 1860s. Coal is the primary input in Darjeeling tea production, and it takes three kilograms of coal to process one kilogram of tea. Darjeeling plantations process nine to ten tons of tea a year, which means they expend twenty-seven to thirty tons of coal each year in a very small area. However, in this regard FLO standards have done little to lessen the environmental impact of tea processing in Darjeeling.

Although coal is a dangerous and unsustainable energy source, and although pesticide use has dropped in Darjeeling, few workers I interviewed expressed serious concerns about these "natural" environment issues. Instead, they discussed persistent problems with their everyday environment, problems that neither fair trade nor the fading colonial system had managed to solve. For example, even though several generations of workers have lived on the plantation, workers have no control over the land on which they live. Workers live in villages within the plantation. They do not own the land that their houses sit on, and while some have title to their houses, others live in fear that the owners could resettle them. A lack of land ownership is a serious obstacle to empowerment. For the workers I interviewed, land and land tenure were the central "environmental" problems they faced.

Since the villages have grown far beyond capacity in the past 150 years and lands are very rarely allotted for new settlements, there is little opportunity for subsistence farming on the plantation. In terms of food security, fair trade discourse resonates with free trade and neoliberal logic, high-lighting that with the revenues from the fair trade social premium, assistance somehow makes it to where it is needed most. Food security remains an overlooked aspect of fair trade agricultural studies. Darjeeling plantation owners justified a lack of family or community garden space by explaining that the forests, protected by Indian land-reform law, are rich in wild vegetables. People are afraid of the forests because for the past ten years, the owner has bred leopards within them. The presence of wildlife in the plantation satisfies FLO's goal of "environmental protection," but fearful workers must buy all their food from small stores on the plantation or at the market at least an hour's walk uphill. At Rs. 58 a day, a worker can afford very little in the way of vegetables and quality grains or meats. Plantation stores often carry only low-quality white rice, flour, potatoes, oil, and sugar. After older residents went to doctors, often at health camps sponsored by NGOs, for treatment of "pressure problems," "sugar problems," or full-blown diabetes, they were told to eat less sugar. Over a meal of potatoes and rice, a female tea plucker with adult-onset diabetes told me that given the constraints of their purchasing power, this is practically very difficult.

Food rations on Darjeeling gardens, mandated by the Labor Act, provide four kilograms of flour and two kilograms of rice per worker every fifteen days. This potentially would last a single worker over a fifteen-day period, but it is not adequate to meet the needs of the extended family members each worker supports. Though this is inadequate, at least the Indian labor law addresses the problem of food security, even though these starches are contributing to the aforementioned silent health epidemics. Fair trade certifiers seem satisfied with the idea of workers purchasing food with their newfound wealth. In congruence with neoliberal policies, fair trade chooses to leave food security issues up to individuals. FLO implicitly assumes that through "democratically elected bodies," fair trade revenue will somehow be distributed where it is needed most. The lack of land tenure, food security alternatives, and purchasing options is creating a slow-moving "human" environmental crisis on fair trade plantations, one that FLO's failure to guarantee economic and social development is only exaggerating.

Conclusion

In this chapter, I have argued that Darjeeling tea-plantation owners are co-opting fair trade and using it to solve postcolonial demand problems and get their tea to market at high prices. The neoliberal aspects of fair trade, namely, the removal of trade barriers, are helping owners compete more effectively; however, in order for a regime of accumulation to succeed, *all* people must ideologically buy into the system. Darjeeling tea workers are not ideologically entrenched in fair trade. Workers seeking better wages and guarantees of social welfare are still turning to the welfare model developed during the colonial regime of accumulation. They are not petitioning civil society organizations to improve labor conditions; they are striking against owners and the state. Workers are not only more ideologically tied to the old system; they are nostalgic for it. Recall the vignette with which I opened this chapter. Over white rice, potatoes, and watery lentil soup, we discussed the role of the Joint Body and the endemic corruption on the plantation. Again, the old woman crouched in the corner, without lifting her eyes from her plate, said, "The British time was better." Town residents and tea workers alike expressed this opinion. Darjeelingers frequently told me that things worked better under colonialism. A Darjeeling schoolteacher even said to me, "I wish that they would just take us over again. . . . We did not have this corruption during the Britishers' time." For tea laborers, the colonial regime represented a time when tea production was stable and the labor conditions were favorable.

In Darjeeling, the implementation of FLO standards has benefited owners, not workers. Although my work in Darjeeling does not lead me to think that the benefits of fair trade should never be extended to plantations, I do think that fair trade standards should reflect that plantations are hierarchical. This hierarchical structure makes it impossible for resources to be managed "jointly." Instead, FLO must privilege workers and take measures to prevent owners from manipulating the system for their own benefit. A quick comparison between a fair trade plantation and a conventional one is instructive. During my 2008–2009 fieldwork, I also spent time at Goodricke Company tea plantations in Darjeeling, as well as cinchona plantations across the district. Workers had expansive gardens and ample water supply, active labor unions, food rations, excellent medical facilities, and good housing, all of which are provided to them by plantation management; however, none of the Goodricke tea gardens and cinchona plantations are certified as fair trade. In fact, workers and managers I interviewed were not at all interested in pursuing certification.

As Fridell (2007) points out, fair trade, as both a movement and a market, extends the neoliberal economic emphasis on nongovernmental regulation and individual empowerment but also challenges the disenfranchisement that such policies cause. I have tried to use a regulation approach to show how neoliberalization reorients the state toward trade at the expense of social justice and how fair trade tries to correct this. When the Darjeeling tea plantations began seeking certification in the late 1990s, Northern consumers' enthusiasm for "socially conscious" products combined with plantation owners' desires to cut costs have inspired Darjeeling gardens to turn to fair trade certification, which has in turn overrun established state apparatuses for regulating workers' welfare. Focusing on modes of regulation in fair trade agriculture should help scholars studying fair trade in other regions shift their scale of analysis to explore the role of state and nonstate regulatory institutions in protecting workers' rights. One possible avenue for improvement is an expansion of FLO and other organizations' understanding of local legal codes and labor histories, something that social scientists are uniquely positioned to provide.

NOTES

1. This research was supported by a Fulbright Hays Fellowship, an American Institute for Indian Studies Junior Fellowship, and a Scott Kloeck Jenson grant from the Center for Global Studies at the University of Wisconsin–Madison.

2. There are five fair-trade-certified producers in Darjeeling: Chamong group, Ambootia group, Tea Promoters of India (TPI), and Makaibari Tea Estate. Each of these, except Makaibari, is a conglomerate. Between them, Chamong, Ambootia, and TPI own over thirty of the eighty-seven gardens of Darjeeling. Makaibari, certified in 1994, is a single estate and heralded by FLO as a model fair trade project (FLO 2005). It became the first plantation of any kind certified by FLO. Over the past fifteen years, many more plantations have become certified. I do not intend this chapter to be an exposé of the practices of Darjeeling plantations, but instead I aim to highlight the difficulties of applying fair trade in hired-labor situations.

3. Change is afoot in Darjeeling. At the time of publication, I am completing research on a separate state movement that heralds the causes of plantation workers' rights and reform in the Darjeeling tea industry.

4. This chapter is based on twelve months of research in Darjeeling (February 2008–January 2009). In Darjeeling, I studied on several fair trade gardens, owned by each of the aforementioned companies. I also worked with the Nepali-speaking laborers on conventional tea plantations as well as cinchona plantations across the district. I collected data through participant observation, informal conversations, and semistructured interviews with tea workers while plucking tea and working in the fields as well as in domestic settings. From my first trips to Darjeeling in 2006 to 2009, I was able to witness how attitudes toward fair trade certification changed among Darjeeling tea planters.

5. CHAI works on several plantations in the Darjeeling district, both fair trade certified and conventional.

WORKS CITED

Althusser, L.
  1971 Ideology and Ideological State Apparatuses: Notes toward an Investigation. *In* Lenin and Philosophy and Other Essays. London: New Left Books.
Bacon, C.
  2005 Confronting the Coffee Crisis: Can Fair Trade, Organic, and Specialty Coffees Reduce Small-Scale Farmer Vulnerability in Northern Nicaragua? World Development 33(3): 497–511.
Barrientos, S., and S. Smith
  2007 Mainstreaming Fair Trade in Global Production Networks: Own Brand and Chocolate in UK Supermarkets. *In* Fair Trade: The Challenges Transforming Globalization. L. Raynolds, D. Murray, and J. Wilkinson, eds. Pp. 103–122. London: Routledge.
Bourdieu, P.
  1977 Outline of a Theory of Practice. Cambridge: Cambridge University Press.
Burghart, R.
  1984 Formation of a Concept of the Nation-State in Nepal. Journal of Asian Studies 44(1): 101–126.
Elkington, J., and J. Hailes
  1989 The Green Consumer. London: Victor Gollancz.
English, R.
  1982 Gorkhali and Kiranti: Political Economy in the Eastern Hills of Nepal. Ph.D. dissertation, Department of Anthropology, New School for Social Research.
Fairtrade Labelling Organizations International (FLO)
  n.d. Have a Nice Cup of Tea! http://www.fairtrade.net/nilgiri_india.html.
  2005 Fairtrade Empowering Women. http://www.fairtrade.net/makaibari_india.html.
  2007a Fairtrade Standards for Tea for Hired Labour. Bonn, Germany: Fairtrade Labelling Organizations International.
  2007b Generic Fairtrade Standards for Hired Labour. Bonn, Germany: Fairtrade Labelling Organizations International.
Fisher, C.
  2007 Selling Coffee, or Selling Out? Evaluating Different Ways to Analyze the Fair-Trade System. Culture and Agriculture 29(2): 78–88.
Fridell, G.
  2007 Fair Trade Coffee: The Prospects and Pitfalls of Market-Driven Social Justice. Toronto: University of Toronto Press.
Friedmann, H.
  1978 World Market, State, and Family Farm: Social Bases of Household Production in the Era of Wage Labor. Comparative Studies in Society and History 20(4): 545–586.
Getz, C., and A. Shreck
  2006 What Organic and Fair Trade Labels Do Not Tell Us: Towards a Place-Based Understanding of Certification. International Journal of Consumer Studies 30(5): 490–501.

Goodwin, M., and J. Painter
  1996 Local Governance, the Crises of Fordism and Changing Geographies of Regulation. Transnational Institute of British Geographers 21: 635–648.
Griffiths, P.
  1967 The History of the British Tea Industry. London: Weidenfeld and Nicolson.
Guthman, J.
  1998 Regulating Meaning, Appropriating Nature: The Codification of California Organic Agriculture. Antipode 30(2): 135–154.
  2004 Agrarian Dreams? The Paradox of Organic Farming in California. Berkeley: University of California Press.
  2007 The Polanyian Way? Voluntary Food Labels as Neoliberal Governance. Antipode 39(3): 456–478.
Harvey, D.
  1989 The Condition of Postmodernity: An Enquiry into the Origins of Cultural Change. Malden, MA: Blackwell.
  2007 Neoliberalism as Creative Destruction. Annals of the American Academy of Political and Social Science 610: 21–44.
Howard, P., and P. Allen
  2006 Beyond Organic: Consumer Interest in New Labeling Schemes in the Central Coast of California. International Journal of Consumer Studies 30(5): 439–451.
James, A.
  1993 Eating Green(s): Discourses of Organic Food. In Environmentalism: The View from Anthropology. Kay Milton, ed. Pp. 205–218. London and New York: Routledge.
Jessop, B.
  2002 Liberalism, Neoliberalism, and Urban Governance: A State-Theoretical Perspective. Antipode 34(3): 452–472.
Kamat, S.
  2004 The Privatization of Public Interest: Theorizing NGO Discourse in a Neoliberal Era. Review of International Political Economy 11(1): 155–176.
Loureiro, M., and J. Lotade
  2004 Do Fair Trade and Eco-labels in Coffee Wake Up the Consumer Conscience? Ecological Economics 53(1): 129–138.
Lyon, S.
  2006a Evaluating Fair Trade Consumption: Politics, Defetishization and Producer Participation. International Journal of Consumer Studies 30(5): 452–464.
  2006b Just Java: Roasting Fair Trade Coffee. In Fast Food/Slow Food: The Cultural Economy of the Global Food System. Pp. 241–258. Lanham, MD: AltaMira.
  2007 Maya Coffee Farmers and Fair Trade: Assessing the Benefits and Limitations of Alternative Markets. Culture and Agriculture 29(2): 110–112.
McCarthy, J.
  2006 Neoliberalism and the Politics of Alternatives: Community Forestry in British Columbia and the United States. Annals of the Association of American Geographers 96(1): 84–104.

McDonagh, P.
    2002 Communicative Campaigns to Effect Antislavery and Fair Trade: The Cases of Rugmark and Cafédirect. European Journal of Marketing 36(5–6): 642–666.
Mintz, S.
    1986 Sweetness and Power: The Place of Sugar in Modern History. New York: Penguin Books.
Murray, D., L. Raynolds, and P. Taylor
    2006 The Future of Fair Trade Coffee: Dilemmas Facing Latin America's Small-Scale Producers. Development in Practice 16(2): 179–192.
Peck, J., and A. Tickell
    2002 Neoliberalizing Space. Antipode 34(3): 380–404.
Renard, M.
    2003 Fair Trade: Quality, Markets and Conventions. Journal of Rural Studies 19: 87–97.
Renard, M., and V. Pérez-Grovas
    2007 Fair Trade Coffee in Mexico: At the Center of the Debates. In Fair Trade: The Challenges Transforming Globalization. L. Raynolds, D. Murray, and J. Wilkinson, eds. Pp. 138–156. London: Routledge.
Rice, R.
    2000 Noble Goals and Challenging Terrain: Organic and Fair Trade Coffee Movements in the Global Marketplace. Journal of Agricultural and Environmental Ethics (14)1: 39–66.
Roseberry, W.
    1996 The Rise of Yuppie Coffees and the Reimagination of Class in the United States. American Anthropologist 94(4): 762–775.
Shreck, A.
    2005 Resistance, Redistribution, and Power in the Fair Trade Banana Initiative. Agriculture and Human Values 22: 17–29.
Shreck, A., C. Getz, and G. Feenstra
    2006 Social Sustainability, Farm Labor, and Organic Agriculture: Findings from an Exploratory Analysis. Agriculture and Human Values 23: 439–449.
Smith, J.
    2007 The Search for Sustainable Markets: The Promise and Failures of Fair Trade. Culture and Agriculture 29(2): 89–99.
Whatmore, S., and L. Thorne
    1997 Nourishing Networks: Alternative Geographies of Food. In Globalising Food: Agrarian Questions and Global Restructuring. D. Goodman and M. Watts, eds. Pp. 287–304. London: Routledge.
Zimmerer, K.
    2006 Geographical Perspectives on Globalization and Environmental Issues: The Inner-Connections of Conservation, Agriculture, and Livelihoods. In Globalization and New Geographies of Conservation. Karl Zimmerer, ed. Pp. 1–44. Chicago: University of Chicago Press.

Part II

••••••••••••••••••••••

Negotiating Difference and Identity
in Fair Trade Markets

In addition to redefining producer-consumer relationships, fair trade's certification standards have prioritized gender equity, the maintenance of local cultural traditions, and democratic participation within producer groups. The three case studies composing this section critically examine the extent to which such standards are implemented among fair trade groups producing coffee, tea, and crafts for the global market. Sarah Lyon's study of a Maya fair trade coffee cooperative in Guatemala raises questions about the effectiveness of these initiatives, at least where gender is considered. Rather than participating in coffee production and the male-dominated cooperative sphere, female cooperative members are eager to find a foreign market for their weavings in order to increase their own earnings. Despite verbal support for a women's weaving project among co-op members, the fair trade group has not actively assisted women in their efforts to seek a foreign buyer, nor has it incorporated women into positions of leadership or decision-making. Notwithstanding the movement's rhetorical commitment to equal participation, its failure to promote women's interests in practice is acutely felt in rural Guatemala, where women are disproportionately indigent, unemployed, and illiterate while often suffering from high levels of personal violence.

With respect to Kenyan tea production, Catherine Dolan similarly notes a disparity between fair trade's rhetorical endorsement of gender equity and its inability to accomplish these goals in practice. She argues that local gender imbalances are related less to inequities in transnational commodity chains than to the fabric of communities cross-cut by longstanding social hierarchies, gendered conventions, and rigid divisions of labor, all of which deflect fair trade's goals of redistributive justice. With regard to decision-making in producers' associations, Dolan finds that fair trade tea growers in Kenya enjoy little discretion over the ways in which social premiums are invested, a fact that vitiates the movement's principles of democratic participation. Here, as well, women are largely absent from the meager involvement that does occur within fair trade producers' groups.

In both Guatemala and Kenya, leaders of local fair trade associations have learned to behave strategically in ways that are rewarded by visiting alternative trade officials from the developed North, whose favor is eagerly sought by producers who depend on continued access to fair trade markets. As seen in Lyon's study, such performances mask persisting inequalities within fair trade associations and the communities in which they operate. Performance of cultural difference also emerges as a theme in Patrick Wilson's study of Ecuadorian craft producers, whose ethnic identities are consciously deployed by alternative trade organizations as a marketing device. Wilson notes that certification standards originating in the developed North impose an essentialized definition of tradition that excludes some indigenous communities from fair trade networks while privileging others. Many of these expectations, such as environmental stewardship, gender equality, and cooperativism, reflect romanticized notions of indigenous traditions, compelling fair trade producers to engage in the performance of "acceptable" cultural practices. Wilson observes that those communities whose members fail to "speak and act 'like an Indian'" by the definition of fair trade certifiers find themselves excluded from the benefits of alternative markets.

These cases all point to the continuing asymmetries in power between commodity producers and those who procure their goods for distribution in the developed North, a fact that seems readily evident to fair trade producers if not the movement's advocates and representatives in developed countries. In contrast to local fair trade officers, many rank-and-file members of the producer groups profiled in this volume possess little or no understanding of the movement's premises or even the fact that their goods are promoted in retail markets as originating in socially just and environmentally sustainable conditions. Tea producers, for example, appreciate the higher prices received from the fair trade market but view the movement as simply a variant of missionary-based charities operating in Kenya since the nineteenth century. Such understandings, as Dolan notes, connote not the reciprocity and equality of fair trade discourse but the noblesse oblige and deference implied in colonial relationships. In Foucauldian terms, she points out that even the emancipatory discourses of fair trade entail systems of differential power, possessing the capacity both to liberate and to dominate those who are subject to them.

A Market of Our Own

Women's Livelihoods and Fair Trade Markets

SARAH LYON

In January 2002, the vice president of Supply Chain Operations at Green Mountain Coffee Roasters (GMCR) visited the fair trade coffee cooperative I was researching on the shores of Lake Atitlan in Guatemala.[1] The vice president traveled from Vermont to check on the progress of the cooperative's construction of new drying patios in its wet mill, which was partially funded by a fifteen-thousand-dollar donation from GMCR. The visiting official explained to the cooperative's president in heavily accented Spanish, "We love the flavor of your coffee, but the most important thing is the coffee quality. Some people like a fruity flavor, but others don't. So we don't want to have it. Therefore you have to be careful of the quality." The president hastily replied that he understood this well and that the cooperative was working hard to improve the coffee's quality. This fruity, or winey, undertone was the exact flavor characteristic that GMCR was hoping to eliminate with the donation and construction of the new drying patios, as the roaster had determined that the flavor resulted from over-fermentation of the coffee cherries due to insufficient drying space.

In order to fete the vice president properly the cooperative organized a celebratory inauguration of the construction project. Before the somewhat awkward ribbon-cutting ceremony, the cooperative's president made a short speech: "The people of our community are very happy. In the name of the 116 families we are thankful for the help you gave us for the patios and the bodegas so that we can produce coffee of good quality." In response, GMCR's vice president stated, "Speaking for the people of my company, I am very happy to be here with you. It's an investment in the quality of the coffee, your lives, and the coffee business." He then cut the ribbon, and each member of the cooperative's board of directors in turn cut a small piece for themselves.

After the ribbon was cut and the wet mill was toured, the cooperative's manager, Guillermo,[2] asked the group to sit down so that he could present an accounting of the patio construction to the vice president. After the detailed accounting, the requisite gift-giving ceremony began. The cooperative's president explained that the organization purchased a small painting that they wanted Green Mountain's vice president to accept on behalf of the company. After posed photos were taken of the vice president receiving the painting, Guillermo explained that there was a special committee in charge of the patio's construction which also wanted to make a presentation. At this point, a cooperative member, Bernadino, came forward and explained, "This painting is for you; the other painting was for the company, but this one is for you." Again, the vice president gratefully received the painting of Maya coffee growers colorfully clad in tattered, local *traje* (the traditional, town-specific clothing worn by many Mayas). Bernadino explained, "We appreciate the company and all the help that you've given us, and we also want to present you with some weavings made here in the community by our wives." The vice president politely received the offerings and said thank you. At this point, Guillermo stood to explain that he wanted to take an additional photograph of the vice president with all his gifts gathered around him. Before he could proceed, however, a middle-aged woman pushed her way into the middle of the exclusively male group. Juana was a cooperative founder back in the late 1970s, and she was the only one of the fifteen female members who spoke fluent Spanish and possessed sufficient self-confidence to speak with foreign visitors. Juana explained, "On behalf of the cooperative members' wives I want to present you with another weaving," as she handed him the gift. Green Mountain's vice president looked slightly bemused but graciously accepted the present. After the ceremony concluded, Guillermo and several members of the cooperative's board of directors (including Juana's husband) walked the vice president to Juana's house on their way to lunch. Juana and several other wives of cooperative members were patiently waiting to show the vice president some of their weavings. While they would have been more than pleased if he had purchased something from them that day, they were clearly hoping the vice president would see the value of their hard work and would arrange to have them weave products for the company and its employees in Vermont. Juana showed him multiple products, such as placemats and shawls, the vast majority of which were woven out of thread dyed in softly muted beiges, purples, and peaches. She patiently explained that the weavings were made with natural dyes and that the women could easily make passport covers, backpacks, jackets, napkins, and other products. Not surprisingly, as a vice president of Supply Chain

Operations, the visitor was noncommittal, and he left the wives empty-handed as he walked off to lunch with the male cooperative members.

The celebration that day illustrates both the strengths and weaknesses of contemporary fair trade coffee markets. Green Mountain's financial donation demonstrates that not only is the company committed to coffee quality but it is also willing to educate suppliers about how to improve quality in order to compete in the marketplace. This is an example of the market information and market access that fair trade markets are celebrated for providing to small farmers (Lyon 2007). Furthermore, the fact that the vice president traveled from rural Vermont to the Highlands of Guatemala demonstrates the company's attempts to nurture face-to-face business relationships with its suppliers. The gift-giving ceremony described above vividly reveals that this transnational business relationship is more than a simple commodity exchange, as the cooperative administrators routinely fete their visiting buyers in exchange for both the secure markets and the "gifts" (in this case donations) they bring. However, it also illustrates the fair trade movement's attempts to minimize the role of intermediaries in supply chains. At the same time, Juana's efforts to make a connection with the vice president that was separate from his relationship with the male cooperative leaders is indicative of the ongoing struggle of female cooperative members and members' wives to develop and maintain a market of their own, one that is comparable to their husbands' foreign coffee market. That market, the women repeatedly told me, was necessary for them to help support their children and their educational expenses while maintaining a small degree of financial autonomy within their households, where their husbands controlled the income from agricultural pursuits, such as fair trade coffee production. Therefore, the women's struggles are indicative of a larger weakness within the fair trade movement: the failure to support gender equality adequately in communities and markets.

Fair trade promotional materials frequently highlight the ways in which the movement contributes to gender equity and women's issues. They foreground groups such as the Peruvian fair trade coffee cooperative Café Feminino, whose seven hundred female members use its premiums to support abandoned and abused women (Allison 2006), and the SOPPEX-CCA cooperative in Jinotega, Nicaragua, which formed an internal association of eighty-five female farmers to produce coffee for Peet's Coffee's "Las Hermanas" blend (Utting-Chamorro 2005). However, this chapter steps beyond the handful of high-profile women's initiatives that are frequently touted as fair trade coffee successes to examine ethnographically women in one fair trade coffee cooperative who continue to struggle to develop a market of their own in order to gain a modicum of financial independence and the relative power that accompanies it in their daily lives. It details the limitations the women face in their attempts to develop new products, such as naturally dyed weavings; new markets, such as a coffee tourism project; and new contacts, such as Juana's attempt to forge an independent relationship with the visiting Green Mountain Coffee Roasters vice president. The chapter ends with concrete suggestions for how fair trade could better accommodate the needs of women in agricultural communities and argues that such an emphasis would help reinvigorate the fair trade movement and make it more than simply an alternative form of development that is fully compatible with neoliberal capitalism.

The chapter relies on ethnographic data gathered primarily through participant observation and qualitative interviews during fourteen months of research in Guatemala (December 2001–February 2003, June 2006). (The larger project also involved six months of research in the United States.) The research focused on the 116 members and the administrators of the fair trade coffee cooperative located in a Tz'utujil Maya community of approximately five thousand people. The cooperative was founded in 1977 and acquired its initial organic certification in 1991 and its initial fair trade certification shortly thereafter. It maintains a long-term relationship with the North American roaster Green Mountain Coffee Roasters, which purchases the majority of its coffee. The community is located on the shores of Lake Atitlan, one of Guatemala's most popular tourist attractions, and while the majority of inhabitants sustain themselves and their families through subsistence agriculture, horticultural farming, coffee production, and weaving, there is also an emerging small-scale tourism industry. The research included ongoing participant observation at community events, at the wet mill during the harvest (December–March), and at internal cooperative meetings and meetings with external market participants, such as coffee importers, roasters, and certifiers. Participant observation was also conducted during the visits made by agronomists and certifiers to members' coffee fields in order to observe production practices and to understand certification requirements better.

Data were gathered through semistructured interviews with each of the available (19) cooperative founders and the collection of life histories from 18 community elders (selected through snowball sampling) in order to illustrate the community's past and recent transformations. Semistructured interviews were conducted with 53 of the cooperative's 116 members

and approximately 30 employees of development agencies, coffee importers, and roasters assisting the cooperative and coffee certifiers. Subjects
were selected judgmentally (on the basis of availability and willingness to
be interviewed) and through snowball sampling. Further data on coffee-
market trends and national production, processing, and marketing initiatives were gathered during participant observation at the Guatemalan
National Coffee Association's annual conference (2000, 2002) and visits
to several fair trade coffee cooperatives located in the Western Highlands
(where informal interviews were conducted with cooperative administrators and board members).

Fair Trade and Gender

Overall, resource transfers within fair trade networks have been significant: transfers from U.S. consumers to Southern coffee farmers resulted
in an estimated additional producer income of $70 million between 1998
and 2005 (Macdonald 2007: 799). The certification standards represent
the backbone of the fair trade coffee network, lending legitimacy to the
product in retail markets and assuring that adequate resources are delivered to the network's intended beneficiaries, small producers. There are
four requirements importers must meet in order to use the fair trade label. First, they must buy their coffee directly from certified small coffee
farmers. Second, they must offer these farmers long-term contracts that
extend at least beyond one annual harvest. Third, they must pay a price
premium of $1.31 per pound ($1.21 fair trade minimum plus $0.10 social
premium) and an additional $0.20 per pound for organic certified coffee.
(It is important to note that the amount paid to individual coffee growers
by an association might be significantly less, depending on an organization's operating expenses.) Finally, they must offer the farmer organizations prefinancing covering at least 60 percent of the annual contract.

Similarly, there are three requirements for participating coffee producers. First, they must be small family farmers. Second, they must be organized into independent, democratic associations. And third, they must
pursue ecological goals (FLO 2005). The certification standards state that
in order to be "an instrument for the social and economic development
of the members" the organization must "have a democratic structure and
transparent administration which enables effective control by the members
and its Board over the management, including the decisions about how the
benefits are shared" (FLO 2005). Specifically, FLO regulations state that (a)

there must be no discrimination regarding membership and participation, (b) there must be a general assembly with voting rights for all members and an elected board, (c) the staff must answer through the board to the general assembly, and (d) there must be one general assembly a year during which annual reports and accounts are approved (FLO 2005: 4).

Fair trade certification standards include the requirements against which producers will actually be inspected. These requirements are divided into minimum requirements, which all producer organizations must meet, and progress requirements, on which producer organizations must show regular improvement (FLO 2007b: 2). Existing fair trade certification standards for smallholder organizations pertain to the generic small producers who are understood to be those who "are not structurally dependent on permanent hired labor, managing their farm mainly with their own and their family's labor force" (FLO 2007b: 4). The standards state that "where workers are casually hired by farmers themselves, the organization should take steps to improve working conditions and to ensure that such workers share the benefits of Fairtrade" (FLO 2007b: 21). However, the standards avoid opening the black box of household relations, including the work conditions of the "family labor force" and the distribution of economic benefits, other than to state that "children may only work if their education is not jeopardized" and that "spouses have the right to off-farm employment" (FLO 2007b: 24). The generic standards for small producers do require certified groups to follow ILO Convention 111, which prohibits discrimination on the basis of gender (among other factors). The existing progress requirements for this standard state that programs relating to disadvantaged and minority groups should be in place within organizations, particularly with respect to recruitment, staff, and committee membership. In implicit acknowledgment of the vagueness of this requirement, a September 2007 consultation document includes a proposed change to these progress requirements which reads, "The organization is expected to show how they directly support members from minority groups to participate actively in organizational matters, e.g. by assuming organizational responsibilities. Special attention should be given to the participation of female members" (FLO 2007a: 10).

The Fairtrade Labelling Organization International's (FLO) website identifies the "empowerment of women" as one of the ten key "impact areas," explaining that "important investments can be made in women's income generating activities that are not related to the farm, thereby strengthening their income, business experience and position in the family" (FLO 2008).

While the production of some fair-trade-certified goods, such as the tea described by Besky and Dolan in this volume (chaps. 5 and 7), is dominated by female agricultural workers, the implicit assumption seems to be that fair trade production is largely a male domain and that alternative sources of income should be identified for female community members. Recently the organization Las Hermanas, a women's cooperative founded by the SOPPEXCCA coffee cooperative in Nicaragua, and a group of female workers in a fair trade tea plantation in India were used to exemplify this "empowerment" (FLO 2008) on the organization's website. FLO's efforts to publicize fair trade's "empowerment of women" are also visible in the organization's 2007 Annual Report, which features eight photos of female fair trade producers (out of a total of nineteen photos of producers). In highlighting the role of women in both certification standards and publicity materials, FLO is responding to the demands of (often female) consumers in Northern markets. A gender study submitted to FLO in 2006 found that women's issues seem to serve as a powerful marketing argument, especially in relation to improved well-being and social projects aimed at child welfare. Wach finds that "community projects related to health or education and the idea to support entire families seem to appeal to consumers. Those topics relate to the traditional role of women and their 'practical needs.' However, it is more difficult to find reference to gender-related empowerment, which relates to strategic interests which challenge traditional role models of both men and women" (2006: 13).

However, despite FLO's publicity efforts, a number of studies indicate that to date fair trade has failed to promote gender equity adequately, especially in regard to active female participation in the democratic processes of fair trade producer associations (Lyon 2008a; Fridell 2007; Utting-Chamorro 2005; Redfern and Snedker 2002; Ronchi 2002; Shreck 2002; Mayoux 2001). In fact, research in varied locales suggests that fair trade has largely failed to alter gender relations that have historically been unequal, despite the transformative goals of equitable participation. There is no direct correlation between the formation of more equitable North-South market relationships and the status of women, so that even if the former are altered by fair trade networks, if women have historically been subordinated within the realm of production or within their households, that subordination is likely to continue. If, on the other hand, there are preexisting (more) equitable gender relations, such as those found in the St. Lucian banana industry described by Moberg (chap. 3, this volume), these are likely to be maintained and even enhanced through fair trade participation.

In implicit recognition of the organization's weaknesses in regard to gender equity, FLO certification standards have been amended. For example, an appendix to the existing certification standards for small farmers states that fair trade premiums may be used by producers for any number of projects, including "programs addressing gender inequality or promoting the participation of women and similar programs for marginalized groups" (FLO 2006: 10). The organization also recently invited applications for a consultant to develop a "Training Approach to Improve Gender Competencies in Fairtrade Producer Support." The advertisement stated, "FLO is committed to include a gender dimension into its mission and integrate gender into the different fields of work in the organization. In this context, the organization aims at improving the gender competencies of relevant staff working in Fairtrade producer support in order to create awareness about and integrate the gender dimension in their certification advisory work" (Kuhlmann 2008: 3).

Why Do Women Want a Market of Their Own?

Historically, Guatemalan Maya households were divided according to gender, with neither the male nor the female domain more important: the group worked as a unit to provide the subsistence needs and luxury desires of the family. Men worked as laborers, farmers, and long-distance traders, whereas women maintained the household by taking care of small children, cooking, cleaning, and making clothing (Little 2004). In the research site, the majority of households more or less maintain these traditions, in that farming is primarily a male domain and women assist in the coffee fields solely during the harvest. This pattern is replicated in some other regions of Latin America, such as Costa Rica and Mexico, where coffee production remains largely a male sphere of economic activity (Fridell 2007; Tallontire 2000; Sick 1997). Female cooperative members and wives were adamant that they did not want to be actively involved in coffee production, and during interviews they frequently told me to ask their husbands when I questioned them about their land or agricultural practices. For example, when I asked one female cooperative member how much land she owned, she told me, "I don't know. The figures are with my husband." While many women in the community owned land due to the local tradition of a gender-neutral partible inheritance system, they generally placed their husbands or sons in charge of its daily maintenance. They repeatedly told me that coffee was men's work and said, "We don't have work in the cooperative. Only the men do. What we need for our family are artisan markets."

The female cooperative members and wives were eager to find a foreign market for their weavings in order to increase their own earnings. In general, the women primarily use these earnings to support their children's educational goals or as a type of nonliquid savings. I once asked a woman to quantify how much she earned from selling her weavings in a month. She told me that this was very difficult to calculate because, she said, "Sometimes I don't sell anything. What I do earn I invest [in more thread] and hope that I am going to sell something. I save my money in my thread. If I buy thread, then I can't spend my money easily on the children or on food. It's better." She, like many women I spoke with, was eager to keep her earnings from weaving separate from the household budget and entirely under her own control. A female cooperative member who belongs to the group's weaving and tourism project explained, "We have to separate the money because this money is ours—it's from our products. It's better that we manage it ourselves so that we can do something with the money." Managing their own money also ensures that they can ensure their children's education, thereby diversifying the next generation's livelihood prospects. A cooperative member's wife stated, "For the moment we are only selling a little bit of our weavings, and it doesn't cover our needs. It's not enough to send the children to school and take care of them in the house." The women are very clear about how the cooperative, and by extension fair trade, can help improve their economic situation, which, in turn, would contribute to a higher standard of living for the household as a whole and help promote gender equity within families and potentially the community at large. However, to date their agenda has not been identified by fair trade certifiers or adequately supported by the cooperative itself.

While the majority of the interviewed women belong to one of the several existing weaving associations in the community, none of them receives significant income from these initiatives, several of which are essentially defunct, while others lack sufficient markets for members' products. The female members of the coffee cooperative and the wives of male members argue that the most obvious way for them to develop a market for their artisan products is through the coffee cooperative, taking advantage of the organization's relatively extensive network of external contacts and administrative and financial expertise. Significant research demonstrates that women's participation in agricultural and artisan cooperatives promotes positive economic and social changes in their communities

(Ehlers 1993; Nash and Hopkins 1976; Olson 1999; Rosenbaum 2000). Specifically, research on female weaving cooperatives indicates that the organizations can help individual artisans to determine the nature of their own participation in global markets, help them gain decision-making power, and increase their economic and political importance locally and regionally (Stephen 2005). Significantly, participation in weaving cooperatives can help women develop more direct links to markets, including those of alternative trade organizations (ATOs) and fair trade networks (Bartra 2003; Eber 2000; Eber and Rosenbaum 1993; Ehlers 1993; Grimes 2000; and Rosenbaum 2000). Thus, membership in weaving cooperatives can help offset the inherent gender segregation in artisan production. As Scrase argues (2003), while craft production is frequently an important industry for the employment of women, the final and most lucrative stage of the process—the selling of the finished goods—remains an inherently masculine task. Finally, Stephen argues that participation in weaving cooperatives can positively affect women's relationships at home by creating "a space in part of the community where gender conventions for weaver women are being reordered—giving women greater independence as artisans, involving husbands, children and others in domestic work and support work for the cooperatives when women leave, and providing women with a sense of respect and appreciation for their economic contributions and efforts on behalf of their families" (2005: 271).

Despite the extensive research documenting the benefits of cooperative membership for women weavers, scholars have also noted potential negative consequences as well, some of which mirror the difficulties facing the women artisans in the Ecuadorian indigenous community that Wilson writes about in this volume (chap. 8). First, it is absolutely critical not to assume that cooperatives always help the neediest in each community (Cohen 2000; Milgram 2000; Stephen 2005). As noted earlier, in the research site there are a number of existing weaving cooperatives. However, several of these are dominated by strong family groups which allegedly parcel out orders and earnings among themselves and their close associates. Although those community members who belong to the coffee cooperative are not necessarily the most impoverished, the certification standards which require members to be *small* family farmers means that the group does contain a cross-section of the community, while simultaneously excluding its wealthiest residents. Furthermore, the fair trade mandates for transparency and democratic participation (through service on an annually elected board of directors) mean that theoretically a weaving project associated with the coffee cooperative would employ more stringent bookkeeping practices and be fully accountable to its members. This is especially critical in the local context, as the stories of managerial corruption in the community's weaving associations are numerous. For example, one of the largest and best known of the associations has repeatedly been forced in the past two decades to fire its managers for embezzlement. One wife of a cooperative member explained, "I was president of that association. We received three donations at that time, and I told the general assembly that we had received this money so that we could decide how to spend the money together. This woman [the manager] got mad at me because she wanted to keep the donations a secret, to keep them only for herself. She then told our members not to be with me, so I left." Several years after this incident, the manager was fired by the group for theft.

Other researchers have noted that participation in artisan associations can result in the harassment (or even murder) of women by family members (Eber 2000; Nash 1993a, 1993b) as local gender relations are challenged. Similarly, Wilson demonstrates that NGOs developing craft production associations in Amazonian Ecuador threatened to undermine gender relations among and between families when their proposed project designs violated local understandings of appropriate gender roles within the family and community (2003). This is not a significant threat in the research site because of the extensive history of weaving associations in the community. However, female members of the coffee cooperative and the wives of male members face significant obstacles in initiating a weaving project and finding a market of their own.

Developing New Products

The market for Guatemalan textiles expanded rapidly in the early 1990s and was associated with the growing youth and backpacking travel to the region (Imhoff 1998). However, Guatemalan artisans, in their race to secure a piece of the burgeoning market, competed with each other to the point of market saturation, oversupply, and declining prices and declining market demand (Scrase 2003). This larger trend is certainly reflected in local and personal histories gathered during interviews with informants. For example, Marta told me that in the late 1990s she and her husband paid Q700 (approximately $95) a month for their son's room and board in the city of Quetzaltenango, in addition to Q2000 (approximately $270) a year in school fees. To help pay for her son's education Marta wove hammocks and backpacks in the courtyard of her home, wares which she sold to a Chinese-Guatemalan man who lived in Guatemala City. For two years she steadily earned Q500 ($68) a month through this market opportunity. However, in 2000 the buyer told her that he could no longer buy her products because "there is no market in the United States for Guatemalan weavings." Like many women in the community, Marta was desperately (and fruitlessly) searching for alternative market opportunities to make up for this lost income at the time of my research.

In 2002 several female cooperative members and the wives of male members were beginning to dye their own threads using natural products in an attempt to create new, muted colors and "environmentally friendly" products that might appeal to tourists and foreign buyers who were eschewing the more traditional, brightly colored weavings for which Guatemala is best known. Juana, the female cooperative member introduced earlier, and her neighbor Lidia, who is the wife of a cooperative founder, were both early adopters of the natural dyes that they learned how to produce from a North American woman who, funded by an international development agency, trained a group of local women in the techniques in 1999. Juana and Lidia often worked together to dye up to ten pounds of thread during one long, hot day of work. Their husbands assisted them by providing firewood to heat the large cauldrons of water and making trips to the surrounding forest or nearby communities to collect or purchase materials such as banana stems, blackberries, Rosa de Jamaica (hibiscus) flowers, and various tree barks. Because of the amount of labor the natural dyes required, Juana and Lidia priced their products significantly higher than comparable weavings made out of chemical dyes. Unfortunately, these higher prices seemed to hinder their attempts both to sell to the occasional tourists who happened through town and to develop wholesale markets with foreign buyers. For example, Lidia explained to me why they did not want to cross the lake to sell their products in Panajachel (a large tourist destination): "because there is so much competition there that it isn't worth it for us. Our natural dyes aren't equal to chemical tints, and therefore they're more expensive." They chose not to make the thirty-minute trip because they experienced difficulty in their attempts to convince tourists of the rationale for their higher prices. Similarly, in 2002 Juana asked me to contact via e-mail a U.S.-based artisan importer who had met with the female cooperative members and members' wives months earlier. The importer had told them their prices were too high, and after consideration the women decided to lower their prices in an attempt to secure his interest. (He told me their prices were still too high and remained uninterested.)

Male members of the coffee cooperative who produce fair trade and organic-certified coffee often spoke with me about the similarities between modern organic agricultural methods and those employed by their grandparents before the introduction of chemical fertilizers. For example, one stated, "We are rescuing the culture and rescuing the older system of production from before" (Lyon 2008b). Similarly, some of the women using natural dyes in their weavings claimed that they were happy with the recently reintroduced methods because it was something that their grandmothers had used before them and it was a way of continuing this tradition. Rosa explained, "My grandmother used a plant that is called 'saca tinta' to give blue color to her skirts." She told me how in past years the women would put their skirts (the community's traditional *traje* includes a deep-navy-colored skirt) into a bath of *saca tinta* to refresh their color when they began to fade. Rosa proudly stated, "I've never used chemicals, only natural. My mother also had many ideas for other things that would give natural dyes. I like to chat with foreigners—they want variety from the chemical dyes."

While some women, such as Rosa, made explicit connections with past cultural traditions when discussing their natural dyes, others argued that these were essentially "invented traditions" (Hobsbawm 1992) and that the connection between contemporary natural dyes and past practices was tenuous at best. They argued that their competitors' attempts to link past and present weaving practices into a narrative of environmentally friendly, indigenous traditions was a marketing ploy aimed at gullible tourists. This argument echoes Wilson's argument (chap. 8, this volume) about ATOs requiring craftspeople to "perform" in ways that acceptably correspond to their understanding of "indigenous" identities and offers a similar example of Southern artisans adapting their production to meet the perceived demands of Northern consumers, as described by M'Closkey in her analysis of the appropriation of Navajo designs by Mexican weavers (chap. 11, this volume). These women weavers are essentially forsaking traditional color preferences in order to accommodate a foreign market predicated on constructed notions of ecological sustainability and "traditional" dying practices. The fact that natural dying techniques were taught to the women by an employee of a North American development agency lends some support to this argument. Regardless of the history of the natural dyes, over the past six years they have become ubiquitous throughout the community as women weavers, desperate for markets and tourist sales, attempt to capitalize on the trend. When I returned to conduct research in 2006, I expressed to Marta my shock over the proliferation of natural dyes in the weavings now offered for sale in the community. She laughed and told me that I needed to learn to look more closely at what weavers were offering. She grabbed two weavings from her own extensive bag of products for sale and demonstrated to me that while both featured pale pastels, only one of the shawls was woven with naturally dyed thread. Just as in the past, when industrious weavers unraveled the used "Ropa Americana" acrylic sweaters from the United States that were sold in the street markets in order to reuse the threads in their own weavings (which they ironically then sold back to United States tourists), entrepreneurial weavers were now using chemically dyed threads in pastel colors in an attempt to increase their earnings without a concomitant increase in labor requirements. Presenting an interesting counterpoint to Wilson's case study of Ecuadorian artisans, in this case, the "performance" of acceptable indigenous identity is accompanied by a degree of local resistance as well. Whereas the natural dyes seemed a novel and promising product development in 2002, it is now obvious that the innovation is not significantly increasing the income of women cooperative members due to competition and the significant labor costs. Furthermore, the products have not become popular in the U.S. market, as demonstrated by the fact that there are few if any of the products offered for sale in third-world import stores or catalogues.

The Ongoing Search for New Markets

In the attempts of the female members of the coffee cooperative and members' wives to develop a market of their own, they have used three primary channels: the fostering of noncooperative associated contacts, participation in a new coffee-tourism project that the cooperative initiated, and subtle pressure on the cooperative's foreign coffee buyers. While the women have attempted several times to make contacts with foreign artisan importers, such as the one mentioned earlier, to date none of these contacts has yielded a market. In 2002, in an attempt to gain access to the local markets, Juana traveled to neighboring communities which possessed regular flows of foreign tourists. She spoke with the owners of several large hotels to ask permission to sell the women's weavings in their lobbies or on their grounds; however, she was repeatedly denied access.

The female cooperative members' efforts at finding a foreign or local wholesale market have been thwarted for several reasons. First, many of them do not speak Spanish fluently. A wife of a coffee-cooperative member explained to me, "The problem that us women have is that we don't speak Spanish well. We are unprepared to explain the problems that women have, to participate and organize." Second, many of them are uncomfortable speaking to foreigners and unwilling to travel long distances. For example, Juana told me that in 2001 a German importer approached her about developing a market for the wives of cooperative members and offered to pay her airfare and expenses for a visit to Germany to discuss the potential relationship. Juana explained, "I said to my husband I wanted to go to Germany and learn about this market, and he said, 'Go ahead.' But none of the other women wanted to go with me, and so we didn't go. What I want is for the women to participate in the selling of the products in other places. I want to go to other communities and sell our products, but no one will help me." Because Maya women traditionally bear the primary responsibility for the care of children and the domestic sphere, they often find their mobility severely restricted. As a consequence, they have limited access not only to jobs but also to education, training opportunities, and, in this case, foreign markets (Goldin et al. 2006). This is in direct contrast to the many male fair trade coffee farmers described by Doane (chap. 10, this volume) who routinely travel to North America from their homes on publicity junkets sponsored by coffee roasters and NGOs such as Global Exchange. Third, the women claim they simply lack the necessary experience. For example, one woman explained to me that they were not actively looking for a market because they "don't know the path to take to look for a market." They are unfamiliar with the Internet and lack training in business administration. Fourth, as stated earlier, there is a long history of corruption and dissatisfaction within the many weaving groups that have formed and dissolved within the community during the past two decades. This serves to curtail some women's willingness to devote significant amounts of time to cooperative work. In summary, the local barriers to gender equity in this case are not solely attributable to male opposition. The structural limitations facing these women, such as monolingualism, low education levels, and a lack of confidence, are significant obstacles which impede their attempts to find a market of their own (Lyon 2008a).

As stated earlier, FLO's website highlights the fair trade market's "empowerment of women" through investments made in "women's income generating activities that are not related to the farm" (FLO 2008). The fair trade coffee cooperative discussed in this chapter has struggled to solidify a female income-generating project; however, other groups have been more successful. For example, across Lake Atitlan a more recently formed fair trade coffee cooperative developed a women's program (run by three women and four men) that runs a catering service which provides meals for local groups that are having meetings and events. (This cooperative also has a female accountant on its staff.) Similarly, Fridell reports that UCIRI has developed a variety of projects "designed to ease the burden of women's work and improve the well-being of the family" (2007: 208). However, he notes that these microprojects, such as small animal husbandry and fruit processing, do not appear actively to ameliorate gender inequality, which would ultimately "necessitate challenging local or 'traditional' notions of the peasant family being run by property-owning, male 'heads of household'" (2007: 133).

Forty-five of the fifty-three interviewed cooperative members (85 percent) agreed that the cooperative should seek markets for non-coffee-related products. Of those forty-five individuals, twenty (44 percent) of them thought that the cooperative should actively seek a market for the weavings made by female cooperative members and wives (as opposed to five who named onions, four who named tomatoes, and three who named avocadoes). Despite this widespread support for a women's weaving project, female members and wives struggled for decades to form a weaving project. However, in 2004 the cooperative initiated two new income-generating programs: a coffee tour and a women's weaving project. The two new projects were not necessarily initiated as a result of suggestions made by fair trade certifiers; however, the administrative skills and market security the cooperative members gained through fair trade market participation undoubtedly helped in the new organizational efforts. While the weaving project remains unprofitable due to the small number of visitors and the larger cooperative's inability or unwillingness to identify foreign markets, it is run entirely by female members and the wives of male cooperative members.

In this regard, the cooperative is making some effort to increase the participation rates of women and promote gender equity. During a 2006 focus-group interview the participating women acknowledged that the training they received and the official role they occupied in the cooperative as a result of the new project helped legitimize the group: "So that we can get support. Because one person alone cannot get support, but now we are in an organization, and we can ask for help from other institutions." However, the women also expressed their frustration at the lack of sales the new project was generating due to the small number of visitors the coffee tour attracted. One woman explained that the training they received from the Guatemalan National Coffee Association (which offered initial project funding) prepared each woman to participate. However, they were enjoying limited success: "If the visitors come, then we sell a bit, but if there are no visitors, we don't sell anything—that's the problem we've been having." Another member explained that the rates of female participation were declining because there were no sales: "That's why people don't go down there anymore [to the coffee tour, which is located in the cooperative's wet mill]. They wanted to earn money to help their husbands, but, like us, you see we are not making anything because we do not have any orders."

Because of the difficulties the female cooperative members and the male members' wives have faced in their attempts to locate a market of their own for their weaving, it is perhaps understandable that they look with envy on their male counterparts in the cooperative, who have enjoyed a secure market for their fair trade and organic-certified coffee for many years. As evidenced in this chapter's introduction, the women attempt to forge connections with the visiting coffee buyers whenever possible. On average the cooperative entertains visits from foreigners (whether GMCR employees or other groups, such as politicians or aid workers) once a month. Whenever the women hear from their husbands that there will be a group visiting, they bring their weavings to the wet mill (which visitors generally tour) and attempt to interest them in purchasing something. Oftentimes the women successfully sell one or two small pieces, which undoubtedly makes them happy. However, in displaying their products they are hoping to identify the elusive wholesale market they so eagerly seek. In their minds, since the foreigners purchase the men's coffee, it is only just that they also purchase the women's products.

In fact, Green Mountain Coffee Roasters does occasionally offer handmade Guatemalan artisan products for sale in its catalogues and on its website. For example, the company's winter 2007 catalogue featured, in its "Exotic Origins of the Americas" coffee section (p. 10), a Guatemalan Pillow Cover ($32.95) and a Guatemalan Mug ($16.95). Both of these products were certified by the Fair Trade Federation, and one description explains, "Because the women who make these pillows are paid a Fair Trade price for their craft, they are not forced to leave their communities to supplement their income." Similarly, the company's website[3] features a "Coffee Wrap Clutch" ($24.95) for sale that was made in Guatemala out of recycled coffee bags. None of these products is made by the wives of cooperative members. It is understandable that this corporation, which is routinely celebrated for its commitment to environmental and social responsibility, has chosen to spread its wealth and business investments across a variety of impoverished Guatemalan communities rather than supporting one lone cooperative. However, this means that, like their other efforts, the female cooperative members' attempts to cultivate these market relationships are failing.

Conclusion

It is not necessarily the aim of the fair trade movement to offer handouts, whether in the form of financial donations or market opportunities, to producers. Rather, the movement aims to provide producers with the skills, information, and contacts necessary for them to locate and maintain their own market opportunities. In this case, it is clear that fair trade is providing these things to male cooperative members but not to their female counterparts. The women's attempts to locate a market of their own have been thwarted by their lack of language skills, discomfort in speaking with foreigners, and unfamiliarity with business administration norms. Fair trade could help promote gender equity in certified cooperatives by providing more specific guidelines for training and skill development.

Furthermore, if fair trade certifiers were to adopt a participatory social auditing model, which places emphasis on the involvement of workers and workers' organizations in the process of code implementation and assessment (Auret and Barrientos 2006), they would be better able to identify the specific needs of male *and* female cooperative members and perhaps work with organizations to set locally appropriate goals for gender equity (Lyon 2008a). Participatory social auditing works to develop partnerships between different actors (such as management, members, and auditors) and a locally suitable approach to improving conditions and promoting gender sensitivity. Snapshot audits tend to focus on formal management compliance rather than helping to support genuine improvement. As a result, they tend to pick up visible issues, such as health and safety, but often fail to pick up issues that are not easily verified, and they are often insensitive to issues of concern to women workers (Auret and Barrientos 2006).

A participatory form of social auditing would help ensure the promotion of gender equity within the fair trade coffee movement and would substantially improve the effectiveness of the existing certification standards. A simple first step would be to require certifiers to speak to a broad range of cooperative members and their wives (since fair trade certifies family farms, not individuals). By speaking to women, certifiers could easily ascertain that women have in fact never served on the board of directors or filled a managerial position at the cooperative. The discussions could be used to identify women's needs, such as a market of their own and more equality, and help pinpoint ways to attain these goals.

This chapter raises a critical issue facing the fair trade movement, which is currently grappling with the role of women in producer communities: what these women want most is a market for their products. They are not pursuing an abstract notion of gender equity that mirrors the concerns and goals of Northern consumers; rather, they are seeking to improve their well-being through locally appropriate channels. As the chapters in this volume demonstrate (especially those by Moberg, Besky, and Dolan), gender roles are socially and culturally determined, and therefore they vary radically among the communities participating in fair trade networks. This reality poses a challenge to the fair trade movement, which, as this chapter argues, needs to develop a gender-sensitive approach that is flexible enough to accommodate highly variable local contexts and yet strict enough to effect real change.

NOTES

1. This research was generously funded by the University of Kentucky Summer Faculty Research Fellowship, the Wenner-Gren Foundation for Anthropological Research, and Fulbright-Hayes. I thank Mark Moberg and four anonymous reviewers for their comments during the revising process.

2. All subjects are identified with pseudonyms.

3. http://www.greenmountaincoffee.com/Accessories/Coffee-Wrap-Purses, accessed June 16, 2008.

WORKS CITED

Allison, M.
  2006 A Cup o' Joe That's Making a Difference. Seattle Times, August 12. Available through TransFair USA, Fair Trade News, http://www.transfairusa.org/content/about/n_060812.php.
Auret, D., and S. Barrientos
  2006 Participatory Social Auditing: Developing a Worker-Focused Approach. *In* Ethical Sourcing in the Global Food System. S. Barrientos and C. Dolan, eds. Pp. 129–148. London: Earthscan.

Bartra, E.

2003 Engendering Clay: Women Potters of Mata Ortiz. *In* Crafting Gender: Women and Folk Art in Latin America and the Caribbean E. Bartra, ed. Pp. 125–157. Durham, NC: Duke University Press.

Cohen, J.

2000 Textile Production in Rural Mexico: The Complexities of the Global Market for Handmade Crafts. *In* Artisans and Cooperatives: Developing Alternative Trade for the Global Economy. K. Grimes and L. Milgram, eds. Pp. 129–142. Tucson: University of Arizona Press.

Eber, C.

2000 That They Will Be in the Middle, Lord: Women, Weaving and Cultural Survival in Highland Chiapas, Mexico. *In* Artisans and Cooperatives: Developing Alternative Trade for the Global Economy. K. Grimes and L. Milgram, eds. Pp. 45–64. Tucson: University of Arizona Press.

Eber, C., and B. Rosenbaum

1993 "That We May Serve Beneath Your Hands and Feet": Women Weavers in Highland Chiapas, Mexico. *In* Crafts in the World Market: The Impact of Global Exchange on Middle American Artisans. J. Nash, ed. Pp. 155–180. Albany: State University of New York Press.

Ehlers, T.

1993 Belts, Business, and Bloomingdale's: An Alternative Model for Guatemalan Artisan Development. *In* Crafts in the World Market: The Impact of Global Exchange on Middle American Artisans. J. Nash, ed. Pp. 181–198. Albany: State University of New York Press.

Fair Trade Labelling Organizations International (FLO)

2005 Fair Trade Labelling Organizations International Annual Report 2004–2005. Bonn, Germany: Fair Trade Labelling Organizations International.

2006 Explanatory Document for the Generic Fairtrade Standard for Small Farmers' Organizations. Bonn, Germany: Fairtrade Labelling Organizations International.

2007a Consultation Document: FLO Draft Generic Fairtrade Standard for Small Producers' Organizations. Bonn, Germany: Fairtrade Labelling Organizations International.

2007b Generic Fairtrade Standards for Smallholder Organizations. Bonn, Germany: Fair Trade Labelling Organizations International.

2008 www.fairtrade.net, accessed on June 25, 2008.

Fridell, G.

2007 Fair Trade Coffee: The Prospects and Pitfalls of Market-Driven Social Justice. Toronto: University of Toronto Press.

Goldin, L., B. Rosenbaum, and S. Eggleston

2006 Women's Participation in Non-Government Organizations: Implications for Poverty Reduction in Precarious Settlements of Guatemala City. City and Society 18(2): 260–287.

Grimes, K.

2000 Democratizing International Production and Trade: North American Alternative Trading Organizations. *In* Artisans and Cooperatives: Developing Alternative Trade for the Global Economy. K. Grimes and L. Milgram, eds. Pp. 11–24. Tucson: University of Arizona Press.

Hobsbawm, E.
  1992 Introduction: Inventing Traditions. *In* The Invention of Tradition. E. Hobsbawm and T. Ranger, eds. Pp. 1–14. Cambridge: Cambridge University Press.
Imhoff, D.
  1998 Artisans in the Global Bazaar. Whole Earth, Fall: 76–81.
Kuhlmann, M.
  2008 Call for Tender for the Development of a Training Approach to Improve Gender Competencies in Fairtrade Producer Support. http://www.fairtrade.net/fileadmin/user_upload/content/Tender_training.pdf.
Little, W.
  2004 Mayas in the Marketplace: Tourism, Globalization and Cultural Identity. Austin: University of Texas Press.
Lyon, S.
  2007 Maya Coffee Farmers and the Fair Trade Commodity Chain. Culture and Agriculture 29(2): 58–62.
  2008a We Want to Be Equal to Them: Fair Trade Coffee Certification and Gender Equity within Organizations. Human Organization 68(3): 258–268.
  2008b What Good Will Two More Trees Do? The Political Economy of Sustainable Coffee Certification, Local Livelihoods and Maya Identities. Landscape Research. 34(2): 223–240.
Macdonald, K.
  2007 Globalising Justice within Coffee Supply Chains? Fair Trade, Starbucks and the Transformation of Supply Chain Governance. Third World Quarterly 28: 793–812.
Mayoux, L.
  2001 Impact Assessment of Fair Trade and Ethical Enterprise Development. http://www.enterprise-impact.org.uk/pdf/IAofFairTrade.pdf.
Milgram, K.
  2000 Reorganizing Textile Production for the Global Market. *In* Artisans and Cooperatives: Developing Alternative Trade for the Global Economy. K. Grimes and L. Milgram, eds. Pp. 107–128. Tucson: University of Arizona Press.
Nash, J.
  1993a Introduction: Traditional Arts and Changing Markets in Middle America. *In* Crafts in the World Market: The Impact of Global Exchange on Middle American Artisans. J. Nash, ed. Pp. 1–24. Albany: State University of New York Press.
  1993b Maya Household Production in the World Market: The Potters of Amatenango del Valle, Chiapas. *In* Crafts in the World Market: The Impact of Global Exchange on Middle American Artisans. Pp. 127–154. Albany: State University of New York Press.
Nash, J., and N. Hopkins, eds.
  1976 Popular Participation in Social Change. The Hague: Moulton.
Olson, J.
  1999 Are Artesanal Cooperatives in Guatemala Unraveling? Human Organization 58(1): 54–67.

Redfern, A., and P. Snedker
    2002 Creating Market Opportunities for Small Enterprises: Experiences of the Fair
        Trade Movement. Seed Working Paper No. 30. Geneva: ILO.
Ronchi, L.
    2002 The Impact of Fair Trade Producers and Their Organisations: A Case Study with
        Coocafé in Costa Rica. Poverty Research Unit at Sussex Working Paper No. 11.
        Brighton, UK: University of Sussex.
Rosenbaum, B.
    2000 Of Women, Hope, and Angels. *In* Artisans and Cooperatives: Developing Al-
        ternative Trade for the Global Economy. K. Grimes and L. Milgram, eds. Pp.
        85–106. Tucson: University of Arizona Press.
Scrase, T.
    2003 Precarious Production: Globalisation and Artisan Labour in the Third World.
        Third World Quarterly 24(3): 449–461.
Shreck, A.
    2002 Just Bananas? Fair Trade Banana Production in the Dominican Republic. Inter-
        national Journal of Sociology of Agriculture and Food 10: 25–52.
Sick, D.
    1997 Coping with Crisis: Costa Rica Households and the International Coffee Market.
        Ethnology 36: 255–275.
Stephen, L.
    2005 Women's Weaving Cooperatives in Oaxaca: An Indigenous Response to Neolib-
        eralism. Critique of Anthropology 25(3): 253–278.
Tallontire, A.
    2000 Partnerships in Fair Trade: Reflections from a Case Study of Cafedirect. Devel-
        opment in Practice 10: 166–177.
Utting-Chamorro, K.
    2005 Does Fair Trade Make a Difference? The Case of Small Coffee Producers in
        Nicaragua. Development in Practice 15: 584–599.
Wach, H.
    2006 Gender Study for Fairtrade: Experiences and Recommendations on How to
        Promote Gender Equity through Fairtrade. Submitted to Fairtrade Labelling Or-
        ganizations International, Bonn, Germany.
Wilson, P.
    2003 Market Articulation and Poverty Eradication? Critical Reflection on Tourist-
        Oriented Craft Production in Amazonian Ecuador. *In* Here to Help: NGOs
        Combating Poverty in Latin America. R. Eversole, ed. Pp. 83–104. New York:
        M. E. Sharpe.

Fractured Ties

The Business of Development in Kenyan Fair Trade Tea

CATHERINE S. DOLAN

Introduction

I stand in one of Kenya's bustling marketplaces waiting for the fair trade representative.[1] In front of me a crowd of men is trading small bundles of the stimulant *miraa* while a discordant mix of hip hop emanates from the "miraa jcts"—the Toyota pickups that wait to ferry this "green gold" to Nairobi and beyond. It is October—the rainy season—and the mud-covered landscape does not present the town in its best light. As I watch the camels of Somali traders crush the layer of wrappers and chewed *miraa* stems that line the roads, the town strikes me as an odd host to Kenya's ethical tea industry.

I have come to this marketplace to begin my escorted tour of the Aruka[2] Fairtrade tea scheme. As we climb a serpentine, red clay road hedged with the plush green carpet of tea fields, we pass groups of women waiting at the buying center for their tea to be collected. Upon seeing them my escort is visibly pleased, informing me, "If everything could go to fair trade, I am telling you that this area would be like London. . . . I am telling you we would change the whole situation here" (interview, 11 October 2006). He is not alone in his zeal for fair trade. Many before him have borne witness to the transformative power of fair trade and the economic conversion made possible through direct exchange.

In recent years the idea that fair trade can alleviate poverty and economic injustice through a market-based form of solidarity exchange has gained traction in development and business circles. Much of the popularity of fair trade and its relationship to contemporary development initiatives, for instance, stems from its ethos as market-friendly, "bottom-up," poverty-reducing growth that positions the private sector rather than development aid as the means to rehabilitate producers caught in the throes of declining commodity prices. This chapter situates fair trade within this broader field of development, examining how "moral" exchange is managed, legitimated, and circumscribed by the prevailing development orthodoxy of market-based solutions. It advances two main arguments. First, it centers on the extent to which the key principles of the fair trade system—empowerment, partnership, and democratic participation—are realized among tea producers in Aruka, suggesting that while such ideals represent the trumpeted tenets of neoliberal development, their achievement is mediated by an array of conflicting interests, as social identities, development legacies, and local politics shape the extent to which fair trade achieves "redistributive" justice and for whom. Second, the chapter raises questions on why this privatization of development and the sociotechnical arrangements it entails reproduce the oft-criticized consequences of conventional development praxis, consequences that are becoming ever more pronounced as fair trade products[3] are mainstreamed, codified, and bureaucratized through corporate participation and globalized ethical and quality standards.

The Kenyan Tea Industry

Tea has long been a mainstay of the Kenyan economy and one of the most important contributors of foreign exchange. Since Kenya's independence in 1963, export volumes have expanded steadily, increasing from 15 million KG to over 345 million KG in 2007 (Embassy of the Republic of Kenya 2008). The country is now the largest exporter and third-largest producer (shared with Sri Lanka) of tea in the world, contributing 17 percent of the country's export earnings and employing over three million people both directly and indirectly (PKF Consulting 2005; African Research Bulletin 2007; Agritrade 2007). In contrast to other tea-producing countries, such as India (described by Besky in chapter 5 of this volume), smallholders play a significant role in Kenyan export production, with four hundred thousand independent growers accounting for 62 percent of the nation's output (van der Wal 2008; Oxfam 2002). All smallholder tea is processed (withered, crushed, fermented, and dried) at factories located near the point of production and marketed as black tea under the auspices of the Kenya Tea Development Agency Limited (KTDA), the largest single exporter of processed tea and the second-largest exporter of black tea in the world (Kinyili 2003; Oxfam 2002). KTDA was privatized in 2000 and now serves as a management agent for the fifty-six KTDA factory companies, purchasing, processing, and marketing tea for both domestic and export markets. Because privatization endowed smallholders with the legal ownership of KTDA's assets, including the factories, these farmers form cooperative structures and are considered as such for the purposes of fair trade.

The tea industry has confronted numerous challenges in recent years. Real primary-producer prices have fallen significantly over the past three decades, negatively affecting the livelihoods of plantation workers and small-scale farmers (van der Wal 2008). According to the World Bank, tea prices fell by 44 percent in real terms between 1970 and 2000, rising marginally between 2000 and 2004, only to fall to 2001 levels in 2005 (World Bank data cited by Agritrade 2007). While real prices for tea in Northern markets have remained stable, average real auction prices in the years 2000–2005 were roughly half those in the eighties and 30 percent lower than in the nineties (van der Wal 2008: 9).

At the same time, tea producers face the formidable market power of global buyers (Agritrade 2007). Ninety percent of the Western tea trade is controlled by seven multinational companies, and six reportedly account for two-thirds of the tea traded at the auction (van der Wal 2008). These companies dominate not only the most profitable activities in the tea commodity chain (blending, packing, and marketing) but the entire global market. Concentration is also pronounced at a retail level: in the United Kingdom, the third-largest tea importer in the world, the top-three packers currently enjoy a 60 percent share of the tea market (van der Wal 2008). These conditions have placed increasing pressures on producer countries to cut costs to remain competitive. As a result, smallholders, who are affected by poor infrastructure (electricity, roads, and water) and resource constraints (land and capital), have confronted declining prices, while wageworkers have experienced a downward spiral in working conditions on tea estates (Tallontire et al. 2001; Traidcraft 2007). It is this set of adverse conditions that fair trade in the tea sector aspires to redress.

The Business of Development

The emergence of fair trade certification parallels the broader paradigmatic shift toward market-friendly approaches to development that emerged in the 1990s as the social costs of structural adjustment came to the fore. The World Bank, the most influential purveyor of development strategy, moved away from the austere neoliberalism of the Washington Consensus toward the "kinder, gentler" development discourses of poverty reduction and social inclusion, reorienting its economic agenda toward market-friendly, poverty-reducing growth (Hart 2004). This approach to poverty reduction—growth in which poor people participate in both its creation and rewards—represented a promising union of free-market ideology and equitable ideals and put social issues back on the development agenda (Stern 2003: 6). It was also a framework that resonated strongly in the United Kingdom, where Africa's rise to the top of the nation's policy priorities was associated with an economic agenda that framed free-market ideals in the language of morality, ethics, and responsibility (Power 2009).

This context, in which development engagement was moving away from states and international financial institutions to the private sector, provided fertile ground for a growth in corporate social responsibility (CSR) initiatives. In contrast to earlier development approaches, CSR positioned business as the key development agent—the driver of economic growth and the steward of social welfare and labor rights—and spawned a wave of policies and programs to harness the forces of globalization to benefit the poor. It is within this framework that pro-poor business models such as bottom-of-the-pyramid (Prahalad and Hart 2002), social entrepreneurship (Dees 1998), microfinance (Leach and Sitaram 2002), and fair trade took root, moving away from a development "culture of dependency" to one of "self-reliance" (Eversole 2007).

Yet while the World Bank and IMF were promoting the merits of market-driven entrepreneurship, such initiatives were not created by the Smithian invisible hand of self-interest alone. Rather, international financial institutions whose "growth-plus-distribution" orientation found a promising vehicle in the marriage of smallholder development and private-sector growth were instrumental in guiding the market. For example, by presenting a financially viable model that could counter the economic as well as social exclusions of Southern producers, fair trade initiatives garnered significant support from development institutions that perceived fair trade as a new way to "solve" the problems of African economies. International development agencies such as the World Bank and the British Department for International Development (DFID) provided significant fiscal support of entrepreneurship opportunities among small-scale producers, including fair trade, with DFID alone awarding approximately £1.8 million in grants to the UK-based Fairtrade Foundation between 1999 and 2007 (Sidwell 2008). Through such backing, development institutions not only bestowed credibility on the private sector's role in poverty reduction but institutionalized their role as a trustee for development. Yet while trusteeship—the intent of one agent to develop the capacities of another—is no stranger to development interventions (Cowen and Shenton 1996), inculcating business with this responsibility opened the possibility for its norms and priorities—profit maximization, efficiency, and growth—to reconfigure development models. Today, as the following discussion of mainstreaming suggests, one strand of fair trade is mirroring and reproducing this architecture of development, casting ethics as commensurate with sales growth and market share.

Changing the Guard: Shifting Alignments in the Fair Trade Movement

Fair trade promotes an ethical vision that seeks to marry tangible financial rewards for developing-country producers with development outcomes such as empowerment, capacity building, and producer participation. Originally formed as a mechanism for humanitarian assistance, by the 1960s the fair trade movement, largely composed of faith-based, campaign, and community organizations (i.e., alternative trade organizations), had recast its mandate as "justice instead of charity," aiming to instill norms of fairness and equality into global exchange through the importation of handicrafts from marginalized producers and workers in the South (Low and Davenport 2005; Barratt-Brown 1993). In the late 1980s these disparate "self-governing and self-certifying" fair trade and alternative trade organizations (FTOs and ATOs) came together to form the International Fairtrade Association (IFAT), an institution accredited under international norms and obliged to adopt third-party certification (Renard 2005). By 2007, IFAT had grown to 330 members, drawn from seventy countries, that embody an organizational commitment to grassroots development and to marketing goods that are produced, imported, and/or distributed through "alternative" market channels (IFAT 2007).

In the 1990s, a second model, spearheaded by the Fairtrade Labelling Organizations International (FLO) was developed to expand the visibility and market access for fair trade goods through mainstream distribution channels (Bezençon and Blili 2006; Renard 2003). Spawned by the establishment of the first fair trade label, Max Havelaar, in 1988, FLO (through its National Initiatives) has become the worldwide standard-setting and certification organization for fair-trade-labeled products, codifying fair trade norms and ideals into a highly regulated certification system.

In contrast to the mission-driven ethos of ATOs, for which fair trade is "more than a market," FLO and its national affiliates are focused on building the business of fair trade, embracing corporate participation as a way to spread development benefits to more producers (Barrientos and Dolan 2006: 181; Raynolds 2009). Fair-trade-labeled commodities are now sold in twenty countries across Europe, North America, and Asia, with their sales in the United Kingdom topping £700 million in 2008 (Fairtrade Foundation 2009). Though not uncontested, corporate engagement has expanded rapidly and now accounts for a growing proportion of market share. Global giants such as Starbucks, Nestlé, McDonald's, and Sam's Club (Wal-Mart) now market fair-trade-certified goods, and in the United Kingdom the major multiples—the Co-op, Safeway, Tesco, and Sainsbury—have all moved into own-brand fair trade products.

The penetration of fair trade into mainstream food production and retailing raises several questions on the type of development the private sector is delivering to small producers and workers. Practitioners and academics suggest that mainstreaming allows companies to capitalize on the "halo effect" of ethical branding, positioning themselves as beneficent global citizens while engendering formidable new barriers to entry (standards, quality requirements, certification, etc.) that cleanse fair trade of its oppositional and transformative elements (Renard 2003; Low and Davenport 2006: 323; Dolan 2008). This "clean washing" assumes various forms, from corporate pursuits of "parallel production"—purchasing only a small proportion of products under fair-trade-certified terms while leaving conventional sourcing strategies intact (Ransom 2005; Mutersbaugh 2005: 398)[4]—to supermarket evasion of FLO licensing by outsourcing roasting, labeling, processing, and packing while wresting maximum price, delivery, and quality concessions from suppliers (Barrientos and Smith 2007).[5] Although the scale and scope of corporate commitment to fair trade can vary significantly (the UK-based Co-operative supermarket, for example, makes demonstrable commitments to fair trade markets and producers [Barrientos and Smith 2007]), the fact that large corporations are capturing increasing shares of the ethical market is raising questions as to who the true beneficiaries of fair trade are. Indeed, while fair trade once denoted a radical break "from the pressures imposed by profit-driven transnationals" (Fridell 2006: 12–13), the case of tea reveals the way in which fair trade can sustain rather than rework the prevailing structures of capitalism.

The Fair Trade Tea Industry

Tea is a relatively new addition to the fair trade portfolio. Although several corporate-responsibility initiatives have emerged in the sector over the past decade, for the most part efforts to institute responsible sourcing practices, such as the UK-based Ethical Tea Partnership and the Rainforest Alliance, have focused on the labor conditions of multinational plantations and tea factories.[6] Tea entered the fair trade market in 1993 when TransFair Germany certified its first tea plantation (Reed 2009), and within a year Clipper Tea had introduced the first certified tea for sale in the United Kingdom (Fairtrade Foundation 2008), spawning the development of a market that has grown steadily over the past ten years. The value of fair trade tea sales increased from £2 million to £30 million from 1998 to 2007, registering a 21 percent increase by volume and a 24 percent increase by estimated retail value from 2006 to 2007 (Fairtrade Foundation 2008).

The Kenya tea industry has capitalized on the growing European Union market for fair trade products. There are currently seventeen certified producer organizations in the country, which supply a number of international tea buyers including Finlays, Cafédirect, Vanrees, Ringtons, and Bettys and Taylors of Harrogate (Mburu 2008).

The case of tea is a fruitful lens through which to examine how the corporatization of fair trade is defining and circumscribing its development trajectory. First, though fair trade's founding principles were oriented toward small and marginalized producers and producer groups, the "product certification route" has included sourcing from larger commercial farms and/or "plantations." This was spearheaded by FLO's standard for banana certification in 1997, which included coverage of minimum labor standards for workers, and has been extended to other products, including bananas, orange juice, cut flowers, pineapples, mangos, plants, and tea. Yet while plantation certification extends the protections and opportunities of fair trade more broadly, ATOs have contested this move on the grounds that larger producers will further marginalize small-scale farmers and strengthen the competitive advantage of agribusiness, thereby reversing the gains of the alternative trade movement (Barrientos and Dolan 2006). As Rink Dickinson, president and cofounder of the ATO Equal Exchange, a U.S.-based company that is committed to buying only from farmer-run cooperatives, argues, "When large, conventional plantations get fair-trade certified for improving practices, we consider that 'fair-trade lite'" (quoted in Gogoi 2008).

Second, in contrast to conventional market channels, ATOs base exchanges on norms of trust, obligation, and long-term buyer commitments (Smith and Barrientos 2005). However, for the most part FLO-certified tea is traded through the conventional supply chains of global buyers, where normative business practices, rather than the ethical ideals of "partnership" and interdependence, structure buyer-supplier relations. For example, the majority (85 percent) of Kenyan tea is supplied to the Mombasa Tea Auction, the second-largest tea auction in the world, which handles the export of tea to over forty-five different market destinations. The auction is a site of short-term market transactions in which "middlemen" (e.g., brokers, agents, traders) mediate the trade between producers and consumers, appropriating value at various stages in the exchange process (Embassy of the Republic of Kenya 2008; Kariuki 2007; Kinyili 2003). While the auction provides producers with market access and potentially higher prices through open bidding, information flows between trading partners are minimized and transactions are fleeting (Vorley and Fox 2006). In contrast to the stable supply-chain relations advocated by fair trade, the auction allows buyers to enjoy flexibility in sourcing and avoid dependence on any one producer country or producer within one country (Oxfam 2002). An importer, for example, may supplement its supply by purchasing from noncertified plantations (as long as 50 percent of the blend derives from fair-trade-certified producers), switch between producers from purchase to purchase, or even buy tea from a certified fair trade plantation as noncertified tea (Bahra 2009). As a result, the auction model serves to consolidate if not deepen corporate power, rendering fair trade tea constitutive of rather than resistant to the prevailing capitalist logic. Thus, in the case of Kenyan tea, the primacy of a business paradigm in FLO's model of development is recasting the ATO covenant between rich and poor into an increasingly opaque encounter.

In the following sections, I examine how a development orthodoxy governed by market, managerialism, and the "institutional hardware" of neoliberalism—standards—are reconstituting the foundational principles and practices of fair trade in the Kenyan tea industry (Peck and Tickell 2002). The purpose of this analysis is not to render a judgment on the effectiveness of fair trade—whether it fulfills (or not) its stated claims—but rather to examine the effects of designating business as a trustee of development, and the interests that are advanced in doing so (Blowfield and Dolan 2008).

The discussion is based on an in-depth study of one KTDA fair-trade-certified factory, Aruka, which incorporates over ten thousand smallholders and two hundred wage employees in ethical production arrangements. All Aruka's tea is cultivated and processed in accordance with the fair trade standards established by FLO International and is subject to FLO's Generic Fairtrade standards for hired labor on large farms, plantations, and factories (FLO 2008), as well as its Generic Fairtrade Standards for Small Producers' Organizations (FLO 2009). Both sets of standards contain requirements for social, economic, and environmental development (e.g., minimum price, democracy, participation, transparency, nondiscrimination, environmental protection) and require adherence with national legislation. The standards for small producers' organizations also require that producers be small family farmers that are organized into independent, democratic associations (FLO 2009), while those for hired labor require that factories and estates comply with various ILO conventions (nondiscrimination, freedom of labor, freedom of association) (FLO 2008). Both workers and smallholders also receive a fair trade premium (€0.50/kg of export value for tea-bag cut, fannings, or crush, tear, and curl [CTC]) targeted for community and/or economic development projects such as boreholes, schools, and daycare facilities (Fairtrade Foundation 2006). Both sets of standards contain minimum requirements which all producers must meet from the moment they join fair trade and a set of progress requirements, which specify the areas in which companies will be expected to improve and in what time frame.

These standards prescribe, codify, and institutionalize the "fairness" of exchange and are the means through which fair trade is rendered legitimate in the eyes of consumers (Fourcade and Healy 2007). The values encoded in standards, for instance, are founded on moral universalism—what Smith (2000) describes as an "ethics of impartiality"—a system that holds that "if something's right for me, it's right for you; if it's wrong for you, it's wrong for me" (Chomsky quoted in Schivone 2007). As the fair trade and organic coffee company Café Campesino describes, "Café Campesino envisions a world in which all trade is based on the tenets of the Golden Rule, [providing] working women and men with equal opportunity, a fair price for the goods and services they produce, the ability to meet their basic needs, and a . . . dynamic future based on a respect for basic human rights, free enterprise and liberty" (Café Campesino 2009).

In the context of fair trade, the Golden Rule presumes that producers and workers face similar risks that can be addressed by the universal rights protections incorporated into standards (Smith 2000: 104). Yet while standards are underpinned by universal ethical values and framed as mechanisms of self-improvement, they are also sociotechnical tools that impose new systems of distinction in producer communities by demarcating the boundaries of ethics and responsibility (Rajak 2008).

The Enigma of the Fair Price

The leitmotif of fair trade is the provision of a minimum guaranteed price that covers the costs of sustainable production and ensures a living wage for growers. FLO standards require that "when the relevant market price (where it exists) or the negotiated price for a product is higher than the Fairtrade Minimum Price, then this higher price must be paid" (FLO 2007a: 5). As the key mechanism through which redistributive justice is secured, the minimum price is the signature element that provides producers the "clearest direct benefit" from their participation in fair trade schemes (Taylor et al. 2005). Yet because the certification of fair trade tea originated in the plantation sector, where the main ethical concern was labor conditions rather than the terms of the trading relationship, tea was originally exempt from FLO's minimum-price condition. Until 2008 all fair trade tea was sold at the standard market price (ranging from US$1.50 to US$2.50), whether at the auction or through direct sales (Kariuki 2007). While the minimum price is the principal vehicle through which fair trade achieves economic development, there are several reasons why it fails to do so among Kenyan tea producers. First, although Cafédirect (which purchases approximately one-quarter of Aruka's Fairtrade tea) introduced a minimum price in July 2007 (US$1.78 per kilogram), and FLO followed suit in February 2008 (US$1.40–US$1.50 per kilogram), both prices are lower than the market price Aruka producers fetch through the auction due to the superior quality of their tea.[7] Second, because the new minimum price is pegged to accommodate varying regional production costs (North India, Rwanda, and South India, for example, have minimum prices of US$2.00, US$1.70, and US$1.40, respectively), it inhibits the associational supply-chain relations that fair trade espouses, as it provides Northern retailers with an incentive to seek a lower-cost producer. In other words, the floor price is counterproductive if it encourages buyers to engage in promiscuous sourcing, seeking more attractive producer prices elsewhere (Blowfield and Dolan, forthcoming). Third, because producers have not experienced a change in tea prices, many are bitter that fair trade does not compensate them for their individual production. As one farmer noted, "Farmers want to be given money. They don't want to be told it is going to a school" (interview, 25 June 2007), referring to the development benefit of the social premium. Similarly, a local KTDA official asserted, "FLO should not talk about the premium. The premium is for the community. We should have something for the farmer and for the factory to maintain the business. . . . You could sell tea below the cost of production even though you are getting a premium. When the factory closes there will be no premium" (interview, 16 October 2006). While an "economy of affection" bounded by moral and kinship obligations is assumed to check the corrosive tendencies of self-interest (Hyden 1980), individual accumulation was, at least rhetorically, privileged. As one farmer noted,

> Those funds should not be taken to the community directly. Those funds should first be used to build for the farmers their homes or help the farmers at their homes before going out to the community. The reason I have for saying this is that something can't spread out before you as the owner receives it. . . . A farmer who doesn't have the fertilizer to put on the tea, and he is still waiting for those funds to build for them a school, if that farmer can't take care of their children as required, where will the community that will go to the school come from?. . . . If God would give me a chance to speak to the *Mzungu* [white person] like I am speaking to you, I would tell him, "Even if that money is there for the community, go back and think about us again. Let even a small percentage come directly to the farmers to uplift him." It's the same as taking a cow and milking it completely. When your cow gives birth and you milk that cow completely, you will make the calf for that cow completely weak. . . . You will sell it [the milk] and get money, but you have made the calf weak. Will you have cows again? It will die. So I take the farmers to be like that calf. They have been denied their rights as the calf has been denied its milk. (Interview, 16 July 2008)

This is not to suggest that the community did not welcome the construction of roads, schools, and health clinics provided through fair trade. The majority (80.2 percent) of smallholders believed that fair trade brought new development to the community, and approximately two-thirds (66.7 percent) claimed to have directly benefited from the community projects or knew other members of the community who had. Yet for some farmers this gratitude was crosscut with a sense of resentment. As one farmer claimed, sharing the social premium with their non-tea-growing neighbor was not right. "It is," he said, "like harvesting where you have not planted. When a class is built, both parties benefit, and a road all will walk on it. This is not fair to tea farmers," whom he perceived as the rightful beneficiaries of the social goods provided through fair trade (interview, 21 June 2007).

Participation and Democracy

Fair trade is founded on a relational ethic, aspiring to construct an emotional as well as material bridge between Northern consumers and Southern producers that embodies trust and mutual respect (Goodman 2004: 893; Wright 2004; Dolan 2007). This relational ethic, founded on principles of dialogue and equality, is wedded to a vision of producers as partners in market exchange, who have not only the right but the opportunity to participate in the key governance decisions of fair trade. Yet while participation is a lauded touchstone of fair trade and the key to FLO's public credibility, producer representation remains a challenge at both international and local levels. The FLO's thirteen-member board, for example, consists of four representatives from producer organizations, while its twenty-three member General Assembly includes only three.[8] This exclusion frustrated some Kenyan stakeholders:

> They [FLO] should involve us, they should involve me. . . . The other day I had sent an email to FLO because I was going through their website and . . . they had only put three factories [there] . . . and we have seven certified factories.[9] And I said, "You guys, you have seven factories, and you are the same people that certified these factories, and you did not put them on your website. . . . How do you expect us to get buyers?" Nobody replied. You tell them to give me a reply. . . . We are willing to participate in FT activities, but nobody ever invites us. . . . We are not asking for money, but we want to be part of it. We want to participate in it, talk about fair trade. (Interview, 25 June 2007).

At a "local" level, participation is construed as the vehicle through which producers will assume responsibility for their own improvement through the democratic structures of fair trade. For instance, FLO standards state that the producer organization must be an instrument for the social and economic development of the members, and the benefits of Fairtrade must reach the members. The organization must therefore have democratic structures in place and a transparent administration, enabling effective control by the members and the Board over the management of the organization, as well as enabling the members to hold the Board accountable for its activities. (2009: 7)

This standard—that producers will secure their own well-being through a governance structure of representative democracy (Macdonald 2007)—mirrors the broader shift in "development" practice away from top-down state solutions to community-led entrepreneurial initiatives. Yet the case of Aruka illustrates that the invocation of consultation and participation, what Rose terms governance through community (Rose 1996), raises a dilemma for how business engages with development concerns.

Fair trade conceptualizes poverty alleviation as an outcome that can be delivered through new sets of relationships, not only between buyers and sellers but through the formation of "responsible, autonomous, self-governing communities" (Li 2007: 241). In Aruka, there are several institutional structures through which fair trade's twelve thousand farmers (divided into six catchment areas) and approximately two hundred workers are represented. These include a workers' committee, buying center committees, a board of directors, and the social premium committee (SPC), the latter of which is the principal forum through which workers and producers are incorporated into the development process of fair trade. As a decentralized institution responsible for representing farmers in the allocation and monitoring of premium funds, the SPC operationalizes fair trade principles of participation, empowerment, and transparency. At the time of this research the SPC comprised fourteen representatives (two from each catchment and two worker representatives) elected by farmers and workers.

The legitimacy of the fair trade system requires that producers and workers participate in the governance processes of the SPC and that the decisions taken by the committee are "thoroughly understood and democratically approved" by them (Sexsmith 2008: 65). Thus, fair trade (in contrast to its sister "ethical trade") valorizes the means as much as the ends, as witnessed in the triad of dialogue, partnership, and participation. It is not, in the eyes of its acolytes, a top-down development initiative but rather a model that achieves producer empowerment through a process of democratic participation. At a minimum, this requires that producers are aware of and understand the objectives of fair trade. Yet as documented in other parts of the world (Shreck 2002; Lyon 2007), most farmers in this study (95 percent) misinterpreted the objectives of "fair trade," perceiving it not as a model of business partnership but as development "aid" in the form of schools and dispensaries funded through the social premium. As a KTDA official said, farmers "don't understand the fair trade concept but see it as a way to get schools free of charge. What the farmer understands is that they produce good tea, send it somewhere, and someone will come and build schools" (interview, 11 October 2006). Indeed most farmers were unaware that fair trade tea garners a higher price in European markets or that buyers purchased it for ethical reasons.

It is clear that the discursive rendering of fair trade that circulates in Northern consumption markets has relatively little purchase among tea producers. At one level the abstract knowledge that underwrites fair trade reflects the "moral genealogies" of Kenyan-UK relations (Mirowski 2001: 432; Dolan 2005), where a "history of caring" has flowed through missionary and development interventions aimed at the "moral and material improvement of distant subjects" (Trentmann 2007: 1080; Lester 2002: 377). This legacy forms a sociohistorical framework through which producers interpret the purpose and benefits conferred through fair trade. For example, while fair trade's moral entrepreneurship casts the marketplace rather than Northern charity as a way to rehabilitate producers, Aruka producers and workers described fair trade in the more familiar language of charitable giving—a gift donated by the benevolent "fair trade *mzungu*" (Dolan 2008).

While such perceptions render the commensurability of exchange somewhat problematic, it is also the case that many workers/producers did not participate in the forums where information on fair trade was disseminated (Dolan 2008). More than half (53.2 percent) of the farmers surveyed and over 95 percent of farmers in focus-group discussions never attended an annual general assembly meeting, and of the former, only 38.9 percent were able to describe the general assembly meeting with any degree of accuracy. As one fair trade auditor remarked,

> If you are working and you ask, "Do you understand what fair trade is?" . . . the sad thing is that more often than not the answer is no. . . . I am telling you everywhere where there is a company or an association of small farmers, if you are working and you ask, "Do you understand what fair trade

is?" some will say yes but will start mumbling when you ask what it is. They
don't have a clue. (Interview, 25 June 2007)

Indeed, while fair trade aims to instill new practices of self-government
that are transparent, participatory, and democratic (Li 2007), producer
involvement in the processes of the SPC was limited. While a significant
proportion of farmers were aware of the SPC and who represented them
(78.2 and 75.3 percent, respectively), only one-third of them (34.1 percent)
actually participated in project selection. One farmer, for example, said
that he neither elected the current representative to the SPC nor knew
that there was one until the fair trade *mzungu* informed him that he
should participate in the fair trade process. He said that he is like most
of the farmers in the area: they do not participate in the selection of the
community projects but rather just "see the project being carried [out]"
(Dolan 2008).

This disjuncture reflects two issues with how democracy and participation are actualized among producers. First, until 2008 voting for social-
premium projects was conducted publicly—through either raised hands
or queuing behind the proposed candidate/project to signal the voter's
preference. Yet openly selecting a development project in an area where
politics and patronage often influence access to resources inevitably
renders the more marginalized members of the community vulnerable
to the will of those with more power and prestige. Second, despite the
fact that FLO states, "You know what you need; you need to make the
choice" (FLO 2007b: 6) and "the best way to find out what is needed in
any organization or community is to talk with the members" (FLO 2006),
FLO also shapes community desires by specifying the parameters for legitimate projects (cf. Li 2007). As a former member of the SPC noted,
"The people from FLO gave us advice and said we should be building
mostly the schools; we should not be constructing things like dispensaries. But we told them these are the community's ideas" (interview, 15 July
2008). Several producers noted that the use of social-premium funds to
construct the road to the tea factory "brought problems," as it was not
the type of project that FLO endorsed, claiming that producers "should
be requesting such kind of things before doing them" (interview, 15 July
2008). This suggests the extent to which African producers and workers
have accepted rather than defined what constitutes an ethical benefit and
the way fair trade may, if even inadvertently, recuperate certain imperial
tendencies.

Drawing a Line in the Sand: The Boundaries · of Moral Consideration

It is not only certain projects that are designated as morally creditable but also producers themselves, as fair trade standards confine their regulatory purview to certain actors, rendering them distinct from those who fall beyond their sphere of obligation (Rajak 2008). For example, the parameters of "responsibility" extend to beneficiaries who are "marginalized," but not so much so that they are unable to invest in the resources necessary to meet the quality standards of Western consumers. As Mutersbaugh's (2002) study of organic coffee producers in Oaxaca, Mexico, demonstrated, standards carve out new forms of distinction and uneven development in rural economies, differentiating between those communities and households that possess the resources to engage in certified agriculture and those that do not (Dolan, in press).[10]

Indeed, as mainstreaming raises the quality bar for participation in supply chains, standards impose a new form of "conditionality" on market entry, eclipsing "some of the poorest and least 'connected' farmers and cooperatives" (Goodman 2007: 1). As a former KTDA official revealed, standards bequeath substantial power to those who control them (Renard 2005):

> These things [standards] come as a condition. Now they have brought in issues to do with mental things [ethics] which are extremely expensive to implement, and they have absolutely nothing to do with even the product they are getting. They will not change the quality or anything. . . . It is just brought in as a condition for certification. . . . So basically the total implication of that is that you are making . . . tea production extremely expensive, and you plough back nothing. What we are saying, I wish for a price differential for that [effort]. For us, there is nothing. (Interview, 20 June 2007)

Notwithstanding standards' potential to create entry barriers to the fair trade market, complying with them can entail rather significant changes to the production processes, work regimens, and daily lives of producers (Blowfield and Dolan 2008; Lyon 2007). Standards thus epitomize what Latour (1987) refers to as "immutable mobiles," objects that circulate across societies without changing form yet possess the power to transform the sites in which they touch down. In the case of fair trade these immutable mobiles generate a tension between the principles of social justice that they seek to emplace and the impersonal and often paternalistic experience that they can create (Dolan, in press).

Who is included in the "community" is thus mediated by the broader political economy of consumption and the certification requirements of social, environmental, and quality standards, which privilege a particular categorization of beneficiary (Blowfield and Dolan 2008). But inclusion is also determined by prevailing socioeconomic relations and the cultural norms, social hierarchies, and gender conventions that shape the extent to which fair trade achieves "redistributive" justice and for whom. For example, even while fair trade aspires to reform gender relations, stipulating that there "must be no discrimination regarding participation, voting rights, the right to be elected," and so on, in the organization (FLO 2009: 9), women remain "invisible" to its "exercise of responsibility" (cf. Rajak 2008; Lyon 2008), constituting 0 to 27 percent of local decision-making structures. This exclusion is manifest in the awareness and understanding that women in the region have of fair trade, with more men than women aware of the existence of the SPC, better able to describe its purpose, and more likely to know their representatives. Men were also more than twice as likely as women (53.8 percent to 19.9 percent) to participate in the process of project selection.

Yet it is not only women's marginality in organizational structures that impedes their participation in customarily "male spheres." As in the Guatemalan case described by Lyon (chap. 6, this volume), among Kenyan tea producers intrahousehold relations, and particularly customary norms of gendered rights and responsibilities, have a considerable impact on the distributional effects of fair trade and its capacity to deliver gender equity for smallholders. In most households in the study, the labor process is governed by social norms that define work allocation by gender, with women and children performing the most labor-intensive tasks such as weeding and tea plucking. At the same time "nonmarket" responsibilities such as childcare and domestic labor are borne predominantly by women, with the majority (78.1 percent) claiming that these responsibilities negatively affected their income-earning options. These time constraints limit women's capacity to serve on committees (SPC, workers' committee, board of directors) or to attend Annual General Meetings (AGMs) and other forums where information about fair trade is typically disseminated and discussed: only 7 of the 240 registered women attended the AGM in June 2007.

Similarly, access to land mediates the benefits of fair trade, not only because you need land to cultivate tea but because participation in KTDA and fair trade governance structures is restricted to those who possess a tea registration number. Those without a registration number cannot receive payment for tea and are excluded from voting for the board of directors or the Social Premium Committee, a situation that disenfranchises the resource-poor and particularly women, who while legally entitled to own land, are socially constrained from doing so. As the manager at one KTDA factory said, "Women are actually the farmers in African culture, but you can't register all these women. What if a man has several wives, then what are you going to do? It could be a problem to give one wife a right to vote" (interview, 12 October 2008). Women, who constitute less than 20 percent Aruka's twelve thousand registered smallholders, are thus not granted legitimate stakeholder status: they are excluded from the main institutional channels through which empowerment is potentially fostered, and their claim to the benefits of fair trade are mediated by husbands, brothers, and sons. The fact that standards are premised on the notion of an ungendered, generic family farmer not only is "a disservice to the female members of producer households" (Lyon 2008: 264) but also points to how fair trade can overlook "the practices through which one social group impoverishes another" (Li 2007: 7).

This gap between what FLO considers a worthy development benefit and the perceptions of producers resembles an established, if oft-maligned, feature of conventional development practice, in which a priori formulations are delivered by benefactors who determine "who can speak, from what points of view, with what authority, and according to what criteria of expertise" (Escobar 1997: 87). Yet while this may be an accurate, if not often witnessed, truth, it also depoliticizes the social and political relations within producer communities and allows the political conflicts inherent in them to slide from view. But as the following case of the SPC illustrates, the ways in which these encounters unfold are also shaped and constrained by political and institutional dynamics in the South.

The Politicization of Fair Trade

As noted, fair trade standards stipulate that producers are organized into democratic associations that elect community representatives to the SPC (which oversees the allocation and monitoring of premium funds) and participate in deciding how the premium is spent. The SPC therefore constitutes the platform through which the principles of "empowerment," "participation," and "partnership" are actualized. In Aruka, however, the composition of the SPC fueled a fractious debate over who can claim the authority to serve as the legitimate representatives of marginalized smallholders and workers.

Because tea is a hybrid model (comprising both plantation workers and smallholders), the constitution of the SPC reflects both the criteria for the Joint Body in hired-labor situations (in which worker and management representatives are responsible for "jointly" managing the premium) (FLO 2007b), as well as those for farmers in which a democratically elected producer organization manages the premium. Following the initial certification of Aruka, FLO initiated a model of the SPC that reflected both these systems—a committee composed of farmer representatives from each of the six catchment areas, as well as worker and management representatives. At the same time, however, a democratically elected body of representatives had long existed in Aruka, as each catchment area elects a director to form the factory board of directors. Although the decision to institute a new structure reflected the international standard for FLO-certified producer organizations, it nonetheless created an unwelcome situation in which two parallel bodies were charged with representing Aruka's smallholders. The KTDA vehemently opposed the composition of the SPC, claiming that FLO was colonizing the "bona fide" structure of farmer representation. As a KTDA manager explained,

> The way that it came was that FLO didn't want to have anything to do with KTDA, [but] . . . this thing of coming to the factory and now setting a fair trade premium committee . . . outside the conventional leadership within the factory became a terrible problem. Because at the factory level, the factory is more or less cooperative based. . . . Now when you come with fair trade and you now tell them to make another body at the same factory— that is highly political. . . . And if the condition is to have a body which is democratically elected, then the sitting board members are democratically elected. (Interview, 20 June 2007)

At the same time, the relationship between the SPC and the board of directors deteriorated into one of frequent recriminations. The KTDA, for example, accused the SPC of using its privileged connections with Europeans to wreak political and economic gain. According to a KTDA manager, the social premium is a "cash cow" whose members acquire "political might" because they are able to dispense funds and therefore curry patronage. It is, he said, a stepping-stone for becoming an MP, a ladder for political ambitions. Whereas the KTDA board members were looking after farmers and their families, the SPC members were giving themselves FLO allowances to visit projects and attend NGO meetings in the swanky hotels of Uganda and Ghana. By contrast, many farmers and NGOs were antagonistic toward the board, which they perceived as corrupt and self-serving, and attributed the recent development in the community to the current SPC, benefits that would have filled the "stomachs" of the board members if they were controlling funds (Dolan 2008).

While the spoils of development are frequently a loadstone for frictions surrounding wealth, opportunity, and political power, the tension catalyzed by the composition of the SPC exacted a high price on fair trade in Aruka, contributing to a nine-month suspension by FLO. Although interpretations of this dismantling are many and clothed in insinuations of money laundering and clandestine meetings, the event nonetheless reveals how development practice and its invocations of empowerment, participation, and transparency can produce as much as diminish unequal power relations. Indeed, as the Aruka case reveals, even when fairness is formalized, rationalized, and managed through well-articulated criteria, what is deemed moral is inflected by the politics and histories of place. This is most evident in the social drama that marked the final days of the SPC, an unexpected turn of events that mired the promise of smallholder revitalization posited by fair trade.

After years of wrangling, the KTDA and the board of directors decided the time was ripe to remove the SPC from office. However, because farmers had democratically elected the SPC members and considered them to be their legitimate representatives, any KTDA-sponsored action would be met with resistance. The KTDA therefore co-opted the Buying Center Committee to summon a meeting to disband the SPC. While the KTDA states that the SPC members were invited to the meeting, the SPC members deny this, claiming that if not for friends and kin, they would have remained unaware of the committee's dissolution. Nonetheless, at the meeting the Buying Center Committee informed members that SPC members were engaged in corruption, bribery, and misallocation of funds and offered them a Faustian bargain: either remove the SPC they had elected or the *mzungu* will go. The choice was an illegitimate one, as FLO regulations stipulate that such decisions must be confined to the AGM and are the prerogative of farmers, not the Buying Center Committee. Yet the AGM that the KTDA subsequently called was also deemed illegitimate, as the SPC and not the KTDA has the right to call an AGM. This incited the SPC chairman to submit a (successful) court injunction to block the AGM, which was subsequently "illegally" held. From this point on, the "facts" of this situation are clouded by allegations of surreptitious meetings, illicit voting processes, and subsequent court orders; however, the outcome is clear: the SPC members were removed from office.

Such stories can be interpreted as clichéd evidence of Africa's reputed corruption, where elites impoverish their neighbors by plundering community resources and embezzling aid funds. However, such an analysis hinges the possibilities of fair trade to the particularities of place. But the neoliberal political economy in which Aruka producers are embedded is not unique; most of fair trade's intended beneficiaries inhabit regions similarly riven by constrained possibilities, where access to development resources are inevitably perceived as a route to economic accumulation. In fact, whether and how fair trade can be sustainable in contexts where states are fiscally crippled by years of structural adjustment, privatization, and associated neoliberal policies is a critical question (Dolan 2008). For example, when I visited the schools, dispensaries, and clinics funded through the social premium, I witnessed the visible benefits of fair trade. Yet in several instances a well-constructed school laid vacant and the shelves of the dispensary bare. As one farmer noted, there are many "projects that have been constructed which are very beautiful. But these projects are not in use. They are just buildings with no use" (interview, 15 July 2008). When I inquired why this was so, I was informed that the government was unable to provide resources for staff and supplies, a situation that created a landscape of "white elephants."

This, of course, is a recognizable picture of development's "failed plotline" (Ferguson 1994), in which many good initiatives have gone sour in the wake of donor departure. While donors' presence in Aruka can hardly be attributed to fair trade alone, the uncoupling of social-premium projects from the institutional context required to sustain them reproduces a compartmentalized view of development, one in which the technical is unmoored from social and political context. As one farmer advised, "The projects should not only be funded by fair trade, because fair trade should only do the projects it can sustain by itself. Like the dispensaries . . . fair trade can't employ doctors and medicine every time" (interview, 7 July 2008). Indeed, the number of projects that fell by the wayside in the absence of state support raises the question of whether a market-driven ethics of care can be expected to deliver a *sustainable* public good. As this study shows, privatizing development through fair trade initiatives may bring certain actors and geographies into the emancipatory embrace of the market, but it leaves others, including national governments, peripheral to fair trade's exercise of responsibility (Rajak 2008).

Conclusion

Fair trade initiatives are promoted as a way to rectify global inequalities and create ethical North-South trading relations through worker empowerment and poverty alleviation. While its form of entrepreneurial developmentalism has enjoyed widespread success in Northern consumer markets, there is growing evidence that clear discrepancies exist between the discourse of "dialogue, transparency, and respect" and conditions that "beneficiaries" experience at the point of production. At one level, this disjuncture reflects the specificities of context and the way divergent histories, institutions, norms, and global interconnections inform the way that fair trade is articulated, actualized, and experienced. At another level, however, it reveals the way that fair trade increasingly pursues development through technologies of certification and corporate supply chains that render the process of exchange an increasingly abstract and virtual encounter for producers. Indeed, although certification authenticates fair trade's moral claim, enabling producers to command a price premium and providing consumers with the confidence that the products they buy have been produced ethically, it is also a regulatory technology that identifies, manages, and packages information on producers to ensure adherence with universal norms, a mode of governance that has implications for the nature of fair trade's relational aspirations (Dolan, in press). Indeed, the bureaucratic processes through which the meanings and experiences of fair trade are produced, conveyed, and validated may not only inhibit but jeopardize the moral contract that the movement seeks to create.

Although fair trade emerged as an alternative development strategy (trade, not aid), its capacity to transform international trade radically may be increasingly remote. With its technologies of market governance (standards, auditing, and certification) and the ever-expanding participation of global retailers and branded manufacturers, it is no longer the alternative trade movement but rather global business that is defining and purveying the meanings and practices of economic development. Indeed, as this chapter has shown, the processes that characterize the exchange of fair trade tea reflect less the inclusionary liberalism of empowerment and participation than the broader moral project of global capitalism, a project that universalizes particular economic, political, social, and ethical norms through the seemingly oppositional strategies of affect and calculation (cf. Blowfield and Dolan 2008). The material practices in the way that fair trade is organized, enacted, and governed, for example, are not only premised on the logics of neoliberalism, which hail the market as the primary means of realizing the public good, but are contingent on capital mobility, private property, and consumption itself (Fridell 2006), a normativity that is veiled by the "alternative" positioning of fair trade's moral claim. It is the symbolic force of this claim that renders the ideational roots of this political economy both unnoticed and unexamined and construes any deficiencies in fair trade as technical rather than as related to the structural and ideological dimensions of neoliberalism that underpin it.

Although fair trade's market-driven ethics of care invokes a moral pluralism, it also operates through a set of practices and discourses that ensure that specific interests hold sway and gain legitimacy in the process of moral exchange. Fair trade standards, for example, legitimize certain norms, identities, and institutions and marginalize others, while systems of patronage and political alliance mediate and circumscribe its development potentialities. The point, however, is not only that fair trade may misconstrue or ignore the experience and subjectivity of African farmers. Rather, it is to question how the power inculcated in a neoliberal, market-driven form of development frames and shapes development outcomes, and in particular, under what terms, by whom, and to what effect such power is exercised. Understanding these processes and their implications for Southern producers is ever more important as business extends its powers as arbiter and steward of development and international justice.

NOTES

1. I thank the National Science Foundation (Grant #0548997) for their generous support of this research.

2. Aruka is a pseudonym.

3. The arguments raised in this chapter refer only to those fair trade products certified by FLO.

4. Compare, for instance, Equal Exchange, a 100 percent fair trade coffee company, to Nestlé's "Partner's Blend," for which fair trade constitutes less than one-tenth of 1 percent of the total volume of coffee (Bacon 2005).

5. Under existing FLO rules, national labeling initiatives such as the UK Fairtrade

Foundation may allow supermarkets the right to include the fair trade logo on their own-brand products without the supermarket itself being licensed by FLO as long as products are sourced from the FLO register of licensed importers (Barrientos and Dolan 2006; Raynolds et al. 2007).

6. Other prominent schemes such as Utz Certified, SAI (SA 8000), BSCI, and Global-GAP (formerly EurepGAP) are in the process of expanding into the tea sector, and the world's largest tea company, Unilever, has announced that all its tea will be certified to Rainforest Alliance standards by 2015 (van der Wal 2008).

7. For a description of Cafédirect's and FLO's minimum-price policy, see http://www. cafedirect.co.uk/pdf/press/2007_july_13_Caf%C3%A9direct_sets_new_standard_in_tea_ pricing.pdf   and   http://www.fairtrade.net/fileadmin/user_upload/content/2009/stan-dards/documents/June09_SOP_Development__of_Fairtrade_Prices_and_Premiums.pdf, respectively.

8. See   http://www.fairtrade.net/fileadmin/user_upload/content/Final_FLO_Gover-nance_Structure.jpg.

9. At present there are 15 Fairtrade-certified factories in Kenya.

10. The costs of FLO certification for a small producer group (between fifty and one hundred members), for example, are approximately €2,500 for initial certification, plus an annual inspection fee of €1,575, a not insignificant sum in countries such as Kenya where the average gross national income per capita hovers at about US$540 (approximately €385) per annum (FLO 2006; World Bank 2005).

WORKS CITED

Africa Research Bulletin
    2007 Burundi Tea. Africa Research Bulletin: Economic, Financial and Technical Series
        44(9): 17568B–17569A.
Agritrade
    2007 Tea: Executive Brief. February. http://agritrade.cta.int/en/content/view/full/2508.
Bacon, C.
    2005 Confronting the Coffee Crisis: Can Fair Trade, Organic, and Specialty Coffees
        Reduce Small-Scale Farmer Vulnerability in Northern Nicaragua? World Devel-
        opment 33: 497–511.
Bahra, P.
    2009 Tea Workers Still Waiting to Reap Fairtrade Benefits. Times Online, 2 January.
        http://www.timesonline.co.uk/tol/news/uk/article5429888.ece.
Barratt-Brown, M.
    1993 Fairtrade, Reform and Realities in the International Trading System. London:
        Zed Books.
Barrientos, S., and C. Dolan
    2006 Transformation of the Global Food System: Opportunities and Challenges for
        Fair and Ethical Trade. In Ethical Sourcing in the Global Food System. S. Bar-
        rientos and C. Dolan, eds. Pp. 1–33. London: Earthscan.
Barrientos, S., and S. Smith
    2007 Mainstreaming Fair Trade in Global Production Networks: Own Brand Fruit and
        Chocolate in UK Supermarkets. In Fair Trade: The Challenges of Transforming

Globalization. L. Raynolds, D. Murray, and J. Wilkinson, eds. Pp. 103–122. Abingdon, UK: Routledge.

Bezençon, V., and S. Blili

2006 Fairtrade Channels: Are We Killing the Romantics? International Journal of Environmental, Cultural, Economic and Social Sustainability 2(1): 87–196.

Blowfield, M., and C. Dolan

2008 Stewards of Virtue? The Ethical Dilemma of CSR in African Agriculture. Development and Change 39(1): 1–23.

Forthcoming Fairtrade Facts and Fancies: What Kenyan Fairtrade Tea Tells Us about Business's Role as Development Agent. Journal of Business Ethics.

Café Campesino

2009 About Us. http://www.cafecampesino.com/aboutus.asp, accessed 21 July 2009.

Cowen, M. P., and R. W. Shenton

2006 Doctrines of Development. London: Routledge.

Dees, J. G

1998 The Meaning of "Social Entrepreneurship." Comments and Suggestions Contributed from the Social Entrepreneurship Funders' Working Group, 6.

Dolan, C.

2005 Benevolent Intent: The Development Encounter in Kenya's Horticulture Industry. Journal of Asian and African Studies 40(6): 411–437.

2007 Market Affections: Moral Encounters with Kenyan Fairtrade Flowers. Ethnos 72(2): 239–261.

2008 The Mists of Development: Fairtrade in Kenyan Tea Fields. Globalizations 5(2): 1–14.

In press   Virtual Moralities: The Mainstreaming of Fairtrade in Kenyan Tea Fields. Geoforum.

Embassy of the Republic of Kenya, Beijing

2008 Overview of the Tea Industry. www.teaexpo.cn/macao/images/subject_2008001_02_04.ppt.

Escobar, A.

1997 The Making and Unmaking of the Third World through Development. In The Post-Development Reader. M. Rahnema and V. Bawtree, eds. Pp. 85–93. London: Zed Books.

Eversole, R.

2007 Making Us Marketable: Reframing Poverty through CED, Ethnodevelopment and Women's Microenterprise. International Journal of Business and Globalisation 1(3): 357–368.

Fairtrade Foundation

2006 Annual Report and Financial Statements. www.fairtrade.org.uk/downloads/pdf/accounts2006.pdf.

2008 Fairtrade Sales Reach Half a Billion Pounds. http://www.fairtrade.org.uk/press_office/press_releases_and_statements/feb_2008/fairtrade_fortnight_launch.aspx, accessed 25 January 2009.

2009 Fairtrade Flows against the Tide. http://www.fairtrade.org.uk/press_office/press_releases_and_statements/april_2009/fairtrade_flows_against_the_tide.aspx.

Ferguson, J.
  1994 The Anti-Politics Machine: Development. Depoliticization, and Bureaucratic Power in Lesotho. Minneapolis: University of Minnesota Press.
FLO
  2006 Explanatory Document for the Generic Fairtrade Standard for Small Farmers' Organisations. http://www.fairtrade.net/uploads/media/Explan_Doc_Small_Farmers_Mar_2006_EN_01.pdf.
  2007a Fairtrade Standards for Tea for Small Farmers' Organizations. http://www.fairtrade.net/fileadmin/user_upload/content/Tea_SF_Dec_07_EN.pdf.
  2007b FLO Training Manual 3.3, Joint Body Premium Project Management. http://www.fairtrade.net/fileadmin/user_upload/content/3.3_FLO_Training_Manual_Joint_Body_Premium_Project_Management_May_2007.pdf.
  2008 Generic Fairtrade Standards for Hired Labour. http://www.fairtrade.net/fileadmin/user_upload/content/Dec08_EN_Generic_Fairtrade_Sandard_HL.pdf.
  2009 Generic Fairtrade Standards for Small Producers' Organizations. http://www.fairtrade.net/fileadmin/user_upload/content/Jan09_EN_Generic_Fairtrade_Standards_SPO.pdf.
Fourcade, M., and K. Healy
  2007 Moral View of Market Society. Annual Review of Sociology 33: 285–311.
Fridell, G.
  2006 Fairtrade and the International Moral Economy: Within and Against the Market. In Global Citizenship and Environmental Justice. T. Shallcross and J. Robinson, eds. Pp. 81–94. Amsterdam: Rodopi.
Gogoi, P.
  2008 Is Fair Trade Becoming "Fair Trade Lite"? Business Week 18 (June).
Goodman, M.
  2004 Reading Fair Trade: Political Ecological Imaginary and the Moral Economy of Fair Trade Foods. Political Geography 23: 891–915.
  2007 "There's Not a Picture of a Smiling Farmer on the Front . . . That Scares Consumers": The Spectral Cultural Political Economies of Fair Trade in the UK. Paper presented to Democracy and Transparency in Certified and Ethical Commodity Networks conference, University of Kentucky, 12–13 October.
Hart, G.
  2004 Beyond Neoliberalism? Development Debates in Historical and Comparative Perspective. Paper presented to 50th Anniversary Conference Reviewing the First Decade of Development and Democracy in South Africa, Durban, South Africa, 21–22 October.
Hyden, G.
  1980 Beyond Ujamaa in Tanzania: Underdevelopment and Uncaptured Peasantry. London: Heinemann.
IFAT (International Fair Trade Association)
  2007 About IFAT. www.ifat.org.
Kariuki, S.
  2007 Kenya Tea Industry Performance Highlights (January–June 2007). Nairobi: Tea Board of Kenya.

Kinyili, J.
2003 Diagnostic Study of the Tea Industry in Kenya. Nairobi: Export Promotion Council.

Latour, B.
1987 Science in Action: How to Follow Scientists and Engineers through Society. Cambridge, MA: Harvard University Press.

Leach, F., and S. Sitaram
2002 Microfinance and Women's Empowerment: A Lesson from India. Development in Practice 12(5): 575–588.

Lester, A.
2002 Obtaining the "Due Observance of Justice": The Geographies of Colonial Humanitarianism. Environment and Planning D: Society and Space 20(3): 277–293.

Li, Tania
2007 The Will to Improve: Governmentality, Development, and the Practice of Politics. Durham, NC: Duke University Press.

Low, W., and E. Davenport
2005 Postcards from the Edge: Maintaining the "Alternative" Character of Fairtrade. Sustainable Development 13: 143–153.
2006 Mainstreaming Fairtrade: Adoption, Assimilation, Appropriation. Journal of Strategic Marketing 14: 315–327.

Lyon, S.
2007 Fair Trade Coffee and Human Rights in Guatemala. Journal of Consumer Policy 30: 241–261.
2008 We Want to Be Equal to Them: Fair Trade Coffee Certification and Gender Equity within Organizations. Human Organization 68(3): 258–268.

Macdonald, K.
2007 Globalising Justice within Coffee Supply Chains? Fair Trade, Starbucks and the Transformation of Supply Chain Governance. Third World Quarterly 28(4): 793–812.

Mburu, S.
2008 Kenya: Farmers Reap Benefits of Fair Trade Teas. Business Daily, 5 May. http://allafrica.com/stories/200805052010.html.

Mirowski, P.
2001 Refusing the Gift. *In* Postmodernism, Economics and Knowledge. S. Cullenberg, J. Amariglio, and D. Ruccio, eds. Pp. 431–458. London: Routledge.

Mutersbaugh, T.
2002 Ethical Trade and Certified Organic Coffee: Implications of Rules-Based Agricultural Product Certification for Mexican Producer Households and Villages. Transnational Law & Contemporary Problems 12(1): 89–108.
2005 Just-in-Space: Certified Rural Products, Labor of Quality, and Regulatory Spaces. Journal of Rural Studies 21: 389–402.

Oxfam
2002 The Tea Market—A Background Study. http://www.maketradefair.com/assets/english/TeaMarket.pdf.

PKF Consulting and International Research Network
   2005 Tea and Coffee Industry in Kenya in 2005. Nairobi: Export Processing Zones
        Authority (EPZA). http://www.epzakenya.com/UserFiles/File/Beverages.pdf.
Peck, J., and A. Tickell
   2002 Neoliberalizing Space. Antipode 34(3): 380–404.
Power, Marcus
   2009 The Commonwealth, "Development" and Post-colonial Responsibility. Geoforum
        40: 14–24.
Prahalad, C. K., and S. L. Hart
   2002 The Fortune at the Bottom of the Pyramid. Strategy and Business 26: 2–14.
Rajak, D.
   2008 In Good Company. D.Phil. thesis, Department of Anthropology, University of
        Sussex.
Ransom, David
   2005 Fairtrade for Sale: David Ransom Thinks Not. New Internationalist, April. http://
        findarticles.com/p/articles/mi_m0JQP/is_377/ai_n13801026.
Raynolds, L.
   2009 Mainstreaming Fairtrade Coffee: From Partnership to Traceability. World Devel-
        opment 37(6): 1083–1093.
Raynolds, L., Murray, D., and J. Wilkinson, eds.
   2007 Fair Trade: The Challenges of Transforming Globalization. Abingdon, UK:
        Routledge.
Reed, D.
   2009 What Do Corporations Have to Do with Fair Trade? Positive and Normative
        Analysis from a Value Chain Perspective. Journal of Business Ethics 86(3): 3–26.
Renard, M.
   2003 Fairtrade: Quality, Market and Conventions. Journal of Rural Studies 19: 87–96.
   2005 Quality Certification, Regulation and Power in Fairtrade. Journal of Rural
        Studies 21: 419–431.
Rose, N.
   1996 The Death of the Social? Re-figuring the Territory of Government. Economy and
        Society 25: 327–356.
Schivone, G. M.
   2007 An Interview with Noam Chomsky: On Responsibility, War Guilt and Intellectu-
        als. Counterpunch, 3 August. http://www.counterpunch.org/schivone08032007.
        html.
Sexsmith, K.
   2008 Power Relations in the Fair Trade Coffee Global Value Chain. M.Phil. thesis, De-
        partment of International Development, Oxford University.
Shreck, A.
   2002 Just Bananas? Fair Trade Banana Production in the Dominican Republic. Inter-
        national Journal of Sociology of Agriculture and Food 10(2): 13–23.
Sidwell, M.
   2008 Unfair Trade. Adam Smith Institute. http://www.adamsmith.org/publications/
        economics/unfair-trade-20080225961/, accessed October 14, 2009.

Smith, D.
2000 Moral Geographies in a World of Difference. Edinburgh: Edinburgh University Press.

Smith, S., and S. Barrientos
2005 Fair Trade and Ethical Trade: Are There Moves towards Convergence? Sustainable Development 12(3):190–198.

Stern, N.
2003 Public Policy for Growth and Poverty Reduction. Center for Economic Studies. CESifo Economics Studies 49(1): 5–25.

Tallontire, A., with M. Blowfield and E. Rentsendorj
2001 Ethical Consumers and Ethical Trade: A Review of Current Literature. Policy Series 12. Chatham, UK: National Resource Institute, University of Greenwich.

Taylor, P., D. Murray, and L. Raynolds
2005 Keeping Trade Fair: Governance Challenges in the Fair Trade Coffee Initiative. Sustainable Development 13: 199–208.

Traidcraft
2007 A Fair Cup: Towards Better Tea Buying. London: Traidcraft.

Trentmann, F.
2007 Before Fair Trade: Empire, Free Trade and the Moral Economies of Food in the Modern World. Environment and Planning D: Society and Space 25(6): 1079–1102.

van der Wal, Sanne
2008 Sustainability Issues in the Tea Sector: A Comparative Analysis of Six Leading Producing Countries. Amsterdam: Centre for Research on Multinational Corporations.

Vorley, B., and T. Fox
2006 Small Producers: Constraints and Challenges in the Global Food System. *In* Ethical Sourcing in the Global Food System. S. Barrientos and C. Dolan, eds. Pp. 163–177. London: Earthscan.

World Bank
2005 GNI Per Capita 2005, Atlas Method and PPP. http://siteresources.worldbank.org/ DATASTATISTICS/Resources/GNIPC05.pdf.

Wright, C.
2004 Consuming Lives, Consuming Landscapes: Interpreting Advertisements for Café-direct Coffees. Journal of International Development 16(5): 665–680.

Fair Trade Craft Production
and Indigenous Economies
Reflections on "Acceptable" Indigeneities

PATRICK C. WILSON

This chapter examines the links between European constructions of indigenous "Others" through catalogues of material practices, and the implications of these cultural understandings for the design and implementation of indigenous artisan fair trade projects.[1] The vast majority of research on fair trade, as well as the bulk of fair trade activities, is oriented toward production of foodstuffs, coffee and chocolate leading the list; but artisan fair trade is a growing, although less clearly defined and regulated, area within this trade niche. Artisan fair trade relies on ethnic difference as a marketing device, where the "cultural traditions" of indigenous peoples and other non-Western populations can be transformed into profitable enterprise through the sale of quintessential ethnic objects. As Eversole (2006) suggests, promoters of ethnodevelopment argue the beneficiaries to be small producers, who gain access to economic alternatives while validating local cultural traditions. In fact, case studies of Mexican artisans by Stephen (2005) and Nash (2001) demonstrate the potential of indigenous artisan production to lead to greater economic prosperity while also contributing to the social and economic empowerment of women.

Yet contrasting cases, such as those depicted by Eversole (2006), for a weaving cooperative in Bolivia, and Lyon (chap. 6, this volume), for Maya weavers in Guatemala, suggest that a range of factors may complicate the viability of these economic activities, including market knowledge; position within regional, national, and international market structures; inequities within communities; and problems of market saturation. These point to the vulnerability of artisans, even within fair trade enterprises (Scrase 2003; Lyon 2007; Smith 2007; Cohen 1998). As highlighted by Lyon and Moberg in the introduction to this volume, recent research (including several of the chapters included here) points to potential contradictions and challenges entailed in a model of fair trade that relies on consumer choice and posits market-based solutions to the many problems that neoliberalism poses to small producers. Further, the present and future potential of fair trade hinges on consumerism and consumer preferences, meaning that the livelihoods of producer groups is partly dependent on consumer whims (Fisher 2007; Lyon 2006b; Scrase 2003).

Social and environmental standards that producers must meet for fair trade certification raise another set of concerns.[2] Fairtrade Labelling Organizations International (FLO) and the World Fair Trade Organization (IFAT, previously the International Fair Trade Association), the two main fair trade certifying bodies, point to these requirements as mechanisms for ensuring that the moral standard backed by these trade initiatives are met in practice, and proponents argue that this defetishizes fair trade commodities by revealing the conditions of production and forging connections between producers and consumers, thereby convincing consumers of their ability to make a difference through the choices they make (Lyon 2006a). As M'Closkey illustrates (chap. 11, this volume), a central part of fair trade marketing for many fair trade stores is the presentation of producer profiles, which provide potential consumers with a sense of personal connection with the producer and evidence, of sorts, that the social and economic goals of fair trade are being met. These vignettes also adhere to at least two critical representational strategies: they establish the authenticity of the products (and therefore the fair trade organizations) by linking them to images of particular producers and by extension to the cultural traditions those producers are thought to represent; and they sanitize the socioeconomic conditions of producer communities by typically presenting portraits framed by an idyllic rural backdrop, reinforcing the notion that fair trade is addressing core problems producers face. Yet the dismantling of the social and economic barriers between producers and consumers is often elusive, as Dolan illustrates in chapter 7 in this volume. The Kenyan tea producers seemed to possess little understanding of the principles of fair trade or of the ultimate destination of their tea and the social composition of those who consume it. Here, fair trade standards were seen as being established from afar, with limited local input in the standards and uneven local participation in the development initiatives funded by the fair trade social premium.

These debates provide us with excellent vantage points from which to evaluate the impacts of alternative trade. Less examined, however, are the symbolic dimensions of fair trade encounters as mediated through the material objects produced, and the role of consumer expectations in shaping productive practices and producers' cultural identities. In this chapter, I am centrally concerned with the materiality of artisan fair trade, and what indexing indigenous peoples through a catalogue of material items might reveal about cultural assumptions driving this form of trade and its economic consequences. Further, and in keeping with recent research on NGOs and sustainable development, I examine how the organization and regulation of fair trade and other forms of "culturally appropriate" sustainable development—as well as indirect exposure to fair trade projects by indigenous communities outside of alternative trade networks— may contribute to the construction of "nongovernmental" practices of governmentality, by NGOs positioning themselves as "experts who know how others should live" (Li 2005: 384). I explore the relationships between materiality and indigeneity in handicraft fair trade production through the examination of a set of alternative trade organization (ATO) projects in Ecuador.[3] The handicraft projects and strategies used to market them reproduce central commonsense Western assumptions of indigeneity by reifying notions of community, the harmonious relationship between indigenous peoples and the environment, gendered complementarity, and particular narratives on history, tradition, and cultural purity, ultimately suggesting that there is an indexical relationship between handicraft items and indigenous peoples. Not only, however, does the marketing of fair trade and the organization of fair trade projects factor into the understandings that potential consumers come to hold of indigenous peoples, conceptualizations that are designed to motivate consumers to purchase fair trade goods, but they also have a ripple effect for indigenous organizations and indigenous peoples not incorporated into fair trade or other national or transnational artisan projects. It is here that ATOs may contribute to the local performance of globally constructed acceptable indigeneities, where the guidelines governing fair trade practices influence the organizational strategies of many indigenous groups, contributing to the solidification of normative forms of "indigenous behavior."

Artisan fair trade occupies a unique place in alternative trade practices precisely because of the explicit link commonly made between the handicrafts produced and the cultural identities of the producers. ATOs[4] frequently market artisan fair trade through visual images of "exotic Others" that point to the cultural distinctiveness between producer and consumer, and accompanying text that reinforces the important role fair trade plays in helping to maintain and valorize minority ethnic identities by supporting specific productive practices. The online fair trade textile shop Indigenous Designs, for example, defines its mission as "elevat[ing] artisans in the poorest regions of South America to world-renowned status in the handicraft textile market while preserving their rich cultural heritage" (2008), and Global Exchange (2008) lists first among its benefits of fair trade that it "values and preserves indigenous cultures." For consumers of indigenous artisan crafts, the products serve as "object lessons" (Mitchell 1989), contributing to a long, Western empiricist tradition that has privileged seeing as the pathway to knowing, and an accompanying tradition, emerging from a penchant that European colonizers had for collecting objects of the colonized, that contributed to categorizations of people in relation to their material possessions or practices (Thomas 1991; Cohn 1996). This is not to deny that material practices are closely tied to the construction of cultural identities (Colloredo-Mansfeld 1999; Appadurai 1986) but rather to illustrate the complexities and assumptions entailed in wedding the production of cultural identities in a simplified manner to productive practices. While, as Meskell suggests, "fabrication is all about making the world while making ourselves" (2005: 3), it has long been apparent that multiple agents are at work in the making of Selves and Others, illustrating the complexities of assigning singular authorship to material practices. In the case of transnational artisan fair trade, the construction of the "producer Self" is a result of multiple dialogic strands that include international and national NGOs, tourists, handicraft purchasers and exporters, and other artisans and community members. Whose identity, then, is actually being constructed through artisan craft production? And who, specifically, has the right to determine the nature and content of the cultural identities produced and displayed in material objects?

Recent research on indigenous craft production has illustrated the potential of these practices to contribute to greater degrees of cultural autonomy, defined in terms of a heightened sense of dignity, garnered through the capacity to sell crafts nationally and internationally (Nash 2001; Colloredo-Mansfeld 2003), yet the multiple actors that shape artisan crafts and the meanings attached to them lead to questions about representational autonomy. In fact, the inability of indigenous artisans to control representational forms and the meanings and interpretations attached to their products can potentially lead to disjunctures between local and nonlocal constructions of indigeneity. This is a point powerfully driven home in M'Closkey's contribution to this volume (chap. 11), in which she illustrates how the limited control that Navajo weavers possess over the appropriation and use of their designs has disempowered women weavers in both economic and sociocultural terms. Similarly, Lyon (chap. 6, this volume) demonstrates how attempts by Guatemalan Mayan weavers to employ natural dyes, possibly a response to the perception that foreign tourists would be drawn to the more environmentally sensitive techniques, confronted a purchasing public unwilling to pay higher prices for these goods and competing production techniques that undercut their prices. The imbalance in the dissemination of representational forms, then, can represent one of the greatest challenges to indigenous cultural sovereignty (Mihelich 2001).

ATOs and Constructing Indigeneity

Since the mid-1990s, the Quito-based ATO Sinchi Sacha has been involved in a range of indigenous handicraft projects funded internationally. In one such project, the ATO was subcontracted by Chemonics, Inc., as part of a large USAID-funded initiative focused on the sustainable management of indigenous territories in Ecuador's Amazon. Sinchi Sacha's specific role was to train Cofán and Huaorani project participants in artisan craft production and to stimulate ecotourism and the commercialization of artisan crafts. A second project, funded by the Cooperación Técnica Belga, was for the construction of an "ethnohistoric museum," called Mindalae, which was designed to promote the strengthening of indigenous cultural identities through the display of artisan crafts and their sale in an attached fair trade store. The two projects, from the vantage point of Sinchi Sacha, were integrative, as the fair trade store in the museum now sells the artisan crafts produced by Huaorani and Cofán artisans involved in the USAID project.

The organization of the store and the museum to which it pertains reveals the specific understanding of indigeneity that guides the projects' design and the methods of marketing indigenous handicrafts. The store meets fair trade standards by selling products produced in ways that promote environmental sustainability and women's social and economic empowerment (as many of the artisan craft activities target women specifically), and they match practices common in broader sustainable-development efforts by privileging the "community" as the basic unit of production. Global, stereotypical understandings of indigeneity are also reflected in and reinforced by these same fair trade standards followed by the ATO: constructions of indigenous communalism, ecological stewardship, and gendered complementarity are among the range of ordered imagery that inform popular North American and European constructions of indigeneity (Strong 1996). These same notions are foundational in edifices of knowledge about Amazonian indigenous peoples (Ramos 1998) that contribute to the formation of expectations that limit acceptable indigenous behavior, and these notions may become salient for assessing who is "really" indigenous in the first place (e.g., Sylvain 2002; Li 2000; Rogers 1996). Artisan craft production is one arena in which the range of acceptable indigeneities can be formulated through the meanings attached to these specific material practices that situate them as iconic evidence of authenticity.

The museum, Mindalae, was inaugurated December 1, 2006, with the mission of "transmitting the historical, cultural, and artistic knowledge and traditions of Ecuadorian artisans, and through this, contributing to the revalorization of these popular creative expressions" (Quito.com 2008). The design and organization of the museum is illustrative of the representational practices that contribute to specific understandings of indigeneity that are closely tied to particular material practices. The museum is housed within a large building, newly constructed in the "Mariscal" neighborhood in the tourist center of Quito and purportedly designed to resemble the pyramids found at the archaeological site of Cochasqui (Florencio Delgado, personal communication). The name is derived from *mindalá*, the term of reference for a class of politically sponsored traders under the Inka (Salomon 1987), but in its current context the role that mindaláes played in the pre-Columbian past in the mobilization of status goods used to cement political authority of elites is ignored in favor of a more generic understanding of mindaláes as merchants or traders.

The museum is organized over five floors intended to be viewed from top to bottom, with each floor dedicated to a particular theme: religious beliefs, ceramics and cotton, weaving, and Amazon worlds, with the fair trade gift shop and café located on the ground floor. Its displays are stylistically sleek, with darkened rooms and motion-sensor spotlights illuminating display cases as visitors enter the different exhibits and move from display to display. Aside from its aesthetic appeal, the museum lacks ethnohistorical or ethnographic detail, providing a vast array of archaeological and contemporary textiles, ceramics, and other handicrafts with almost no explanation or text. Objects, when labeled, are identified by name and region but not contextualized within broader social or economic practices of different societies, and there is no text that associates artisan crafts with sociocultural beliefs, except a small display that generi-cally discusses "indigenous cosmology" by reference to Canelos Kichwa ceramics (from Ecuador's Amazon region). In this display, again without reference to the cultural specificities of the Canelos pottery, accompany-ing text provides an interpretation of the significance of individual pieces. The text accompanying one piece is illustrative:

> Juri Juri Huarmi: Beautiful anthropomorphic figure. It was carried through the village by the men who pursued the Amasanga (shape-shifting forest spirit) but they decided not to kill her. Later back in the village, men be-gan to disappear. They discovered that she had a mouth on the nape of her neck, under her hair, and that she used that mouth to eat the men. There-fore, they killed her.

The failure to elucidate specific cultural traditions and situate material practices through their embeddedness in other aspects of social life is, ul-timately, a failure to embrace the meanings of materiality. By separating the material product from the producer, one is left with an impoverished understanding of the relationship between material goods, crafts or other-wise, and the context-specific production of cultural identity; this short-coming contributes to reductive interpretations of artisan craft produc-tion, where the crafts themselves can become representative of "a people" rather than being products of—and integrated in—specific webs of social relationships (Meskell 2005).

Gaitán Ammann (2006) examines the tensions of historical narratives in the Gold Museum of Bogotá, where the pinnacle of indigenous civi-lizations is pegged to pre-Columbian goldwork and is juxtaposed with a vision of contemporary indigenous peoples as corrupted victims of co-lonialism and capitalism. The main text accompanying the displays in Mindalae similarly paints a picture of history that confirms hegemonic Western constructions of indigeneity, reinforcing the tendency to portray desirable indigeneities as "pure" preconquest forms, those not polluted by colonialism and associated cultural change (read as cultural loss). The narrative of history presented here is of a golden preconquest age tempo-rarily interrupted by conquest and colonization, and now—thanks to the initiatives of ATOs such as Sinchi Sacha—a rebirth, a Pachakutic of sorts, where indigenous handicraft traditions are being recuperated thanks to the wave of culturally appropriate sustainable-development projects. For North American and European viewers, this matches commonsense' understandings of indigeneity in which the dehistoricizing of indigenous peoples is part of a metanarrative that contributes to their utility as figures that contrast with and serve as corrective measures to Western immorality and excesses (Friedman 1999); at the same time, the museum fits neatly within a long Latin American tradition of *indigenista* thought, with its internal debates about the relative merits or disadvantages associated with "racial" and cultural mixing, and the glorification of (and attempt, in fact, to re-create) uncontaminated Indians (de la Cadena 2000).

In Sinchi Sacha's work with USAID and Chemonics, Inc., it paid particular attention to the marketing of artisan crafts, contributing to the construction of artisan stores and small ethnographic museums in Amazonian urban centers in proximity to the territories of the indigenous protagonists of the projects. "Product communication" was a central component of this marketing process, and Sinchi Sacha designed ethnic logos that facilitated the identification of handicrafts with people. In fact, the name of the ethnic group became the "product line," whereby display banners, shopping bags, tags, and stickers would all bear the name of the ethnic group with its own stylistic font and accompanying imagery. Each ethnic group was also assigned a color—the Cofán green and the Huaorani red and black—that was used in the design of the aforementioned communication devices. The logo, in the case of the Cofán, uses leafy vegetation as the background image and emphasizes the "beautiful combination of the Cofán name with the forest" (Brito, Araya, and Galvan 2005), forging linkages between products, people, and nature. The Huaorani logo employs a spear in the design, an unfortunate choice, as it continues a long tradition of viewing this group as hostile and warlike and lends credence to assertions that the Huaorani are the "least civilized" of Ecuador's Amazonian peoples. In sum, the material representations of indigenous peoples through their handicrafts as seen in the ethnohistorical museum and the fair trade shop illustrate the capacity to assert an identifiable relationship between people and things, while extracting things, their uses, and by extension the people attached to them from cultural contexts of meaning making. As I suggest later, these practices may shape ATO and consumer judgments about indigenous peoples, frame the economic activities in which indigenous peoples engage, and have possible repercussions for some indigenous social-movement organizations, especially those that have coalesced around alternative forms of community development.

Development and Molding Indigenous Organizational Goals

One of the assumptions guiding fair trade is that the economic benefits entailed in fair trade projects will strengthen grassroots organizations, productive cooperatives, and indigenous federations. This suggestion is tied to the recognition of structural inequalities that have historically disadvantaged peasant and indigenous producers in Latin America and elsewhere; however, it also simplifies the pathway to empowerment by suggesting that economic opportunities will override more pervasive social inequalities fueled by enduring racisms and stigmatization within dominant social-class hierarchies. It also fails to explore how fair trade projects, as specific kinds of sustainable-development efforts, may be interpreted locally, and the impacts these projects may have on local and regional subaltern politics. There is potential, however, that valorization of cultural difference, and ethnic politics more generally, may provide strategies for progressive social-movement organizing. As Turner (2007) points out, despite the threats neoliberalism and the economic deregulation accompanying it represent for indigenous groups, the current context preserves the strategic relevance of ethnicity and racial difference by providing opportunities for political leverage through avenues of identity politics.

Yet it does not appear that all those who are labeled "indigenous" are equally able to benefit from these practices, leading to questions regarding the potential benefits identity politics offers all those who may participate in indigenous organizing. These limitations seem to be at work in the role that alternative development may play in empowering local producers. For example, the unevenness of NGO-sponsored development (Bebbington 2004), in terms of the spatial distribution of projects, access to project benefits, and varied project outcomes, suggests the need to examine the sociocultural context of development practice and how its cultural content may contribute to shaping local practices. Therefore, while individual cases can be put forward to decree alternative trade to be the pathway to empowerment for marginal groups or to condemn such trade as simply the latest in a long line of exploitative development practices, both extremes selectively ignore the nuances and contradictions of development encounters. If we are to take seriously Bebbington's observation about the unevenness of development and even move it beyond his original discussion, we need to examine the internal sociocultural constitution of producer organizations, thereby exposing the contours of fair trade and its uneven accessibility and distribution of benefits. This also points to the symbolic importance of performances of indigeneity in the ability of individuals and groups to gain the attention of fair trade organizations and favorably position themselves within fair trade market niches. In the end, growing economic disparities among producers, the exacerbation of class hierarchies within groups, contention within and competition among producer organizations, and marginalization of some producer groups or regions illustrate the multiple dimensions of economic differentiation that can result from these development interventions (Smith 2007; Scrase 2003; Colloredo-Mansfeld 1999). While the causes of these disparities are partly structural and related to market forces, they are also partly performative and in that sense outcomes of the deployment of strategic essentialisms in pursuit of economic goals.

In this section, I argue that, for the case of the Napo Kichwa of Ecuador's Amazon, the interactions between an indigenous federation and its member communities and a range of NGOs, ATOs, state agencies, and multinational corporations participating in "sustainable development" (some of which would be classified as fair trade, some of which would not) serve disciplinary roles by framing appropriate and inappropriate social and economic behavior of indigenous participants. Access to state or NGO resources and project funding has historically been contingent on indigenous organizations and their member communities pursuing economic agendas that meet external expectations. The certification requirements of fair trade represent yet another form of discipline to which indigenous groups respond in their strategic positionings; and the consistently disciplinarian logic governing development intervention over time illustrates the impossibility of disentangling fair trade from other development initiatives in the Amazon, as local understandings of fair trade initiatives are shaped by broader development trends in the region. Federation leaders and community members, in fact, rarely make sharp distinctions among the range of development actors, seeing state agencies, NGOs, and multinational corporations as all potential (yet fickle) sources of project funding (see also Lyon's contribution to this volume).

Since the formation in 1969 of FONAKIN, the primary Napo Kichwa indigenous organization, it has been keenly aware of the changing development terrain and has attempted to position itself strategically to benefit from the "development moment," in all its changing forms. Through relationships with state agents, NGOs, and ATOs, federation leaders and members have constructed forms of strategic, essentialized representations that seek to mirror the expectations of these different external agents;

although these do not determine the course of federation politics, they have influenced the particular forms and objectives they take. At the same time, only a tiny fraction of the federation's membership possesses the linguistic skills, cultural knowledge of these external agents, and even leisure time to become active participants in many of these development projects.

The Federation of Organizations of Kichwa Nationalities of Napo (FONAKIN) is the largest of the indigenous organizations in Napo Province, with roughly 150 member communities. In its early years, FONAKIN (at that time FOIN) focused its efforts on securing land title for its member communities and promoting economic development by seeking credits and loans for agro-pastoral projects, with cattle ranching and corn, rice, and cacao production topping the list of economic activities. These two goals (land titling and agricultural development) were joined through state policies implemented by Ecuador's Institute of Agrarian Reform and Colonization (IERAC), which made market-oriented productive practices preconditions for receiving official recognition for land claims. In the context of state-sponsored colonization of the Amazon, spurred along by road construction and the limited infrastructure provided by Texaco in conjunction with exploitation of its Amazonian oil fields, the requirements tied to land titling favored colonists who were typically Andean or coastal peasants accustomed to those economic practices more than were Amazonian indigenous peoples, whose economic activities were more commonly associated with small-scale horticulture, hunting, and gathering. In this setting, FONAKIN effectively positioned itself as a recipient of state-sponsored credits, while also benefiting from a small number of primarily religiously affiliated charity and agricultural-development NGOs, such as Pan Para el Mundo and CEDOC, that provided organizational training and support for the young federation and financed agricultural commercialization projects coordinated by the indigenous organization. FONAKIN's ability to attract agricultural credits, offer training workshops, forge contracts with agricultural exporters for the purchase of their member communities' products, and negotiate favorable terms with IERAC for the drawing of community boundaries and the titling of land was fundamental to its success in the early years. In fact, so successful were FONAKIN's efforts to establish legal title to land and promote agricultural commercialization that by the 1980s cattle ranching was a dominant economic feature of most of these communities (MacDonald 1999).

FONAKIN's promotion of cattle ranching and market agriculture and its attention to the importance of land titles for its member communities illustrate the ability of federation leaders to read the sociopolitical landscape accurately and to situate its organization and member communities advantageously within emerging policy frameworks. At the same time, these federation initiatives also contributed to state goals of "modernizing" the Amazon, by cementing indigenous communities spatially and orienting at least part of their economic activities toward productive practices for external markets, both of which implicated the federation in the pursuit of state goals of constructing legible geographies and associated socioeconomic practices. More generally, FONAKIN's actions point to how the federation, even from its earliest years, tied organizational objectives to community development and surveyed policy trends to determine how best to serve its members' interests given the development climate of the moment.

Promoting "Acceptable" Indigeneities

Issues of land tenure and agro-pastoral development dominated federation politics in its first fifteen years or so of existence (from 1969 to the mid-1980s), but since the 1980s, the federation has taken advantage of the NGO boom by becoming the primary interlocutor in the region between international and national NGOs promoting sustainable development and rainforest conservation and the indigenous communities that compose the federation and receive these projects. This shift in focus has ushered in a transformation in organizational goals, as well as members' changing perceptions of the federation itself. The federation, by the late 1980s, became active in the writing of project proposals and funding requests to an array of sustainable-development, conservation, and human-rights international NGOs, and the federation's archives reflect the growing rhetoric of ecological nobility that was a trademark of indigenous organizing in the Amazon during this period and that illustrates the strategic importance of global indigeneities for regional indigenous social movements. Yet, as Conklin (1997) and Ramos (1998), among others, suggest in their analyses of the closing gap between environmentalism and indigenous social movements, the expectations created through essentialized indigeneities ultimately expose indigenous leaders and their member communities to unrealistic scrutiny of their socioeconomic practices, with potentially harmful consequences for the durability of alliances between indigenous groups and international advocates, as well as the possible consequences that the erosion of these alliances might have for the indigenous movements themselves.

The scrutiny to which the federation was subject by NGOs was not lost on FONAKIN's leadership, which was keenly aware that the expectations to which NGOs held them were among the criteria used to assess where and with whom to implement development projects, and furthermore that these expectations were not static. This has led, in some cases, to the direct and indirect restructuring of indigenous organizations and their stated goals to match the prerequisites these NGOs have for project involvement. In fact, FONAKIN modified its institutional goals and organizational structure in such a manner, with the hope of increasing its attractiveness to international donor organizations. Responding to the predominance of sustainability in alternative development, the federation—and even individual member communities—began submitting funding proposals for ecotourism projects directly to national and international NGOs, illustrating awareness of the prominence of environmental conservation in global development ideologies and the capacity for Amazonian peoples to capitalize on it.

Similar observations can be made for the influence that "gendered" requirements in NGO development has had on indigenous organizations and communities. In the mid-1990s, for example, recognizing the growing tendency for grassroots development to target women and women's groups, FONAKIN established a Women's Group (Grupo de Mujeres) within the federation and opened a seat on the Federation's Executive for an elected official to serve as Women's Representative. Further, it encouraged its base communities to establish similar women's organizations in order to be competitive in attracting NGO projects, leading to the formation of these groups in many of the federation's base communities. A result was the growing centrality of women as protagonists in NGO-sponsored development projects in the region, mirroring the growing importance of gender in development theory and practice. Lyon (chap. 6, this volume) notes similar trends within fair trade agricultural projects.

In the mid-1990s, Sinchi Sacha began working closely with a second-tier member organization of FONAKIN, the Unión Huacamayos, on a set of sustainable-development projects oriented around women's production of handicrafts. The Unión Huacamayos, now largely dormant and disbanded, at that time represented eleven communities (all of which were also members of FONAKIN); the impetus for the formation of the Unión itself came from Sinchi Sacha and a conservation NGO, PROBONA. Sinchi Sacha's projects with the Unión trained women in ceramics production and encouraged them to focus attention on the production of other handicrafts: jewelry made from black, red, brown, and orange seeds collected from plants that grow locally; shigras (carrying bags woven from a fiber produced from tree bark and dyed with natural and artificial coloring); feathered crowns; and "typical" outfits used in cultural performances. These, as well as the ceramics, were to be sold in the gift shops forming part of the other Sinchi Sacha–Unión Huacamayos projects, including an ethnographic museum and an ecotourism lodge, and were also to be purchased by the NGO to sell in its large, indigenous-handicraft store in Quito. This store, Tianguez, is located in the heart of colonial Quito, on the ground floor of the San Francisco Cathedral, a prominent destination for tour groups and individual travelers (the fair trade store at Mindalae is Sinchi Sacha's second handicraft store). To promote women's participation in these activities, Sinchi Sacha encouraged the Unión to form women's groups in each of its member communities, which it did.

Sinchi Sacha's motivations for promoting women's participation in handicraft production related to rectifying gendered hierarchies in these communities by improving women's economic standing, the belief that women—as bearers of tradition—would preserve the cultural traditions inscribed in artistic practices, and the belief that women are more "rational" economizers than their male counterparts (see Wilson 2003a, 2003b). Sinchi Sacha's interaction with the Unión and its member communities, however, also illustrates the disciplinary dimensions of its activities. As Sinchi Sacha deliberated over which community should serve as the location for a large ceramics plant, to be used to train women in ceramic techniques and ultimately to be the site of large-scale ceramic production, the NGO eventually settled on one community, Santa Rita, that demonstrated itself to have a strong and active women's organization. The design of the project itself ended up marginalizing the other communities of the Unión and their respective women's organizations by locating the project in a single community and privileging the members of Santa Rita's women's organization as the project beneficiaries. Over time, the men from Santa Rita, as well as the majority of women from that community not involved in the women's organization or the ceramics plant, similarly complained of being excluded from the project and its benefits. The process by which particular communities and individuals within those communities were selected to be involved in Sinchi Sacha's projects is a result of both performances of indigeneity for NGO representatives and the strategic appropriation of NGO resources by indigenous leaders. On the one hand, the ATO determined in which community to build the ceramics plant based on the extent to which the chosen community seemed to have integrated a strong gendered component to its sociopolitical organization. On the other hand, leaders of the Unión also took advantage of their ability to influence the destination of NGO resources by having the ecotourism complex constructed in the community of the Unión's president and by placing the management of the ethnographic museum in the hands of young, cosmopolitan leaders closely allied with the president.

The Unión Huacamayos, by the late 1990s, came to be dominated by the three member communities that were most directly involved in the different components of Sinchi Sacha's projects. Participation by the remaining eight member communities dipped over time; by 1999 two of those communities had withdrawn from the organization, and only rarely did representatives from the other communities attend Unión Huacamayos meetings. The structure of the development projects was antithetical to empowering the indigenous organization as a whole, because of the disparities it created and accentuated among the member communities. Even within the three communities active in the projects delivered by Sinchi Sacha, project involvement was uneven, exacerbated economic differentiation (or the perception of such differentiation) within the community, and led some of those not directly involved in the projects to bring forth accusations of corruption and hoarding of economic gains against those individuals more centrally involved.

Furthermore, personal histories were important determinants of involvement in these projects. In the case of the museum and the ecotourism lodge, those who were involved in the projects were set apart from other members of their communities by high levels of education, their past and present roles and experiences as leaders in their communities, the Unión Huacamayos and FONAKIN, and in many cases their relative prosperity in comparison to other community members. In Santa Rita, where the level of education was not as significant a marker of distinction within the community, ownership of land (a scarce resource in this community) was; this set apart a few families with substantial land holdings from the vast majority of community members. Of the seven women who consistently worked at the plant, five of them were members (grandmothers, mothers, or daughters) of one of the four families with sizable amounts of land. The other two were widows who were beyond their productive years. Class and educational distinctions, and experience as leaders within their communities and organizations, provided these individuals with economic resources and practical experiences that better enabled them to take time away from other activities to dedicate to these development projects. Even more, these same traits also made them more sought after by NGO staff to be the participants in these projects.

The class differences are important, but so are the corresponding differences in cultural capital they often entail. The elite individuals in these communities, because of their access to education and previous experiences interacting with NGOs through their roles as leaders of FONAKIN or the Unión, are more accustomed to interacting with White, upper-middle class NGO representatives from Quito or representatives from foreign development institutions. These past experiences help to frame social interaction; given the perceptiveness of federation leaders in evaluating the expectations NGOs hold of them, leaders have performed in accordance with those expectations in order to curry favor with the NGOs. This "facework" (Goffman 2003) contributes to rhetorical processes that form part of performances of indigeneity for their national and international NGO audiences, performances that tend to emphasize core elements of NGO expectations of environmentalism, communalism, and gendered equality and complementarity. Rogers (1996) has demonstrated the relevance of these performances as they form some of the selection criteria determining where and with whom NGOs choose to work. Therefore, learning how to speak and act like an "Indian" may be crucial in successfully attracting NGO support.

In the context of fair trade, the regulatory functions of certification may take this dynamic one step further, by eliminating groups from consideration for inclusion in fair trade artisan projects if they do not perform indigeneity in ways that are in tune with the values enforced through certification oversight. In research with a former community member of the Unión Huacamayos, Stein (n.d.) observed the reluctance of a fair trade organization to work with the community because of its "child labor" practices. Members of the artisan cooperative regularly included teenagers in different aspects of handicraft production, from collecting raw materials to the actual production of the crafts. The director of this fair trade organization was unwilling to risk reprimand from international regulatory bodies because of the possibility that these practices would be deemed "child labor," while the president of the cooperative merely saw these practices as passing on traditional knowledge to the next generation. The expectations that many sustainable-development NGOs held for Amazonian indigenous communities in the 1980s and 1990s—ethics of cooperativism, environmentalism, and gendered complementarity—have been codified as components of IFAT's principles of fair trade, meaning that the performance of particular forms of indigeneity remains at the core of fair trade, as it has for other manifestations of culturally appropriate sustainable development. As such, fair trade, in its current form, does not offer the potential of transforming the trade relationships between the Global North and South in a general sense, as some proponents have suggested. Although it may offer some members of indigenous communities access to alternative markets for their handicrafts, it excludes many more that do not perform indigeneity to expectations (which are in fact requirements for fair trade certification), while also excluding even more that do not possess the economic means to afford themselves leisure time to spend on handicraft production. Fair trade seems to be an option most available to elite members of indigenous communities and organizations while offering only limited possibilities to other members; this may ultimately exaggerate economic differences in these communities without addressing the needs of these communities' most marginal members.

Fair trade regulations promoting cultural preservation, gendered equality, and ecological protection contribute to commonsense understandings of an essentialized indigeneity that run the risk of elevating particular material practices to privileged symbolic status as evidence of indigenous authenticity. The regulation of these practices reveals the role fair trade may play in framing normative socioeconomic behavior, as it limits the kinds of economic activities in which indigenous peoples are expected to engage and the types of products that should result from their labor. Fair trade handicraft production continues the association between indigenous peoples and the aesthetics and sensuality of their products, where the value of the products is related to the emotional satisfaction their aesthetic qualities bring to Western consumers. In fact, indigenous products are of little utilitarian value, as illustrated by the handicrafts produced for Sinchi Sacha by Huaorani artisans: feathered headdresses, necklaces, bracelets, spears, blowguns and darts, earrings, axes, and flutes are among their products. Even those with utilitarian value, such as fishnets, are worthy of purchase because of their aesthetic value and not their use-value for Western consumers. The tight association between indigenous peoples and a limited set of material practices narrows the range of economic activities that would fall under the rubric of acceptable indigeneities, thereby constraining the range of potential economic outlets that would be supported by fair trade for indigenous producers. Further, the social and environmental conditions tied to fair trade contribute to the transformation of indigenous organizations and communities and shape social-movement goals and objectives, which may contribute to local constructions of indigeneity and reinforce essentialized global ones. While the representation of indigenous Amazonians as "ecologically noble savages" may be an effective marketing device for their handicrafts, and in this sense may match the economic goals of those involved in handicraft production, these representations are not reflective of the self-images or everyday economic practices of most indigenous Amazonians. The end result of these material practices and their representations for marketing purposes may be the marginalization of indigenous peoples, rather than their empowerment in a broad sense, as their contributions to larger society are limited to a narrow set of artistic skills or serving as barometers to regulate the excessive consumption of Westerners.

Proponents of fair trade suggest its potential to liberate historically marginalized producers trapped in commodity chains in which they find themselves at or near the bottom of the hierarchy. This potential may exist, and as fair trade continues to grow and solidify international markets for its products as well as grapple with some of the contradictory trends revealed through recent research, the goals of alternative trade may become reality for more ATOs and producer organizations. For this to be the case, however, greater attention needs to be paid to the impacts of particular development approaches and models on the intended beneficiaries themselves, and critical reflection is required to expose the underlying assumptions, cultural beliefs, and ideologies woven into the design of specific development projects. The organization of these projects and the formulaic interaction between NGOs and indigenous peoples may inadvertently marginalize groups and individuals who do not perform indigeneity in expected ways. As is now commonly recognized by anthropologists, development agendas have the tendency to frame specific economic pursuits as "natural," obfuscating the social transformations and cultural ideologies entailed in them, and this recognition has long been at the center (in different ways) of Marxist and poststructuralist critiques of capitalism and international development (Nash 1979; Taussig 1980; Ferguson 1994; Escobar 1995). Similar critical attention needs to be paid to the potential of fair trade and other alternative forms of development to narrow the scope of acceptable indigeneities by rewarding those who perform indigeneity according to dominant expectations and castigating those who do not— with possible disciplinary consequences for indigenous peoples and their representative organizations that do so.

NOTES

1. Different phases of this research were funded by grants from Fulbright IIE (1997–1999), a University of Lethbridge Research Envelope (2004), and an Internal Social Sciences and Humanities Research Council of Canada Grant (2007). I thank Sarah Lyon and Mark Moberg for inviting me to write this chapter and Sarah Lyon and an anonymous reviewer for helpful comments that have contributed to greatly improving this text.

2. While FLO has established a set of standards for a variety of agricultural products, no specific certification standards exist for fairly traded handicrafts. Most of the fair trade organizations that buy and distribute handicrafts are members of IFAT and are required to comply with IFAT's "10 Principles of Fair Trade" and "Code of Practice." Many of these principles closely mirror FLO's generic producer standards. Among IFAT's principles of fair trade are working for gender equality and promoting environmental sustainability; and stated in its code of practice is that fair trade organizations should respect and promote producers' cultural identity through their work.

3. Research was conducted in 2007 in Quito, at the ethnohistorical museum and fair trade shop Mindalae, and in Tena (located in Ecuador's Amazon basin and home to the offices of the indigenous Kichwa federation, FONAKIN), and in the Kichwa community of Jondachi. In Tena between 1997 and 1999, I conducted extensive archival work in the federation's office, I conducted semistructured and unstructured interviews with past and present federation leaders, and I participated in regular federation meetings. In Jondachi in 2004 and again in 2007, I worked with a recently formed artisan cooperative seeking linkages with fair trade organizations.

4. Fair trade groups can roughly be divided into two strands, the ATO strand and the FLO labeling strand, although there is a shared commitment between these two groups in their fair trade goals and a degree of overlap and blurring of boundaries between them. The ATO model remains most relevant for the handicraft fair trade industry, as handicrafts continue to fall outside the rubric of certified commodities, and the bulk of handicrafts sold are through alternative and ethical shops and the producer-purchaser link is often more direct than that of the certified strand represented by FLO (Raynolds and Long 2007).

WORKS CITED

Appadurai, A.
    1986 The Social Life of Things: Commodities in Cultural Perspective. Cambridge:
        Cambridge University Press.
Bebbington, A.
    2004 NGOs and Uneven Development: Geographies of Development Intervention.
        Progress in Human Geography 28(6): 725–745.
Brito, M., H. Araya, and Y. Galvan
    2005 Informe Final: Productos, Imagen y Comunicacion. USAID Mission to Ecuador.
        Conservation in Managed Indigenous Areas Project. Available at http://pdf.
        usaid.gov/pdf_docs/PNADF538.pdf, accessed October 31, 2009.

Cohen, J. H.
  1998 Craft Production and the Challenge of the Global Market: An Artisans' Cooperative in Oaxaca, Mexico. Human Organization 57(1): 74–82.
Cohn, B.
  1996 Colonialism and Its Forms of Knowledge: The British in India. Princeton, NJ: Princeton University Press.
Colloredo-Mansfeld, R.
  1999 The Native Leisure Class: Consumption and Cultural Creativity in the Andes. Chicago: University of Chicago Press.
  2003 Tigua Migrant Communities and the Possibilities for Autonomy among Urban Indígenas. *In* Millennial Ecuador: Critical Essays on Cultural Transformations and Social Dynamics. Norman E. Whitten, ed. Pp. 275–295. Iowa City: University of Iowa Press.
Conklin, B. A.
  1997 Body Paint, Feathers, and VCRs: Aesthetics and Authenticity in Amazonian Activism. American Ethnologist 24(4): 711–737.
de la Cadena, M.
  2000 Indigenous Mestizos: The Politics of Race and Culture in Cuzco, Peru, 1919–1991. Durham, NC: Duke University Press.
Escobar, A.
  1995 Encountering Development: The Making and Unmaking of the Third World. Princeton, NJ: Princeton University Press.
Eversole, R.
  2006 Crafting Development in Bolivia. Journal of International Development 18: 945–955.
Ferguson, J.
  1994 The Anti-politics Machine: Development, Depoliticization, and Bureaucratic Power in Lesotho. Minneapolis: University of Minnesota Press.
Fisher, C.
  2007 Selling Coffee, or Selling Out? Evaluating Different Ways to Analyze the FairTrade System. Culture and Agriculture 29(2): 78–88.
Friedman, J.
  1999 Indigenous Struggles and the Discreet Charm of the Bourgeoisie. Australian Journal of Anthropology 10(1): 1–14.
Gaitán Ammann, F.
  2006 Golden Alienation: The Uneasy Fortune of the Gold Museum in Bogotá. Journal of Social Archaeology 6(2): 227–254.
Global Exchange
  2008 Fair Trade: Economic Justice in the Marketplace. http://www.globalexchange.org/campaigns/fairtrade/stores/fairtrade.html, accessed December 21, 2008.
Goffman, E.
  2003 On Face-Work: An Analysis of Ritual Elements in Social Interaction. Reflections 4(3): 7–13.

Indigenous Designs
    2008 Artisans. http://www.indigenousdesigns.com/section/garment/artisans, accessed
        December 21, 2008.
Li, T. M.
    2000 Articulating Indigenous Identity in Indonesia: Resource Politics and the Tribal
        Slot. Comparative Studies in Society and History 42(1): 149–179.
    2005 Beyond "the State" and Failed Schemes. American Anthropologist 107(3):
        383–394.
Lyon, S.
    2006a Evaluating Fair Trade Consumption: Politics, Defetishization, and Producer Par-
        ticipation. International Journal of Consumer Studies 30(5): 452–464.
    2006b Migratory Imaginations: The Commodification and Contradictions of Shade
        Grown Coffee. Social Anthropology 14(3): 1–14.
    2007 Maya Coffee Farmers and Fair Trade: Assessing the Benefits and Limitation of
        Alternative Markets. Culture and Agriculture 29(2): 100–112.
MacDonald, T.
    1999 Ethnicity and Culture amidst New "Neighbors": The Runa of Ecuador's Amazon
        Region. Boston: Allyn and Bacon.
Meskell, L.
    2005 Introduction: Object Orientations. In Archaeologies of Materiality. Lynn Meskell,
        ed. Pp. 1–17. New York: Blackwell.
Mihelich, J.
    2001 Smoke or Signals? American Popular Culture and the Challenge to Hegemonic
        Images of American Indians in Native American Film. Wicazo Sa Review 16(2):
        129–137.
Mitchell, T.
    1989 The World as Exhibition. Comparative Studies in Society and History 31(2):
        217–236.
Nash, J.
    1979 We Eat the Mines and the Mines Eat Us: Dependency and Exploitation in
        Bolivian Tin Mines. New York: Columbia University Press.
    2001 Maya Visions: The Quest for Autonomy in an Age of Globalization. New York:
        Routledge.
Quito.com
    2008 Museo Mindalae. http://www.quito.com.ec/index.php?page=shop.product_
        details&flypage=shop.flypage&product_id=47&category_id=7&manufacturer_
        id=&option=com_virtuemart&Itemid=89, accessed December 21, 2008.
Ramos, A.
    1998 Indigenism: Ethnic Politics in Brazil. Madison: University of Wisconsin Press.
Raynolds, L. T., and M. A. Long
    2007 Fair/Alternative Trade: Historical and Empirical Dimensions. In Fair Trade: The
        Challenges of Transforming Globalization. Laura T. Raynolds, Douglas Murray,
        and John Wilkinson, eds. Pp. 15–32. New York: Routledge.

Rogers, M.
   1996 Beyond Authenticity: Conservation, Tourism, and the Politics of Representation in the Ecuadorian Amazon. Identities 3(1–2): 73–125.
Salomon, F.
   1987 A North Andean Status Trader Complex under Inka Rule. Ethnohistory 34(1): 63–77.
Scrase, T. J.
   2003 Precarious Production: Globalization and Artisan Labour in the Third World. Third World Quarterly 24(3): 449–461.
Smith, J.
   2007 The Search for Sustainable Markets: The Promise and Failures of Fair Trade. Culture and Agriculture 29(2): 89–99.
Stein, P.
   n.d. Fair Trade Divergences: The Case of Child Labor and Sustainability in the Ecuadorian Amazon. Unpublished manuscript.
Stephen, L.
   2005 Women's Weaving Cooperatives in Oaxaca. Critique of Anthropology 25(3): 253–278.
Strong, P.
   1996 Animated Indians: Critique and Contradiction in Commodified Children's Culture. Cultural Anthropology 11(3): 405–424.
Sylvain, R.
   2002 "Land, Water, and Truth": San Identity and Global Indigenism. American Anthropologist 104(4): 1074–1085.
Taussig, M.
   1980 The Devil and Commodity Fetishism in South America. Chapel Hill: University of North Carolina Press.
Thomas, N.
   1991 Entangled Objects: Exchange, Material Culture, and Colonialism in the Pacific. Cambridge, MA: Harvard University Press.
Turner, T.
   2007 Indigenous Resurgence, Anthropological Theory, and the Cunning of History. Focaal—European Journal of Anthropology 49: 118–123.
Wilson, P. C.
   2003a Ethnographic Museums and Cultural Commodification: Indigenous Organizations, NGOs, and Culture as a Resource in Amazonian Ecuador. Latin American Perspectives 30(1): 162–180.
   2003b Market Articulation and Poverty Eradication? Critical Reflection on Tourist-Oriented Craft Production in Amazonian Ecuador. In Here to Help: NGOs Combating Poverty in Latin America. Robyn Eversole, ed. Pp. 83–104. New York: M. E. Sharpe.

Part III

Relationships and Consumption in Fair Trade Markets and Alternative Economies

The final three case studies in this volume approach alternative trade from the vantage point of consumption. Despite the expanding range of certified fair trade commodities in recent years, most goods remain entirely outside fair trade networks. This applies even to those items (especially manufactured goods) involving great inequities in their production and sale. Faidra Papavasiliou examines concepts of "fairness" that animate alternative currency movements, drawing on the example of the HOURS system in Ithaca, New York. The HOURS alternative currency circulates in a market parallel to that of dollars, but it is geared exclusively to the consumption of local goods and services. Hence, it is viewed as a means of strengthening social relationships and retaining wealth within the community rather than facilitating exchange over more distant geographical horizons. HOURS signals more equitable relations of exchange among its participants, indicating a new consumption discourse that challenges the neutrality of money as simply a measure of value. As such, it is both a direct counterpart to and embodiment of alternative trade initiatives that seek greater justice and strengthened bonds between producers and consumers. Yet, as Papavasiliou admits, the alternative trade network imperfectly substitutes for the dollar economy, as the vast majority of commodities and exchanges in Ithaca remain fully outside its sphere of exchange. The limited circulation of HOURS, despite the system's nearly two decades of existence, itself serves as a metaphor for fair trade networks that benefit a privileged minority of commodity producers.

Molly Doane's chapter contrasts the meanings that fair trade activists and roasters in the United States impute to "relationship coffees" with the attitudes that fair trade coffee growers in Mexico invest in the new trading networks. North American fair trade roasters tend to be well-educated and highly traveled professionals who emphasize the transnational relationships established between producers and consumers of fair trade coffee. These encounters are almost always framed in the idiom of reciprocity and mutual respect. Much as is suggested by Lyon and Dolan in part

2, similar views are also (strategically) invoked by the leaders of Mexican coffee cooperatives who communicate regularly with their fair trade partners in the United States or who travel to conferences there. However, these discourses of reciprocity rarely penetrate beyond the small minority of well-traveled leaders from fair trade producer groups. Most coffee producers themselves possess little knowledge of the fair trade system or its purposes, viewing it instead as part of a longstanding strategy of seeking improved incomes, better living standards, and greater autonomy. Indeed, Mexican producers speak at length about the rigorous demands of organic and fair trade certification, but almost never about the "relationships" and "justice" that animate consumers' and roasters' discussions at the retail end of the commodity chain.

Relationships between indigenous groups and the appropriation of native craft traditions by the fair trade movement form a central theme in Kathy M'Closkey's contribution. Navaho and other Southwest Indian weaving designs were introduced to South and Central American weavers by Peace Corps volunteers as early as 1970. Novica, the world's most visited website for fair trade arts and crafts, markets a large number of textiles based on such designs. Yet these textiles are more often produced by Zapotec and other weavers in the developing world than by the Southwest tribes who created the designs in the first place. The appropriation of Southwest Indian aesthetic styles by rug manufacturers outside the United States has undercut the market for authentic Navajo weavings. Such trends are responsible, M'Closkey contends, for increasing unemployment on some reservations from an already high 40 percent to an astronomical 70 percent. Ironically, promoting one group's market position through fair trade has weakened the cultural identity and economic viability of another, as the word "Navaho" is appropriated to market rugs of non-Navaho origin to Internet consumers. In the process, this has fueled the very "race to the bottom" that the fair trade movement was originally intended to challenge.

Clearly, fair trade has provided measurable and in some cases significant economic benefits to many farmers and artisans who have gained access to alternative markets. Because of limited demand for fair trade goods at the retail level, however, most producers of any given commodity lack such access. As a result, the higher commodity prices received by fair trade producers are likely to result in growing economic disparities between a fortunate few and those who, for whatever reason, are unable to qualify for fair trade certification. The result can also entail heightened competition for access to the fair trade market, as seen with tragic consequences in M'Closkey's case study. Given the greater demands of certification on fair trade producers' labor and resources, it is little surprise that producers themselves rarely describe their marketing relationships in terms of fair trade's much-extolled "new world" of mutual respect and social justice. Indeed, a common perception reported in many of the case studies throughout this volume is that fair trade producers regard foreign certifiers and other fair trade officials in the same light as they do other powerful and seemingly arbitrary agents of global economic structures. This by no means diminishes the real economic advantages that the fair trade market has conferred on hundreds of thousands of agricultural and craft producers in the developing world. It does suggest, however, that fair trade's overriding goal of transforming the structure of global market relations may have instead been transformed by those markets, if not largely fallen victim to them.

9

....

Fair Money, Fair Trade
Tracing Alternative Consumption in a Local Currency Economy

FAIDRA PAPAVASILIOU

I AM A GOLD COIN

Behold! I am a twenty-two-carat Ottoman Sultani gold coin and I bear the glorious insignia of His Excellency Our Sultan, Refuge of the World. My image is here before you, yet I myself can be found in the money purse of your dear brother Stork, the illustrious miniaturist. He's rising now, removing me from his purse and showing me off to each of you. Hello, hello, greetings to all the master artists and assorted guests. Your eyes widen as you behold my glimmer, you thrill as I shimmer in the light of the oil lamp, and finally, you bristle with envy at my owner, Master Stork. You're justified in behaving so, for there's no better measure of an illustrator's talent than I. I take pride in being recognized as a measure of talent among artists and in putting an end to unnecessary disagreements.

Over the last seven years in Istanbul I've changed hands 560 times, and there's not a house, shop, market, bazaar, mosque, church or synagogue I haven't entered. As I've roamed about, I've learned that much more gossip has been spread, many more legends told and lies spun in my name than I'd ever suspected. I've constantly had my nose rubbed in it: nothing's considered valuable anymore besides me, I'm merciless, I'm blind, I myself am even enamored of money, the unfortunate world revolves around, not God, but me, and there's nothing I can't buy. But despite all such heartless comparison and thoughtless slander, I've realized that a large majority do sincerely love me.

If I didn't exist, however, no one would be able to distinguish a good artist from a bad one, and this would lead to chaos among the miniaturists; they'd all be at each other's throats. So I haven't vanished. I've entered the purse of the most talented and intelligent of miniaturists and made my way here.

If you think you're better than Stork, then by all means, get hold of me.

—excerpted from Orhan Pamuk, *My Name Is Red*

Money is so divisive. We want to turn that completely on its head.

—Stephen Burke, Ithaca Hours, Inc., board of directors

Money, Stage Left

In 1991, the town of Ithaca in upstate New York became a dual currency zone. A growing variety of goods and services, food, shelter, clothing, necessities, and luxuries, as well as labor, can also be exchanged with a kind of money other than the familiar, blue-green U.S. dollar. This currency, called the HOUR, to mark labor time, was not issued by any legal, financial, or political authority and was meant to circulate on a voluntary and consensual basis, parallel to the U.S. currency. Its exchange rate was determined somewhat arbitrarily to 1 HOUR = US$10, only later to be linked to the average hourly wage for the region of ten dollars per hour. The market system it came to define is fluid and inconsistent, and in the beginning HOURS circulated among fewer than a hundred people. Yet this unusual initiative steadily grew. In a pivotal moment for grassroots collective action, Ithaca's "other money" became both the model for and the example of innovative, bottom-up efforts to revitalize and empower economies and societies at the local level by challenging the monetary conventions of globalized finance. HOURS came to be at the forefront of a less well known but dynamic global social movement variously known as the local, alternative, parallel, community, or complementary currency movement.

Economics recognizes the emergence of alternative currencies as a response to crisis, when national currencies and economies may fail. However, complementary currencies have been emerging in the context of social mobilization promoting alternative trade and sustainable economies since the 1980s. By 2003 over four thousand systems were recorded, with numerous cases appearing in North America, Europe, and Japan, as well as in Argentina, Brazil, New Zealand, and Australia (Lietaer 2004), and more recently complementary currencies are reported in South Africa and various countries in Asia, including China (Complementary Currency Resource Center 2009). The size, mechanisms, trajectories, and success of alternative money systems are highly variable. In general, however, complementary currency is meant to promote exchange within the locale, community, or network within which it circulates, reaping the advantages of strengthened internal exchange in wealth, social relations, and local control (and preservation) of resources. As such, it can be situated among the burgeoning field of alternative development and trade initiatives that seek to infuse notions of fairness in the global economy. "Alternativity," of course, requires a "conventionality," and in this case the mainstream which defines the frame from which these initiatives seek to depart is the one put in place by the triptych of capitalism-globalization-modernity and the logic of conventional development and free trade, with their well-documented connections to global inequality, exploitation, and, as acknowledged a bit more recently, ecological crisis (Edelman and Haugerud 2004). Against this dystopic globalization, alternative trade initiatives counterpoise a vision that evokes a global civil society (Appadurai 1996; Lyson 2003), in which action focuses on local realities.

While complementary currency is specifically concerned with "the local," its connection to fair trade is more than a moral and ideological affinity for economic, social, and environmental justice. By promoting local exchange, alternative money seeks to address the conditions that have produced the "periphery within the core," which mirror the processes that sustain North-South inequities: the inability of small-scale, local production and business to compete with large-scale corporate enterprises in deregulated, global markets, where overseas cheap labor and manufacturing in conjunction with diminishing state support have been leading to the destabilization and sometimes outright decline of regional economies. The northeastern United States, where the local currency system I am discussing emerged, is a case in point, where economies formerly dependent on industry now form the aptly named, economically depressed "rust belt," in which solid manufacturing positions have been replaced by low-paying, low-security service jobs. These conditions have also promoted a consumer economy oriented toward the cheap imports made possible through "free trade" (Shuman 1998; Benson and Papavasiliou 2004). Under such conditions, fairly traded goods, as well as other alternative, "social value added" commodities such as organics, are considerably less likely to attract cash-strapped consumers. Even in prosperous (often urban) contexts, flexible accumulation capitalism is associated with flexibility, hence volatility, in the labor market (Harvey 1991), which can translate to equally "flexible" consumer demand, as the current economic crisis illustrates rather starkly.

The complementary currency movement, however, offers something more than just another illustrative case of collective action signaling the need and desire for change in the terms of global trade in order to promote more equity. Its broader significance hinges on the fact that instead of managing trade, it takes on money. The "financialization" of the global economy, including both the problematic of access to credit and structures of debt and the exponential growth and acceleration of capital flows, is broadly recognized as a key characteristic, and arguably a driving force, of late capitalism (Appadurai 1996; Harvey 1991; Maurer 2005). Yet the nature of this financialization and the extent of its effect have generally been treated obliquely, either on the level of systemic abstraction, where money and financial structures become part of generalized categories in the order of "market forces" or "factors" (Gledhill 2004), or in the terms of tallying the global distribution of cost and benefit. Money, in other words, is taken as a gauge, or a diagnostic, for evaluating the impact of trade under free-trade regimes.

Yet money is profoundly symbolic and political. It inscribes and communicates not only a quantity but also a *quality* of economic value.[1] In the epigraph to this chapter, Pamuk's clever gold coin, musing on its own nature, captures an entire economic worldview rather well: the medium of exchange is both the measure and proof of value but also the purpose or goal of any activity. It creates and affirms social divisions by seemingly obliterating qualitative difference. Tracing this confluence of meanings onto modern (fiat) money, Hornborg (2007) suggests that the abstraction of economic value effected by modern, general-purpose money is a serious obstacle to both envisioning and enacting sustainable economies, because modern money works to conceal completely the basic incommensurability of value between labor, subsistence, and other commodities, by expressing them in a single, generalized, numerical metric. And if discourses on sustainability and fairness, just like those on conventional development and free trade, deal with money with the same naturalized neutrality, they may

miss an important aspect of the mechanism that supports the trade conditions they wish to redress. By addressing money, or the means through
which market exchange takes place, therefore, the complementary currency movement presents an opportunity to query money directly, not
only about how it is distributed—that is to say, who has more and who (or
which places) end up with less of it—but about what it does as a form, a
"thing" that carries information for conceptualizing and acting on value,
exchange, and consumption. If the institution of money itself has an active
role in shaping economic relations, would a different kind of money, such
as Ithaca's alternative currency, promote a different and perhaps more equitable and sustainable economic reality, and how? I first trace the role of
"conventional" modern money in the production and perpetuation of our
current global model of trade relations and then turn to the question of
how the use of an alternative kind of money may shape alternative economic relations and notions of fairness in Ithaca.

Money as Thing
1. Conventional Money

For money's omnipresence, it is a strange, curious thing. Both a means
and an end of economic activity, it represents the distilled, quantitative
measure of economic and social success (Hart 2001; Davies 2002; Hornborg 2007). Particularly in its modern, generalized iteration, money represents the ultimate, extracted essence of material reality. As such, it has
been historically seen as simply a neutral tool that facilitates economic
transactions. Simmel viewed money as colorless and lacking intrinsic
value, as it objectively signifies all value and is thus indifferent to origins,
social distinctions, or interests (2004: 297–312). Similarly, for Marx, "Just
as in money every qualitative difference between commodities is extin-
guished, so too for its part, as a radical leveler, it extinguishes all distinctions (in social relations)" (1990: 229). Like Simmel, Marx saw money as
the grease in the modernist, fetishizing capitalist machine, lending his
philosophical weight to a far too common sentiment: "nothing's considered valuable anymore besides me, I'm merciless, I'm blind, I myself am
even enamored of money, the unfortunate world revolves around, not
God, but me, and there's nothing I can't buy" (Pamuk 2001: 105).

That the meaning of value and the trade and consumption relationships
it fosters are mutable and contingent cultural practices is hardly news for
anthropology, which has a long history of uncovering and comparing the

diverse meanings and practices that produce the world at the intersection of culture and material practice (Mauss 1964; Strathern 1990; Wilk and Cliggett 2007). Nevertheless, anthropological examinations of value and materiality have often failed to escape a "modernist historicization" that maps simple dichotomies on space (West vs. non-West, or North vs. South) and time (modern vs. premodern) and sees family, community, and market in a taxonomical sequence of complexity, thus invoking a "familiar pair of ethical positions," the "march of progress" versus the preservation of the small, local, and authentic (Danby 2004: 70).

This dualism is particularly evident in the scholarship on money. Anthropology largely structured its studies around the core of modern money as constructed by classical, neoclassical, and also Marxist perspectives that place it at the center of capitalist development. Modern money, the kind analyzed (and promoted) by the classical economists, Adam Smith and, importantly, David Ricardo (Hornborg 2007), stands out as what Bohannan and other anthropologists studying currency have called general-purpose money (Bohannan 1959; Douglas 1967; Salisbury 1962; Pospisil 1963).

Money is an archetypical (perhaps the archetypical) case in the rise of quantification as synonymous with scientific objectivity, mutually supported by metrology and the spread of numeracy in the modern world. By contrast, in noncapitalist settings, different kinds of value were recognized and correspondingly counted with different kinds of money, marking hierarchically compartmentalized "multicentric economies." For instance, among the Siane in New Guinea yams could be used to buy subsistence goods, but to pay bridewealth one needed a more prestigious currency such as shells or axes (Salisbury 1962). Although conversion from sphere to sphere was not entirely impossible, it was also highly undesirable and problematic, as the different types of money should not move from their sphere of value. This, though, was "primitive money," reflecting both the historical trajectory money took in "evolving" toward standardized generality[2] and the inevitable march of modern capitalist dominion sweeping up all "traditional societies" in its way.

While the neutral, disinterested, and precise objectivity of modern money is a didactic reflection on the rational, calculating *homo economicus*, the axiom of the perfect orthologism and neutrality of modern money is violated in daily practice both in the small scale, by people on the ground, and in the large scale of organizations and states, where fully generalized currency is subjected to complex rules of allocation, restrictions, and classifications reflecting social and cultural meanings and boundaries. Zelizer's pioneering work elucidated the strategies people use to "earmark" or separate generalized (and hence undifferentiated) modern money into qualitatively distinct classes, usually on the grounds of its origin or intended use (Zelizer 1994; Hermann 2006). Similarly, U.S. states launder "dirty" money that comes from morally ambiguous sources, such as gambling and the various lotteries, by allocating it for "clean" causes, primarily for funding schools.

The complexities of money are not limited to informal cultural rules of appropriateness and allocation. Money as distilled value is pure, quantitative reason. And yet there is a magic to it that, sometimes in the form of transubstantiation and sometimes in the form of a sleight of hand, commands not only dedication but confusion and awe from the mass of its users. How it operates, or even what it is, is if not an outright mystery, then certainly the domain of deeply esoteric knowledge and power, governing the construction and flows of modern financescapes (Appadurai 1996). This only aids in the abstraction effected by money, concealing potentially incommensurate things under a homogenized and murky, yet familiar and naturalized, numerical mask.

2. Currency Critique and Alternatives

What the problematic of financescapes suggests is that fairness may not only be a matter of unequal access to money. Rather, the forms, rules, and even the intentions of money as an institution can come to shape social realities. Alternative or complementary currencies as a movement begin to probe into the problematic reality of the modern, "conventional" monetary system by turning to the basic question of what it is that money is supposed to do. According to the Federal Reserve, money is "anything that serves as a generally accepted medium of exchange, a standard of value and a means to save or store purchasing power."[3] Money, then, has many functions, and not all of them are necessarily complementary or, more importantly, always congruent. In the modern system, the two main functions of money are the medium-of-exchange function, in which currency serves to facilitate transactions, and the store-of-value function, in which money serves to save value reliably so that it will be predictably retrievable and usable at any time. These functions frequently clash on the level of policy, where different financial regimes may privilege the "quantity" or the "quality" of money (Boyle 2002; Davies 2002).

The current global financial regime has been heavily influenced by the philosophy of monetarism, neoliberalism's financial counterpart (Davies 2002; Friedman 1987). While neoliberalism favors the deregulation of markets, monetarism favors closely regulating the money supply as a primary means for economic stability, and ascribes price phenomena, such as inflation, to an overly (and detrimentally) expanded money supply. Monetarism therefore privileges money's function as a store of value, rather than as a medium of exchange, and is concerned with the quality, not the quantity and availability, of money, seeing the latter as inherently inflationary. In this way, the regime gives primacy to financial rather than to productive capital. On the one hand, finance is liberalized through the production of new and increasingly complex financial instruments, while money as currency proper is tied up as a macroeconomic regulator that can control spending, somewhat independently of actual demand and supply of goods and services on the ground. The perpetual struggle between the means-of-exchange versus the store-of-value functions of money means that scarcity is endemic to the system (Raddon 2003; Davies 2002).

Additionally, the ways in which money is placed in circulation influence the directions of economic activity. Modern money is what is known as credit money, created by the state, which then loans it to private banks, from which it is issued to circulation through further, "retail" lending. The implication of this system is that the very creation of money is predicated on the need to return more of it than was originally given out, setting up a perpetual cycle of debt. This also means that a third function of money, money as a means of payment, becomes key, as borrowers strive to pay back their loans and the accrued interest, thus placing additional demands on the existing money supply in a cycle where, at all points, there is more debt than the means to pay it. This fuels the need for perpetual economic growth, further entrenching both the condition and the experience of scarcity (Rowbotham 1998: 8; Hutchinson et al. 2002). This growth furthermore both supports and is supported by the logic of free trade to match the rapid pacing and short temporal frames of financial markets.

What these perspectives point to is that money is hardly a neutral marker of distilled "essential value." As Hornborg succinctly puts it, "the moral" (and I would add cultural and political) "semiotics of money—in other words, how exchange is culturally conceived—can have very significant material implications" (2007: 64). Nevertheless, the main way in which money figures in the study of global economic conditions is over-whelmingly in the question of inequality of access and distribution. Money itself remains depoliticized, its workings as an institution obscured.

Against the scarce and convoluted modern money, the alternative pro-posed by the complementary currency movement is to connect people and things in a direct, and hence demystified and defetishized, exchange. In a basic sense, the function of complementary currencies is to create a type of money "with a boundary around it" (Glover 1995), usable only within a predetermined space, an area, or network of people that define a com-munity. Following the logic of localism, the movement promotes the cre-ation of an alternative medium of exchange that is community issued and bounded and that circulates on a voluntary and consensual basis (Glover 1995; Boyle 1999a, 1999b, 2002; Cahn 2004; Raddon 2003). Like local-food and sustainable-agriculture initiatives, complementary currency systems are usually grassroots efforts that attempt to redress unequal economic relationships at the local level and to empower individuals and communi-ties within the networks where they circulate. Unlike most other alterna-tive trade initiatives, however, complementary currencies do not focus on specific economic relations or commodity chains, but they cast a wider net, addressing the general domain of trade and consumption.

For the movement, a currency that is intended to function mainly as a means of exchange challenges the axioms of scarcity and competition, as it operates on the fact that economic problems at the local level are not always a question of adequate demand or supply but a shortage of cash, that is to say, the means to exchange. With this as its starting point, a par-allel currency circulating just outside of but in tandem with the normal or mainstream economy confers a number of advantages, according to the movement, that span economic, social, and even environmental lines. The claim is that a complementary currency as a source of extra cash but with bounded circulation will stimulate local trade, while also assuring that profits will remain and proliferate within the network of its users, instead of being funneled out into the vast unknown of transnational corporate networks. Stimulating local-level economic activity can encourage local development of resources. Local control of resources leaves more room for incorporating issues of ecological sustainability and social equity in the economy. In other words, the movement claims to empower people as economic beings at the local level, placing them in a position with more possibilities, better options, and, mainly, more control. It is here that al-ternative currency's ideological kinship with the fair trade movement becomes most apparent. By promoting local trade, complementary currency emphasizes the significance of direct relationships between producer and consumer as the catalyst against competition from global, "free trade" commodities and services, whose prices do not reflect the social and environmental costs of their production and whose consumption pits the short-term benefit of cheaper prices against the long-term cost of deteriorating local economic and social conditions (Boyle 1999a, 1999b, 2002; Glover 1995; Shuman 1998; Cahn and Rowe 1992; Cahn 2004).

The HOURS Currency in Ithaca, New York

Studying local currency means that one is simultaneously considering both an organization (the "movement" part, as it were) and a market. The study from which this discussion draws is based on sixteen months of fieldwork in Ithaca that included interviews with both participants (n = 75) and nonparticipants (n = 21) in the HOURS currency system, as well as extensive participation in the local currency economy. The study involved elements of participatory action research in the sense that I assisted the volunteer board of directors that administers Ithaca's local currency system, which afforded a much more detailed view of the dynamics between the organization and the community at large.

Situated in the economically depressed "rust belt" of upstate New York, Ithaca exhibits several distinctive characteristics, largely connected to the presence of the two major educational institutions, Cornell University and Ithaca College, which act as economic, social, and cultural centers but do not subsume the town. The presence of the universities has to some extent buttressed Ithaca against extended economic depression caused by the loss of manufacturing but has also produced a largely university-oriented service economy with a number of consequences for the town, including an income bifurcation between high-end, highly skilled positions and low-end service jobs (Jacob et al. 2004a, 2004b). Nevertheless, far from being a "typical" college town, Ithaca is distinctly diverse as a community. Characterized by a highly progressive segment having grown around, but independently of, the universities since the 1950s and '60s, as well as a historically strong and sizable black community, it is also marked by racial, ethnic, and class inequalities and tensions.

In this context, HOURS are primarily intended to operate as an alternate source of cash, which feeds back into the local economy. Before delving into the details of the system, an example will help illustrate how local currency can work to promote alternative development on the ground. The following is an account from an early user who started working as a carpenter through the HOURS network in 1995, two years after the official start of the system:

> I can't quite remember exactly how I found out about it. I probably saw the list and then talked with Paul [Paul Glover, the founder of the system]. I think it was the first list [a circular listing offers and demands by people willing to trade in local currency] that ever came out, and I called Paul. I thought it was a stroke of genius at work. I thought it was going to be a small-business incubator. and I wanted to run a small business. It was also a free way to advertise. In the fall of 1995 I started part-time, and in 1996 I started full-time. I filed papers for sole proprietorship of my company in 1996. Before that I was a grad student in natural resources. I have a master's degree in natural resources from Cornell (coal ash landfills and water quality in such landfills). I learned carpentry and such from my father while growing up, plus through all sorts of experiences, on the job training and the like. I decided to take it up professionally in January of 1995 after looking for work at least locally and turning most every stone that I knew to turn. We were not ready to move. I enjoy doing carpentry and developed enough confidence to become proficient in both carpentry and plumbing. When I heard about the list in 1995, I thought this was for me. A great way to see if people who wanted to try out a business could see if they could do it without much investment. And since people would hire you directly from the list, there was a sense of community. Like "we're all in this boat together," and we'd all turn around and spend the HOURS. When I first started working, I worked almost entirely for Ithaca HOURS. That lasted for about a year. One way we used Ithaca dollars [sic] was to finish our home renovation. We paid for dry wall finishing entirely with HOURS.

Ideally, then, local currency is a type of money whose use is restricted to "the community" as defined by the network of participants. It allows people to "save" national currency, though it is not meant to be saved itself but rather used to proliferate in-network economic activity, promoting defetishized social engagement and participation.

Over the years, the user base of Ithaca's local currency has become increasingly diversified, but the core group of users remain the town's progressive, "cultural creative" segment (Ray and Anderson 2000), which tends to be young to middle-aged, white, and well educated, though widely differentiated with regard to income or employment. Ithaca's social diversity, including its progressive scene, makes it difficult to trace participation in the local currency economy as a factor of social class or socioeconomic status in the classical sense, as ideological/political leanings, race, and ethnic identities trump the assumption of commonality based on income, work, or education. For Ithaca, this is one manifestation of a larger problem facing alternative trade mobilization. Specifically, I am referring to contrasting "the community" to "global capitalism" and designating it as the space of alternative economic action, without sufficient attention to internal differentiation (Gibson-Graham 2006). "Locality," however, does not immediately imply community in the sense of shared experience, desires, or even shared identities, and despite the system's stated mission of inclusivity, it has not managed to undo the town's racial, class, or political barriers. Minority and generational low-income participation, for instance, is markedly low.

With these issues in mind, Ithaca's HOURS currency has still been quite successful as a grassroots initiative. It has been in circulation (and growing) since 1991, unlike the majority of complementary currency experiments, which tend to be short-lived (Collom 2005). After several years operating at various levels of informality, the system became incorporated as a not-for-profit in 1998 and is now administered by a board of elected volunteers. As an organization, the HOURS system runs on nearly no national money, operating largely on volunteer work and local currency. The currency circulates in denominations of 2, 1, 1/2, 1/4, 1/8, and 1/10 HOURS ($20, $10, $5, $2.50, $1.25, and $1, respectively), and it is put to circulation in three ways: through small "disbursements" (2 to 4 HOURS, that is, US$20 to US$40) given to registered members of the organization, through small interest-free loans to local businesses, and through grants to community organizations, projects, and events.

The name "HOURS" is meant to evoke the principle of labor exchange and that a unit of time is equal for everyone, a nod to social equity, though in practice that does not mean that every participant's hour is "the same." Participants are free to decide on their own terms of acceptance, and users are encouraged to negotiate their own individual deals. While some participants do so (one of the most notable cases being a dentist who accepted full payment in local currency and, as some people told me, used a sliding fee scale and would consider a fee of an HOUR per hour on a case-by-case basis), pricing usually corresponds to that of the conventional market. The issue of pricing generates much debate among alternative currency activists and users, as prices (and the power to set and control them) are a key problem in reforming trade. Nevertheless, there are strong arguments for following standard market prices and maintaining coherence and continuity, both for the practical difficulties of everyday market exchange in multiple price scales but also, and rather significantly, for the issue of building and maintaining confidence in the alternative currency. Particularly after global abandonment of the gold standard, the value of all modern money is based on consensus, or the confidence of its users that the currency token will continue to be honored at a more or less stable rate. Standard national currency, however, which also bears the insignia of the state, has come to be seen as inherently real and valuable, so much so in fact that the idea of an alternative currency appears odd and immediately raises doubts about not only value but legality[4] for most people. Thus, the alternative currency movement already has a hard sell to make by asking people to use a nonstandard token of value. An additional point to be made is that, in principle at least, local, small-scale exchange is supposed already to reflect fairer or more livable pricing (which is also what initially renders it less competitive), so that by encouraging local trade, alternative currency also indirectly supports fairer practices.

More or less anyone can participate. To be an official member in the organization one has to live or work in a radius of roughly twenty miles from the community. The system counts about one thousand members, though one does not have to be a registered member to use the currency, and hence the user base is actually larger. The town numbers about twenty-five thousand permanent residents and about another twenty-five thousand students. The universities, however, are largely unengaged with the HOURS system. Participants tend to be people with long-term investment in the community. The fluidity of cash means that anyone can use the currency, though formal membership does confer some advantages, primarily inclusion in the system's directory of participants that serves as a local version of the yellow pages.

In the directory one can find about fifteen hundred offers for goods and services payable on HOURS that cover 250 different categories. These range from food, crafts, and entertainment to consumer goods, legal and professional services, and both alternative and mainstream healthcare. Nevertheless, though this list is markedly diverse, it is not viable as a full market alternative for most people. The majority of participants restrict how much local currency they are willing to accept, by either limiting acceptance to a fixed amount or percentage of price or accepting payment in HOURS for specific goods and services or on certain days of the week. This restricts the flow of HOURS, an effect partly encouraged by the organization as a way to maintain confidence and stability by allowing people to become involved at their own level of comfort and interest, but it adds a layer of complication to HOURS transactions. Users do not only have to contend with the somewhat counterintuitive HOURS denominations but may find it difficult both to earn and to spend local currency to the degree they desire. These difficulties of earning and spending were, in fact, the primary complaints about the currency that the users with whom I spoke expressed, and they are a direct cause of the slow growth of the HOURS economy.

To date, around 15,000 HOURS, the equivalent of US$150,000, have been issued for circulation. Although this number may seem small, advocates are quick to point to the multiplier effect of local currency: the size of the local currency economy is contingent not on the amount of money that exists but on how fast it circulates, and one macroeconomic study has determined that the velocity of HOURS is greater than that of the dollar in Ithaca (Yoshida 2002). Yet in the currency's seventeen years of circulation, it has not grown to account for a significant share of the local economy, representing much less than 1 percent of the county's economy, according to an interviewed administrator. While there is distinct variability in the size and significance of direct HOURS transactions among participants, over 80 percent of the seventy-five users with whom I spoke estimated that they earned less, and in most cases much less, than US$1,000 annually, with 39 percent reporting earning less than US$100.

Nevertheless, there are a number of other, supporting or auxiliary economic functions performed by local currency, which such quantitative snapshots would miss. HOURS can serve as a networking tool, as a resource for credit, and as a form of security against economic crisis, indicating that at least in some cases, the alternative currency economy can have a significant material impact. Consider the following case: In 2002, a local retailer, Juana's Gifts, had taken out a moderately sizable business loan in U.S. currency, through a financial firm connected to the HOURS network. By 2003, Juana's found itself unable to meet its payments and was dangerously close to defaulting on the loan and possibly declaring bankruptcy. Juana's was in this position as a result of alleged wrongdoing by employees that had gone undetected for an extended period of time. The case could not be proven, and the losses were unrecoverable. In order to avoid defaulting and potentially losing the business, the owners of Juana's Gifts, also long-term participants in the HOURS system, agreed with the financial firm to obtain a loan in HOURS with which to repay their debt. This "refinancing" was done in the considerably favorable terms of HOURS business loans, which bear no interest, require no collateral, and are negotiated on a case-by-case basis. The requirement on the part of the local businesses is to make a case that they offer something valuable to the community and submit a plan showing where and how the funds will be spent, to assure that the borrower does in fact have viable connections to the local economy and that the loan will indeed be infused into the local economy. Payment schedules are negotiated to be manageable, and the borrower can pay back the loan in either local (most often the case) or federal currency. Juana's was thus able to take advantage of these favorable terms to recover and rebuild the business.

Consumption in the Local Currency Economy

The financing aspect of alternative currency conjures the image of microlending and microfinance schemes and underscores the primacy of financial means and the role of credit and debt in determining "fairness" in local-level material realities. But the deeper effect of participation in Ithaca's local currency system had to do with the emergence of an alternative discourse within the HOURS economy, surrounding exchange and consumption. In this discourse, as it emerged from users' narratives, regular money and alternative money came to imbue trade and consumption with different and even contrasting meanings, where dollar exchange was associated with suspicion, danger, and even powerlessness, while HOURS exchange was associated with empowerment and fairness. This difference furthermore was not a function of the things exchanged but of the currency with which they were exchanged. This first appeared in the way the local currency economy allows negotiation, in ways that begin to challenge the uncontested dominance of the terms set by the quantitative rationality and standard maximization calculus that, as discussed earlier, have come to define the "modern economy." And this effect was possible even if HOURS never directly figured in the transactions. As one person related with respect to some unskilled manual labor he had performed some years ago, the fact that the work came through the local currency economy made possible different ways of thinking about fair exchange. Instead of the established minimum wage, payment was negotiated in the terms of a living wage: "The guy who called me from the HOURS list paid in dollars but agreed to pay ten dollars an hour. I asked for that rate, but it was the HOURS hourly rate that gave me the inspiration. That is what I would have gotten in HOURS. Otherwise I may not have asked for that."

Another theme indicating a currency-specific view of exchange and consumption had to do with the notion of scarcity as a fundamental tenet of the economy. If scarcity is the "shadow" of abundance in the Jungian sense, abundance is what is promoted in Ithaca's alternative currency economy. And this abundance is not only figurative and symbolic but can be taken quite literally. Like fair trade, the local currency movement, certainly in the way that it has developed in Ithaca, is emphatically not a simplicity or anticonsumerist movement. The promotional rhetoric of the system not only encourages people to put dreams and talents to work for fun and profit but also emphasizes the delight and fun to be found in spending (local) money. The bills themselves are a humorous rendition of the U.S. dollar, proudly proclaiming, "In Ithaca We Trust," and sporting colorful and whimsical designs with Ithaca-centered themes, celebrating the natural and human riches of the region. Various slogans play on these themes: "We are rich when we hire each other" or "Local currency is good for the community. Use it and have fun!" Most system publications encourage readers to patronize HOURS businesses. They advertize local products and services and often present this as an opportunity for Ithacans to discover new and special delights available in the local economy. Local currency in Ithaca advocates anything but austerity. On the contrary, much like other development schemes both standard and alternative, and certainly including the fair trade movement, local currency invites consumption, as spending leads to development: the more local currency circulates, the more local wealth is created and recirculated, and so on.

Accordingly, there is a large range and volume of "nonessential" or "finer" goods and services available in the HOURS network, which is also reflected in one of the main stereotypes about HOURS that I heard from users as well as nonparticipants, that they are mainly good for "pottery and massages" and for those who want and can afford them. Although this characterization is technically inaccurate (primary or subsistence items are well represented in the HOURS economy), it does reflect the larger problematic common to alternative trade initiatives, and the potentials and limitations of consumption as a tool for global economic transformation. Can the very same practices and mechanisms of material practice that propelled the current system into dominance serve the purposes of sustainability and fairness? But the complementary currency rhetoric also claims that this economic activity, by virtue of having "a boundary around it," however permeable that boundary may be, is by definition different: more controlled, more aware, more sustainable. Like purchasing fair trade coffee, consumption in local currency is moralized as *productive consumption* (Trentmann 2006), one that elevates the individual and promotes the collective good rather than being a sign of personal and social corrosion. The inscription on the back of the 1/8 HOUR (US$1.25) reads, "TIME IS MONEY. This note entitles the bearer to receive one eighth hour labor or its negotiated value in goods or services. Please accept it, then spend it. Ithaca HOURS stimulate local businesses by recycling our wealth locally, and they help fund new job creation. Ithaca HOURS are backed by real capital: our skills, our time, our tools, forests, fields and rivers."

On the other hand, while in theory growth of local consumption will ideally substitute for external goods and services (the line of thought that has caused local currency to be compared to import substitution), one of the particularities of the Ithaca system is that it is (in principle at least) a fully generalized currency that can be used for trading just about anything between two consenting parties. Therefore the act of consumption does not have to be limited to only local products and services. However, if filtered through the alternative money network, even global goods can be made appropriate, humanized, indeed infused, through the awareness of consumption engendered in local exchange, with local value. In this way, alternative currency goes quite a bit further than other consumer and sustainability movements in engaging consumption. It does not set predefined targets, particular commodities, trade relationships, or consumption practices but addresses consumption as a whole field. It does not matter what one trades for, as long as one trades *with* local money, the logic goes. The money itself will recirculate to restore the balance.

This is clearly a contentious assertion when economic fairness is at issue. In Ithaca it is indeed possible to purchase at least some conventional goods from the global (free) market with local currency. Even if this may confer some kind of benefit to seller and consumer, it does nothing to account for the inequitable and harmful conditions of production associated with free trade. In practice, however, this scenario was notably missing from users' reports about consumption with local currency. On the contrary, perhaps the most significant effect that HOURS appeared to have on users was a reorientation of consumption toward things that were deemed ethical yet not entirely appropriate in the terms of the rational quantitative calculus that standard money underpins. As discussed earlier, standard money presents a face of value commensurability, with the implication that proper consumption decisions are overwhelmingly based on price and quantity as the two most important (and most readily available) types of information in economic decision-making (Hornborg 2007). In Ithaca, however, the effect of alternative currency was to begin to decouple consumption from the neoclassical economic calculus and to admit alternative values and relationships in the decision-making process that were inscribed on the alternative money itself.

This proliferation of values in consumption appeared both directly and indirectly. Indirectly, HOURS were associated with a different exchange experience that relates to negotiation as fundamentally linked to trust and to the necessity for shared representations of value (Danby 2004). It is here that the tenacious identification of HOURS with barter becomes most salient. HOURS are unequivocally a money system: they create a generalized, durable, and divisible token of value for the purposes of exchange. Yet the most widely used way to explain the admittedly difficult concept of what they are and how they function is in the terms of barter. The literature is rife with references to barter: "Ithaca HOURS is a paper barter currency" (Hermann 2006: 3). "Barter dollars" or "barter bucks" are common euphemisms for alternative currency, Ithaca being no exception. While I enquired about people's other barter activities and received a wide range of responses (barter was a favored hobby, a significant mode of exchange, an occasional activity among friends, something that never happened, or something actively disliked), barter as a trope also appeared in another way in Ithacans' narratives about HOURS exchange. One of the very early and still active users shared,

> I had been plagued to the same thinking that the dollar bill was tangibly this thing that had value, and really when you think about it, it's about having faith in each other. And that's what HOURS represent for me. It didn't take long if you think of the ramification to that, that it can really formalize a way a community can barter. But somehow Ithaca HOURS, put in your pocket . . . if you want more, you could go after getting more. Somehow I guess if I did a transaction with HOURS with somebody, I just felt like they were part of the same thinking, more community; it just represented more thinking outside . . . community development stuff.

Others commented, "HOURS works like barter but exists for the same reason that money does" or "It is more like barter within the wider community." One person happily reminisced about being introduced to HOURS and being drawn to it: "I understood it immediately, because I love to barter!" A substantial number of the people with whom I spoke referenced other barter activities in the community, ranging from child-care networks to labor, crafts, and other products and services, and saw HOURS as a way to expand that barter activity. Conversely, some Ithacans indicated that they engaged in direct barter because of the difficulties they had in productively entering the HOURS network. Lastly, some nonusers explained their lack of interest in participation in the HOURS economy as a function of the fact that they did not like or had no use for barter.

This parallelism is not idle but has significant implications for framing consumption and value. Barter is widely held to be the precursor to money. The inconvenience of exchanging in kind, the story goes, was the impetus for the creation of a universal equivalent of value. It was a brilliant moment of abstraction from which much greatness has flowed. This evident history of where money comes from is the account given in encyclopedias and textbooks on finance. It also happens to be quite false. Historical and anthropological work in particular has shown that money and barter are in fact distinct branches of the economic tree (Davies 2002; Hart 2001; and the authoritative anthropological volume on barter edited by Humphrey and Hugh-Jones [1992]). Money has historically held multiple and diverse functions, not all of which were always primarily concerned with exchange. Barter, on the other hand, has been and continues to be a direct exchange of resources. An additional point of proof for the separate and distinct history and function of money and barter is that barter has never really been replaced by money, but it is still going strong not only among individuals in the small scale of informal, day-to-day exchanges but also among corporate entities that find advantage in the direct and unmediated exchange of materials to the order of billions of dollars annually. And while modern money is widely seen as the hallmark of the contemporary global economy, Hart (2001), among others, has pointed out that the closest one can get to an idealized free market is, in fact, barter, a sort of direct one-to-one trade which involves free, independent choice; direct exchange of equivalent values; lack of "strings" and perpetuated commitments, as exchange is a one-time event that fulfills all obligations on both sides; and no outside regulation. Nevertheless, the story of barter as the antiquated, primitive, and clearly less efficient ancestor of money persists, and today, community barter holds a wholesome charm, evoking idealized notions of community-embedded economies or personal, face-to-face relations of honesty, cooperation, and responsibility. It is in this sense that, as several feminist scholars have argued, barter and other small-scale, alternative economic spaces such as garage sales are "feminized" and relegated to a "gray," far less significant, and not properly "economic" sphere of activity (Raddon 2003; Hermann 2006).

While some types of local currency operate on the principle of labor time exchange and could thus be more easily seen as systems of exchange in kind, the HOURS model that originated in Ithaca is unequivocally a money system. HOURS have all the markers of form and function to be recognized as money. They are a paper currency that is denominated, durable, recognizable, and of declared value, which can also serve a number of the functions ascribed to money: medium of exchange, store of value, unit of account, and so on. Equating alternative money with barter, therefore, makes for a technically faulty but evocative comparison, particularly if the focus is on the idea of the free exchange of equivalent values. Unlike market exchange, barter does not carry the same connotations of risk and the possibility of unequal transfers where one party gains while the other loses. At its basic, barter is about everyone getting what he or she wants. And if local currency evokes that sense of bartering, as many of the users' narratives indicate, exchanges in local currency also carry a sense of "fairness," the security of an equal and mutually beneficial transaction without the suspicion (or assumption) of hidden costs or risks.

Anthropological literature on money shows that the medium of exchange, and not just the type or institutional context or mechanism of exchange (market vs. nonmarket, capitalist vs. noncapitalist), has a bearing on the construction and representation of value that governs both the material and social and cultural aspects of economic activity. This was further reflected in the markedly diverse and inconsistent ways users perceived HOURS compared to "real money," and more specifically, earning and spending HOURS versus earning and spending dollars. So what did it feel like?

> Definitely it felt like money, and I had this cool fascination about it, knowing it is useful like regular money but totally outside the U.S. economy and would have to stay here. Also it was fun to keep them in my wallet and show people who were new to Ithaca. They are colorful, with a colorful meaning and story behind them.

I think I did a pretty good job convincing myself this is real money, mainly because I was around people who did *not* think of it as money but more as a coupon. But I did see it a little like free money . . . something different.

Or,

What it feels like? Does it feel like real money? I think it's good! I like the system. Yes! It is real money. It's cool. It's *our* money. I like it.

Or,

It made it possible to spend for things I would not spend cash on. It made me feel like I could afford it. Also it makes me feel good to know that the person will spend it locally. It is a sort of double value.

Or,

It feels like money, definitely. I like the idea of spending and knowing it's local. It's like nice money.

Or,

Yes. It is playful money, but it is real. In a sense it's more real because it stays around. The other money, I don't know where it comes from, where it gets printed, etc. Here I know the artists. It's really concrete.

Be they "free money," "nice money," "our money," "playful money," and even "concrete money," HOURS hold diverse meanings and functions that set them apart from "regular" money, while still remaining "real." For many users, however, this "realness" shifted depending on the direction of the currency's flow, distinguishing earning from spending. For some, getting paid in local currency carried the same weight as getting paid in any other fashion, yet spending that money amounted to something different, something special, even denoting a treat, a sort of prize or stroke of luck. A couple with longstanding ties to, and by all accounts extensive experience in, the local currency economy shared:

What does earning HOURS feel like?
    It feels quite real, like real money—you pay real bills with them. And for example, Turbacks [an upscale Ithaca restaurant that is no longer in operation], we would not have even eaten there if it weren't for HOURS. We went there for her birthday. It was a seventy-five-dollar bill.

What does spending feel like? Is it like dollars?
Yes and no. There is a part of me that feels like I'm getting away with something. You know, like monopoly money. Also we would spend them at places we'd never get out the cash for. Spending feels a little surreal, and we are not very careful with them at all.

Things and payment still change hands, but the value somehow differs. The issues of risk, equity, and possibility (of "fairness" in a certain sense) ran through users' narratives in other forms as well. One participant elaborated:

[Earning HOURS] differs in certain ways from earning dollars. I am conscious of whether, whichever currency I am getting, I'm under pressure to need. Right now I am out of HOURS and aware of the lack.
   Spending is different. It is a more proactive thing. Much spending is passive—you write checks for bills. But with HOURS I have two rules:
   1. I try not to be cheap when spending HOURS.
   2. I do allow leeway—it is okay to periodically buy something with HOURS.
This is shifting over time though. It is not as true as it was. A good working definition of money is, can you buy food with it? And with this you can, so I have a hard time justifying spending it when you can use it for necessities. But I do get some treats with HOURS.

This presents an interesting dialectic between value and utility. This user carefully monitors the balance of currencies at his disposal. In terms of use, however, having more "regular" use for local currency is cause for restricting spending, presumably putting HOURS closer in line with federal dollars and perhaps moving away from the possibility that local currency defines a different sphere of value. However, there is still a different set of rules for using federal and local currency and, significantly, a distinction about what it means to spend passively versus spending actively. And so value is no longer a simple issue of quantitative equivalencies. The money does not only carry but affects and informs the value of the commodity and the tenor of the exchange.

Discussion

The personal meanings articulated by users indicate that even tenuous contact with the local currency system produced experiences evoking "senses of community." There is the ability to obtain and enjoy "special" goods that connect them to place in a fundamentally material way, or the opportunity to create bonds (either temporary or sustained) with new people, made intelligible by the common participation in the alternative network. There is the realization of belonging and the affirmation of a local identity, shared by the participants and admired by those from the outside. And for some, this network offers a space in which to examine critically and even to challenge the established economic norms of the "regular" market.

Regardless of the small size of complementary currency exchange, it reflects the emergence of an alternative consumption discourse, where the mainstream money (dollars) is connected to necessity, to the danger of scarcity, and to obligation, while the alternative currency is connected to something different, frequently a sort of reward, sometimes a potential burden, but overall something that opens both material and conceptual space for people to reexamine the naturalized conflation of value with price and validate and promote the inclusion of meanings such as social and environmental justice and equity into the calculus of consumption. In Ithaca, the money used colors the experience, understandings, and as a result the direction of material exchange, demonstrating that if, as Keith Hart has aptly argued, the medium of exchange is primarily a vehicle of information, then different currencies can codify and promote different ways to trade and consume. Minimally, this challenges the neutrality of money as an economic metric of objective value. The case of alternative currency indicates that money can shape how we understand, represent, and count economic value. In the search for fairness, we may thus need to reproblematize and repoliticize not only specific trade activities but the medium by which they are carried out as a force that affects the terms as well as outcomes of global trade.

NOTES

1. Money's symbolic power in shaping economic realities is well illustrated by two examples of recent work on money. Mahir Şaul (2004) traces the use of money as a political tool by colonial authorities in West Africa to break down the preexisting regional

trade networks that used cowry shells and to establish colonial economies. Beth Notar (2004) traces how money was used to build identities and networks of political/ideological loyalties in China.

2. Money is a very ancient institution, but even a cursory examination of numismatic history will show that in ancient monetized economies, not all state-issue coinage was meant for standard commercial use but reflected the existence of different "spheres of value" (Alpha Bank Numismatic Collection Online, 2007, http://www.alphabank.gr/page/default.asp?id=686&la=2).

3. I would like to draw attention to the fact that the glossary available on the website of the Chicago Branch of the Federal Reserve Bank calls money not a store of value, which is the overwhelmingly common wording for that function of money, but a store of *purchasing power* (http://www.chicagofed.org/glossary/).

4. In the United States, alternative currencies are perfectly legal under the federal Constitution and under most state constitutions, provided that income is reported and taxes are paid.

WORKS CITED

Appadurai, A.
  1996 Modernity at Large: Cultural Dimensions of Globalization. Minneapolis: University of Minnesota Press.
Benson, L., and F. Papavasiliou
  2004 The Social Equity Challenge: Creating and Sustaining a Diverse Community by Means of Local Currency. Paper presented at the Local Currencies in the Twenty First Century Conference, Bard College, New York, June 25–27.
Bohannan, P. J.
  1959 The Impact of Money on an African Subsistence Economy. Journal of Economic History 12: 491–503.
Boyle, D.
  1999a Alternative Currencies, Alternative Identities. London: Center for Reform.
  1999b Funny Money: In Search of Alternative Cash. New York: HarperCollins.
  2002 Money Changers. London: Earthscan.
Cahn, E.
  2004 No More Throw-Away People. Washington, DC: Essential Books.
Cahn, E., and J. Rowe
  1992 Time Dollars: The New Currency That Enables Americans to Turn Their Hidden Resource—Time—into Personal Security and Community Renewal. Emmaus, PA: Rodale.
Complementary Currency Resource Center
  2009 World Map of Complementary Currency Systems. http://www.complementary-currency.org/ccDatabase/maps/worldmap.php, accessed January 2009.
Collom, E.
  2005 Community Currency in the United States: The Social Environments in Which It Emerges and Survives. Environment and Planning A 37(9): 1565–1587.

Danby, C.
   2004 Conceptions of Capitalism: Godelier and Keynes. *In* Values and Valuables: From
      the Sacred to the Symbolic. C. Werner and D. Bell, eds. Pp. 67–78. Lanham, MD:
      AltaMira.
Davies, G.
   2002 A History of Money from Ancient Times to the Present Day. Cardiff: University
      of Wales Press.
Douglas, M.
   1967 Primitive Rationing: A Study in Controlled Exchange. *In* Themes in Economic
      Anthropology. R. Firth, ed. Pp. 119–148. London: Tavistock.
Edelman, M., and A. Haugerud
   2004 The Anthropology of Development and Globalization: From Classical Political
      Economy to Contemporary Neoliberalism. New York: Blackwell.
Friedman, M.
   1987 Quantity Theory of Money. *In* The New Palgrave Dictionary of Economics, vol.
      2. S. N. Durlauf and L. E. Blume, eds. Pp 3–20. London: Palgrave Macmillan.
Gibson-Graham, J. K.
   2006 A Postcapitalist Politics. Minneapolis: University of Minnesota Press.
Gledhill, J.
   2004 Neoliberalism. *In* A Companion to the Anthropology of Politics. D. L. Nugent
      and J. Vincent, eds. Pp. 332–348. Oxford, UK: Blackwell.
Glover, P.
   1995 Hometown Money: How to Enrich Your Community with Local Currency.
      Ithaca, NY: Ithaca Money.
Hart, K.
   2001 Money in an Unequal World. London: Profile Books.
Harvey, D.
   1991 The Condition of Postmodernity. Oxford, UK: Blackwell.
Hermann, G.
   2006 Special Money: Ithaca HOURS and Garage Sales. Ethnology 45(2): 125–141.
Hornborg, A.
   2007 Learning from the Tiv: Why a Sustainable Economy Would Have to Be "Multi-
      centric." Culture & Agriculture 29(2): 63–69.
Humphrey, C., and S. Hugh-Jones
   1992 Barter, Exchange and Value: An Anthropological Approach. Cambridge:
      Cambridge University Press.
Hutchinson, F., M. Mellor, and W. Olsen
   2002 The Politics of Money. Towards Sustainability and Economic Democracy.
      London: Pluto.
Jacob, J., M. Brinkerhoff, E. Jovic, and G. Wheatley
   2004a HOUR Town—Paul Glover and the Genesis and Evolution of Ithaca HOURS.
      International Journal of Community Currency Research 8.
   2004b The Social and Cultural Capital of Community Currency, an Ithaca HOURS
      Case Study Survey. International Journal of Community Currency Research 8.

Lietaer, B.
2004 Complementary Currencies in Japan Today: History, Originality and Relevance. International Journal of Community Currency Research 8(1): 1–23.

Lyson, T. A.
2003 Global Capital and the Transformation of Rural Communities. *In* Handbook of Rural Studies, T. Marsden, P. Cloke, and P. Mooney, eds. Pp. 292–303. London: Sage.

Marx, K.
1990 Capital, vol. 1. London: Penguin Classics.

Maurer, B.
2005 Mutual Life, Limited. Princeton, NJ: Princeton University Press.

Mauss, M.
1964 The Gift. New York: Norton.

Notar, B.
2004 Ties That Dissolve and Bind: Competing Currencies, Prestige and Politics in Early Twentieth Century China. *In* Values and Valuables: From the Sacred to the Symbolic. D. Bell and C Werner, eds. Pp. 128–157. Lanham, MD: AltaMira.

Pamuk, O.
2001 My Name Is Red. New York: Vintage Books.

Pospisil, L.
1963 Kapauku Papuan Economy. New Haven, CT: Yale University Publications.

Raddon, M. B.
2003 Community and Money: Men and Women Making Change. Montreal: Black Rose.

Ray, P. H., and S. R. Anderson
2000 The Cultural Creatives. New York: Harmony Books.

Rowbotham, M.
1998 The Grip of Death: A Study in Modern Money, Debt Slavery and Destructive Economics. Charlbury, UK: Jon Carpenter.

Salisbury, R. F.
1962 From Stone to Steel. London: Cambridge University Press.

Şaul, M.
2004 Money in Colonial Transition: Cowries and Francs in West Africa. American Anthropologist 106(1): 71–84.

Shuman, M. H.
1998 Going Local: Creating Self-Reliant Communities in a Global Age. New York: Free Press.

Simmel, G.
2004 The Philosophy of Money. Translated by T. Bottomore and D. Frisby. New York: Routledge.

Strathern, M.
1990 The Gender of the Gift. Berkeley: University of California Press.

Trentmann, F.
2006 The Modern Genealogy of the Consumer: Meanings, Identities and Political Synapses. *In* Consuming Cultures, Global Perspectives: Historical Trajectories, Transnational Exchanges. J. Brewer and F. Trentmann eds. Pp. 19–69. Oxford, UK: Berg.

Wilk, R. R., and L. Cliggett
  2007 Economies and Cultures: Foundations of Economic Anthropology. Boulder, CO: Westview.
Yoshida, N.
  2002 Estimating Multiplier Effects of Ithaca Hours. Ithaca Hours Inc. Archive, History Center in Tompkins County, Ithaca, NY.
Zelizer, V. A.
  1994 The Social Meaning of Money. New York: Basic Books.

Relationship Coffees

Structure and Agency in the Fair Trade System

MOLLY DOANE

> You are directly supporting a better life for farming fam-
> ilies through fair prices, direct trade, community devel-
> opment, and environmental stewardship.
> —text next to the fair trade certification seal on a
> Harvest coffee bag

Introduction

In this chapter I explore the fair trade market in the U.S. Midwest as it is seen by activist students and coffee roasters, and in Mexico among professionals who market fair trade coffee and producers who sell to midwestern consumers. Many of these informants are involved in buying, selling, marketing, shipping, or producing the beans produced by Solidarity Coffee Cooperative in Chiapas, Mexico. Fair trade is a globally regulated system intended to build social-justice criteria into market transactions between core consumers and peripheral commodity producers (Raynolds et al. 2007). On its face, fair trade seems to offer a correction to the impersonal mechanisms that govern trade and to allow for the direct negotiation of value and price between producer and consumer. It promises to open the "black box" that hides the social relations behind commodity production and exchange (Collins 2003).

However, it seems to me that this discourse invokes an ideal "Smithian" vision of how markets function. The language of choice, equal exchange, and direct relationships obfuscates the political economy of fair trade markets, which are a complex and well-organized system of privatized regulation that help to stabilize the smallholding coffee sector as well as the world's supply of gourmet coffee. Rather than shed light on the ongoing challenges faced by producers and the solutions they have fashioned, fair trade practice highlights the power of personal choice and agency of consumers. Thus, rather than defetishize the commodity, fair trade may well "refetishize" it—hiding the social relations of the fair trade system even as we try to reveal them through our discourse. This is not surprising—fair trade coffee is sold on free markets and within a U.S. market-culture lens that emphasizes personal agency and efficacy in a neoliberal structure that itself reinforces ideas about individual agency and diminishes the crucial role of socially agreed upon rules (such as market regulations and commodity agreements) that make civility possible. That the cultural models of consumers affect the way they envision alternatives is supported by contrasting their perspectives on the fair trade system with those of producers at the front end of this commodity chain. Coffee producers see the fair trade system through an organizational perspective that reflects a longstanding practice of organizing commodity transactions through the state, agricultural cooperatives, and campesino unions.

David Harvey (2006) defines the neoliberal era as a regime of accumulation characterized by "accumulation through dispossession" in which new wealth is acquired not through production (as in Fordism) but when social wealth (such as that invested in infrastructure) is redistributed to individuals via privatization measures, effectively transferring wealth potentially available to the bottom economic tiers to private interests at the top. At the political level, accumulation through dispossession can be accomplished only with a compatible program of deregulation for industries and markets. In the case of coffee, deregulation of coffee prices undercut the efforts of producer nations to keep coffee prices high enough to generate foreign exchange for the global south (Raffaelli 1995; Daviron and Ponte 2005).

The origins of the coffee crisis have been summarized in several places (Goodman 2008; Daviron and Ponte 2005; Raynolds et al. 2007; Raffaelli 1995; Talbot 2004). Beginning in the Great Depression, coffee-producing nations began to control world coffee prices through programs of targeted crop destruction and to pressure consumer nations to agree to minimum pricing standards. The United States, committed to a policy of cheap staple groceries (including coffee and bananas), resisted any agreements. However, by the 1960s the efforts of producer nations resulted in the International Coffee Agreement (Raffaelli 1995). According to a USAID official, the International Coffee Agreement, which stabilized coffee prices globally, lost relevance within the international community after the fall of the Soviet Union (IADB 2002). Apparently, by keeping coffee prices relatively high, policymakers sought to discourage leftist sentiments among peasant producers, or at least to remove any incentive for allegiance with Soviet-backed regimes. However, in the neoliberal era policymakers have also reacted to instability in the coffee production system. Coffee growers suffered from rock-bottom prices again in 2001, leading to congressional hearings and a USAID/World Bank initiative to bring large corporate coffee buyers such as Starbucks into the fair trade system (U.S. Congress 2002). Thus, the fair trade market experienced its largest expansion partly as a result of concerted policy efforts to institutionalize a privatized form of regulation. In November 2005, full-page ads in the *New York Times* celebrated that Starbucks was now the largest buyer of fair trade coffee in the world.

Sassen (2006) looks at governance systems as constellations of rules organizing territory, establishing (state) authority, and setting the limits of individual rights and benefits. She argues that in the past few decades, authority has gradually shifted from the public and legislative arena to the executive branch and that private organizations and markets have taken on more regulatory authority as nation-states forgo these activities. Sassen's work can be used to frame and contextualize fair trade, a movement that works to reform or regulate markets, now an important locus of authority. At the same time, as fair trade disseminates the idea that markets can trade in justice, the fair trade movement helps to legitimize the market as an independent agent of change. Just as the locus of state authority has changed from the legislative and bureaucratic domains to the executive domains and the market, social movements that once tried to redirect state policy via legislation now engage with a new locus of authority, the market.

In this context, fair trade has emerged as a complexly intertwined specialty market and social movement (Jaffee 2007). The fair trade social movement operates in an environment in which it is no longer legitimate to expect global regulation or price supports. Activists either can agitate to strengthen state regimes, or they can find new foci of reform. That the marriage of market and movement is uncomfortable and fraught with challenges has been pointed out in many places (Fisher 2007; Lyon 2007a, 2007b; Jaffee 2007; Mutersbaugh 2005; Raynolds et al. 2007; Smith 2007). Not least of these discomforts is the commodification of political action inherent in fair trade (Fisher 2007). The commodification of politics in fair trade presents particular challenges because market success—which is the result of many people acting on their political impulses—can result in the failure of the fair trade system (Jaffee 2007).

Jaffee (2007) recently argued that the social-justice mission of fair trade is endangered as fair trade goods become more and more widely distributed in the market. He refers to the ideas of Karl Polanyi, who, like Marx, highlighted the inability of markets to achieve socially desired moral ends. In the case of fair trade, as it becomes more mainstream—available as brands offered by companies with poor corporate reputations but large market investments in fair trade—the fair trade product is disembedded from fair practice. This dilutes the impact of fair trade in several ways: it severs the product from its critique of unfair "free" market practice, it puts fair trade activists and proponents in a difficult position in relation to corporations it may wish to monitor and criticize, and it contributes to and legitimizes "market thinking" among the professionals who are collectively responsible for setting fair trade prices and standards. That is, fair trade regulators have incentives to regulate fair trade in accordance with an abstract idea of the market and what the market will bear rather than in accordance with the producer's cost of living. Thus, as the fair trade movement succeeds in making fair trade products more available on the market, it sows the seeds of failure for its social-justice mission.

Not all researchers are as wary of fair trade mainstreaming as Jaffee. Raynolds et al. (2007) and Goodman (2008) seem to think that mainstreaming is the only possible way to expand fair trade's benefits to producers meaningfully. My concern here has less to do with mainstreaming and more to do with the nature of regulation in the neoliberal context. In the case of coffee, when commodity agreements that stabilized prices were abrogated (unilaterally by the United States), massive instability for both producers and markets ensued, and now, albeit in limited ways, private forms of regulation are being pursued. But these forms of regulation are limited to a relatively small number of growers who participate in one of several certification programs, such as organic, fair trade, or shade grown (Goodman 2008). Moreover, regulation is not organized, written, and enforced by producer countries but rather by consumer countries. This represents a disturbing shift in power relationships.

In what follows I sketch out the shifting cultural meanings of the fair trade market as it moves along a continuum from coffee shop to coffee plot. I am particularly interested in the complex interplay of structure and agency, and ideas about structure and agency, within a global movement that plays out in distinctly different historical and spatial contexts. My observations are based on research with roasters, activists, consumers, and producers conducted between 2005 and 2008, funded by grants from the National Science Foundation and the Wenner Gren Foundation. Data comes from participant observation on the consumer side at public events and conferences; consumer focus groups; and more than sixty interviews with roasters, coffee shop managers, and fair trade "leaders" from fair trade regulatory agencies and NGOs that work on fair trade projects. On the producer side, data comes from seven months of ethnographic fieldwork, including participant observation with coffee producers in their coffee plots and homes and during cooperative meetings, and forty semistructured interviews with coffee producers. I explore the fair trade movement in three venues: the roaster-consumer milieu in the Midwest; the regulatory context that takes place globally but that is most easily observed where professionals gather, such as at professional and student conferences; and in Chiapas, Mexico, where coffee is produced.

Selling Coffee in the Midwest: Market Culture and Choice

The Chiapas Chili Cook-Off was held at St. Mary's, a Catholic church on the liberal east side of Milwaukee, a large midwestern city, on a crisp winter day. The basement of the church was full of casually dressed people—jeans, T-shirts, and colorful hand-knit sweaters from the Andes to fend off the February cold. A dozen pots of chili of various sorts, including bratwurst, veggie, and turkey, were lined up on a long cafeteria table. Wine and beer flowed, and the din of conversation warmed the room. Crafts from Chiapas, bottles of tequila, and bags of fair trade coffee were auctioned off to raise money for San Pedro, the sister parish of St. Mary's in Chiapas. It was a parishioner of St. Mary's Church who originally (ca. 1999) brought a sample of organic coffee from the Tenjapa region of Chiapas to Harvest Roasters in Milwaukee. Fair trade coffee from Mexico and other places now makes up almost half of Harvest Coffee's wholesale inventory, and the company ranks among the top fifteen wholesalers of fair trade coffee in the nation. Locally, Harvest Coffee is wildly popular for its earthy coffee shops. It is carried by local food cooperatives and gourmet groceries. It sponsors community events such as music and film festivals and advertises on community and public radio. In the culture of Milwaukee, both Harvest Coffee and fair trade coffee are mainstays of the progressive cultural scene.

Like other coffee shops in the area, Harvest Coffee sold specialty coffee before fair trade coffee existed as a phenomenon in the United States. Doug Lerner, owner and founder of Harvest Coffee, got into the coffee business in the early nineties, after changes in the regulatory system and in the industry made it possible for relatively small roasters to import inventory (see Roseberry 1996). As his company expanded in scale, he was able to import coffee directly from origin. However, some coffee markets were still tightly controlled by particular importers. Like many roasters, Harvest looked for a wider variety of sources in order to buy coffee in large volumes:

> Lots of origins—Colombia, Sumatra, Guatemala, Mexico, Costa Rica—a lot of these origins are places we can buy that kind of volume from. As you cross that barrier with each successive origin, we try to get our people down there and start talking to people that we've been familiar with through years previous working through brokers. . . . Maybe we'll go visit the farm, . . . and he wants to pursue a direct relationship, so you develop a relationship with him or her. So it's a very organic process, as your capacity to find those kinds of quantities comes and your capacity to do that kind of travel and your capacity to endure the risks of direct purchasing. If your coffee gets on a boat and gets saturated with seawater, as a guy buying one container of coffee you probably don't have a lot of leverage to rectify that situation. And what court is going to enforce monetary actions between you and Colombia? None. So really these international transactions are born on the back of relationships, and as a small relationship, your leverage is small. . . . And you also don't gain tremendous economy by buying direct from origin. It's not just that you're saving a lot of money by cutting out the middleman; you save some, but not a lot. Really it's—the value is in being able to get the relationships and capture the right quality from the right grower. That's really the value there. But you endure the risk as well because quality goes up, but it also goes down. (Doug Lerner, interview with author, Milwaukee, Wisconsin, July 17, 2007)

Specialty coffee shops such as Harvest popped up all over the country as changes in the global regulatory system that controlled coffee prices for producers broke up, creating new opportunities for small roasters. The expansion of coffee cropping from large plantations (the main suppliers of the coffee giants) to small peasant-held properties expanded coffee production into areas not controlled by the coffee giants. Roseberry (1996), following N. Harvey (1990), described the plantation model as "Fordist" (capital intensive, nationally regulated), in contrast to the smaller, more flexible "post-Fordist" roasters. In a very real sense the post-Fordist coffee market displayed a flexibility and openness to innovation that transformed coffee selling and purchasing. Both roasters and consumers were exposed to a wide variety of new coffee flavors and origins, reflecting the post-Fordist sensibility of both choice and quality through the market. In this new model, the profit that derived from enormous efficiencies of scale in the Fordist coffee market were replaced by profit derived from premiums assessed for quality and originality. Not insignificantly, within the new political economy of coffee, roasters all over the country also became coffee buyers and importers, traveling all over the world in the process. In the new model, companies of massive scale (e.g., Nestlé or Maxwell House) are replaced by lone businesspersons, defined by Lerner as risk takers and innovators and mirroring the flexible, creative, and youthful model of business entrepreneurship in the digital economy. In this model, risk is mediated not by enormous scale but by calculating chance against knowledge—in this case of coffee quality.

As Roseberry (1996) has pointed out, specialty roasters are a new breed of businessperson. They do not take up roasting as a family trade and therefore come to the business with little or no experience in coffee roasting. There is a surprising demographic consistency among the mid-western roasters I interviewed. All are thirty- to forty-something men, most with young families. All are at the very least college educated, some with advanced degrees, all in the social sciences. Coffee roasters tended to like the coffeehouse culture, to be inquiring and educated, and to enjoy a certain amount of adventure—through foreign travel to origin as well as through quite commonly shared interests such as adventure sports like cycling. They are innovative, risk-taking individuals with a strong belief in the power of personal efficacy to change the world.

Steve Lansing from Synergy, a local chain of coffee roasters also located in Milwaukee, explained that his business success made him want to "give back" to the community:

> I've felt that I could make a difference in the world, but . . . money is really one of the keys to making that happen. So it was my belief that I could start a company, and I could use the energies and the knowledge and all the in-fluence that a company could have to actually influence social change. (Steve Lansing, interview with author, Milwaukee, Wisconsin, January 26, 2007)

Jason Brown, the manager of Culture and Communications at Harvest Coffee, created his own position at the company. He had seen fair trade coffee taking off during his master's research in Latin America. Upon his return in 2001, he convinced the owners of Harvest Roasters that fair trade coffees would be a valuable addition to their specialty offerings. Harvest was in a good position to source and import fair trade coffees, and it was already importing coffee from Solidarity Coffee on an informal fair trade basis—that is, importing the coffee at a fair trade price but without Trans-Fair licensing.

Jason communicates with producers, travels to origin to familiarize himself with particular cooperatives, and manages public relations in Milwaukee. He presents papers at professional conferences and works with student groups that promote fair trade. Over the years, Jason has developed a strong personal relationship with Juan Mendez, a Tzeltal Maya-speaking coffee producer whose excellent command of Spanish and general business and organizational skills have made him a cooperative leader and a conduit between roasters and the general cooperative membership. Like Doug Lerner, Jason highlights the "structural" aspects of the fair trade system:

> What I like about fair trade is that it allows—specifically in the coffee example—allows small-scale coffee farmers to continue to produce. And as we saw with the coffee crisis of 2001 and 2002, those small-scale producers were the ones who were the most vulnerable to the price crash, and they're the ones who were uprooted from their farms, their small farms, or who couldn't find work on the big estates and who ended up having to move to the cities and live in shanty towns and in some cases try to immigrate illegally into the U.S. And what fair trade does with those farmers, if those farmers are fortunate enough to be selling through the fair trade market, they have at least some support to help them to continue to produce coffee because if you've got a farmer out there who doesn't really have a system to fall back on, that farmer is essentially hostage not just to coyotes but also to market fluctuations and things as simple as lack of transportation, lack of market access, remote locations. So these are factors that can essentially make or break a coffee farmer's life and the life of his or her family. And so I think fair trade contributes to sustainability in that it allows these farmers to *be* farmers and to produce the coffee that is demanded for the export market.

However, for Jason, consumer agency is ultimately the driving force of the fair trade movement. He explains:

I usually define fair trade as a consumer—"consumer-based movement" to guarantee that small-scale producers of agricultural products grown in the developing world and consumed in the developed world receive a higher or fair price for that product. That's kind of how I describe fair trade because I believe it really is consumer based—that you can have all of these fair-trade-certified producers around the world, and if their products are not being sold to the fair trade market, then their certification doesn't really matter. So it's really up to the end consumer to make the conscious choice to buy the fair trade product. (Jason Brown, interview with author, Milwaukee, Wisconsin, April 20, 2006)

Consumer agency in supporting the welfare of farmers is stressed during public events, where the presence of coffee farmers is often the main draw. In 2006, a farmer from Tanzania, featured in a nationally released film called *Black Gold,* came to an annual fair trade event at the Milwaukee Museum of Art. A panel of fair trade leaders from local roasters, food co-ops, and the certifying agency TransFair explained to the assembled public the purposes and benefits of fair trade. In these presentations, farmers, such as Tadesse from Tanzania, become the visual proof of the direct and humane market relationships that underlie the fair trade market. Public events celebrating fair trade ubiquitously feature coffee farmers, whose presence on a midwestern stage is a synecdoche for the global relationship.

Roasters are aware that there is a distance between what consumers understand about fair trade and the way the system works. Roasters themselves have a more chary view of the economies of cutting out middlemen. They know that even "direct" relationships are mediated by a series of buying, marketing, shipping, warehousing, and contracting agents that move coffee from field to roasting location. They know that the fair trade price is set by regulatory bodies dominated by large-scale wholesalers, where producers are scarcely represented. Jason Brown from Harvest Coffee expressed surprise at the general hullabaloo around fair trade coffee, which he feels should not be set up as an answer to political or economic change in the world. Instead, he sees fair trade as a pragmatic, albeit socially responsible, approach to business:

I would have to say that before I came to work for Harvest Coffee I was fairly cynical about the private sector and business in general. This is my first real job in the private sector, and it is definitely not what I would call typical or corporate America or anything like that. But what I've learned in my time here is that our world and our civilization is essentially based on commerce, and people essentially live based on the buying and selling of products, services, and ideas. And for us it's obviously a product. (Brown interview)

Consuming Fair Trade in the Midwest

In contrast to fair trade professionals such as roasters and certifiers, consumers of fair trade coffee do not have "roaster" knowledge or structural position. Their attitudes about fair trade are largely determined by fair trade marketing. Fair trade marketing appears informational—designed for an educated and activist consumer. Graphics on coffee bags evoke images of nature or southern climes or even reproduce images of coffee growers themselves. Fair trade in name and on coffee bags suggests that choosing one particular coffee over another will promote a host of progressive values, not least an equitable economic exchange between consumer and producer. Why is this message so powerful?

Scholarship on consumer society shows that modern advertising is never simply informational. Rather, it is emotional, seeking to connect products to pleasant emotions and deeply desired states, such as happiness, love, friendship, and a sense of efficacy. Williams (1980) described advertising as a "magic system" because commodities—dead things— are invested with life-affirming properties: they have the power to grant beauty, happiness, health, and so on. The connection between products and feelings is quite entrenched in our culture and relates to a manufacturing political economy in which the very survival of the political economy is linked to consumption practices (Cohen 2004). Environmental values might be expressed through shopping at nature-themed stores such as the Body Shop (Price 1996) or through the consumption of certain brands associated with the outdoors (see Klein 2002). The hallowed place of nature in middle-class U.S. culture has long philosophical and political roots (Gottlieb 2005); its emotional importance has increased as the middle classes lose connections to manual and outdoor work, forging new associations between nature and leisure or pleasure (White 1996).

Fair trade marketing also taps into feelings of personal, political, and economic alienation. It is a fantasy of community and place in a displaced context. In a highly decentralized industrial world, where layers of outsourcing increasingly obscure the connections between producers, products, and consumers, fair trade promises a direct connection between a producer, a product produced wholly in place, and a consumer. In this decentralized world where accountability is difficult, and consumers with the highest standards of social justice may be unknowingly benefiting from the products of child labor or criminally cheap labor, fair trade promises just economic relationships. In a world characterized by industrial forms of food production, it is a conduit to family forms of agricultural production.

Between spring 2005 and summer 2007, I interviewed several dozen students individually and in focus groups. All were students active in campus fair trade initiatives or familiar with fair trade through their involvement in student social-justice groups at Marquette, a Catholic university in Milwaukee. According to these students, direct relationships are one of the chief advantages of fair trade products. Direct relationships correct the commodity relationship. According to Anna, who was asked what defined fair trade,

> I don't know, I think the term *free trade* is a bit of a misnomer. I mean, it's free for the person that's in an advantageous economic position, you know, whereas the other person is doing it out of necessity, and they're willing to take lower prices for whatever they're selling 'cause they feel that's the only thing they can get for it. But fair trade, it's, you know, fair. It's not about getting as much money as you can possibly get. It's about being reasonable and seeing that the person that you're engaging with is a person too, and they need to eat and live as much as you. (Marquette University, August 2006)

In this excerpt, Anna is particularly concerned about adjusting or correcting the abuses of the market. The idea that fair trade removes some specified or unspecified layers or obstructions comes up repeatedly when students are asked to define or characterize fair trade:

> I describe fair trade as a consumer movement that is a lot about farmers' rights and environmental sustainability and gender equality and giving people, both consumers and farmers and coffee growers and other growers, resources and access to each other and access to a fair market instead of a system they don't understand. (Beth, Marquette University, August 2006)

Students stressed direct trade, transparency, and most commonly, cutting out the middleman. However, it is important to note that most student

consumers did not interpret fair trade relationships as a radical move—
a defetishization of the commodity in Marxian terms (Marx 1976). Most
students in the focus groups vastly preferred to buy fair trade coffee where
available, but they were also accepting of conventional coffee. This is ex-
emplified well by the following conversation among students after dis-
covering, in the context of a February 2006 campus fair trade event, that
Harvest Coffee Roasters, the campus fair trade coffee supplier, sells 70
percent conventional coffees and only 30 percent fair trade coffee within
its total sales.

> MICHELLE: I don't think fair trade and free trade coffees are neces-
> sarily incompatible.
> DOUG: Absolutely. Fair trade would not be possible without the free
> trade system.
> JENNY: I know—I have tried to explain that to my mother. She won't
> buy fair trade coffee because she thinks it is protest. I have told her
> that it is *not* protest.
> DOUG: That's right. Anyway, some day all free trade will follow the
> fair trade model. It will all be fair trade.

This sentiment—that fair trade is not a radical move and is more rightly
viewed as a correction to a prevailing model—was echoed in a focus group
conducted by one of my research assistants in May of the same year:

> STUDENT: I think part of the confusion is I don't think, like, fair trade
> and free trade wouldn't be opposites. From my understanding, it's a
> pretty different thing. Free trade has to do with tariffs on imports
> and exports, and fair trade is cutting out the middleman and pay-
> ing growers more. So I don't think—I think it confusing to think of
> them as [pause] . . .
> RESEARCH ASSISTANT: Complete opposites.
> STUDENT: Yeah, 'cause I don't think they're opposites.

On the whole, student views of fair trade on an active but not radical
campus struck me as fundamentally Smithian. Fair trade, rather than exposing the fundamental contradictions of the global commodity markets
and demanding, as a logical extension, radical political economic change,
seemed to serve as a necessary corrective to a system that sometimes could
get out of hand. It used the basic principles of neoclassical economics to

critique and correct the system, which has been restored to an ideal state of transparency and efficiency.

The idea that capitalist economic exchange is contractual, based on mutual negotiation and mutual desire, and most properly conducted between individuals (not states) is an entrenched cultural ideal. As has been argued in many places, Smithian ideas of the market permeate U.S. ideas not only of the market itself (Carrier 1997) but also the general understanding of individual life history, social life, and social action (Bellah 1996; Holland 1998; Newman 1988). Carrier (1997) argues that the market itself is best understood as a "cultural model." This cultural model consists of several central beliefs: (1) Society is composed of free individuals who act voluntarily and is nothing more than the sum of these independently operating parts. (2) In economic matters, the world consists of buyers and sellers. Both want the best price (over any other noneconomic wish or preference) and exercise choice to select the best (and cheapest) product from the seller. The market is thus a means of communication between buyer and seller. (3) Restricting choice is morally reprehensible because it upsets the free and voluntary negotiations between buyer and seller. In this virtual reality, markets are naturalized, following the Smithian model that markets are the inevitable outcome of human nature and its proclivity to "truck and barter." Thus, markets are a fundamental part of human nature, rather than a creation of human political economies. Markets are neither good, bad, fair, nor unfair—they are simply the outcome of interpersonal negotiations among free individuals acting in their own interests.

Since markets do not in reality function freely but rather are subject to myriad regulations that are the outcome of political negotiation, the free market can exist only as an ideal. However, this ideal is frequently treated as an a priori assumption, informing and underlying real-world policy decisions. Thus, in a culture of the market, "virtualism" dominates—actors must play by the rules of a fake reality superimposed on the actual, underlying political economy. For example, IMF officials impose structural adjustment policies that demand that debtor nations abandon subsidies and price supports for their own farmers in order to participate in a global free market. However, lender nations are not required to drop their own subsidies and price supports for farmers (Carrier and Miller 1998). Thus, one effect of market virtualism is to reinscribe historical inequalities between core and periphery while appealing to progressive ideals of freedom and participation. At this moment, fair trade operates not within free markets but rather within neoliberal markets. Neoliberalism does not make markets function more "freely" (it tends to regulate in favor of capital markets rather than in favor of particular national commodities), but its rhetoric of free global markets helps to reinforce popular ideology about the market.

Privatizing Regulation and the Crisis in Fairness

The neoliberal restructuring of the market described by David Harvey (2006) contributed to the periodic coffee crises after 1989, during which the coffee market was characterized by volatility and overall price decline. The volatility of markets affected coffee quality, global coffee supplies, and in a feedback loop, coffee prices. This volatility was particularly bad for small farmers (large plantations can better weather annual price fluctuations) who faced periodic subsistence crises as a result, sometimes choosing to exit the coffee business altogether. It was also bad for specialty coffee roasters, who had trouble predicting supply, price, and quality under these conditions. Fair trade commodity chains have helped to reregulate that market through private and voluntary agreements, constituting a new system of privatized regulation. This system of privatized regulation has been arrived at as a result of years of organization among activist networks, the development of international and national NGOs dedicated to creating a verifiable system of fair commodity trade, and a network of coffee roasters and shops that have expanded the consumer niche for fair trade coffee. Privatized regulation developed within the new neoliberal contexts that destabilized more inclusive commodity agreements among trading nations.

In order briefly to elucidate the privatized regulatory structure, I now turn to an ethnographic examination of the regulatory framework of fair trade coffee. The richest venue for ethnographic research concerning the regulatory framework is the annual convergence of the United Students for Fair Trade (USFT), where representatives from the development world, certification professionals, small roasters, corporate representatives, and fair trade activists meet for educational fora and informally to hash out policy and goals.

One of the great controversies that emerged during the 2007 convergence involved standards of fairness within the system. At this time, the fair trade licensing organization (FLO) was considering a proposal to raise the minimum guaranteed price of fair trade coffee. FLO is an international NGO that has twenty affiliates in consumer countries, including TransFair USA. FLO has a board of directors, until 2006 drawn exclusively from twenty consumer countries that set the price of fair trade coffee. In 2007, three producer unions—one from Latin America, one from Asia, and one from Africa—were officially included within the FLO membership. Critics of the system from the United Students for Fair Trade and Cooperative Coffees have been troubled that the price of fair trade coffee has not been raised by FLO in the eleven years since its inception. The base price for fair trade coffee (nonorganic) in 2006 was $1.21 per pound paid to the individual producer, plus a five-cent social premium per pound that went to the cooperative for social development projects. In 1989, when global coffee prices were deregulated, the world coffee price was $1.21 per pound. In March 2007, FLO decided against raising the base price for fair trade coffee, instead opting to raise the social premium from five to ten cents. The FLO board is heavily weighted toward the coffee industry.

In the United States, roasters are licensed to sell fair trade coffee by a nongovernmental organization, TransFair. TransFair has the sole right to label FLO-certified fair trade coffee within the United States and to license individual roasters and retailers that wish to carry TransFair coffee. Another major debate in the fair trade system is over the propriety of licensing large corporations to sell TransFair coffee. Within the fair trade system, a small minority of roasters have rebelled against TransFair and FLO. They elect to pay higher prices for fair trade coffee but do not pay for a TransFair license. TransFair USA and its corollaries in other consumer countries represent a privatized system of regulation that operates to guarantee enough stability in the marketplace that coffee production is not compromised. At the same time, the social premium, often invested in coffee-related projects such as drying patios, fermentation tanks, and new trees guarantees the higher-quality coffee for which consumers pay a premium as actual coffee prices for roasters and retailers decline.

TransFair labels allow individuals to operate as activist consumers, letting their choices, commodified through the market, shape the political economic landscape. Political action is boiled down to individual choice and behavior and is also benignly recast as a socially responsible act, akin to charity, rather than as a political act akin to protest. This reinforces a benign, self-regulating ideology of the market system—democracy can naturally flow from one's economic transactions within it. One of the hinges of Marx's critique of capitalism is commodity fetishism. Commodities sold on the market derive their value from the labor that transformed them from raw materials to useful objects. However, the value of that labor in time and effort, the human contribution to things, is not visible to consumers who buy goods on the market, and ultimately the value added by labor comes to be viewed as an objective property of the thing itself. As objects become detached from their origins in production, consumers of things no longer consider the people who produce them. Fair trade marketing, because it stresses direct relationships between producers and consumers, suggests that fair trade effectively "defetishizes" the commodity being traded. That is, the labor that produces the commodity is no longer invisible; it is no longer alienated from the consumer, and consumer and producer are now linked in a mutually negotiated, moral relationship. In a recent article, Fisher rightly argues that fair trade cannot possibly effect this defetishization: the power differences between producers and coffee buyers and consumers are too great to allow for meaningful negotiation. Fisher goes on to argue that fair trade, rather than representing a defetishization of the commodity, actually represents a commodification of political action, or rather the creation of a new commodity where the (labor) value added is political action (Fisher 2007). The commodification of political action has become ubiquitous in fair trade, green consumption, and politics itself.

However, as fair trade expands from the college coffee shop to the local Dunkin' Donuts, it is not clear that the political message of fair trade, however imperfect, is commodified along with the product. I argue that what is increasingly sold is a message about the ideal functioning of the privately regulated, rigorously audited, transparent market system. As fair trade enters new and more traditional markets, it is "refetishized." The truly complicated workings of the system remain invisible. But now the critique of the global political economy at the root of fair trade and the years of solidarity work and political action for global justice that went into its creation are equally obscured.

That market language deradicalizes the fair trade message is understood by Peter Henley, the founder of Revolution Roasters, a one-hundred-percent fair trade roaster headquartered in a liberal midwestern college town:

> I thought the idea for a long time that most of our political discourse is happening through the market. And that's what we're told to believe, like somehow capitalism and democracy are the same thing now. And they talk about voting with your dollar, and I really have always hated that language. I don't think it's a good place to go, but what I sort of came to finding is

that there's a certain reality to it, and you can fight against it and turn your back on it. And that's one way that you can sort of oppose, or you can roll up your sleeves and kind of get into it and decide, I'm going to use the language of market exchange, the language of capitalism, and I'm going to turn it on its ass. Fair trade is a redistribution of wealth, and that scares them: "Oh, that's communism." And that's what it's all about, just keep pushing and asking for more and keep thinking about fair trade as a way to change the relationships between consumers and producers and businesses. It's a movement of economic and social justice, and we can't let it not be that way. We can't let it be a brand, and that's why we left the system; that was our response. (Peter Henley, interview with author, USFT Conference, Boston. February 17, 2007)

Peter has a bachelor's degree in anthropology and a master's in Latin American studies and a long history of involvement in activism on Latin American issues. His interest in coffee roasting was sparked on a trip to Chiapas, where he was exposed to the Zapatista movement, as well as to a community that wished to find a fair trade buyer for its coffee. Not able to locate a coffee shop willing to buy the Chiapas coffee he brought back, Peter eventually opened his own roaster in the midwestern college town of Madison. His roaster belongs to an association called Cooperative Coffees, a group of one-hundred-percent fair trade coffee roasters that also run their own businesses as cooperatives. Revolution Roasters has grown into a large coffee roaster, wholesaler, and retailer. One of its cooperatives in Guatemala was established on an old plantation that was settled by ex-guerilla fighters. Revolution Roasters and other members of Cooperative Coffees are the most vocal critics of fair trade branding and "fairwashing," the practice of marketing fair trade coffee in order to create a positive corporate image.

Revolution Roasters no longer buys licensing to carry the TransFair label, which in the United States indicates that coffee has been produced under the social and ecological criteria set out by TransFair. One of the major points of contention is that TransFair has brought many large corporations into the fair trade system, including Starbucks, Dunkin' Donuts, and Wal-Mart. These corporations can carry the TransFair label on certified fair trade coffee and carry it among their other retail offerings. Although the coffee itself is produced using fair trade guidelines—within democratically organized cooperatives and according to certain sustainability criteria, all of which must be transparent for certifiers—the roasters and retailers themselves need not be democratic or transparent and may in fact pursue egregious labor and production practices.

The justification for an open-door policy on licensing, according to Jane Campbell of TransFair, is to increase the sheer volume of fair trade coffee that is being sold worldwide and to bring it to a wider public, including those who do not live in cities with a vibrant local coffeehouse culture. The certification of large companies with conventional business practices to sell fair trade products has been controversial within the fair trade movement, especially for progressive roasters and the USFT. At the 2004 USFT conference, the contradictions of admitting Starbucks into the fair trade system were highlighted in a panel entitled "Scaling Up or Selling Out?" At the 2005 meetings of the Specialty Coffee Association of America (SCAA), progressive coffee roasters participated in a panel concerning the ethics of marketing: when does fair trade stop being progressive and instead become a brand or a fairwashing technique for unpopular companies? In Jane's view, regulatory structure, as it might be imposed by FLO and TransFair, was subject to the natural workings of the market. Of course, regulatory frameworks are and have always been heavily influenced by the large corporations they seek to regulate. But the fair trade parlance of negotiation, relationships, and fairness makes this bending to the bottom line problematic to many participants in the system, some of whom feel that large companies such as Starbucks are running away with their alternative market system.

At the same time, the solution of dropping out of the TransFair system, adopted by Revolution Roasters as well as a small number of companies that call themselves "direct" trade companies, is not popular with current USFT leadership. Although USFT leaders are trenchantly critical of TransFair's watered-down version of fair trade, they are unwilling to abandon TransFair and the years of organizing, negotiation, and work it represents. Rather than abandon TransFair and FLO, they would prefer to push TransFair and FLO to adopt regulations that are more favorable to producers than they currently are. Moreover, USFT leadership values the fact that TransFair/FLO makes producer cooperatives central to fair trade. TransFair/FLO regulations require that to be certified coffee must be produced within family- or worker-owned cooperatives rather than on plantations. This helps to support the subsistence sector and to promote and reinforce strong community organizations among rural workers (Tracey Black, USFT, personal communication, November 23, 2008).

View from Mexico

In June 2007, on a rainy day in a tiny hamlet within the municipality of Tenejapa, Chiapas, members, mostly officers, of Solidarity Coffee Coop-erative gathered in a long, concrete-block building that serves as coopera-tive headquarters and as a drop-off and temporary storage site for Har-vest Coffee. After a while, a truck arrived from Comitan, bringing in a group of professionals who work at Mas Café, a marketing cooperative that brings together six producer cooperatives such as Kulaktik. Later, a bureaucrat from the Ministry of Rural Development arrived to meet with the cooperative treasurer, who carefully counted out a stack of cash pesos handed to him by the bureaucrat. The money was paid out as part of a government program to promote organic markets and was meant to offset the costs of certification inspections required by FLO and Certimex, an agency that certifies organics within Mexico and that is in turn empow-ered to provide documentation to international agencies such as FLO.

Solidarity Coffee Cooperative produces fair trade, organic coffee that is sold, marketed, processed, and transported with the help of three nested cooperatives and that receives social support from various government agencies. The cooperative is located in the hills of Tenejapa, a municipal-ity (county) of highland Chiapas located about twenty-five miles from San Cristobal de Las Casas, the regional city. The cooperative is made up of over two hundred producers who come from more than twenty sur-rounding communities or settlements.

Coffee production in the region is relatively new: until the late seven-ties, these farmers produced corn and beans for subsistence, working on coastal coffee farms, known as *fincas*, to earn necessary cash. Coffee is not the first cash crop remembered by informants. During the fifties and six-ties, peanuts were introduced as a cash crop for sale in the world market, but demand for that crop subsequently declined. The story of Antonio, which I have translated and condensed from interview material, is fairly typical of the changes and hardships experienced by older informants:

> I am an orphan. My father died when I was ten of drink. My Mother died when I was twelve of fever. So I had to go work on the coffee *finca*. I went for the first time when I was ten to support my mother. At first I worked in the kitchen because I was too young to work in the fields. When I was twelve, I began agricultural work on the *finca*, under the care of a man

from my own community. The man felt sorry for me and was kind, making sure that I got to pick the most loaded trees so I could fill my bags quickly and earn well. I worked for twelve years on this *finca*. As an adult the work was much harder. You had to get up at two or three in the morning to work until five in the evening. I worked from about 1950 until about 1975 on the *finca* and often felt lonely in my heart.

Eventually I inherited six hectares from my father's estate and was able to marry. At first, we grew peanuts, corn, and beans, and I continued to work seasonally on the *finca*. About thirty years ago we started growing coffee, which was promoted through a government agency called INME-CAFE, and I no longer had to work on the *finca*.

In the seventies, coffee was grown in small quantities and by a few farmers who had brought home seeds from the coffee *fincas,* but it became a major local enterprise after a coffee-planting program was introduced to the area by INMECAFE, the National Coffee Institute. IN-MECAFE provided subsidies, seeds, fertilizers, and pesticides through a loan program and free ongoing technical assistance. During this period, the hillsides of Tenejapa were transformed. Plots once largely deforested and planted in corn were seeded with Chalum trees to shade the coffee bushes.

Schooled in both green-revolution technology and the ideals of the de-campesinista movements (left-oriented activists focused on rural development for marginalized rural people), technicians discouraged farmers from growing food-bearing shade trees and encouraged them to immerse themselves in "modern" farming techniques. Coffee producers spoke very favorably of INMECAFE. Its technicians helped campesinos to build terraces, plant shade trees, grow coffee bushes from seed, prune and maintain plants, and regulate shade. During this period (late seventies to mid-eighties) prices were supported at the national level, and producers were organized into co-ops. Producers described this period as a good one, both for the empowerment of the training they received and for the price of coffee:

> When INMECAFE arrived, they brought technicians who came to tell us and convince us that there was a market for coffee. But still people didn't know if it was true. But then when it really did work, little by little people got organized and began to sell a little coffee and then a little more. This is how INMECAFE worked—they sent a technician to convince the people,

the people agreed they wanted to do this work, and then they planted coffee, like that, little by little. I don't know how many years I worked in my coffee plot before INMECAFE died. (Pancho, interview with author, November 8, 2006)

Many producers described the introduction of coffee marketing in Tenejapa by the Mexican Coffee Agency INMECAFE in similar terms. INMECAFE was described as animated or personified, as a positive force, and as fostering organization. The disappearance of INMECAFE in the late eighties was described as its having "died." After its death, a period of social chaos ensued, during which campesinos, like so many orphans, suffered social abandonment and isolation. This liminal period after the death of INMECAFE gave way to the current period, which started after the formation of Solidarity Coffee Cooperative. Solidarity was formed in the wake of the deregulation of coffee prices internationally and globally. After the disappearance of INMECAFE, prices for coffee dropped radically, because international regulations on prices were abandoned. Coffee farmers experienced this time as chaotic or anarchic, when middlemen or coyotes preyed on the campesinos, who now had no way of knowing what the market price for coffee was but had to take the word of any buyer who showed up at the door:

> Many coyotes arrived in Tenejapa and San Crisotbal and in the community to buy coffee. Yes, we sold the coffee to them, except that they really ripped us off. When they weighed the coffee, a lot of times they shorted us on the weight a few kilos per sack. (Diego, interview with author, December 14, 2006)

Coffee farmers responded to this situation by organizing themselves. Diego went on to explain:

> At that point, I began to think and weigh my options and listen: what would be better than this? Where is there a good organization. Where will they weigh my coffee fairly? That is why I am here [with Kulaktik] today.

Through a network of Catholic churches, local farmers became aware of a coffee coop in Oaxaca (UCIRI) that had begun growing organic coffee for sale in Europe. This co-op put the Tenejapa farmers in contact with a co-op in Chiapas that was also selling organic coffee. In 1992 Solidarity gained entry into the organic fair trade market. Gabriel described the process this way:

> When we were alone—my father was working in coffee during those times—we saw that it wasn't working out with each producer working alone trying to sell his coffee. That is why we formed an organization that gave us the right to sell our coffee to other nations. We saw that if we organized ourselves we would have opportunities—we saw that it is better to be organized. The truth is that really you get some freedom through the association. (Gabriel, interview with author, June 4, 2007)

The history of the cooperative attests to the importance of organization—whether religious, community, or producer based—in maintaining acceptable social and economic conditions. When Solidarity joined the organic cooperative based in the Lacandon forest, they associated themselves with an agenda of political economic autonomy later articulated by the Zapatistas. This led to a break with the local community authorities, at that time (1992) affiliated with the political party PRI, which had ruled in Mexico for almost seventy years. Organic and fair trade coffee production was adopted in the context of a number of other local- and national-level changes. This local history is significant because it is exemplary of the political organization among rural people, who—whether sympathetic to the Zapatistas or not—have found new agency in the past two decades.

This new agency is attributed by many scholars to a democratic opening in Mexico. Along with many anthropologists (Collier and Quaratiello 1994; Collier and Stephen 1997), I think that it has much to do with the retreat from a revolution-era social contract and the declining hegemony of social democracy in general: society as a whole is no longer the source of security for the poorest of its members. This in turn loosens the bonds of clientelism that kept rural people committed to the ruling political party at the national and local levels (Bobrow-Strain 2007). In the current era of market solutions, rural people experience their relative political freedoms in a context of extreme economic insecurity, since there is little protection from the market. Fair trade partnerships and markets offer the best form of security available. However, producers did not prefer the new arrangements to the arrangements that prevailed under INMECAFE and generally found that their earnings were about the same or less than they had been in the late eighties, although the time spent cultivating coffee had increased.

The Harvest-Solidarity commodity chain is an example of a "relation-ship" commodity chain. Harvest is a coffee importer as well as a roaster and retailer. Representatives from Harvest periodically visit Solidarity Co-operative to make recommendations for improving production levels and quality. They have made a long-term commitment to buy Solidarity's cof-fee, despite some problems with coffee quality that arose earlier in their association. Moreover, Harvest has a "give-back" program that returns twenty-five cents to the cooperative for every pound of bagged Solidarity coffee sold in stores. This amounts to thousands of dollars annually that the cooperative can use for necessary equipment or infrastructure, subject to the approval of Harvest. When a landslide decimated the coffee plot of one of Solidarity's members, Harvest sent the producer several thousand dollars to help offset the loss of the crop. Solidarity members value their relationship with Harvest for the support the roaster has extended over the years. Moreover, Solidarity is supported by a strong network of coop-eratives that have built a strong and efficient coffee market for its mem-bers. Solidarity sells all its certified coffee to organic, fair trade buyers and does not have to unload an excess of fair trade beans to conventional coffee buyers, as many coffee cooperatives must (Goodman 2008; Bacon et al. 2008). Thus, this fair trade commodity chain represents a best case scenario within the fair trade world.

However, some of the problems with the system pointed out in a grow-ing literature on the subject were also experienced by my informants. As the fair trade system has become institutionalized through audited prac-tices, it has also become expensive and onerous. Producers with whom I have talked at USFT conferences complain about the costs of certifica-tion. In my field site, dual organic and fair trade certification costs re-sulted in higher costs and necessitated the centralization or merging of separate cooperative structures to create more effective economies of scale and thus save on costs. Producers not only bear the burden of fees imposed by FLO and Certimex, but they also bear the burden of quality control, a cost borne by the buyers in conventional coffee markets (Mut-ersbaugh 2005). This was a major complaint of coffee producers in my study—that under the current system organic coffee is much more labor intensive than conventional coffee. The coffee bushes must be carefully pruned, pests removed, and moss scraped from the bark. The shade trees must also be pruned. Organic coffee bushes require compost, which has to be assembled according to certain specifications and cured by produc-ers. It must be later lugged by the bagful to the often distant coffee plots, requiring a producer to carry, for example, a one-hundred-pound sack of compost a few kilometers up a steep hill. All heavy loads are hauled by means of a *mekapal*—a woven band worn against the forehead and connected by rope to an object tied to one's back. During harvest times, organic production is especially onerous. Ripe coffee cherries have to be selected carefully for picking and reselected during processing. Producers complain that conventional producers can pick anything and even sell the rocks that get mixed in with the coffee beans. Farmers argue that the extra work required to produce high-quality organic coffee is not reflected in the current fair trade price for coffee. The burdens of certification and of the extra work demanded by niche coffee production has been discussed in detail by fair trade coffee researchers (see Jaffee 2007; Lyon 2006; Mutersbaugh 2002).

In my interviews, the coffee system was almost always referred to as "organic." I found that, with the exception of a few cooperative leaders, coffee producers have little or no knowledge of the fair trade system or its purposes. The most frequent response to my question, "What is fair trade?" was "I forget." Most thought it was the same as the organic market—a higher-priced and higher-quality niche. They were not sure why it was "fair" and viewed the fair trade market as "the market that we have right now." A reasonable market for producers was not a matter of values but rather a matter of price. That is, producers did not organize themselves into cooperatives—a considerable investment of time and energy—in order to preserve shade for birds (Lyon 2006), promote organics, or transform the global economy. They did it to create economies of scale and administrative structures large enough and efficient enough to make it possible to compete in the global market and to receive the best possible prices for their products. These structures in no way guarantee that coffee production constitutes a good living for farmers—my research, as well as that of others (Bacon et al. 2008; Jaffee 2007; Lyon 2007a, 2007b; Smith 2007), points to serious problems with fair trade pricing as well as access to fair trade markets.

Conclusion

The producer view provides an interesting contrast to the consumer view, in which work and price are eclipsed by stories about relationships and justice. In this chapter I have tried to provide a glimpse into the structures that condition feelings about the fair trade market system. In "knowable communities" Raymond Williams provides a template for understanding structures of feeling (Williams 1975). He uses the novels of George Eliot to take us on a tour of the country seats of the English gentility during the transition to industrial capitalism. He argues that in the English country-side, knowable communities are not defined by spatial proximity. Each country house stands isolated, miles from the next island of social equals. People living in the immediate proximity of each country house are social inferiors—renters, small farmers, craftsmen. Whereas the inhabitants of other great houses some miles distant are known in their full dimensionality, the proximate neighbors are generally absent or invisible, appearing as scenery and occasionally in caricature. There is an enormous social gulf between the poor and the rich, and this gulf makes them unknowable to each other. In the literature discussed by Williams in *The Country and the City*, the poor appear as a sort of moral backdrop, sometimes associated with an unspoiled countryside of the past. In daily transaction, they set off the virtue of the heroine, who regularly makes her charitable round of visits to the poor and needy. But who are the poor and needy? They are the renters and cottagers, postfeudal peasants whose rents and taxes support the great houses in Eliot's novels. This makes each act of charity an instance of mystification—performing the act of giving to mask the original act of taking. Thus, in Williams, the sum of one's actions does not equal the structure. That is, good deeds do not make a good society. But they do make up a structure of feeling in which each lived reality makes moral sense to each person.

In the U.S. context, coffee professionals understand the structural precursors for fair trade (e.g., deregulation of the coffee market and neoliberal production and consumption models), particularly that low prices for coffee endangered the supply of high-quality coffee as farmers pulled up their coffee bushes in favor of other crops. Notwithstanding this structural knowledge, they typically describe and experience fair trade participation as an exercise in agency and choice, reflecting prevailing U.S. cultural understandings of the political economic system, which is seen in Smithian terms as the sum of many individual actions, so that agency is the genitor of structure. In both conversation and marketing, roasters associate fair trade coffee with foreign travel, distant communities, and new friendships. In fact, most fair trade roasters put considerable effort into building personal relationships with individual producers. They tend to see the fair trade market as a way in which to exercise agency and choice in their careers and to gain a sense of personal efficacy and social

engagement through the adoption of fair trade practices. They see consumer choices as essential to perpetuating a fair trade market. Consumers
themselves share this view, and because they believe that their consumer
choices have social-justice outcomes, they also gain a sense of agency and
efficacy through the market.

For producers, in contrast, agency is a minor theme. It is not entirely
absent: the most successful producers are those who control larger than
average amounts of acreage, and wealthier producers attribute control
of acreage to their own actions, such as working hard on coffee plantations in their youth to earn the money to buy additional land. However,
the marketplace itself looms large as a defining and limiting structure in
producer interviews. In contrast to the consumer view, efficacy in the
producer sphere comes from organization and structure itself. Although
some cooperative leaders have personal relationships with individual
roasters, and some have even traveled to the United States to learn about
roaster operations, producers seldom talk about these personal relationships. Instead, producer discussions of fair trade tend to emphasize the
importance of cooperative structures and networks of relationships. That
consumers tend to see agency where producers see structure is not a function of structural knowledge. As a rule, roasters have more historical and
structural context about the fair trade and conventional coffee markets
than producers do, and therefore they have every "opportunity" to think
structurally. However, it is producers, who have less knowledge of the institutional relationships and historical circumstances of fair trade, who
tend to think in structural terms. Whether fair trade is experienced as a
phenomenon of agency or structure is most related to one's position on
the consumer-producer continuum and the associated structure of feeling
that gives contour to that experience.

WORKS CITED

Bacon, C. M., V. E. Méndez, S. R. Gliessman, D. Goodman, and J. A. Fox, eds.
  2008 Confronting the Coffee Crisis: Fair Trade, Sustainable Livelihoods and Ecosys-
    tems in Mexico and Central America. Cambridge, MA: MIT Press.
Bellah, R.
  1996 Habits of the Heart: Individualism and Commitment in American Life. Berkeley:
    University of California Press.
Bobrow-Strain, A.
  2007 Intimate Enemies: Landowners, Power and Violence in Chiapas. Durham, NC:
    Duke University Press.

Carrier, J.
  1997 Meanings of the Market: The Free Market in Western Culture. Oxford, UK: Berg.
Carrier, J., and D. Miller
  1998 Virtualism: A New Political Economy. New York: Berg.
Cohen, L.
  2004 A Consumer's Republic: The Politics of Mass Consumption in Postwar America.
      New York: Vintage.
Collier, G. A., and E. L. Quaratiello
  1994 Basta! Land and the Zapatista Rebellion in Chiapas. Oakland, CA: Institute for
      Food and Development Policy.
Collier, G. A., and. L. Stephen, eds.
  1997 Ethnicity, Identity and Citizenship in the Wake of the Zapatista Rebellion.
      Special edition, Journal of Latin American Anthropology 3(1).
Collins, J.
  2003 Threads: Gender, Labor, and Power in the Global Apparel Industry. Chicago:
      University of Chicago Press.
Daviron, B., and S. Ponte
  2005 The Coffee Paradox. London: Zed Books.
Fisher, C.
  2007 Selling Coffee, or Selling Out? Evaluating Different Ways to Analyze the Fair-
      Trade System. Culture & Agriculture 29(2): 78–88.
Goodman, D.
  2008 The International Coffee Crisis: A Review of the Issues. *In* Confronting the
      Coffee Crisis: Fair Trade, Sustainable Livelihoods and Ecosystems in Mexico and
      Central America. C. Bacon et al., eds. Pp. 3–25. Cambridge, MA: MIT Press.
Gottlieb, R.
  2005 [1993] Forcing the Spring: The Transformation of the American Environmental
      Movement. Washington, DC: Island.
Harvey, D.
  2006 Spaces of Global Capitalism: Towards a Theory of Uneven Geographical Devel-
      opment. London: Verso.
Harvey, N.
  1990 The New Agrarian Movement in Mexico, 1979–1990. London: Institute of Latin
      American Studies.
Holland, D. C.
  1998 Identity and Agency in Cultural Worlds. Cambridge, MA: Harvard University
      Press.
IADB (Inter-American Development Bank)
  2002 Managing the Competitive Transition of the Coffee Sector in Central America.
      Discussion paper prepared for the regional workshop The Coffee Crisis and Its
      Regional Impact in Central America: Situation and Lines of Action, Antigua,
      Guatemala, April 3–5.
Jaffee, D.
  2007 Brewing Justice: Fair Trade Coffee, Sustainability, and Survival. Berkeley: Univer-
      sity of California Press.

Klein, N.
  2002 No Space, No Choice, No Jobs, No Logo. New York: Picador.
Lyon, S.
  2006 Migratory Imaginations: The Commodification and Contradictions of Shade
      Grown Coffee. Social Anthropology 14(3): 377–390.
  2007a Guest Editor's Introduction. Culture & Agriculture 29(2): 58–62.
  2007b Maya Coffee Farmers and Fair Trade: Assessing the Benefits and Limitations of
      Alternative Markets. Culture & Agriculture 29(2): 100–112.
Marx, K.
  1976 [1867] The Fetishism of the Commodity and Its Secret. In Capital: A Critique of
      Political Economy. New York: Vintage Books.
Mutersbaugh, T.
  2002 The Number Is the Beast: A Political Economy of Organic-Coffee Certification
      and Producer Unionism. Environment and Planning A 34: 1165–1184.
  2005 Fighting Standards with Standards: Harmonization, Rents, and Social Ac-
      countability in Certified Agrofood Networks. Environment and Planning A 37:
      2033–2051.
Newman, K.
  1988 Falling from Grace: Downward Mobility in the Age of Affluence. Berkeley: Uni-
      versity of California Press.
Price, J.
  1996 Looking for Nature at the Mall: A Field Guide to the Nature Company. In
      Uncommon Ground: Rethinking the Human Place in Nature. W. Cronon, ed.
      Pp. 186–203. New York: Norton.
Raffaelli, M.
  1995 Rise and Demise of Commodity Agreements. Cambridge, UK: Woodhead.
Raynolds, L., D. Murray, and J. Wilkinson, eds.
  2007 Fair Trade: The Challenges of Transforming Globalization. New York: Routledge.
Roseberry, W.
  1996 The Rise of Yuppie Coffees and the Reimagination of Class in the United States.
      American Anthropologist 98(4): 762–775.
Sassen, S.
  2006 Territory, Authority, Rights: From Medieval to Global Assemblages. Princeton,
      NJ: Princeton University Press.
Smith, J.
  2007 The Search for Sustainable Markets: The Promise and Failures of Fair Trade.
      Culture & Agriculture 29(2): 89–99.
Talbot, J. M.
  2004 Grounds for Agreement: The Political Economy of the Coffee Commodity
      Chain. Lanham, MD: Rowman & Littlefield.
U.S. Congress
  2002 The Coffee Crisis in the Western Hemisphere. Hearing before the Subcommittee
      on the Western Hemisphere of the Committee on International Relations. House
      of Representatives, 107th Congress, 2nd session.

White, R.
  1996 Are You an Environmentalist, or Do You Work for a Living? *In* Uncommon
      Ground: Rethinking the Human Place in Nature. W. Cronon, ed. Pp. 171–185.
      New York: Norton.
Williams, R.
  1975 The Country and the City. Oxford: Oxford University Press.
  1980 Advertising: The Magic System. *In* Problems in Materialism and Culture. Pp.
      170–195. London: Verso.

Novica, Navajo Knock-Offs, and the 'Net

A Critique of Fair Trade Marketing Practices

KATHY M'CLOSKEY

Recently, *Networks*, the newsletter of the Fair Trade Federation, quoted Gandhi: "Poverty is not only about a shortage of money. It is about rights and relationships; about how people are treated and how they regard themselves; about powerlessness, exclusion and loss of dignity. Yet the lack of adequate income is at its heart" (Morrison 2006). These words are apropos to the predicaments faced by thousands of Navajo weavers who have seen the demand for their rugs plummet in contrast to the massive escalation in knock-offs produced by weavers in Mexico and abroad.[1]

In a *Cultural Survival Quarterly* article published over twenty-five years ago, Israel (1982) profiled a popular exhibit and sales event featuring Amazon Indian cultures and sponsored by Macy's department store. She described the slide show run by an anthropologist, depicting smiling natives living in harmony with their natural environment. The selective presentation avoided mentioning their current struggles involving land rights and exploitation of resources by multinationals: "Native artifacts are more saleable if they come from an idyllic paradise than if they come from hungry, angry or exploited Indians." Israel concluded by noting how Navajo and Pueblo Indians from the southwestern United States had managed "successful development of [their] craft industries" (1982: 16). Israel's narrative of the depiction of "smiling natives" evokes images crafted by ethnologists describing Native American artisans. The theme of this book, global ethnographies of fair trade, provides a platform to reveal the dramatic decline in incomes that many Native American artisans have suffered over the past three decades due to appropriation of their designs. Unlike their counterparts in less developed regions, such as southern Mexico, Native American artisans are not benefiting from inclusion in the alternative networks promoted by the fair trade movement.

In the introduction to this volume, the editors comment on how global sourcing of new products has heightened awareness of global wealth disparities of concern to fair trade advocates. Yet the plight of thousands of Native American artisans from the southwestern United States lacks scholarly engagement. Although the Navajo reservation is geographically part of the North, many Diné experience third-world poverty. In a request to the Obama-Biden Transition Team for nearly three billion dollars in aid, Navajo Nation president Joe Shirley Jr. described the significant economic and social needs due to "too few employers, . . . thousands of miles of rough dirt roads, . . . [and] inadequate means of communication. More than half of our families heat their homes with wood they cut themselves, drink water hauled in barrels from windmills, and light rooms with kerosene and gas lanterns" (Navajo Nation 2009).

This chapter explores how Novica, the high-profile fair trade artisan organization headquartered in Los Angeles, supports the reproduction of historic Navajo designs by Zapotec weavers located in Oaxaca, Mexico. Such appropriation is compounded by gendered injustice, as male Zapotec weavers copy historic designs originally created by generations of anonymous Navajo women. Like many fair trade organizations, Novica has captured a niche market catering to relatively affluent consumers who seek commodified morality in their purchases (Fridell 2007; Moberg and Lyon, introduction to this volume). By harnessing the symbolic capital of indigenous goods bearing well-known designs originated by another group, Novica's support for such appropriation exemplifies the tension between ethics and the marketplace. I suggest that Novica's actions violate a plank in the fair trade platform: to encourage producers to develop products based on their cultural traditions and promote their artistic talents in order to sustain cultural identity.[2] In order to understand the magnitude of the problem and place this critique in perspective some historical context is necessary.

A Short History of Commodification

During the last quarter of the nineteenth century, the diversity of Indian societies in the Southwest provided the most enticing ethnographic area of North America (Hinsley 1981). As a result, the federal government financed much large-scale collecting in the region. Museums became directly involved in commercializing the region under the auspices of salvaging the material culture of what were assumed to be soon extinct populations, prompting a frenzied removal of artifacts (Berlo 1992; Hardin 1989; Hinsley 1989; Parezo 1985; Thompson and Parezo 1989). Ethnology curators served influential roles as cultural translators and adjudicators of the authenticity and artistic merit of artifacts (Mullin 2001; Parezo and Hardin 1993; Wade 1985). For generations ethnologists were primary contributors to publications on Native American art (Amsden 1934; Hedlund 1989, 1992, 1997; Reichard 1934, 1936, 1939; Tanner 1968; Wheat and Hedlund 2003; Whitaker 1998, 2001), yet they ignored the postreservation politico-economic context of production (M'Closkey 2000, 2002, 2004; M'Closkey and Manuel 2006).[3]

Currently over two hundred thousand Navajos, or Diné, occupy an eight-thousand-hectare reservation in the southwestern United States. Historically they managed a broad subsistence base that included farming, herding, raiding, and trading, but they gained a major portion of their subsistence from weaving and livestock production. After the formation of the reservation in 1868, the federal government licensed traders to buy and sell Navajo products. Although the Navajo are one of the most studied peoples on earth, an enormous amount of evidence, languishing in archives, suggests how the inimical effects of free trade over a century ago triggered Navajo impoverishment in a manner not revealed in other analyses (M'Closkey, forthcoming). The ideology of weavers as "domesticated housewives," based on the gendered spheres of productive waged labor and nonproductive, nonwaged housework, masked the relations that link weavers' productivity to tariff revisions legislated by Congress. Witherspoon (1987) conservatively estimates that one hundred thousand women wove one million textiles over the past two centuries. Extant analyses of the Navajo economy have failed to take adequate account of weavers' production because women wove at home and not in factories. Amsden described the gendered dynamics of Navajo weaving production:

> With weaving, these [favorable] circumstances are spare time and cheap wool. Traders long ago noticed that most of their rug purchases are made in the spring because most weaving is done during the long idle days of winter. . . . The Navajo woman weaves when she has nothing better to do, or when the family wool crop cannot be sold to better advantage in the raw. . . . Wool in rug form brings a little more money. (1975: 235)

The few published government reports that identify Navajo women as weavers designate the production of hand-spun, dyed, and woven textiles as an industry that, because women produced for an external market, also fell under the category of commercialization (Sells 1913). The statistical portions of annual Indian agents' reports to the Commissioner of Indian Affairs often included the quantity and value of weaving: the information is incorporated in the livestock and wool production figures, demonstrating how bureaucrats perceived weaving as an extension of the livestock industry (M'Closkey, forthcoming). Although thousands of Navajo women and girls were weaving at this time, participation in the informal economy translated into invisibility.

After 1890, women wove over 25 percent of the annual coarse wool clip sheared from *churros* into saddle blankets and rugs. Women weaving fleece into textiles provided a more secure means of diversification for reservation traders faced with continual oscillations in the international wool market because of the duty-free importation of over one hundred million pounds of Class III carpet-grade wool annually, much of it from China. Thus, Navajos underwent a unique kind of structural adjustment not experienced by other American growers subject to tariff protection for clothing wools after 1898 (M'Closkey, forthcoming). By the late nineteenth century all other domestic growers raised either finer-wooled flocks for clothing wools (Class I) or cross-breeds for mutton and combing wools (Class II), used in manufacturing worsted yarns. These wools were protected by high duties and ad valorem. Although the federal government periodically attempted to "breed up" Navajo flocks, the heavier breeds had difficulty adapting to the Navajo range. Many animals died, and some traders, anxious to capitalize on the more profitable rug trade, resisted up-breeding (M'Closkey, forthcoming). The light fleeced *churro* was a hardy breed capable of surviving on meager forage in an arid environment. Its long-stapled, hairy, greaseless wool was ideal for hand processing and served as the most suitable wool for weavers.

By 1930, women's textile production peaked at one million dollars— one-third of the income earned by Navajo households. Until the 1960s, nearly all textiles were acquired from weavers by weight. Women received credit, not cash, and their saddle blankets and rugs were sold to regional wholesalers for three to eight times the value of Navajo fleece. Traders treated saddle blankets and rugs like other renewable resources, such as goatskins and sheep pelts. They graded, bundled, and sold them wholesale by weight (M'Closkey 2002). Textiles and hides were shipped to jobbers on a weekly basis and were credited against traders' monthly balances with regional wholesalers (M'Closkey, forthcoming). Thus, traders used weaving as a more lucrative means to market the nonstandardized wool clip. The voluminous records of the Hubbell family (1865–1965) substantiate the importance of textile production to the regional economy. The extended family probably controlled one-seventh of the reservation trade at the height of its economic prowess. The Hubbells shipped over two hundred tons of hand-spun woven textiles between 1892 and 1909 (M'Closkey 2002: 76). Today these "pound blankets" fetch record prices at auctions. For example, "eye dazzlers" woven of Germantown yarns circa 1890s earned weavers ten to twenty dollars in credit when exchanged for household goods at the trading post. Today they are routinely auctioned for five thousand to fifty thousand dollars (M'Closkey 2002: 186).[4]

Although the religious aspects of Diné culture have undergone extensive examination for over a century (Faris 1990; Matthews 1902; Reichard 1950; Wyman, 1970, 1983), the context and importance of weaving remains detached from Navajo spirituality in most publications. This is due to fragmentation of Native lifeways into categories based on dualistic thinking. In the Navajo example, generations of scholars juxtaposed the ceremonialism of medicine men with women's secular commodity production for external markets (Kent 1981, 1985; Reichard 1934, 1936, 1950; Tanner 1960, 1968). Over seventy years ago Reichard (1936) implicitly sanctioned the categorization of functional textiles as "nonsacred" craft commodities because commercialization by traders not only submerged any sacred associations but also obliterated a distinctly Navajo aesthetic. Museumologists' statements support her thesis (Kent 1976, 1985; Wheat 1984). Until very recently anthropologists and popular writers have convinced the reading public that Navajo weavers' patterns are derivative (Kaufman and Selser 1985; Kent 1985; Tanner 1968). For example, textile scholar Kate Peck Kent (1976: 101) maintained that "Navajo weaving has no deep historical roots in cultural tradition. Essentially it has always been a commercial link with other Indians, Spanish, and Anglo-Americans. As such it has thrived on innovation, change, and outside contacts."

The emphasis on the empirical and quantifiable aspects of individual rugs, and the evolution of various styles, receives inordinate attention, coupled with the cult of personality expressed by the good taste of various collectors and connoisseurs, both past and present (Berlant and Kahlenberg 1977; Blomberg 1988; Hedlund 1992, 1997; Whitaker 1998). Currently a select number of weavers, perhaps one hundred out of a population of twenty thousand, enjoy national or international standing. Their success as tapestry artists blinkers the public's understanding of the threats to Navajo lifeways engendered by the increasing importation of knock-offs, coupled with the escalation in the investment market for historic textiles.

Zapotec Weaving

Within the past three decades, an increasing number of scholars have documented the political economic changes occurring within Latin American indigenous communities. Utilizing theoretically informed, analytically sophisticated, and comprehensive analyses of textile production shaped initially by tourist demand, and more recently by accommodation to the demands of neoliberalism, currency devaluation, increasing transnationalism, and accelerated globalization, such studies are widely cited in the anthropological literature (Cohen 1998, 2000; Stephen 1991a, 1991b, 1993, 2005; Wood 2000a, 2000b). Wood (2008) describes the emergence of a variety of production units including pieceworkers, subcontractors, merchants, and independents, reflecting the accommodation to flexibility driven by globalization. Stephen (2005: 262) notes that the overall impact of commercialization has been contradictory: "Everyone in Teotitlán has benefited from the successful commercialization and export of textiles since the late 1970s, some have benefited much more than others." Stephen in particular provides gender-sensitive analyses, utilizing detailed data extracted from government sources in tandem with extensive interviews that reveal the close attention paid to the importance of women's labor in sustaining their household economies. Overall these authors delineate how the Mexican government, local merchants, and dozens of foreign exporters continue to transform Zapotec ethnic identity into a commodity.

Many Zapotec weavers have benefited from government support, NGOs, access to training programs, and the development of business plans, including web-based technologies (Stephen 2005: 264). During the 1990s government-linked peasant organizations, agencies such as INI and FONART, and several political parties encouraged artisans to form cooperatives. Stephen (2005) documents the increase in the number of women's textile cooperatives and marks their success. Weavers' increased income has also enhanced their participation in community political life.

Wood (2008: 31–52) deftly unpacks the "construction and consumption" of Zapotec artisans in the historic travelers' literature and its appropriation by entrepreneurs currently active in the field who conveniently expunge the nature of commercial relations in their narratives. Portions of his description of the construction of Zapotecs could easily be applied to the construction of Native American artisanal history north of the border in "the land of enchantment," as the Zapotecs are similarly described as "remote, timeless, picturesque, living remnants of the past" (Wood 2008: 47).

Although Wood (2008: 78, 101) claims that entrepreneurs have faced hurdles selling Zapotec textiles in the southwestern United States, it is difficult to sustain his argument in light of the increasing number of retailers and Indian casino gift shops that now sell them. Zapotec woven textiles bearing Navajo designs are often the featured décor in regional hotels and restaurants. The very fact that an exponential increase in knock-off sales has occurred north of the border over the past three decades is testament to the success of this reputed invasion. Wood's (2008: 186–98) description of the challenges faced by a Zapotec weaver attempting to duplicate a *Yei* (Holy Person) figure copied from a Navajo sand painting illustrates the fact that he and other scholars are potentially overlooking the cultural patterns that gave rise to traditional weaving patterns, such as the Navajo *Yei*. Wood seemingly overlooks the extensive evidence offered in Willink and Zolbrod (1996) and M'Closkey (2002: 205–255) that demonstrates the cultural and spiritual values sustained by Navajo weaving.

The Contemporary Economics of Navajo Weaving

Thus, although Stephen and Wood document various aspects of the production and consumption of Navajo designs by Zapotec weavers and American consumers, respectively, they ignore the negative consequences of such practices on the originators of the historic designs. Given the glaring poverty on the Navajo reservation, how can scholars persist in ignoring the effects of this appropriation? Perhaps one explanation is to be found in the deficient narratives crafted by generations of ethnologists working in the southwestern United States. For example, the dearth of publications on the political economy of weaving is reflected in Bahr's recent comprehensive bibliography (1999) of Navajo scholarship: more than six thousand articles and books were published about Diné between 1970 and 1990. In the subject index under "weaving," Bahr lists four entries under "economics" and more than fifty-five under "catalogues," "collections," and "exhibitions." A review of references in most texts and catalogues on weaving reveals just how overdetermined the topic is. Much of this literature is scripted by traders, collectors, and dealers (Berlant and Kahlenberg 1977; Dedera 1990; Kaufman and Selser 1985; Maxwell 1984; Moore 1987; and Valette and Valette 1997). The sustained emphasis on connoisseurship that dominates historic Navajo textile studies (Baizerman 1989) is contrary to the reflexive analyses embraced by many scholars today.

The market relations characterizing Navajo weaving today are similar to those facing the impoverished small farmers who potentially benefit from fair trade in countries outside the United States, such as a lack of direct trade relationships, relative powerlessness, and low prices. With few exceptions, private enterprise continues to control the marketing of Navajo weaving. Dealers caution buyers about commissioning rugs directly from weavers, relating horror stories about unsuccessful attempts (Montgomery 1982: 27; Trevathan 1997: 37). Such rhetoric appearing in popular publications perpetuates dealers' control over marketing weavers' creations, with markups as high as 500 percent. Thus, excessive markups by retailers have inhibited strong sales of contemporary Navajo weaving.

In my conversations with weavers, they inform me that they frequently receive far less than the retail cost of high-end knock-offs. Entrepreneurs and middlemen continue to make most of the profits, and weavers themselves face several factors that constrain their direct market opportunities. Specifically, the huge reservation lacks market towns, and over 80 percent of the roads are unpaved; 50 percent of the population lacks plumbing and/or electricity, and until 2002, only 20 percent had phone service. The reservation trading-post system has vanished, primarily a consequence of the Federal Trade Commission's 1976 ruling that imposed long-overdue stringent regulations on pawning and credit practices (Powers 2001). No reservation-wide infrastructure exists to assist artisans with marketing. The monthly rug auction held in Crownpoint, New Mexico, is nearly 60 miles from the closest motel accommodations in Gallup, and over 110 miles from Albuquerque, New Mexico. The auction was started during the 1960s, by the local trader and several weavers, because the weavers averaged six to eight dollars per rug. For years the auction was attended by hundreds of bidders, featured up to one thousand rugs, and ended well after midnight. By 2001, weavers averaged $250 per rug, prior to a deduction of a 15 percent fee to the organizers. More recently attendance has declined, with fewer than three hundred rugs entered; one-third fail to sell, and another 30 percent typically sell for the opening bid (M'Closkey 2002: 199).Currently, only an estimated eighty to one hundred visitors will request bidding numbers.

Because poverty among Navajo weavers is a neglected topic, consumers lack awareness of current circumstances. Weavers have always relied on traditional knowledge and skills to meet their livelihood needs, but they were also dependent on trading posts and curio shops catering to tourists to sell their textiles. Like their contemporaries described by Wills (2006), weavers used the proceeds from their weavings to feed and clothe their families, and they continue to do so with increasing difficulty. During 2004, in an effort to increase returns to wool growers when wool prices declined to eight cents per pound, the Natural Resources Conservation Service of the USDA provided three thousand dollars to support a value-added project in the Four Corners area that funded a handful of Navajos to weave their wool into rugs (NRCS 2004). In light of the sustained impoverishment in the region, such minuscule funds are almost laughable. While filming *Weaving Worlds: Navajo Tales of How the West Was Spun* (PBS, 2008), in the Hard Rock area of the Navajo reservation, we encountered experienced weavers who had given up weaving.[5] Because they lacked access to dependable transportation to border towns, they were unable to market their rugs. Several fine weavers now make three-tiered skirts to sell at local flea markets; members of households lacking electricity use treadle sewing machines. With the changes in welfare and the increase in neoliberal governmental policies over the past decade, poverty has risen dramatically. The median household income of families in the Hard Rock area averages eight thousand dollars a year. Trading posts and pawn shops located in reservation border towns such as Gallup, New Mexico, are overstocked with pawned items including Pendleton blankets, jewelry, rugs, saddles, and even vehicles. Payday-loan outlets proliferate, driving the local and reservation populations deeper into debt.

Yet the production of weaving and other arts and crafts has significant impact on the regional economy and on thousands of Native American families. Indians, along with the scenery, are primary attractions in New Mexico and Arizona, and tourism brings billions of dollars into the region annually. However, since the Indian arts-and-crafts boom in the 1970s, unemployment has increased dramatically on reservations where arts-and-crafts production provides an important source of income (Abeita 1999, 2001). Isleta Pueblo fetish carver Andy Abeita (2006) acknowledges that "the world renowned recognition of southwest arts and crafts does not reflect what goes on within impoverished makers' homes." This is an astonishing statement given the numerous publications authored by generations of ethnologists. Currently over 50 percent of nearly two-billion-dollar sales annually of "Indian" products is either produced by non-Indians and imported into the United States or assembled from stones imported from Southeast Asia and China by Navajo working in near sweatshop-like assembly-line factories (Brooke 1997; Rowling 1998; Shiffman 1998). This is perfectly legal under the Indian Arts and Crafts Board Act. Retailers break the law *only* if they label an object "Indian-made" when it is not made by a Native American who is a member of a federally recognized tribe. Other terms used to confuse consumers include "Indian-inspired," "Navajo-inspired," the "Southwest look," or the "Santa Fe style." Thus, knock-offs flood the shelves of hundreds of retailers and thousands of Internet sites, including eBay. In a recent conversation with Navajo weaver Barbara Teller Ornelas, I mentioned that textiles from Bangladesh can be purchased on the Internet with the click of a button. She replied, "Yeah, but no one ever steals their designs. . . . When people ask why I don't have a website, that's the reason." Navajo weavers have experienced increasing impoverishment due to globalization, which has furthered the practice of minimal or misleading labeling of artisanal products. This situation is paralleled by the experience of some Southern artisans as well. For example, Smith and White (2002) describe the plight of Kenyan weavers who make kiondo bags from sisal. Although the bags were once Kenya's fourth-largest export, the market has declined dramatically with the mass-produced imitations imported from Southeast Asia. In order to compete with the lower-priced imports, Kenyan weavers had to reduce their prices and now no longer recoup the costs of production.

In 1995, New Mexico spent over twenty-five million dollars advertising Indian arts and crafts. Today, the state spends less than seven million dollars, and most of that is for whimsical "folk art." In 1998, Andy Abeita actively campaigned for a Democratic candidate who was running for attorney general. If elected, the candidate had promised to halt the importation of all types of knock-offs into New Mexico. Shortly before the election, he lost a large percentage of his support from the business community, demonstrating the importance of the knock-off market to the regional economy: retailers and banks are too vested in its success. Although several elderly Gallup traders are very outspoken about the pernicious effects of knock-offs on Native artisans, many trading posts now sell them because they are 25 percent of the cost of the authentic Navajo work.[6] The increase in the importation of imitation Navajo products first drew widespread attention in the late 1990s. A 1998 issue of *Cowboys and Indians* magazine carried an article titled "The Scandal of Fake Indian Crafts" (Smith 1998). It reported that the appropriation of many of the popular southwestern designs created by artisans from Zuni, Navajo, and Hopi tribes had triggered an escalation in unemployment from 40 to 70 percent: "a lot of families have had their vehicles taken, their lights shut off." Deanna Olson, president of Silver Sun gallery in New Mexico, said, "this situation is not only resulting in Indian artists practically starving, but it is destroying Native cultures" (Smith 1998). Similarly, the ailing arts industry was the topic of discussion at the first Navajo Arts and Crafts (NACE) Forum held during June 1998. NACE passed a resolution requesting the Navajo Nation Council to explore the possibility of a Navajo trademark to fight proliferation of fakes and imports. A decade later, in 2008, the New Mexico state legislature amended the Indian Arts and Crafts Sales Act to increase the penalties from five hundred to five thousand dollars, associated with misrepresentation or false or fraudulent sales of authentic Indian arts and crafts (New Mexico State Legislature 2008).

The history of Navajo textile, as crafted by museumologists, embraces a linear trajectory—craft production by previous generations of weavers is now repositioned within an art-historical framework. The future of weaving lies in appreciating it as an art form and the weaver as an artist and cultural trendsetter. The ethnoaesthetics model that museumologists espouse emphasizes the aesthetics of individual creativity. This way of thinking intersects with postmodern concepts embracing stylistic hybridity and translocality, and it complements much of the consumption literature in anthropology (Appadurai 1986; Mansvelt 2005; Miller 1997). Perhaps this explains why there has there been no response from scholars concerning the wholesale appropriation of Navajo patterns by entrepreneurs, and by several fair trade organizations, that escalated dramatically over the past three decades. Thus, the object-based aesthetics embraced by southwestern ethnologists unintentionally sustain parallel worlds: the upscale Santa Fe and Taos scenes populated with antiquities dealers, galleries, collectors, and museums housing comprehensive, historic collections, and the seedy side of contemporary production reflected in the "Gallup grind," a reservation border town in western New Mexico, where hundreds of Native Americans labor in sweat shops owned by local or foreign companies.

Fair Trade and Navajo Designs

Fair trade organizations are deeply committed to supporting people-centered rather than profit-driven development. As exporters and retailers, they work directly with artisan groups to ensure makers are paid a fair wage and work in a healthy and safe environment. They offer technical and business expertise and monitor product quality. For example, the *Networks* column "Trend Spotting" provides updates on fashion trends and lists helpful websites (Networks 2006). Some fair trade organizations use designer consultants to ensure that artisans produce salable articles, since good design is one of the keys to increasing sales. Because of the popularity of the "Santa Fe" style or "Southwest" look, Navajo patterns are frequently used. For example, Peace Corps workers first introduced Navajo designs to South American weavers during the 1970s. Today, a number of fair trade organizations in North America market knock-offs woven in Mexico and Peru. In April 1999, an associate with SERRV admitted that the fair trade organization acquired textiles bearing Navajo designs from Peruvian weavers. Another fair trade retailer has Zapotec weavers copy Navajo patterns from the Smithsonian's collection. During October 2002, I contacted two dozen fair trade organizations and queried whether they carried textiles using Navajo patterns. Five organizations confirmed that they carried such stock, and six others apologized for not having the merchandise I requested. Why have individuals and organizations supportive of social justice assumed that this is an acceptable practice?

Fair trade organizations such as Novica assist artisans in marketing their wares directly to consumers. Novica's byword, "the world is your market," seeks to create a bridge between consumers and talented artisans globally. Novica dispenses with middlemen so the artisan and the consumer can gain the greatest benefits from each transaction. Affiliated with *National Geographic*, the organization was cofounded by Roberto Milk, a Stanford University alumnus with Peruvian roots; his Brazilian-born actress wife; and her mother, a former United Nations human-rights officer. Investors include the founders of the Hollywood Stock Exchange and Island Records. The organization maintains an office in West Los Angeles. By 2000, the one-year-old "upstart" employed over 130 people in seven regions globally, featured a roster of over one thousand artisans (which has since doubled), and launched an ambitious, long-term $3.5 million ad campaign directed at travel and interior-design enthusiasts. Advertisements were placed in magazines such as *Condé Nast, Sunset,* and the *New Yorker* (Romney 2000). Catherine Ryan, Novica's "Wander Woman," commented in an NPR interview that even though the company uses one of the principal tools of globalization, the Internet, it helps local communities "sustain their distinct art and traditions" (NPR 2000). The website garners over one million hits per month (Romney 2000). The organization's web-based catalogue, featuring a range of well-designed products, continually attracts buyers, as is evident from numerous testimonials posted on its website from satisfied consumers. In 2004, Novica received a "2004 Fast 50 Winner" award from Fast Company for "thinking globally, acting locally" (Fast Company 2004).

The Ruiz Bazan family from Oaxaca, featured almost continuously on Novica's website, is one of the most prominent families among the organization's artisans. Weavers in this family have woven a number of Navajo knock-offs. On March 2, 2007, I e-mailed the Product Selections Department, expressing my concern about the inappropriateness of a fair trade organization's supporting such activity:

> I'm writing as a concerned anthropologist regarding the use of both Navajo designs and the term "Navajo" in marketing non-Navajo woven textiles. I was hoping to meet with a Novica employee involved in marketing while I was in Los Angeles recently. However, the individual I spoke with said that was impossible, but that I could provide a list of product ID's and forward them to you.
>
> ID 98373 is named "Navajo Blues."
>
> ID 17152 "Red Geometry" is appropriated from a coffee table book on historic Navajo weaving. The description states it's "inspired by Navajo designs."
>
> ID 107166 "Fire" is a design appropriated from a textile in the William Randolph Hearst Collection housed at the Los Angeles Museum of Natural History.
>
> ID 107167 "Fire of Dawn" is also a copy of a 19th century Navajo chief's blanket, as is
>
> ID 25034 "Red Fire Crosses" [this textile is one of the ten most popular products on the website].
>
> The most egregious example is ID 17147 "Children" which depicts sacred *Yei* figures created in Navajo sand painting ceremonies. [This textile is described as follows: "From the imagination of Zapotec artisans, a geometric fantasy is crystallized for celebrating the universal miracle of childhood. Hand-woven with pure wool, this rug is adorned with transversal lines uniting the composition. A sweet message of hope and happiness, this polychrome dream will add a warm and cozy accent to any children [*sic*] ambience."]

Although it is technically not illegal to use these designs and terms under US law, is it ethical for an organization that promotes fair trade to do so? Unlike the Ruiz Bazan family who are now world famous, only a handful of over 20,000 weavers on the Navajo reservation enjoy such publicity. Per capita income remains 20% of the national average, and until 2002, 80% of the population had no phone service.

I look forward to your reply.

On March 12, 2007, Jose Cervantes, vice president of Sales and Operations at Novica, replied:

Dear Kathy

We'd like to thank you once again for bringing this issue to our attention. As you know, Novica is committed to preserving traditional arts and crafts of indigenous peoples throughout the world. Please note that we have decided we will be eliminating those tapestries that you have noted are direct copies. With regards to those tapestries that have Navajo-inspired designs but that are of the artisans' own creation, we will appropriately credit them as "Navajo inspired" in the cases where we haven't already done so.

We hope this will address your concerns. Many thanks for the time and care you have taken to provide us with this detailed information, and we continue to welcome your feedback.

Sincerely, Novica in Association with National Geographic

PR Department.

Throughout 2007, I periodically tracked Zapotec rug designs on Novica's website. The Ruiz Bazan family of Teotitlán del Valle was frequently profiled, and Novica mentioned their interviews on NPR's *Morning Edition* and in numerous magazines and newspapers in the United States and Europe. Novica also profiles the testimonials of many satisfied customers on its website: a minister wrote that he had looked at hundreds of Zapotec rugs while touring the southwestern United States, but the Ruiz Bazan family's rugs that he had purchased through Novica were superior. Another reader commented on how the craftsmanship reminded her of quality Navajo rugs. This family and others profiled by Novica illustrate the "shaped advantage" provided by fair trade (Fridell 2007), in which a selective group of producers is privileged over their counterparts competing within the neoliberal market economy.

On March 3, 2008, I found "Fire," ID 56629, and "Fire of Dawn," ID 107167, by Alberto Ruiz, still available. To my dismay, I found a new pattern, ID 142718, titled "Nazca and the Inca" and woven by Nestor Suarez. The design description claims the rug is inspired by pre-Incan geoglyphs located on the Nazca plain in Peru. Curious as to the possible similarities between Navajo and pre-Incan designs, I scanned two websites containing drawings and photographs of well-known Nazca geoglyphs.[7] None of more than two dozen images was even remotely similar to the design used in ID 142718. On the contrary, the textile conforms to the layout and design of the well-known Navajo "storm pattern" rug, of which two examples are depicted in the J. B. Moore catalogue (1911). Renaming an appropriated design is a tactic commonly used by other major supplies of Navajo knock-offs. For example, El Paso Saddle Blanket Company currently refers to dozens of knock-offs as "Maya" designs. The company's book *Rugs to Riches* (Henson and Henson 2001) chronicles the increase in the company's fortunes through production of hundreds of Navajo designs by Zapotec weavers and producers located in India and Romania. Ten years ago, the company advertised "10,000 rugs"; today, with fifty thousand copies of the company's book in print, its one-acre headquarters now advertises "200,000 rugs." Sadly, unlike other groups, as described by Hollowell (2007), Navajo weavers are no longer able to capitalize on their heritage designs because of such extensive appropriation and aggressive marketing. This is a human-rights issue, as weavers are increasingly deprived of a livelihood.

According to Andy Abeita, because of such massive appropriation, craft production by southwestern Native American artisans, a crucial aspect of cultural preservation, is being driven to oblivion (Abeita 2006). The phenomenal success of the knock-offs marketed by Novica and other retailers of fair trade artisan products produced in the global South violates one of the planks of the fair trade platform: "to provide equal employment opportunities for all people, particularly the most disadvantaged." Using the term "Navajo-inspired" to describe Zapotec woven rugs is an example of the cultural appropriation that is negatively affecting the ability of Navajo artisans to maintain their livelihoods and cultural traditions of weaving.

One Bright Light

To date, only one fair trade organization assists Navajo weavers. Black Mesa Weavers for Life and Land was cofounded in 1998 by a group of Diné and Carol Halberstadt of Boston, to help restore economic and social self-sufficiency to the region through the preservation of traditional lifeways based on sheepherding and fair trade marketing of wool, mohair, weavings, and other related products. This organization's work is focused in the Black Mesa region of Arizona, an area that garnered attention during the infamous Navajo-Hopi Land Dispute (Brugge 1994). Black Mesa Weavers maintains a website, http://blackmesaweavers.org and sells Diné weavings, churro wool, mohair, and other items via the Internet, Cultural Survival bazaars, and other venues. Faced with the problems of economic and cultural survival in a fragile and threatened ecosystem, the organization empowers local Diné communities to expand their traditional economy within the contemporary marketplace through sustainable development and reinvests in the strength of the community. The association retains a very small percentage of each sale to sustain the organization.[8]

Black Mesa demonstrates how an all-volunteer grassroots group can improve the lives and well-being of artisans. It has expanded the limited market access to which Diné have been restricted and empowered them to bring their products to a wider market by fair trading from the source. In September 2000, Black Mesa began selling fleece in addition to weavings on its website after seeing bags of churro wool sitting unsold in the sun on Coal Mine Mesa because the local market rate was only four to six cents per pound. During the June 2004 wool buy, growers from fifty-three households received $1.60 per pound for their churro wool, and the following year growers sold over thirty-four hundred pounds at $1.85 per pound. Since Black Mesa's inception, over five hundred weavings and fifteen thousand pounds of wool and mohair have been sold at fair prices. This organization is a model for sustainable development and ecologically balanced agriculture and production and certainly provides inspiration for those who are concerned about the future of Native North American indigenous cultures and their traditional livelihoods, which in this case are dependent on herding and weaving. Although this organization also features a colorful and informative website, it differs greatly from Novica.

Conclusion

Complex patterns of relations were occluded through the epistemological lens of the colonizers, followed by ethnographers. The bifurcation of sacred and profane as constructed by anthropologists historically has thrust Navajo weaving into an alien field. Today, when documenting the creolization of expressive forms through developments facilitated by globalization, anthropologists have unwittingly adopted a stance that sanctions processes by which commoditized forms of culture are disembedded from their social matrix and marketed through simulations of cultural performance. After the session on fair trade (out of which this volume emerged) ended at the 2007 American Anthropology Association's annual meeting in Washington, DC, I searched for the ladies' room in a crowded lobby. Suddenly a middle-aged woman rushed past me and commented, "I've been in product development for NGOs for years—there's nothing you can do about this. You might as well forget it!" Stunned by her comment, I tried to see her nametag, but she disappeared into the crowd.

Novica, in its desire to promote equitable returns to Zapotec weavers, has inadvertently contributed to the impoverishment of Navajo weavers. Although feminist political economist Lynn Stephen (2005: 190) claims that the Zapotec have appropriated "elements" of Navajo designs, Novica's website, and those of other Internet-based retailers, reveals the extent of the knock-off trade by advertising duplicates of historic Navajo textiles. This is a social-justice issue with ethical dimensions that remain understudied. Scholars committed to fair trade need to consider how ethically to pursue product development and design innovation to attract consumers in a heavily competitive marketplace, *without* impoverishing artisans whose ancestors originated designs that now reside in the public domain. The very circumstances that led NGOs and others to improve artisans' lives in the Third World through fair trade now confront Native American artisans living in a domestic "third world" of sweat shops, mass production, and deteriorating working conditions for many jewelers and the marginalization and sustained impoverishment of many Navajo weavers. The growing number of coffee-table books on "Indian Art" authored by scholars who support an object-based aesthetics typically feature highly successful individual artists while neglecting the vast majority of struggling practitioners. Native American artisans were and continue to be depicted as "cultural performers," not "workers"—hence the dearth of political economic analyses of their livelihoods. And unlike the Inuit of northern Canada and many other groups supported through fair trade initiatives, their artisanal abilities were never linked to development projects. Instead, culture and political economy have remained separate concerns for scholars researching Native American artisanal creations.

To continue to use patterns designed by Navajo weavers and ignore Navajo poverty evokes the behavior of corporations driven by capitalist motives. Stimulating the production of Navajo-sourced designs by offshore indigenous weavers has greatly contributed to the glut of such designs in the global market. Textiles bearing non-Navajo patterns are now woven in over twenty different countries and imported into the United States, greatly diminishing the demand for rugs woven by Navajo weavers. Novica's support for such appropriation exerts an even greater threat to Navajo weavers because it neutralizes copying through the prism of ethical marketing.

Although fair trade is a globally regulated system that seeks to build social justice into market transactions, this chapter makes a similar argument to Doane's contribution to this volume (chap. 10), demonstrating how fair trade practices actually refetishize the commodity relationships "through a US market-culture lens that emphasizes personal agency and efficacy in the global arena over the consideration of enduring structural inequalities" (Doane 2007: 57). As Henrici pointedly states in this volume's final chapter, trading rights globally often supersede human rights at the local level, and it is absolutely critical that in our rush to improve one set of labor, land, and environmental rights (for example, among Zapotec weavers in Mexico) that we not ignore the conditions elsewhere (for example, among the Navajo). The evidence related here demonstrates the powerful contradiction between the fair trade network's compatibility with neoliberal reforms and the belief that the network is a fundamental challenge to neoliberalism. The shaped advantage gained through appropriation has greatly enhanced financial returns to a specific group of Zapotec weavers to the detriment of thousands of Navajo weavers also competing in the global marketplace. Capitalism requires its dominant participants to behave in an exploitative and destructive fashion to increase competitive advantage (Fridell 2007: 279–281). By sanctioning the production of knock-offs, fair trade organizations such as Novica capitulate to, rather than counter, capitalism's mandate.

Perhaps this story serves as a regrettable example of the critique voiced by Karim (1996: 129) at the 1996 Oxford decennial: "Is anthropological knowledge generated to enrich the western intellectual tradition or destitute populations from which this knowledge was appropriated? . . . Why is it that as the field of theoretical anthropology is enriched by every new discourse it adopts, the people of the world from which anthropology makes its name become culturally impoverished by the day?" Perusing the information revealed here challenges conventional thinking that Diné weavers and other southwestern Native artisans have benefited from the anthropological gaze. In fact, as demonstrated in this chapter, they continue to endure formidable odds in their attempt to ensure cultural survival in today's competitive marketplace (Abeita 2006).

NOTES

1. I thank editors Sarah Lyon and Mark Moberg, Andy Abeita, Carol Halberstadt, and Navajo weavers who shared their stories with me. This research was funded by an operating grant #410-2004-0170 from SSHRC, Social Science and Humanities Research Council of Canada, 2004–2007.

2. The plank of the fair trade platform I refer to is, "Providing equal employment to the most disadvantaged." This plank, along with seven others, is listed on the back page of every *Networks* newsletter published by the Fair Trade Federation.

3. M'Closkey and Manuel (2006: 226–241) review over a century of history, contrasting the sustained colonial relationships between Canadian museums and First Nations material culture with the appropriation of Native American material culture by U.S. museums initiated in the early nineteenth century to serve nationalist interests. That chapter utilizes a model developed by Cory Willmott (2006: 212–225).

4. The "Auction Block" column authored by Harmer Johnson and published quarterly in the *American Indian Art Magazine* lists the selling price of Native-created antiquities sold by prominent auction houses. See M'Closkey 2002 for an overview of the political economy of "collectibles" concomitant with the transformation of Navajo weaving from "craft" to "art."

5. I served as research director of this documentary directed by Navajo Bennie Klain and produced by Leighton Peterson of Trickster Films, LLC, Austin, Texas.

6. Southwestern retailers selling Indian arts and crafts often capitalize on the nostalgia and romanticism associated with the "old west" by calling their stores "trading posts." Although the post in Cameron, Arizona, is sited within the boundaries of the Navajo Nation, it is located on private property homesteaded prior to the expansion of the western edge of the reservation nearly a century ago. That post has sold knock-offs for decades and hosts a popular auction annually featuring historic Native American "collectibles."

7. "The Enigmatic Lines of the Nazca Pampa," labyrinthina.com, http://www.labyrinthina.com/nazca2.htm, and "Nazca Lines: Inca," Lost Civilizations website, http://www.lost-civilizations.net/inca-nazca-lines.html.

8. Carol Halberstadt has published several articles in *Cultural Survival Quarterly,* including "Fair Trading from the Source" (Winter 2003) and "Black Mesa Weavers for Life and Land" (Winter 2001).

WORKS CITED

Abeita, A.
   1999 Protection Laws. *In* Collecting Authentic Indian Arts and Crafts: Traditional Work of the Southwest. Indian Arts and Crafts Association, ed. Pp. 109–118. Summertown, TN: Book Publishing Company.
   2001 American Indian Arts and Crafts: A Study on Handcrafts and the Industry. *In* Safeguarding Traditional Cultures: A Global Assessment. P. Seitel, ed. Pp. 78–82. Washington, DC: Smithsonian Institution.

2006 Pressing Concerns for the Future of Authentic Native American Arts and Crafts. Presentation at the Navajo Studies Conference, University of New Mexico, Albuquerque, November 2.

Amsden, C. A.
1975 [1934] Navajo Weaving, Its Technique and History. Salt Lake City: Peregrine Smith.

Appadurai, A.
1986 The Social Life of Things. New York: Cambridge University Press.

Bahr, H.
1999 Navajo Bibliography to the 1990s. Lanham, MD: Scarecrow.

Baizerman, S.
1989 The Study of Material Culture: The Case of Southwest Textiles; The Legacy of Kate Peck Kent. Museum Anthropology 13: 14–18.

Berlant, T., and M. H. Kahlenberg
1977 Walk in Beauty: The Navajo and Their Blankets. Salt Lake City: Peregrine Smith.

Berlo, J. C., ed.
1992 The Early Years of Native American Art History. Vancouver: UBC Press.

Blomberg, N.
1988 Art from the Navajo Loom. The William Randolph Hearst Collection. Tucson: University of Arizona Press.

Brooke, J.
1997 Sales of Indian Crafts Rise and So Do Fakes. New York Times, August 2: A6.

Brugge, D.
1994 The Navajo-Hopi Land Dispute: An American Tragedy. Albuquerque: University of New Mexico Press.

Cohen, J. H.
1998 Craft Production and the Challenge of the Global Market: An Artisans' Cooperative in Oaxaca, Mexico. Human Organization 57(1): 74–82.
2000 Textile Production in Rural Mexico: The Complexities of the Global Market for Handmade Crafts. *In* Artisans and Cooperatives: Developing Alternative Trade for the Global Economy. K. Grimes and B. L. Milgram, eds. Pp 129–142. Tucson: University of Arizona Press.

Dedera, D.
1990 [1975] Navajo Rugs: How to Find, Evaluate, Buy, and Care for Them. Flagstaff, AZ: Northland.

Doane, M.
2007 Structure and Agency in the Fair Trade System. Anthropology News, December: 57–58.

Faris, J.
1990 The Nightway: A History and History of Documentation of a Navajo Ceremonial. Albuquerque: University of New Mexico Press.

Fast Company
2004 2004 Fast 50 Awards. http://www.fastcompany.com/fast50_04/winners/novica. html, accessed June 22, 2009.

Fridell, G.
   2007 Fair Trade Coffee: The Prospects and Pitfalls of Market-Driven Social Justice.
      Toronto: University of Toronto Press.
Hardin, M. A.
   1989 Using Museum Collections in Ethnographic Research: A Zuni Example. *In* Per-
      spectives on Anthropological Collections from the American Southwest. Anthro-
      pological Research Papers 40. A. L. Hedlund, ed. Pp. 99–111. Phoenix: Arizona
      State Museum.
Hedlund, A. L.
   1989 The Study of the 19th Century Southwestern Textiles. *In* Perspectives on An-
      thropological Collections from the American Southwest: Proceedings of a
      Symposium (Anthropology Research Papers) 40, Pp. 121–138. Phoenix: Arizona
      State University.
   1992 Reflections of the Weaver's World: The Gloria F. Ross Collection. Denver:
      Denver Art Museum.
   1997 Navajo Weavings from the Andy Williams Collection. St. Louis: St. Louis Art
      Museum.
Henson, D., and B. Henson
   2001 Rugs to Riches: The Amazing Story of the El Paso Saddle Blanket Company. El
      Paso, TX: Trego-Hill.
Hinsley, C.
   1981 Savages and Scientists: The Smithsonian Institution and the Development of
      American Anthropology 1846–1910. Washington, DC: Smithsonian Institution
      Press.
   1989 Zunis and Brahmins: Cultural Ambivalence in the Gilded Age. *In* Romantic
      Motives: Essays on Anthropological Sensibility. G. Stocking Jr., ed. Pp.169–207.
      Madison: University of Wisconsin Press.
Hollowell, J.
   2007 Heritage Goods as Economic Capital: Heritage Lost or Reframed? Paper
      presented at the American Anthropology Association Annual Meeting, Washing-
      ton, DC, December.
Israel, P.
   1982 The Amazon in Plexiglass. Cultural Survival Quarterly 6(4):15–17.
Karim, W. J.
   1996 Anthropology without Tears: How a "Local" Sees the "Local" and the "Global."
      In The Future of Anthropological Knowledge. H. L. Moore, ed. Pp. 115–138.
      London: Routledge.
Kaufman, A., and C. Selser
   1985 The Navajo Weaving Tradition 1650 to the Present. New York: E. P. Dutton.
Kent, K.
   1976 Pueblo and Navajo Weaving Traditions and the Western World. *In* Ethnic and
      Tourist Arts. N. Graburn, ed. Pp. 85–101. Berkeley: University of California
      Press.
   1981 From Blanket to Rug: The Evolution of Navajo Weaving after 1880. Plateau 52(4):
      10–21.

1985 Navajo Weaving: Three Centuries of Change. Santa Fe, NM: School of American Research Press.

Mansvelt, J.
2005 Geographies of Consumption. Thousand Oaks, CA: Sage.

Matthews, W.
1902 The Night Chant: A Navajo Ceremony. New York: American Museum of Natural History.

Maxwell, G.
1984 [1963] Navajo Rugs: Past, Present and Future. Palm Desert, CA: Desert Southwest Publications.

M'Closkey, K.
2000 "Part-Time for Pin Money": The Legacy of Navaho Women's Craft Production. *In* Artisans and Cooperatives: Developing Alternative Trade for the Global Economy. K. Grimes and B. L. Milgram, eds. Pp. 143–158. Phoenix: University of Arizona Press.
2002 Swept under the Rug: A Hidden History of Navajo Weaving. Albuquerque: University of New Mexico Press.
2004 The Devil's in the Details: Tracing the Fingerprints of Free Trade and Its Effects on Navajo Weavers. *In* Native Pathways: American Indian Culture and Economic Development in the Twentieth Century. B. Hosmer and C. O'Neill, eds. Pp. 112–130. Boulder: University Press of Colorado.
Forthcoming Why the Navajo Blanket Became a Rug: Excavating the Lost Heritage of Globalization. Albuquerque: University of New Mexico Press.

M'Closkey, K., and K. Manuel
2006 Commodifying North American Aboriginal Culture: A Canada-US Comparison. *In* Historicizing Canadian Anthropology. J. Harrison and R. Darnell, eds. Pp. 226–241. Vancouver: University of British Columbia Press.

Miller, D.
1997 [1987] Material Culture and Mass Consumption. New York: Wiley-Blackwell.

Moore, J. B.
1987 [1911] Collection of Catalogues Published and Crystal Trading Post, 1903 and 1911. Albuquerque, NM: Avanyu.

Montgomery, B.
1982 Navajo Blankets and Rugs. Collector-Investor, March: 22–27.

Morrison, M.
2006 Letter to members from executive director of the Fair Trade Resource Network. Networks, November.

Mullin, M.
2001 Culture in the Marketplace. Durham, NC: Duke University Press.

Navajo Nation
2009 Navajo President Joe Shirley, Jr., Sends $2.9 Billion Needs Request to Obama-Biden Transition Team, Asks that Navajo Not be Forgotten. The Navajo Nation, Office of the President and Vice President, Press Release, January 10.

Networks

 2006 Trend Spotting. Newsletter of the Fair Trade Federation. Winter: 7.

New Mexico State Legislature

 2008 Indian Arts and Crafts Penalties Bill. Passed January 21, 2008. http://legis.state.
  nm.us/Sessions/08%20Regular/firs/HB0210.html, accessed June 18, 2009.

NPR (National Public Radio)

 2000 Website Helps Artists' Business Thrive. Interview with Catherine Ryan. Morning
  Edition. Host Bob Edwards with correspondent Gerry Hadden. September 11.

NRCS (National Resources Conservation Service)

 2004 RC&D Aids Navajos to Make Value-Added Rugs. USDA. June 14. Copÿ in
  author's possession.

Parezo, N. J.

 1985 Cushing as Part of the Team: The Collecting Activities of the Smithsonian Institution. American Ethnologist 12: 763–774.

Parezo, N. J., and M. A. Hardin

 1993 In the Realm of the Muses. *In* Hidden Scholars: Women Anthropologists and the
  Native American Southwest. N. Parezo, ed. Pp. 270–293. Albuquerque: University of New Mexico Press.

Powers, W. R.

 2001 Navajo Trading: The End of an Era. Albuquerque: University of New Mexico
  Press.

Reichard, G.

 1934 Spider Woman. New York: Macmillan.

 1936 Navajo Shepherd and Weaver. Glorieta, NM: Rio Grande Press.

 1939 Dezba, Woman of the Desert. Glorieta, NM: Rio Grande Press.

 1950 Navajo Religion: A Study in Symbolism. New York: Pantheon.

Romney, L.

 2000 Web Firm Profits by Enriching Both Artisans and Buyers. Los Angeles Times,
  June 14. http://www.novica.com/news/index.cfm?action=printarticle&articleI
  D=17, accessed December 17, 2006.

Rowling, R.

 1998 Indian Jewelers Fight for Life: Imports Crushing Demands for Wares. Arizona
  Republic, August 16.

Sells, C.

 1913 Annual Report of the Commissioner of Indian Affairs. Washington, DC: Government Printing Office.

Shiffman, J.

 1998 Indian Art: Buyer Beware; $1 Billion Industry Reeling as Faux Crafts Flood
  Market. USA Today, April 8: 1A.

Smith, N., and M. White

 2002 Freedom to Craft a Future? The Impact of Trade Liberalization on Grassroots
  Craftswomen. http://www.womensedge.org/trade/craftwomen.htm, accessed
  October 7, 2002.

Smith, S.

1998 The Scandal of Fake Indian Crafts. Cowboys and Indians. http://www.cowboys-indians.com/articles/archives/0998/fakecrafts.html, accessed October 22, 2005.

Stephen, L.

1991a Culture as a Resource: Four Cases of Self-Managed Indigenous Craft Producers in Latin America. Economic Development and Culture Change 40(1): 101–130.

1991b Export Markets and Their Effects on Indigenous Craft Production: The Case of the Weavers of Teotitlan del Valle, Mexico. *In* Textile Traditions in Mesoamerica and the Andes. J. B. Margot Blum Schevill and E. Dwyer, eds. Pp. 381–399. New York: Garland.

1993 Weaving in the Fast Lane: Class, Ethnicity and Gender in Zapotec Craft Commercialization. *In* Crafts in the World Market. J. Nash, ed. Pp. 25–57. New York: State University of New York Press.

2005 Women's Weaving Cooperatives in Oaxaca: An Indigenous Response to Neoliberalism. Critique of Anthropology 25(3): 253–278.

Tanner, C. L.

1960 Crafts of Arizona Indians. Arizona Highways 36: 8–35.

1968 Southwest Indian Craft Arts. Tucson: University of Arizona Press.

Thompson, R., and N. Parezo

1989 A Historical Study of Material Culture Studies in Anthropology. *In* Perspectives on Anthropological Collections from the American Southwest. A. L. Hedlund, ed. Pp. 33–65. Phoenix: Arizona State University.

Trevathan, B.

1997 Contemporary Navajo Weaving: A Collector's Guide. Indian Artist, Fall: 32–37.

Valette, J., and R. M. Valette

1997 In Search of Yah-nah-pah: The Early Gallegos "Yei" Blankets and Their Weavers. American Indian Art Magazine, Winter: 56–69.

Wade, E.

1985 The Ethnic Art Market in the American Southwest, 1880–1980. *In* Objects and Others: Essays on Museums and Material Culture, vol. 3. G. Stocking, ed. Pp. 167–191. Madison: University of Wisconsin Press.

Weiss, L.

1984 The Development of Capitalism in the Navajo Nation: A Political Economic History. Studies in Marxism 15. Minneapolis: MEP.

Wheat, J.

1984 The Gift of Spiderwoman: Southwestern Textiles, the Navajo Tradition. Philadelphia: University Museum, University of Pennsylvania.

Wheat, J., and. A. L. Hedlund

2003 Blanket Weaving in the Southwest. Tucson: University of Arizona Press.

Whitaker, K.

1998 Common Threads: Pueblo and Navajo Textiles in the Southwest Museum. Los Angeles: Southwest Museum.

2001 Southwest Textiles: Weavings of the Pueblo and Navajo. Seattle: University of Washington Press.

Willink, R., and P. Zolbrod

 1996 Weaving a World: Textiles and the Navajo Way of Seeing. Santa Fe: Museum of New Mexico Press.

Willmott, C.

 2006 The Historical Praxis of Museum Anthropology: A Canada-US Comparison. *In* Historicizing Canadian Anthropology. J. Harrison and R. Darnell, eds. Pp. 212–225. Vancouver: University of British Columbia Press.

Wills, C.

 2006 Fair Trade: What's It All About? *In* Business Unusual: Successes and Challenges of Fair Trade. A. Osterhaus, ed. Pp. 7–27. Brussels: Fair Trade Advocacy Office.

Witherspoon, G.

 1987 Navajo Weaving: Art in Its Cultural Context. Monograph 37. Flagstaff: Museum of Northern Arizona Press.

Wood, W. W.

 2000a Flexible Production, Households, and Fieldwork: Multisited Zapotec Weavers in the Era of Late Capitalism. Ethnography 39: 133–148.

 2000b The "Invasion" of Zapotec Textiles: Indian Art "Made in Mexico" and the Indian Arts and Crafts Act. Presentation at the Textile Society of America Annual Meeting, Santa Fe, New Mexico, September.

 2008 Made in Mexico: Zapotec Weavers and the Global Ethnic Art Market. Bloomington: Indiana University Press.

Wyman, L.

 1970 Blessingway: With Three Versions of the Myth Recorded and Translated from the Navajo by Father Berard Haile, O.F.M. Tucson: University of Arizona Press.

 1983 Navajo Ceremonial System. *In* Handbook of North American Indians, vol. 10, Southwest. A. Ortiz, ed. Pp. 536–557. Washington, DC: Smithsonian Institution.

Naming Rights
Ethnographies of Fair Trade

JANE HENRICI

Fair trade agendas and methods are various, but researchers have come to regard these initiatives as part of a rapidly expanding movement. Anthropologists are especially committed to examining these new forms of exchange in light of the discipline's concerns about interactions among different societies, particularly smaller-scale groups that are increasingly challenged merely to survive, let alone to prosper, in the global economy. Such inquiries also reflect a longstanding anthropological interest in economic systems that are "alternative" to the present world market or linked to nonmarket traditions. Through a variety of ethnographic contexts and methods, the anthropological research presented in this volume seeks to identify both general patterns and diverging details within the amorphous and varied relationships based on "alternative trade." In addition, several of the authors here make suggestions for improving fair trade in practice.

In chapter 1, Mark Moberg and Sarah Lyon offer an extensive review of fair trade history, policy, and theorization since the origin of the term in the post–World War II period. They suggest that the attempt to make an economic system "fair" while operating within the existing "free" trade system produces paradoxical results, particularly since fair trade's formation was counter to today's penchant for unregulated markets: "Hence, the fair trade movement in its earliest incarnation was opposed in principle to the deregulation embraced by later neoliberal policies" (this volume, p. 2). Moberg and Lyon argue that fair trade—in its modern guise as a variant of free trade—might well produce puzzling and ironic results. Among these is the possibility of involvement with corporations that seek "commodified morality" rather than social justice. However less than ideal, fair trade arrangements also have their own logic(s), examples of which are revealed in the case studies in the chapters in this volume. The authors illustrate how the global expansion of the current free-trade system, pushed by its advocates to demand nothing but escalating profits and muzzled governmental intervention, has provoked a set of practices intended to aid the producers and consumers who claim to unfairly bear the costs of free trade arrangements. Therefore, fair trade from its beginning has been pushed by a perception of both a need to counter free trade practices and a right to a fair share of those practices. At the same time, the volume's contributors point out that most of those who advocate an expansion of fair trade networks reinforce free trade's dependence on consumer spending and its emphasis on privatization. As Catherine Dolan notes with respect to the rhetoric of consumers of Kenyan tea, fair trade shoppers prefer to yield part of their funds to the safety net of the larger society—typically defined in global terms—through the selective purchasing of fair-trade-labeled goods and services rather than through giving tithes, making donations, or paying taxes. Anthropological inquiries such as Dolan's demonstrate that fair trade is deeply embedded in the current configuration of free trade and its underlying assumptions, regardless of how fair trade's practitioners describe them. However, while fair trade might operate in ways that support world capitalism, most of the chapters demonstrate that fair trade fails except in the short term and within specific instances to make either local exchanges or the global market more equitable and secure. The authors help us to reconsider the relationships among these systems so that we recognize fair trade for both its contributions and its shortcomings, especially as these relate to the distinctive societies that anthropologists seek to understand, and their exchanges within a larger and increasingly unstable system.

In addition to adding to the anthropology of fair trade, the contributors to this volume have greatly expanded the analysis of various types of fair trade commodities. Fair trade and the body of scholarship that deals with it have histories that developed primarily within Latin America, and these have centered largely on the buyers and sellers of coffee and bananas. This volume extends ethnographic consideration to a wider range of goods and geographic areas, some of them overlapping with the more traditional sites of fair trade inquiry and others moving in entirely new directions. Among these are the ethnographic examinations of fair trade tea growers undertaken by Sarah Besky in India and Catherine Dolan in Kenya. Currently, tea is treated differently from coffee within fair trade in that it is not backed by stable minimum prices and its certification is extended to plantations as well as small farmer cooperatives. As a result, both case studies suggest notable differences from other, better-known certified fair trade commodities. In Besky's study of labor relations between tea plantation workers and owners in Darjeeling, India, she observes that the 1951 legislation passed by a newly independent Indian state codified extensive responsibilities toward laborers on the part of employers. Although Indian law has long mandated these protections for workers, Besky points out that in practice their actual enforcement involves ongoing renegotiation and contestation by unions and farm owners. Drawing on the differing experiences and often conflicting perspectives of Darjeeling plantation owners and the workers they employ, Besky's ethnographic interviews reveal that farm owners resent the labor laws as costly and unnecessary burdens. Their viewpoint is indirectly endorsed by fair trade, since plantations may obtain certification without demonstrating support for unions or any legal guarantee of labor rights. In place of rigorous government enforcement, infrequently monitored compliance with weak certification standards is now regarded as sufficient protection for worker welfare, leaving workers newly vulnerable to mistreatment. Volunteerism has become not only one of fair trade's defining attributes but its primary weakness in this and other cases.

Mark Moberg similarly presents interview and ethnographic data from both those who labor on farms and those who act as intermediaries, in this case small-scale St. Lucian banana farmers and the island's fair trade representatives. Like Besky, Moberg also focuses on the relationship between fair trade and deregulation. In this case, a World Trade Organization ruling ended a preferential banana trade agreement with the European Union and devastated the Caribbean banana industry, but it also encouraged surviving farmers to work with European alternative trading organizations (ATOs) to identify fair trade markets. Despite their reluctant acceptance of fair trade certification requirements, the banana farmers in Moberg's study complain of a need for even more access to the fair trade market and even fewer restrictions, like the producers of fair trade tea, coffee, crafts, and flowers described by other contributors to the book. In addition, decision-making about labels and rights to them is disproportionately controlled by fair trade "outsiders" rather than among all participants, which also appears as a common dilemma in other case studies. Nonetheless, St. Lucian banana farmers, at least according to the fair trade intermediary quoted by Moberg, have come to view positively the social premiums generated by fair trade sales, which enable farmers to invest profits in community development. Unlike the situation of the Kenyan tea farmers that Dolan interviews, banana producers in the Eastern Caribbean appear to share in the values of solidarity and community development espoused by shoppers at the retail end of the commodity chain.

Following Moberg, Julia Smith presents an overview of fair trade coffee certification and a critique of its potential to improve conditions for growers. Her chapter's overall focus is on the shared social and moral obligations expressed by many consumers regarding their preference for fair trade. According to Smith, the certification standards for fair trade coffee have with time and marketing come to favor specific beans for their quality and regional origin regardless of their costs of production. Meanwhile, producers who cannot afford to meet these standards or pay for organic growing methods, but who nonetheless maintain labor standards and social equity, might be denied fair trade labeling. Conversely, many growers are attracted to the broader specialty-coffee market that frequently offers higher prices than fair trade without as many requirements. With the long-term stagnation in fair trade producer prices, Smith argues that the fair trade trademark has lost much of its original appeal and meaning for growers. Smith's point is mentioned by others as well; that is, fair trade practices can support unity among either consumers or producers but not necessarily for both, although that remains one of the movement's guiding ideals. Further, fair trade's emphasis on a particular product and production method as valued by the consumer retail market involves an unequal distribution of decision-making power. This in turn suggests that the priorities of the consumer market are privileged over the interests of producers, a point that both Dolan and Kathy M'Closkey also emphasize.

Catherine Ziegler also presents a comprehensive if less ethnographic overview of the global exchange of a single commodity, fair trade cut flowers. Her chapter focuses on flower growers from Ecuador, Colombia, and Kenya and their relationship to distributors across the European Union, the United Kingdom, and the United States. Unlike traditional fair trade arrangements that seek to benefit small growers of such commodities as coffee and bananas, cut flower producers operate large and heavily capitalized farms that employ wage labor. As a result, many of the same issues of equity and the distribution of fair trade benefits raised by Besky on tea plantations apply to cut flower production as well. Apart from careful monitoring by fair trade certification auditors, there is no guarantee that the benefits of fair trade markets will diffuse down to laborers on flower plantations. Further, the manner in which flowers are sold and repackaged as bouquets at the retail level often impairs the ability of consumers to select a fair trade purchase consciously, since it is rarely apparent from the label that a given batch of flowers was grown under fair trade conditions. Nevertheless, Ziegler's general conclusion is that the environmental, labor, and social standards from fair trade certification and monitoring have improved existing practices in cut flower production. What remains to be seen is whether these improvements can be sustained without careful and continued scrutiny or can be more widely distributed given the peculiarities of the cut flower retail market that inhibit fair trade labeling.

Meanwhile, Sarah Lyon considers a potentially unfair aspect of fair trade but one that is perhaps more fundamental to any aid effort: its promoters must select who among the needy to assist, given their inability to reach everyone. In the Guatemalan Mayan village studied by Lyon, women weavers operate a parallel economy to that of male villagers, often their own husbands, who are fair trade coffee growers. Lyon shows that the growing economic division between men who work with coffee and women who do not simultaneously highlights and contradicts fair trade ideals. One of the notable features of Lyon's chapter is the detailed depiction of multiple efforts by Mayan women to seek, on their own behalf, access to the same fair trade markets with which their husbands work. These efforts, as Lyon shows, are impeded not by the men of the community but by the narrow scope of the fair trade market as well as women's general inability to navigate the culture and language outside their communities. Lyon's chapter is not a condemnation of fair trade arrangements but rather an examination of their currently limited form; as she notes, these arrangements can entail gender biases in the distribution of benefits.

Like Besky, Catherine Dolan examines fair trade tea producers, but Dolan centers her discussion on the often opaque and arduous relationship between farmers and the international buyers who purchase their produce. Dolan portrays the tea auction as a divide across which Kenyan tea farmers and foreign buyers are prevented from entering into more direct relationships and communication. The tea auction simultaneously lumps together all teas and formulaically divides fair trade as a portion from the whole. As a result, no direct exchange or social relationship exists between the producers and the distributors or consumers of their products, despite fair trade's rhetoric to the contrary. The lack of direct communication between tea producers and buyers not only contradicts fair trade's claim of social equity but prevents shared decision-making on the use of profits in the form of social premiums. In contrast to the pattern that Moberg describes for the Eastern Caribbean, in Kenya social premiums are invested in ways that outsiders deem to be the greatest good, much to the resentment of tea producers themselves. Dolan's study thus reveals a significant and troubling shortfall between ethnographic reality and the goals of transparency and local decision-making embraced by fair trade advocates.

A community's differentiated access to wealth does not in and of itself indicate "unfair" or externally imposed trade or some sort of rigid hierarchical and exploitative system; neither does it reveal a successful "free" market. Conversely, as both Dolan and Patrick Wilson illustrate in this volume, to ignore local divisions, or to attempt to invoke imaginary community solidarities, instead might exacerbate existing divisiveness. As I have encountered in my own work, such friction can be found at every level of exchange, and, in agreement with M'Closkey, hiding that fact can often worsen inequities (Henrici 2002, 2007). This is particularly true between the men and women in Dolan's study; in the case that Wilson describes, fair trade has opened disparities between men and women, among women in different communities, and between ethnically distinct communities. Despite readily apparent differentiation among the Ecuadorian indigenous groups featured in Wilson's chapter, fair trade marketing typically portrays these societies to be communal and egalitarian. Like Smith, Dolan, and M'Closkey, Wilson observes that fair trade seeks to tailor the activities of local producers to external values and perceptions, rather than build on the preferences and identities of producers themselves.

Wilson's chapter nicely integrates the existing literature on tourism, development, fair trade, and ethnicity to show how the marketing of indigenous crafts within global capitalism draws in part on simplified and romanticized representations of ethnic and tribal groups. In addition, he demonstrates how such practices preferentially assist individuals and households that already enjoy privileged access to wealth and symbolic capital in the form of "acceptable" indigenous identities. Wilson examines a development project that sought to train indigenous groups in varieties of craft production valued by the fair trade market. This initiative, intended to reinforce an imagined order of community solidarity and gendered complementarity, exclusively targeted one women's group for instruction in ceramics while bypassing others. Even as fair trade aid efforts herald equality, this case reveals how in practice they can reinforce its opposite, with the priorities of the consumer end of the commodity chain again determining how the benefits of fair trade are distributed at the producer end.

Just as intergroup differentiation is often neglected or ignored by fair trade initiatives, Faidra Papavasiliou introduces another topic often overlooked in accounts of fair trade: the monetary. In the United States, the financial and commercial are considered distinct for policy purposes, but both are supported by assumptions about individual agency, competition, and rights. Papavasiliou explains that complementary currency is meant to link members of a society through their exchange medium so that, while it can remain tied to individual choice, it also can compel people to communicate more directly with one another about how they value goods and services as well as foster more locally based production. In her ethnographic description of the HOURS complementary currency system in Ithaca, New York, Papavasiliou points out that standard currency has been discussed as seeming neutral or stable but is in fact neither. In contrast, complementary currency, or alternative money, seems more openly subjective and contextual to those who use it. In Ithaca, the HOURS currency is sometimes relegated to purchases of "luxury" items or events, which would make its use both unstable and unsupportive of sustainable work. However, the alternative money goes well beyond such limited applications, to stimulate its users to scrutinize standard currency critically and to perceive themselves as part of a unity of like-minded persons. Although the local economy might not be well maintained at this point by its distinctive money alone, its currency has encouraged a social connectedness among individuals that otherwise might lack a means to express a shared identity and set of values. In contrast to the other studies in this volume, Papavasiliou examines a local group in which there exist direct relations between buyers and sellers, notwithstanding some social and economic differentiation among them. This finding seems similar to that of Moberg in showing how fair trade practices can encourage new awareness and concern for the societal among its participants, almost in spite of its marketing claims that the groups within fair trade come predisposed to a communal ideal.

Fair trade proponents often argue that the initiative integrates geographically and culturally distant producers, consumers, and distributors into a single global partnership based on shared values and goals. In contrast to Papavasiliou's study of alternative currency users, Molly Doane's research among fair trade coffee producers in Mexico and the buyers of their coffee in the United States raises doubts about such unity. Like Wilson's examination of craft producers, the consumers' perception of coffee producers is one of homogeneity even as their products, as Smith points out, are sold as if highly varied and distinctive. Again, producers and consumers of fair trade items appear to operate with profoundly differing understandings of the alternative markets in which they commonly participate. Doane suggests that the extensive travel and educational experiences among fair trade consumers and roasters make them particularly conscious of differences in living standards and well-being between producers and consumers involved in the international coffee trade. Simultaneously, such experiences lend themselves to a kind of mystification that transforms geographic, cultural, and socioeconomic differences between regions into a sameness that can be smoothed even further by individual choice in the consumption of coffee. As a result, in spite of efforts and claims of success by coffee roasters and coffee drinkers in the U.S. Midwest in fostering social relationships with producers in Chiapas, Mexico, the producers that Doane interviews do not imagine their relationships with the midwesterners to be aspects of a unified society but rather are aware of it as part of an abstract economic system. The farmers instead focus on the ever-rising demands of fair trade certification and of securing better marketing opportunities for their coffee, not unlike the growers of bananas and tea described elsewhere. In other words and in contrast to what consumers envision about fair trade, the producers of fair trade goods tend to struggle with the difficulties associated with fair trade labeling in the hope of obtaining higher prices but without the belief that they have much control over the terms of fair trade exchanges.

Kathy M'Closkey, for her part, expresses anger at the increased distancing of Navajo artists from the profits made from their designs within the international marketplace, particularly given the dire economic state of the Navajo Nation. M'Closkey is also appalled that neither more anthropologists nor fair trade advocates seem concerned about the ongoing appropriation of Navajo rug designs by non-Navajo weavers. Like others who focus on intellectual property rights and claim them as an aspect of social and economic justice, M'Closkey seeks to guide the discussion about Navajo art production away from merely asserting authenticity through a restricted or stereotypic view of indigeneity and toward linking ethnic or tribal invention to protected compensation. She points out that organizations claiming to be fair are particularly open to criticism when they knowingly contract and sell goods made by one group that appropriates the ideas and imagery of another, especially when the latter receive nothing from those transactions. Whether of English cheddar cheese, Ethiopian crucifix jewelry, Chiapas coffee beans, or Navajo trade rugs, copies do more than alter the object, its associations, and its affect: copies arguably prevent profits from returning to the source of the product. Endorsing cultural creativity and privileging the point of origin of material goods as well as guaranteeing shared compensation among producers truly would reinvent fair trade as an alternative market system. Ironically, enforcing that endorsement through copyrights, patents, and inspections for plagiarism would require governmental regulation, or comparable binding oversight, requiring a return to the original statist definition of fair trade as discussed in chapter 1 of this volume. Enforcing such agreements would also entail even more time, vigilance, and costs for producers themselves.

Since the reproducible will continue to be reproduced and images reconfigured into patterns torn from their original context, a case could be made that fair trade organizations should deny labeling rights and privileges to those who appropriate the designs of others. Conversely, distributors of ethnic artistry might increase their self-regulation, create as a group their own label to show standards of origin, or seek a fair trade certification for the design as well as ethnic or national origin of their products rather than just for the items' labor and environmental standards. However, in addition to depending on a volunteerism that the authors have shown varies in dependability among fair traders, that option would be unhelpful to many producers whose experiences have been documented in this volume. As the chapters by Besky, Smith, Dolan, Wilson, and Doane suggest, such arrangements would continue to divide rather than unite based on one set of participants' values instead of ideals that are common to all. Conversely, as Moberg, Ziegler, Lyon, and Papavasiliou discuss, social values can be reinforced through fair trade practices where benefits are seen in association with mutuality and community investment.

Many proponents consider fair trade to be transcendental in that it invokes by its very existence both a substitute for free trade and an improvement over it. However, to deliver either would require a different sort of discipline and reward model than traditionally hierarchical economic systems foster, and putting that into action is easier said than done. Consistent with many models intended for change, fair trade in fact often repeats, if not exacerbates, the structural inequalities of conventional exchanges even when it is fully intended to help a wider spectrum of people: we find in these chapters that size matters in fair trade, as does gender, race, and ethnicity. Specifically, as Moberg and others in the book

describe it, the limited size of fair trade markets, as well as restrictive certification standards, inevitably limit the benefits of fair trade participation
to a fortunate few in a much larger sea of producers. Neither volunteerism nor the intervention of alternative trade organizations appears able to
avert this inequitable aspect of fair trade, which may at an extreme foster
stratification and even conflict between fair trade beneficiaries and those
excluded from such markets (Garsten and Jacobsson 2007).

Another issue with respect to devolution is that "community-based" or
"locally controlled" activities may appear both egalitarian and empowering but, short of accountability and transparency, can simply lapse into
muddy rhetoric. The result is something akin to the following discussion
about communal land and land reform in Scotland:

> If notions like *"stewardship"* (and we have touched on others such as *"com-
> munity planning"*) point to a more constructive relationship between the
> state, NGOs, local communities and individuals, and a more equal and
> transparent division of power between them, then they may be useful con-   .
> cepts. If on the other hand they are used to obfuscate the real issues, such
> that no one knows what kind of power is being exercised by whom, then
> they merely constitute rhetorical devices cloaking the real interests and
> conflicts involved in the processes of devolution and land reform. As such
> they hinder realistic analysis of the issues, even if they may on occasion
> help to bring people together. (Bryden and Hart 2000: 10)

Meanwhile, those left to the side or perhaps shunted there by fair trade
opportunities—most often women and members of lower-status ethnic
groups—must challenge and maneuver within so-called alternative solutions or sink even further into relative poverty and limited circumstances.
As many of the authors in this volume argue, that is made more difficult
by the fact that fair trade can seem rigged to privilege some groups over
others where, as in Lyon's study, it is targeted at one set of household economic activities (coffee) over others (textiles). Indeed, the experience of
Guatemalan weavers seems to beg an obvious question that is rarely asked
of fair trade proponents: why does alternative trade embrace certain commodities (particularly of an agricultural or artisan nature) and not others
(manufactured goods such as clothing and electronics) that also involve
great inequities in their production? This question becomes even more
salient given the recent willingness of FLO and other fair trade organizations to extend certification to large-scale, plantation-based forms of

production as well as to the goods marketed by agribusiness corporations such as General Mills, Cadbury, and Nestlé.

While Fair trade practices can occasionally yield wider opportunities for participants along the commodity chain, as Ziegler and Moberg describe, the retail consumer seems to play a smaller role in any such transformation than he or she is encouraged to believe. That might disappoint those of us who hope that our care in selecting purchases and investments has promoted our ideals or at least mitigated the harm done to them by the world market. Yet, as Papavasiliou observes in her chapter, perhaps the most promising aspect of fair trade is that actual shifts in economic relations do seem to occur when producers and consumers enter into exchanges based on genuine equity.

Within any context the act of labeling is necessarily one of agency. The power and right to classify and name a thing or person is intrinsically greater than that of the status that is granted. Even if the label becomes weakened because its selection criteria widen or diminish, certifiers who stamp and star have authority over the producers they choose and reject, whether or not they recognize this power (Henrici 2003). That such authority might be mystified, mishandled, and mercenary is a risk within any institution or system. Within fair trade, where labels form both the message and the marketing, inconsistencies distort the very basis of the effort at equality and, to an extent, amount to a private and guildlike form of governance even as broader state intervention is shunned.

In very interesting and incredibly diverse ways, the chapters in this volume talk about making deals, and about conversations about making deals, within the world's overarching capitalist system and whether those deals can ever *not* hurt the less powerful in the exchange. Indeed, a dilemma seems to arise within each chapter, and that comes as a choice made by those studied between either a better link to the global economy through higher salaries, sales, or subsidies, or a stronger sense of local community through some other expression of shared values. The researchers seem to find in their respective studies that, regardless of the context, groups of people currently can either receive better support from their employers or trading partners within fair trade or have better connections among their own people. On occasion both aims may be achieved, but typically only if there were already present many other preconditions, such as literacy and formal education, a command of the nonlocal language and culture, familiarity with regional trade agreements, and so on. This problem might be a good place to go forward: how can conditions be improved within a work or trade arrangement and a social system that seems at this point disconnected from it? Despite common objections that benefits will be lost for consumers if conditions are made better for producers, or that social networks are expenses rather than investments, anthropologists can build on their research to challenge these zero-sum arguments and increase policy support for what can be fair within trade.

Currently, the right to make a profit takes precedence within international trade policy and practice over other rights. Like the right to shelter or food, the right to a profit—or at the least an adequate return to labor— is fiercely protected for some individuals and groups while all but denied for others. Multilateral agencies such as the World Trade Organization are able to defend corporations' rights to property and access to global markets with the force of law, while saying little about the economic and human rights of those who labor for such entities. Indeed, unlike universal rights endorsed but rarely enforced by United Nations entities such as the High Commissioner for Human Rights or the International Labor Office, legal guarantees for profit-oriented corporations within much of the present world economic system seem virtually unassailable. Arguments for and against free-market policies and the prerogatives of private capital often take a moralistic stance, but seldom is it asked exactly whose morality is invoked in debates about trade. Can trade ever be fair, or free, between people whose values conflict? Conversely, are all our values so inherently distinct as to be incompatible? If we are to work toward improvements in the fair trade system, we must, as Raynolds et al. (2007) argue, first find out whether we agree on what those values should be.

As this volume demonstrates, an anthropological approach to fair trade provides critical insights needed to improve the equity and transparency of exchange. The socioeconomic and cultural aspects of a people's perspectives about bettering their lives provides a context that can aid our understanding as we try to combine viewpoints among the societies and nation-states that compose the world system. Anthropologists have found that one group's view of morality in trade may reflect a concept of charity, while another's depends on its kinship or social connectedness, and another's provides a remedy to fraud. Regardless of these differences, anthropologists also have found among many cultures that there exists a common set of moralities concerning subsistence that tend to emphasize the long term and societal in contrast to the short term and self-regarding, often considering the unqualified pursuit of the latter to violate the spirit of a moral economy. In other words, anthropologists can show both how cultures differ in their treatment of trade and how they are alike in their forms of savings and security, even as they might seem in conflict over the short term. The next step, then, is to learn how we might find common positions among these variations in morality from which to discuss our world's exchanges (Gudeman 2001).

While working as a graduate student I attempted to ask residents of a well-known Peruvian tourist village about their concerns with making and selling goods for nonlocals, and whether they can preserve their traditional culture while doing so. My informants responded that I was asking the wrong questions. Combining laughter with courtesy, the villagers explained to me that to learn the right questions I first would need to go back "to where the money comes from," by which they meant the United States, and study my "own people's product." They added in the same vein that they would look forward to my return. I have been fortunate in that the people of that village, as well as the staff of NGOs and ATOs who work to help the villagers, continue to educate me. Indeed, the preceding chapters are evidence that, despite the complexities and disparities of transnational exchange, people all along commodity chains are willing to try to help us understand their experiences and motives. Those we interview often talk with us in the hope that we will be able to enlighten others and to bend policy in a direction that might improve rather than worsen relations, a fact that in no way lessens the generosity of their assistance. However, it does make it even more of a challenge to offer what we can in return. As we who study cultures and economics often recognize, our activities of research and publication are also transactions, some more reciprocal than others. In particular, an ethnographic approach asks a great deal from those being observed and interviewed: the editors of this book emphasize that it is the very intensity and duration of an ethnographic encounter that can contribute to what we might grasp about others' economies as well as examples from our own. In the end, I returned to the village for my doctoral and subsequent studies and brought new questions with me. However, my old questions received responses as well; my initial inquiries were not wrong so much as they needed repositioning.

Clearly, local values and identities are of critical importance, but they are also part of a broader set of economic and political relations (Roseberry 2002). As we think about the chapters of this volume, we ask new questions; in a sense, we inquire about our own identities and relationships to one another. This book's authors, like fair traders, push us to reconsider our economic relationships. For us to be equal with one another as trading partners we have to recognize the unequal power some of us have to categorize and name; we also need to acknowledge the power some of us yield to others in the global economy (Hart 2001). Without abandoning hope for future improvement in the equity of global exchange, these chapters reveal that fair trade risks oblivion as long as we allow ourselves, or others, to falsely frame it as

1. unquestionably an improvement for producers over past systems;
2. an opposition to the free market;
3. lacking friction and conflict among those involved;
4. fully voluntary and equitable in its operations;
5. entirely "locally," "community," or "consumer" controlled;
6. intrinsically moral;
7. involving deals, products, and people that are inherently more authentic, organic, or legitimate or have greater stewardship rights, without questioning the right to label;
8. removed from all national or international governmental regulation or protection; and
9. effectively the same, for better or worse, regardless of who claims to do it.

Standards, categories, and values *must* exist in all exchanges. Our task, then, is to figure out what we agree about them and work together to see them both as our ideal goals and as models that we might tweak over the long term. In the process, we must avoid letting others define these rules and values for us. Indeed, I assert that all of us should become participatory in reading our own accounting practices, and those of our nations, and in thinking about our needs for and definitions of protections, securities, and rights. We might discover that we are not so removed from those with whom we conduct our research or undertake our fair trade and that we need to demand agency over the labels we ourselves receive. Fair trade must not succumb to the same processes that have allowed a smaller and smaller subset of the planet's population to control a larger and larger portion of its resources and profits.

At one and the same time, the need to remain sensitive to the differences of place is critical, as Besky and Dolan point out. It is Besky who also reminds us that there is a relational articulation among places and peoples, and we can begin to take responsibility for that as we take it for ourselves. For example, it is the very lowered assessment of the reproducibility of the rugs made by those who M'Closkey studies that then pressures those who Wilson studies to stuff giant steel shipping containers full of their products. It is the very existence of commercial monocropping, such as coffee, that decades ago displaced women household farmers in Guatemala and other parts of Latin America so that the growers that Lyon studies enjoy a privileged position over their female kin and neighbors, who now weave for marginal and unstable returns. All the items that we as consumers buy, and their relations of production and marketing—coffee, bananas, tea, flower, money, handicrafts—are relational in this sense. How then are we to improve labor, land, and environmental rights in one corner of the world economy if we ignore those elsewhere?

In other words, and in conclusion, we might need to think not only in terms of the supranational organizations that strive to monitor and sanction unjust actions at the hands of states and corporations but also in clearer terms—"key words"—of universal trading rights, analogous and perhaps related to those of human rights. The challenge emerges from these case studies to discover our common values, if they do exist, on which to base our exchanges and rights. By doing so, we further the effort to make our exchanges more equitable in ways that privilege all trading partners over that which they trade. The authors of this book want fair trade to continue, but they also want it to come clean. Without transparency, or self-critique, on the part of its participants, including ourselves, the aspects of fair trade with the potential to serve as an alternative to a world market governed by free trade may very well fail. For our trade to be equitable and sustainable, we must use more fully our consciousness as well as our conscience.

WORKS CITED

Bryden, J., and K. Hart
  2000 Land Reform, Planning and People: An Issue of Stewardship. Arkleton Centre for Rural Development Research, University of Aberdeen, Scotland. Available at http://www.caledonia.org.uk/land/stewardship.htm, accessed June 22, 2009.
Garsten, C., and K. Jacobsson
  2007 Free Trade—Fair Trade: The Moralizing Claims of Global Market Regulations. Paper presented at the Annual Meeting of the American Anthropological Association, Washington, DC, November 28–December 2.
Gudeman, S.
  2001 The Anthropology of Economy. Malden, MA: Blackwell.

Hart, K.
  2001 Money in an Unequal World: Keith Hart and His Memory Bank. New York: Texere.
Henrici, J.
  2002 "Calling to the Money": Gender and Tourism in Peru. *In* Gender/Tourism/Fun? M. Swain and J. Momsen, eds. Pp. 118–133. Elmsford, NY: Cognizant Communication Corporation.
  2003 Non-governmental Organizations, "Fair Trade," and Craft Producers: Exchanges South and North. Visual Anthropology 16(2–3): 289–314.
  2007 Free Trade, Alternative Trade, and Women in Peru: A First Look. Journal of Developing Societies 23: 145–157.
Raynolds, L., D. Murray, and J. Wilkinson, eds.
  2007 Fair Trade: The Challenges of Transforming Globalization. New York: Routledge.
Roseberry, W.
  2002 Understanding Capitalism—Historically, Structurally, and Spatially. *In* Locating Capitalism in Time and Space: Global Restructurings, Politics, and Identity. D. Nugent, ed. Pp. 61–79. Stanford, CA: Stanford University Press.

....

About the Contributors

SARAH BESKY is a Ph.D. candidate in the Department of Anthropology at the University of Wisconsin–Madison.

MOLLY DOANE is Assistant Professor at the University of Illinois at Chicago. She is working on a book on fair trade coffee. Her current research builds on earlier research concerning the politics of the environment in Mexico.

CATHERINE S. DOLAN is Fellow of Green Templeton College and a University Lecturer in the Marketing, Culture and Society Programme at the University of Oxford. She is coeditor of the volume *Ethical Sourcing in the Global Food System: Challenges and Opportunities to Fair Trade and the Environment.*

JANE HENRICI is Study Director at the Institute for Women's Policy Research with a focus on disparities and development. She has published on women and poverty, health care, job training, tourism development, free trade, fair trade, and nonprofits/NGOs. Henrici is coauthor of *Poor Families in America's Health Care Crisis: How the Other Half Pays* (2006) and editor of, and contributor to, *Doing Without: Women and Work after Welfare Reform* (2006).

SARAH LYON is Assistant Professor of Anthropology at the University of Kentucky.

KATHY M'CLOSKEY is Adjunct Associate Professor in the Department of Sociology, Anthropology and Criminology at the University of Windsor, Ontario, Canada. She authored *Swept under the Rug: A Hidden History of Navajo Weaving* (2002, paperback 2008) and recently served as research director for the PBS documentary *Weaving Worlds,* directed by Bennie Klain from Tuba City, Navajo Nation, Arizona.

MARK MOBERG is Professor of Anthropology at the University of South Alabama. He is the author or coeditor of five books dealing with development issues and globalization in Central America and the Caribbean.

FAIDRA PAPAVASILIOU received her Ph.D. from Emory University and is Lecturer in the Department of Anthropology at Georgia State University.

JULIA SMITH is Assistant Professor of Anthropology at Eastern Washington University. She has written elsewhere about small-scale coffee farming in Costa Rica.

PATRICK C. WILSON is Associate Professor of Anthropology at the University of Lethbridge. Among his publications is a coedited volume (with Frank Hutchins), *Editing Eden: A Reconsideration of Identity, Politics, and Place in Amazonia* (2010), and *Federaciones Indígenas, ONG, el Estado: El Desarrollo y la Politicazión de la Cultura en la Amazónia Ecuatoriana* (2009).

CATHERINE ZIEGLER's anthropological research focuses on consumer culture and global trade. Her most recent book is *Favored Flowers: Culture and Economy in a Global System.*

Index